THE WORKS

OF

LORD BYRON

The Works
of
Lord Byron

With an introduction
by
LESLIE A. MARCHAND

BLACK'S READERS SERVICE

ROSLYN, NEW YORK

PRINTED IN THE UNITED STATES OF AMERICA

INTRODUCTION

BY LESLIE A. MARCHAND

THE NAME of Byron became in the nineteenth century, and remains today, a symbol for a mood, an attitude of mind, and a view of life. "Byronism" was generally associated with a kind of haughty romantic melancholy of a defiant and Satanic turn. This interpretation, popularly distilled from *Childe Harold,* dominated the critical approach to the poet through the past century and is still current. But now the name of Byron is becoming more and more frequently associated with a tough-minded realism and a trenchant satire often hilarious but always grounded in a basic sanity and a knowledge of human nature.

Though he sometimes shocked them, Byron intrigued many of his contemporaries because he expressed so well the mood of those whose romantic aspirations for the ideal had suffered the various disillusionments that attended the Napoleonic and post-Napoleonic periods: the disappointment that came with the failure of the French Revolution to usher in the brotherhood of man and to end the abuses in government and in social and economic life; the disillusionment of those who, like certain followers of Godwin, had hitched their wagons to the star of perfectibility and an idealized human nature and who were forced to resign themselves at last to the sad spectacle of man's irrationality and imperfection.

To other contemporaries, and to many of the Victorians, Byron seemed altogether dangerous and immoral, not so much for his presentation of immoral action or skeptical sentiment as for his failure to treat seriously the romantic ideal of dreaming true, of the mastery of mind over matter, of the ultimate attainment of the ideal by force of mind and will.

And yet Byron exerted a powerful influence on the minds of many of the Victorians in their youth (for they were all children of the Romantic Movement). Tennyson, at 15, wandered out disconsolate in 1824 and wrote on a rock: "Byron is dead." Carlyle, courting Jane Welsh, encouraged her to read Byron, and after the news arrived from Greece, she wrote to him: "Byron is dead! I was told it all at once in a roomful of people. My God, if they had said that the sun or the moon had gone out of the heavens, it could not have struck me with the idea of a more awful and dreary blank in the creation." Carlyle replied that Byron's was "the noblest spirit in Europe"; he felt as if he "had lost a brother." John Ruskin, brought up by puritanical parents, still was permitted to read Byron, and Browning's first poetry was inspired by him. It is true that most of the Victorians later repudiated Byron and decried his influence for various reasons—all, however, probably springing from a common denominator of moral squeamishness or reticence or from their passion for moral reform and their optimistic trust in material progress, a trust that they found Byron did not share.

Those who have tried to achieve critical detachment and a more balanced view of Byron have often been baffled by the extremes of romance and realism in his personality and work. But the romantic and realistic (or satiric) veins are not evidence that irreconcilable impulses directed his poetic productions nor that there was any basic inconsistency in his character. They spring from the same source: an imponderable longing for an ideal and dissatisfaction with the reality whose impact on his sensitive temperament always brought disillusionment.

The moods of both *Childe Harold* and of the later satires in which the fair face of reality is stripped away and shown to be only a mask are present in Byron's first published poems. Though most of the verses in *Hours of Idleness* are imitative and lacking in originality of form or content, a few rise to heights of lyrical beauty and sincerity, particularly those which deal with evanescent young love—fascinating because it was unattainable and because its pleasure rested in the imagination, and sad because even at that early age he had known the disillusionment of satiety. Granted that they lack Shelleyan perfection, several of his early lyrics such as "The First Kiss of Love" and "When I Roved a Young Highlander," contrived as they are, reveal a determination to deal with experience directly and a promise at least of that greater felicity of phrasing which produced the finest stanzas of *Childe Harold* and the most romantic flights in *Don Juan* as well as the lyric grace of some of the *Hebrew Melodies*.

An even greater interest attaches to these early pieces, however, because many of them reveal the realistic and satiric spirit which moved Byron as early as his residence at Harrow and Cambridge, but which did not gain full expression before the relaxation of his Italian exile. That fact is apparent to anyone who has read Byron's letters, but so much stress has been put on the sentimental and melancholy aspects of his early poems that the few of a different cast have been neglected. "To a Knot of Ungenerous Critics" and "Soliloquy of a Bard in the Country" are in a sense forebears of *English Bards and Scotch Reviewers,* while there is evident in "Reply to some Verses of J. M. B. Pigot," "To the Sighing Strephon," "The Girl of Cadiz," and "Queries to Casuists" something akin to the satiric spirit of *Don Juan,* though they are of course inferior to it in ease of manner and expression. The fact to bear in mind is that Byron's penchant for mockery did not spring suddenly into life with *Beppo* but was a constant facet of his personality, though mostly suppressed from his earlier publications.

More deeply wounded than he would admit in later years by the *Edinburgh Review's* caustic critique of his juvenile verses, Byron converted a satiric poem he had begun on the writers of the day into *English Bards and Scotch Reviewers,* lashing out in a manner of which he was soon ashamed at all of his contemporaries except a few who followed the Popean pattern. The remarkable thing about the poem, however, is not its cleverness in imitating the *Dunciad,* or its more immediate models the *Maeviad* and *Baviad* of William Gifford, Byron's great idol, but rather the originality that often transcends the limitations of the model. When working with material within his own observation and experience Byron could never be entirely conventional or commonplace. The satire in its best passages bears the stamp of Byron's personality. When he speaks of Wordsworth showing "both by precept and example," "That prose is verse and verse is merely prose" and when he ridicules Betty Foy, "The idiot mother of 'an idiot boy,' " he has already captured the rollicking mood of *Don Juan.*

The Byronic moods of disillusionment and melancholy stand out most clearly in *Childe Harold.* In an attempt to make it appear that he was not as bad as he pictured himself, Thomas Moore and other early biographers had fostered the view that Byron didn't mean what he said when he proclaimed that he had lived through all experience at an early age and "felt the fulness of satiety." But biographical evidence recently made available points to the fact that *Childe Harold* is a pretty literal record of Byron's sincerest feelings and moods if not the facts of his life. After the publication of the first two cantos in 1812, Byron wrote: "I awoke one morning and found myself famous." The reason was not alone that the world recognized in it a self-portrait despite Byron's protestations, nor that it expressed so well the disillusioned view of life congenial to the "lost generation" of the post-Revolutionary and Napoleonic eras. The deeper reason was that, despite the mawkishness of overstrained emotion and the affectations of an attempted Spenserian style (both discarded in later cantos), it displayed an honesty of self-revelation that had been absent from English literature for many years and a sincere attempt to grapple with problems of the ego that had previously been attacked only by indirection. He surprised people in their innermost thoughts, and thereby disarmed even those who could not approve of his unconventional views. Without being profound in the philosophic sense, he had faced squarely the central problem of romantic egoism: the disparity between desire and fulfillment, the unbridgeable gap between the romantic ideal and the world of reality.

To study *Childe Harold* properly (not the first two cantos alone, but all four) is to discover the very essence of the honest romantic mind. Byron's melancholy sprang directly from his uncompromising idealism (complicated by the fatalism of the early Calvinistic training from which he never wholly escaped). It is the record (poignant or sentimental as one chooses to view it) of the failure of things, emotions, people, landscapes, historic places, even his own nature, to measure up to the rigid demands of the ideal.

Its moods are those inspired by a constant and foredoomed search. The "Satanic pose" is with Byron something more than a pose. It is recognition of the fact that human nature, including his own, does not satisfy the romantic ideal. The "lonely soul" mood grew out of anguished yearnings for companionship which could never be satisfied, for the demands of the ideal left too much to be desired in human beings, male or female. He was most alone in crowds and he felt himself "the most unfit / Of men to herd with Man." "He would not yield dominion of his mind / To spirits against whom his own rebell'd." He found an impermanent peace among the mountains, and the waves and other wild and boundless aspects of nature symbolized his own unutterable thoughts and unattainable longings.

The far away and long ago, which could be clothed with the mind's ideal conceptions, were untrammeled by the gross realities of the here and now. The desire to travel and forget was inspired by a haunting restlessness, a forlorn searching for something, though his experience had already taught him to expect the fail ure of his quest. It is a characteristic of Childe Harold to find the lands and cities of his travel picturesque at first view and then to see them fade into something less than the light of common day. Lisbon from the Tagus was a thing of beauty where "fruits of fragrance blush on every tree." But the nearer view brings inevitable disappointment: the town is dirty and the people ignorant and proud. So when he enters Spain and views the site of recent battles, he dwells upon the splendor and the pageantry of the fighting, but he soon reflects that honor is sophistry and the best that it does is to feed the crow and fertilize the field, while tyrants continue their sway.

The "sic transit gloria mundi" theme, the vanity of ambition, is one of the most characteristic in *Childe Harold*. Typical is the description of the field at Waterloo preceded by the flashy dramatic stanza beginning "There was a sound of revelry by night." Byron does not fail to draw the obvious moral from the career of Napoleon. So with his moralizing on the ruins of ancient grandeur and on historical sites. The longing for the ideal in character, for something to match the mind's finest images in deeds and monuments is rudely shocked by contact with the real personalities and events. A couplet rounds out the conclusion: "One breast laid open were a school / Which would unteach mankind the lust to shine or rule."

Alternate longing for the ideal and disillusionment in the face of reality forms the pattern of *Childe Harold*. From transcendental aspirations (probably inspired by Shelley with whom he was associated while he was writing the third canto) he descends to world weariness or to cynicism and worldly wisdom. And again the plaintive cry of the uncompromising idealist goes up to emptiness: "Oh Love! no habitant of earth thou art . . . / But never yet hath seen, nor e'er shall see / The naked eye, thy form, as it should be; / The mind hath made thee, as it peopled heaven, / Even with its own desiring phantasy." And still again: "Where are the forms the sculptor's soul hath seized?— / In him alone. Can Nature show so fair? / Where are the charms and virtues which we dare / Conceive in boyhood and pursue as men, / The unreached Paradise of our despair."

Nowhere is Byron's self-revelation more patent or more eloquent than in his description of Rousseau. Though he later made a point of denying that he bore any resemblance to the French philosopher, "the self-torturing sophist, wild Rousseau," Byron must have felt a sympathetic kinship when he wrote of "The apostle of affliction, he who threw / Enchantment over passion, and from woe / Wrung overwhelming eloquence." And again: "he knew / How to make madness beautiful, and cast / O'er err·

ing deeds and thoughts a heavenly hue / Of words, like sunbeams, dazzling as they past / The eyes, which o'er them shed
tears feelingly and fast." Still more must Byron have seen himself
in the portrait when he continued: "But his was not the love of
living dame, / Nor of the dead who rise upon our dreams, / But
of ideal beauty, which became / In him existence, and o'erflowing
teems / Along his burning page, distempered though it seems."

Occasionally, from the depths of disillusionment, Byron turns
in sheer exhaustion to a kind of tranquillity beyond tragedy, but
he is not tranquil for long and the whole agonized quest begins
again, for "quiet to quick bosoms is a hell." Then the pleasant
plateau of the picturesque, particularly in nature, woos him once
more, for still "There is a pleasure in the pathless woods, / There
is a rapture on the lonely shore." But by this time his "theme has
died into an echo," and except for occasional short poems he gave
over the moods of *Childe Harold* after completing the fourth
canto and found relief in mockery and satire.

But before he had turned to irony and laughter he had gone
even further than Childe Harold in his arraignment of the universe. More experience at first strengthened Byron's fortitude and
stoicism in the face of what he felt to be the fated failure of the
world of nature and of man to measure up to the romantic ideal
which he still longed for, though hopelessly. In the middle years,
when he was writing *Manfred, Darkness, The Dream,* and the
third canto of *Childe Harold,* his melancholy reached the lowest
depths precisely because he aspired more intensely and more
vainly toward an unattainable ideal. Like Childe Harold he recognized that "there is a fire / And motion of the soul which will
not dwell / In its narrow being, but aspire / Beyond the fitting
medium of desire." And when in *Manfred* he complains that we
are "half dust, half deity" he has reached the ultimate of romantic
revolt against reality. Nothing real in the human and tangible
world could ever satisfy one who aspired to the freedom of spirit
and the omniscience and omnipotence of deity. And later, in
Cain, he went one step further. For when Lucifer had taken Cain
on a voyage through the spirit world and shown him things "Beyond all power of my born faculties, / Although inferior still to
my desires / And my conceptions," he came to the bitter conclusion that even deities may not be happy. All knowledge does
not bring all happiness. And so he fell back on a kind of unhappy
stoicism—a reliance on his own unconquerable will and a fortitude born of recognition of the hopelessness of all aspirations.

This was only the reverse side of the later satiric Byron whose poetic faculties and native wit flowered into such exquisite exuberance in *Beppo* and *The Vision of Judgment*. His final yielding to the fact that the ideal was unattainable left him free to approach the world once more at its own level, and though he found it still absurd, he gained more pleasure than pain from pricking the bubbles of its pretensions. Irony replaced melancholy, and in an increasing proportion of his poetic productions he turned his eyes (no less keen in their observation of the disparity between the real and the ideal) toward the comedy rather than the tragedy of the earthly stage. Now mockery and good-natured raillery marked his unmasking of the self-deceits of humanity in general and of his own contemporaries in particular. But the old longings never died out in Byron. Even after he had found his true bent in the satire of *Don Juan*, the melancholy contemplation of the fleeting ideal drove him to write the fourth canto of *Childe Harold* and shortly before his death at Missolonghi he composed a poem on his thirty-sixth birthday that is filled with the pathos of forlorn aspiration.

It was after his self-exile and particularly during his residence in Italy that Byron really found himself as a poet, though he wasted much effort in writing poetic drama which, like everything that didn't spring from his own experience, was outside his bent. Byron's two most successful efforts in the vein of ironic high comedy, aside from *Don Juan*,* are undoubtedly *Beppo* and *The Vision of Judgment*. The first, a direct product of his Italian experience, takes clever back-handed shots at English weather and English hypocrisy, "Our cloudy climate, and our chilly women." Using for the first time the *ottava rima* in imitation of Frere's *Whistlecraft*, he played with it, exercising almost all the ingenuity that he was soon to display in *Don Juan*: the digressions, the ironic deflation of sentiment, the comic rhymes which he used as "punch lines" in the couplets at the ends of stanzas, the leisurely conversational tone, the disarming realism, and the unheroic portraits of the characters.

The Vision of Judgment, Byron's parody of Laureate Southey's impossible apotheosis of George III, is a more balanced and a more finished satire than any other that he wrote. Here with a minimum of digression the comic action mounts to a crescendo of ridicule as the devils run howling down to hell when Southey begins reciting his works. Byron was never more felicitous in his phrasing nor more successful in his handling of a narrative. The

* *Don Juan* is arbitrarily omitted from this volume because of its length but is published separately in THE MODERN LIBRARY.

irresistible logic of the absurdities builds up to a tremendous impact of good-humored comedy which is utterly devastating to the Laureate.

Byron is coming more and more to be valued as a letter writer as increasing numbers of his epistles are published. The naturalness and wit of his letters is a delightful revelation to many who have known him only through his heavier *Weltschmerz* poems. Some of his *jeux d'esprit* in verse, mostly dashed off in letters to his friends, share the informal spirit of his correspondence and are worthy of inclusion, at least as leavening, in any volume of his poetry. Such lively pieces as the "Lines to Mr. Hodgson," the graceful "So we'll go no more a roving," addressed to Tom Moore, and the roguish "My Dear Mr. Murray," show that Byron was not always *Childe Harold.*

Byron has been accused of being a "poseur," and certainly he was conscious of dramatizing his own feelings, particularly in the first two cantos of *Childe Harold,* but it is a mistake to suppose that the basic personal, emotional, and intellectual problems which he faced were not real to him, or that he did not meet them with an honesty and sincerity which should command our respect, however much he may have overstrained the sentiments involved in the expression.

BIOGRAPHICAL SKETCH

GEORGE GORDON, sixth Lord Byron, was born in London on January 22, 1788. His early years were spent in Aberdeen, where he was brought up in narrowed circumstances by his widowed mother, the last of the Gordons of Gight, whose wastrel husband had spent her considerable fortune before he died in 1791. Lame from birth, he early developed a sharp sensitivity to his deformity which stayed with him through life. In 1798, when he inherited the title and the ancient Byron estate at Newstead Abbey, his mother took him to England. He was enrolled at Harrow in 1801 and at Trinity College, Cambridge, in 1805. His first book of poems, *Hours of Idleness*, was published in 1807. Before his next work, *English Bards and Scotch Reviewers*, a rejoinder to a harsh review of his early poems, was published in 1809, he was embarked on a tour of Europe and the Levant which took him through Portugal, Spain and Albania to Greece, Asia Minor and Constantinople. When he returned in 1811 he carried with him the manuscript of the first two cantos of *Childe Harold*. On its publication the following year he became famous overnight and was lionized in the drawing rooms of a high society of which he had known very little before he went abroad. Handsome, with a Greek beauty of profile, he was much sought after by women of that society and became involved in several intrigues before he was married on January 2, 1815, to Anne Isabella Milbanke, who bore him a daughter (Augusta Ada) in December of that year. In January, 1816, Lady Byron left him and returned to her parents. The reasons for the separation never having been made public, the darkest crimes were hinted, including incest with his half sister Augusta Leigh. (Later evidence rather conclusively indicates that Byron was involved in a liaison with Augusta before his marriage, but since Lady Byron was not aware of it until after the separation, it could not have been the cause.) To escape the éclat of the scandal, Byron left England in April, never to return. After a summer on Lake Geneva, where he first met Shelley, he proceeded to Italy, which was his home for more than six years. Settling first in Venice, he entered into the dissipations of the place, and had nearly ruined his health (though at the same time he had written some of his best poetry in that environment, including *Beppo* and the first cantos of *Don Juan*) when he met and fell in love with the Countess Teresa Guiccioli. Following her to Ravenna (1819–1821), he became involved through her family in the Italian revolutionary movement. After her separation from her husband, he continued the liaison, which was generally beneficial to his health and spirits. They lived for a time at Pisa (1821–1822), where he was again associated with Shelley until the latter was drowned in July of 1822 (Byron was present at the cremation ceremony on the beach at Viareggio). After a year at Genoa, Byron left in July, 1823, to aid the Greeks in their struggle for independence from Turkish rule. He died of a fever at Missolonghi, in Western Greece, on April 19, 1824, and his body was returned to England. Refused burial in Westminster Abbey, the remains were deposited in the ancestral vault at Hucknall Torkard near Newstead Abbey.

SELECTED BIBLIOGRAPHY

EDITIONS

The Works of Lord Byron, Poetry. ed. E. H. Coleridge. 7 vols. London: John Murray, 1898–1904; *Letters and Journals.* ed. R. E. Prothero. 6 vols. London: John Murray, 1898–1901.

The Complete Poetical Works of Lord Byron. Cambridge Edition. ed. Paul Elmer More. Boston: Houghton Mifflin, 1905. The best complete one-volume edition, based on E. H. Coleridge's seven-volume edition.

Lord Byron's Correspondence. ed. John Murray. 2 vols. London: Murray, 1922. Revealing letters to Lady Melbourne, Hobhouse, and Kinnaird.

Byron: A Self-Portrait, Letters and Diaries, 1798 to 1824. ed. Peter Quennell. 2 vols. London: John Murray, 1950. Includes some hitherto unpublished letters.

BIOGRAPHIES AND CRITICAL INTERPRETATIONS

Blessington, The Countess of. *Conversations of Lord Byron with the Countess of Blessington.* London: Colburn, 1834. A shrewd contemporary interpretation.

Borst, William A. *Lord Byron's First Pilgrimage, 1809–1811.* New Haven: Yale University Press, 1948. Useful background for the study of *Childe Harold.*

Boyd, Elizabeth F. *Byron's Don Juan, a Critical Study.* New Brunswick, N. J.: Rutgers University Press, 1945. The poem seen against the background of Byron's reading and personality.

Calvert, William J. *Byron: Romantic Paradox.* Chapel Hill: University of North Carolina Press, 1935. An interpretation of the poetry in relation to the man.

Chew, Samuel C. *Byron in England: His Fame and After Fame.* London: John Murray, 1924. Contains excellent bibliography of Byroniana.

Fuess, Claude M. *Lord Byron as a Satirist in Verse.* New York: Columbia University Press, 1912.

Lovell, Ernest J., Jr. *Byron: the Record of a Quest.* Austin: University of Texas Press, 1949. Studies in the poet's con·

cept and treatment of nature. Excellent critical postscript on "The Contemporaneousness of Byron."

Maurois, André. *Byron.* tr. Hamish Miles. London: Jonathan Cape, 1930. Still the best and most readable biography.

Mayne, Ethel C. *Byron.* London: Methuen, 1924. A detailed biography but often strangely warped in interpretation.

Medwin, Thomas. *Journal of the Conversations of Lord Byron.* London: Colburn, 1824. Not wholly reliable but catches the tone of Byron's realistic and satirical wit.

Milbanke, Ralph (Earl of Lovelace). *Astarte.* New edition with many additional letters, ed. Mary Countess of Lovelace. London: Christophers, 1921. Evidence of Byron's relations with his half sister Augusta.

Moore, Thomas. *Letters and Journals of Lord Byron: with Notices of His Life.* 2 vols. London: John Murray, 1830. The first official life.

Nicolson, Harold. *Byron: The Last Journey.* London: Constable, 1924. Detailed and interesting account of Byron's last voyage to Greece and of his death.

Origo, Iris. *The Last Attachment.* London: Jonathan Cape and John Murray, 1949. The story of Byron and the Countess Teresa Guiccioli as told in their unpublished letters and other family papers. An illuminating study of Byron as lover.

CONTENTS

HEBREW MELODIES

SATIRES

TALES

ITALIAN POEMS

DRAMA

SELECTED POETRY
OF LORD BYRON

CHILDE HAROLD'S PILGRIMAGE

A Romaunt

[The first two cantos of *Childe Harold* were written during Byron's travels in the Eastern Mediterranean countries. Canto I was begun at Janina, Albania (now Greece), October 31, 1809, and Canto II was finished at Smyrna, March 28, 1810. It was published in March, 1812, and brought Byron immediate fame, surpassing that of any young poet, perhaps of any poet during his lifetime. Canto III was mostly written while Byron was living at the Villa Diodati near Geneva. It was begun early in May and finished at Ouchy, near Lausanne, on June 27, 1816, and was published the same year. The fourth canto, inspired by Byron's trip to Rome in the spring of 1817, was begun on June 26 and a first draft was finished on July 20, but he added many more stanzas before the poem was published in 1818.]

"L'univers est une espèce de livre, dont on n'a lu que la première page quand on n'a vu que son pays. J'en ai feuilleté un assez grand nombre, que j'ai trouvé également mauvaises. Cet examen ne m'a point été infructueux. Je haïssais ma patrie. Toutes les impertinences des peuples divers, parmi lesquels j'ai vécu, m'ont réconcilié avec elle. Quand je n'aurais tiré d'autre bénéfice de mes voyages que celui-là, je n'en regretterais ni les frais ni les fatigues."—*Le Cosmopolite, ou, le Citoyen du Monde,* par Fougeret de Monbron. Londres, 1753.

PREFACE

[TO THE FIRST AND SECOND CANTOS]

THE following poem was written, for the most part, amidst the scenes which it attempts to describe. It was begun in Albania; and the parts relative to Spain and Portugal were composed from the author's observations in those countries. Thus much it may be necessary to state for the correctness of the descriptions. The scenes attempted to be sketched are in Spain, Portugal, Epirus, Acarnania and Greece. There, for the present, the poem stops: its reception will determine whether the author may venture to conduct his readers to the capital of the East, through Ionia and Phrygia: these two cantos are merely experimental.

A fictitious character is introduced for the sake of giving some connection to the piece; which, however, makes no pretension to regularity. It has been suggested to me by friends, on whose opinions I set a high value, that in this fictitious character, "Childe Harold," I may incur the suspicion of having intended some real personage: this I beg leave, once for all, to disclaim— Harold is the child of imagination, for the purpose I have stated.

In some very trivial particulars, and those merely local, there might be grounds for such a notion; but in the main points, I should hope, none whatever.

It is almost superfluous to mention that the appellation "Childe," as "Childe Waters," "Childe Childers," etc., is used as more consonant with the old structure of versification which I have adopted. The "Good Night" in the beginning of the first Canto, was suggested by Lord Maxwell's "Good Night" in the *Border Minstrelsy*, edited by Mr. Scott.

With the different poems which have been published on Spanish subjects, there may be found some slight coincidence in the first part, which treats of the Peninsula, but it can only be casual; as, with the exception of a few concluding stanzas, the whole of the poem was written in the Levant.

The stanza of Spenser, according to one of our most successful poets, admits of every variety. Dr. Beattie makes the following observation:—

"Not long ago I began a poem in the style and stanza of Spenser, in which I propose to give full scope to my inclination, and be either droll or pathetic, descriptive or sentimental, tender or satirical, as the humour strikes me; for, if I mistake not, the measure which I have adopted admits equally of all these kinds of composition." Strengthened in my opinion by such authority, and by the example of some in the highest order of Italian poets, I shall make no apology for attempts at similar variations in the following composition; satisfied that, if they are unsuccessful, their failure must be in the execution, rather than in the design sanctioned by the practice of Ariosto, Thomson, and Beattie.

London, February, 1812.

ADDITION TO THE PREFACE

I HAVE now waited till almost all our periodical journals have distributed their usual portion of criticism. To the justice of the generality of their criticisms I have nothing to object; it would ill become me to quarrel with their very slight degree of censure, when, perhaps, if they had been less kind they had been more candid. Returning, therefore, to all and each my best thanks for their liberality, on one point alone I shall venture an observation. Amongst the many objections justly urged to the very indifferent character of the "vagrant Childe" (whom, notwithstanding many hints to the contrary, I still maintain to be a fictitious personage), it has been stated, that, besides the anachronism, he is very *unknightly*, as the times of the Knights were times of Love, Honour, and so forth. Now it so happens that the good old times, when "l'amour du bon vieux temps, l'amour antique," flourished, were the most profligate of all possible centuries. Those who have any doubts on this subject may consult Sainte-Palaye, *passim*, and more particularly vol. ii. p. 69. The vows of chivalry were no better kept than any other vows whatsoever; and the songs of the Troubadours were not more decent, and certainly were much less refined, than those of Ovid. The "Cours d'Amour, parlemens d'amour, ou de courtoisie et de gentilesse" had much more of love than of courtesy or gentleness. See Rolland on the same subject with Sainte-Palaye.

Whatever other objection may be urged to that most unamiable personage Childe Harold, he was so far perfectly knightly in his attributes—"No waiter, but a knight templar." By the by, I fear that Sir Tristrem and Sir Lancelot were no better than they should be, although very poetical personages and true knights,

"sans peur," though not "sans reproche." If the story of the insti-
tution of the "Garter" be not a fable, the knights of that order
have for several centuries borne the badge of a Countess of
Salisbury, of indifferent memory. So much for chivalry. Burke
need not have regretted that its days are over, though Marie-
Antoinette was quite as chaste as most of those in whose honour
lances were shivered, and knights unhorsed.

Before the days of Bayard, and down to those of Sir Joseph
Banks (the most chaste and celebrated of ancient and modern
times) few exceptions will be found to this statement; and I fear
a little investigation will teach us not to regret these monstrous
mummeries of the middle ages.

I now leave "Childe Harold" to live his day such as he is; it
had been more agreeable, and certainly more easy, to have drawn
an amiable character. It had been easy to varnish over his faults,
to make him do more and express less, but he never was intended
as an example, further than to show, that early perversion of
mind and morals leads to satiety of past pleasures and disappointment in new ones, and that even the beauties of nature and the
stimulus of travel (except ambition, the most powerful of all
excitements) are lost on a soul so constituted, or rather misdi-
rected. Had I proceeded with the Poem, this character would
have deepened as he drew to the close; for the outline which I
once meant to fill up for him was, with some exceptions, the
sketch of a modern Timon, perhaps a poetical Zeluco.

TO IANTHE

Not in those climes where I have late been straying,
Though Beauty long hath there been matchless deemed,
Not in those visions to the heart displaying
Forms which it sighs but to have only dreamed,
Hath aught like thee in Truth or Fancy seemed:
Nor, having seen thee, shall I vainly seek
To paint those charms which varied as they beamed—
To such as see thee not my words were weak;
To those who gaze on thee what language could they speak

Ah! may'st thou ever be what now thou art,
Nor unbeseem the promise of thy Spring—

As fair in form, as warm yet pure in heart,
Love's image upon earth without his wing.
And guileless beyond Hope's imagining!
And surely she who now so fondly rears
Thy youth, in thee, thus hourly brightening,
Beholds the Rainbow of her future years,
Before whose heavenly hues all Sorrow disappears.

Young Peri of the West!—'tis well for me
My years already doubly number thine;
My loveless eyes unmoved may gaze on thee,
And safely view thy ripening beauties shine;
Happy, I ne'er shall see them in decline;
Happier, that, while all younger hearts shall bleed,
Mine shall escape the doom thine eyes assign
To those whose admiration shall succeed,
But mixed with pangs to Love's even loveliest hours decreed.

Oh! let that eye, which, wild as the Gazelle's,
Now brightly bold or beautifully shy,
Wins as it wanders, dazzles where it dwells,
Glance o'er this page, nor to my verse deny
That smile for which my breast might vainly sigh
Could I to thee be ever more than friend:
This much, dear Maid, accord; nor question why
To one so young my strain I would commend,
But bid me with my wreath one matchless Lily blend.

Such is thy name with this my verse entwined;
And long as kinder eyes a look shall cast
On Harold's page, Ianthe's here enshrined
Shall thus be *first* beheld, forgotten *last:*
My days once numbered—should this homage past
Attract thy fairy fingers near the Lyre
Of him who hailed thee loveliest, as thou wast—
Such is the most my Memory may desire;
Though more than Hope can claim, could Friendship less require?

CANTO THE FIRST

I

Oh, thou! in Hellas deemed of heavenly birth,
Muse! formed or fabled at the Minstrel's will!
Since shamed full oft by later lyres on earth,
Mine dares not call thee from thy sacred Hill:
Yet there I've wandered by thy vaunted rill;
Yes! sighed o'er Delphi's long deserted shrine,
Where, save that feeble fountain, all is still;
Nor mote my shell awake the weary Nine
To grace so plain a tale—this lowly lay of mine.

II

Whilome in Albion's isle there dwelt a youth,
Who ne in Virtue's ways did take delight;
But spent his days in riot most uncouth,
And vexed with mirth the drowsy ear of Night.
Ah me! in sooth he was a shameless wight,
Sore given to revel, and ungodly glee;
Few earthly things found favour in his sight
Save concubines and carnal companie,
And flaunting wassailers of high and low degree

III

Childe Harold was he hight:—but whence his name
And lineage long, it suits me not to say;
Suffice it, that perchance they were of fame,
And had been glorious in another day:
But one sad losel soils a name for ay,
However mighty in the olden time;
Nor all that heralds rake from coffined clay,
Nor florid prose, nor honied lies of rhyme,
Can blazon evil deeds, or consecrate a crime.

IV

Childe Harold basked him in the Noontide sun,
Disporting there like any other fly;
Nor deemed before his little day was done
One blast might chill him into misery.
But long ere scarce a third of his passed by,
Worse than Adversity the Childe befell;
He felt the fulness of Satiety:
Then loathed he in his native land to dwell,
Which seemed to him more lone than Eremite's sad cell.

V

For he through Sin's long labyrinth had run,
Nor made atonement when he did amiss,
Had sighed to many though he loved but one,
And that loved one, alas! could ne'er be his.
Ah, happy she! to 'scape from him whose kiss
Had been pollution unto aught so chaste;
Who soon had left her charms for vulgar bliss,
And spoiled her goodly lands to gild his waste,
Nor calm domestic peace had ever deigned to taste.

VI

And now Childe Harold was sore sick at heart,
And from his fellow Bacchanals would flee;
'Tis said, at times the sullen tear would start,
But Pride congealed the drop within his ee:
Apart he stalked in joyless reverie,
And from his native land resolved to go,
And visit scorching climes beyond the sea;
With pleasure drugged, he almost longed for woe,
And e'en for change of scene would seek the shades below.

VII

The Childe departed from his father's hall:
It was a vast and venerable pile;
So old, it seeméd only not to fall,
Yet strength was pillared in each massy aisle.

Monastic dome! condemned to uses vile!
Where Superstition once had made her den
Now Paphian girls were known to sing and smile;
And monks might deem their time was come agen,
If ancient tales say true, nor wrong these holy men.

VIII

Yet oft-times in his maddest mirthful mood
Strange pangs would flash along Childe Harold's brow,
As if the Memory of some deadly feud
Or disappointed passion lurked below:
But this none knew, nor haply cared to know;
For his was not that open, artless soul
That feels relief by bidding sorrow flow,
Nor sought he friend to counsel or condole,
Whate'er this grief mote be, which he could not control.

IX

And none did love him!—though to hall and bower
He gathered revellers from far and near,
He knew them flatterers of the festal hour,
The heartless Parasites of present cheer.
Yea! none did love him—not his lemans dear—
But pomp and power alone are Woman's care,
And where these are light Eros finds a feere;
Maidens, like moths, are ever caught by glare,
And Mammon wins his way where Seraphs might despair.

X

Childe Harold had a mother—not forgot,
Though parting from that mother he did shun;
A sister whom he loved, but saw her not
Before his weary pilgrimage begun:
If friends he had, he bade adieu to none.
Yet deem not thence his breast a breast of steel:
Ye, who have known what 'tis to dote upon
A few dear objects, will in sadness feel
Such partings break the heart they fondly hope to heal.

XI

His house, his home, his heritage, his lands,
The laughing dames in whom he did delight,
Whose large blue eyes, fair locks, and snowy hands,
Might shake the Saintship of an Anchorite,
And long had fed his youthful appetite;
His goblets brimmed with every costly wine,
And all that mote to luxury invite,
Without a sigh he left, to cross the brine,
And traverse Paynim shores, and pass Earth's central line.

XII

The sails were filled, and fair the light winds blew,
As glad to waft him from his native home;
And fast the white rocks faded from his view,
And soon were lost in circumambient foam:
And then, it may be, of his wish to roam
Repented he, but in his bosom slept
The silent thought, nor from his lips did come
One word of wail, whilst others sate and wept,
And to the reckless gales unmanly moaning kept.

XIII

But when the Sun was sinking in the sea
He seized his harp, which he at times could string,
And strike, albeit with untaught melody,
When deemed he no strange ear was listening:
And now his fingers o'er it he did fling,
And tuned his farewell in the dim twilight;
While flew the vessel on her snowy wing,
And fleeting shores receded from his sight,
Thus to the elements he poured his last "Good Night."

CHILDE HAROLD'S GOOD NIGHT

1

"ADIEU, adieu! my native shore
  Fades o'er the waters blue;
The night-winds sigh, the breakers roar,
  And shrieks the wild sea-mew.
Yon Sun that sets upon the sea
  We follow in his flight;
Farewell awhile to him and thee,
  My native Land—Good Night!

2

"A few short hours and He will rise
  To give the Morrow birth;
And I shall hail the main and skies,
  But not my mother Earth.
Deserted is my own good Hall,
  Its hearth is desolate;
Wild weeds are gathering on the wall;
  My Dog howls at the gate.

3

"Come hither, hither, my little page!
  Why dost thou weep and wail?
Or dost thou dread the billows' rage,
  Or tremble at the gale?
But dash the tear-drop from thine eye;
  Our ship is swift and strong:
Our fleetest falcon scarce can fly
  More merrily along."

4

"Let winds be shrill, let waves roll high,
  I fear not wave nor wind:
Yet marvel not, Sir Childe, that I
  Am sorrowful in mind;

For I have from my father gone,
    A mother whom I love,
And have no friends, save these alone,
    But thee—and One above.

5

"My father blessed me fervently,
    Yet did not much complain;
But sorely will my mother sigh
    Till I come back again."—
"Enough, enough, my little lad!
    Such tears become thine eye;
If I thy guileless bosom had,
    Mine own would not be dry.

6

"Come hither, hither, my staunch yeoman,
    Why dost thou look so pale?
Or dost thou dread a French foeman?
    Or shiver at the gale?"—
"Deem'st thou I tremble for my life?
    Sir Childe, I'm not so weak;
But thinking on an absent wife
    Will blanch a faithful cheek.

7

'My spouse and boys dwell near thy hall,
    Along the bordering Lake,
And when they on their father call,
    What answer shall she make?"—
"Enough, enough, my yeoman good,
    Thy grief let none gainsay;
But I, who am of lighter mood,
    Will laugh to flee away.

8

"For who would trust the seeming sighs
    Of wife or paramour?

Fresh feeres will dry the bright blue eyes
   We late saw streaming o'er.
For pleasures past I do not grieve,
   Nor perils gathering near;
My greatest grief is that I leave
   No thing that claims a tear.

9

"And now I'm in the world alone,
   Upon the wide, wide sea:
But why should I for others groan,
   When none will sigh for me?
Perchance my Dog will whine in vain,
   Till fed by stranger hands;
But long ere I come back again,
   He'd tear me where he stands.

10

"With thee, my bark, I'll swiftly go
   Athwart the foaming brine;
Nor care what land thou bear'st me to,
   So not again to mine.
Welcome, welcome, ye dark-blue waves!
   And when you fail my sight,
Welcome, ye deserts, and ye caves!
   My native Land—Good Night!"

XIV

On, on the vessel flies, the land is gone,
And winds are rude in Biscay's sleepless bay.
Four days are sped, but with the fifth, anon,
New shores descried make every bosom gay;
And Cintra's mountain greets them on their way,
And Tagus dashing onward to the Deep,
His fabled golden tribute bent to pay;
And soon on board the Lusian pilots leap,
And steer 'twixt fertile shores where yet few rustics reap.

XV

Oh, Christ! it is a goodly sight to see
What Heaven hath done for this delicious land!
What fruits of fragrance blush on every tree!
What goodly prospects o'er the hills expand!
But man would mar them with an impious hand:
And when the Almighty lifts his fiercest scourge
'Gainst those who most transgress his high command,
With treble vengeance will his hot shafts urge
Gaul's locust host, and earth from fellest foeman purge.

XVI

What beauties doth Lisboa first unfold!
Her image floating on that noble tide,
Which poets vainly pave with sands of gold,
But now whereon a thousand keels did ride
Of mighty strength, since Albion was allied,
And to the Lusians did her aid afford:—
A nation swoln with ignorance and pride,
Who lick yet loathe the hand that waves the sword
To save them from the wrath of Gaul's unsparing Lord.

XVII

But whoso entereth within this town,
That, sheening far, celestial seems to be,
Disconsolate will wander up and down,
'Mid many things unsightly to strange ee;
For hut and palace show like filthily:
The dingy denizens are reared in dirt;
Ne personage of high or mean degree
Doth care for cleanness of surtout or shirt,
Though shent with Egypt's plague, unkempt, unwashed, unhurt.

XVIII

Poor, paltry slaves! yet born 'midst noblest scenes—
Why, Nature, waste thy wonders on such men?
Lo! Cintra's glorious Eden intervenes
In variegated maze of mount and glen.

Ah, me! what hand can pencil guide, or pen,
To follow half on which the eye dilates
Through views more dazzling unto mortal ken
Than those whereof such things the Bard relates,
Who to the awe-struck world unlocked Elysium's gates!

XIX

The horrid crags, by toppling convent crowned,
The cork-trees hoar that clothe the shaggy steep,
The mountain-moss by scorching skies imbrowned,
The sunken glen, whose sunless shrubs must weep,
The tender azure of the unruffled deep,
The orange tints that gild the greenest bough,
The torrents that from cliff to valley leap,
The vine on high, the willow branch below,
Mixed in one mighty scene, with varied beauty glow.

XX

Then slowly climb the many-winding way,
And frequent turn to linger as you go,
From loftier rocks new loveliness survey,
And rest ye at "Our Lady's house of Woe;"
Where frugal monks their little relics show,
And sundry legends to the stranger tell:
Here impious men have punished been, and lo!
Deep in yon cave Honorius long did dwell,
In hope to merit Heaven by making earth a Hell.

XXI

And here and there, as up the crags you spring,
Mark many rude-carved crosses near the path:
Yet deem not these Devotion's offering—
These are memorials frail of murderous wrath:
For wheresoe'er the shrieking victim hath
Poured forth his blood beneath the assassin's knife,
Some hand erects a cross of mouldering lath;
And grove and glen with thousand such are rife
Throughout this purple land, where Law secures not life.

XXII

On sloping mounds, or in the vale beneath
Are domes where whilome kings did make repair;
But now the wild flowers round them only breathe:
Yet ruined Splendour still is lingering there.
And yonder towers the Prince's palace fair:
There thou too, Vathek! England's wealthiest son,
Once formed thy Paradise, as not aware
When wanton Wealth her mightiest deeds hath done,
Meek Peace voluptuous lures was ever wont to shun.

XXIII

Here didst thou dwell, here schemes of pleasure plan,
Beneath yon mountain's ever beauteous brow:
But now, as if a thing unblest by Man,
Thy fairy dwelling is as lone as Thou!
Here giant weeds a passage scarce allow
To Halls deserted, portals gaping wide:
Fresh lessons to the thinking bosom, how
Vain are the pleasaunces on earth supplied,
Swept into wrecks anon by Time's ungentle tide!

XXIV

Behold the hall where chiefs were late convened!
Oh! dome displeasing unto British eye!
With diadem hight Foolscap, lo! a Fiend,
A little Fiend that scoffs incessantly,
There sits in parchment robe arrayed, and by
His side is hung a seal and sable scroll,
Where blazoned glare names known to chivalry,
And sundry signatures adorn the roll,
Whereat the Urchin points and laughs with all his soul.

XXV

Convention is the dwarfish demon styled
That foiled the knights in Marialva's dome:
Of brains (if brains they had) he them beguiled,
And turned a nation's shallow joy to gloom.

Here Folly dashed to earth the victor's plume,
And Policy regained what arms had lost:
For chiefs like ours in vain may laurels bloom!
Woe to the conquering, not the conquered host,
Since baffled Triumph droops on Lusitania's coast!

XXVI

And ever since that martial Synod met,
Britannia sickens, Cintra! at thy name;
And folks in office at the mention fret,
And fain would blush, if blush they could, for shame.
How will Posterity the deed proclaim!
Will not our own and fellow-nations sneer,
To view these champions cheated of their fame,
By foes in fight o'erthrown, yet victors here,
Where Scorn her finger points through many a coming year?

XXVII

So deemed the Childe, as o'er the mountains he
Did take his way in solitary guise:
Sweet was the scene, yet soon he thought to flee,
More restless than the swallow in the skies:
Though here awhile he learned to moralise,
For Meditation fixed at times on him;
And conscious Reason whispered to despise
His early youth, misspent in maddest whim;
But as he gazed on truth his aching eyes grew dim.

XXVIII

To horse! to horse! he quits, for ever quits
A scene of peace, though soothing to his soul:
Again he rouses from his moping fits,
But seeks not now the harlot and the bowl.
Onward he flies, nor fixed as yet the goal
Where he shall rest him on his pilgrimage;
And o'er him many changing scenes must roll
Ere toil his thirst for travel can assuage,
Or he shall calm his breast, or learn experience sage.

XXIX

Yet Mafra shall one moment claim delay,
Where dwelt of yore the Lusians' luckless queen;
And Church and Court did mingle their array,
And Mass and revel were alternate seen;
Lordlings and freres—ill-sorted fry I ween!
But here the Babylonian Whore hath built
A dome, where flaunts she in such glorious sheen,
That men forget the blood which she hath spilt,
And bow the knee to Pomp that loves to varnish guilt.

XXX

O'er vales that teem with fruits, romantic hills,
(Oh, that such hills upheld a freeborn race!)
Whereon to gaze the eye with joyaunce fills,
Childe Harold wends through many a pleasant place.
Though sluggards deem it but a foolish chase,
And marvel men should quit their easy chair,
The toilsome way, and long, long league to trace,
Oh! there is sweetness in the mountain air,
And Life, that bloated Ease can never hope to share.

XXXI

More bleak to view the hills at length recede,
And, less luxuriant, smoother vales extend:
Immense horizon-bounded plains succeed!
Far as the eye discerns, withouten end,
Spain's realms appear whereon her shepherds tend
Flocks, whose rich fleece right well the trader knows—
Now must the Pastor's arm his *lambs* defend:
For Spain is compassed by unyielding foes,
And *all* must shield their *all*, or share Subjection's woes.

XXXII

Where Lusitania and her Sister meet,
Deem ye what bounds the rival realms divide?
Or ere the jealous Queens of Nations greet,
Doth Tayo interpose his mighty tide?

Or dark Sierras rise in craggy pride?
Or fence of art, like China's vasty wall?
Ne barrier wall, ne river deep and wide,
Ne horrid crags, nor mountains dark and tall,
Rise like the rocks that part Hispania's land from Gaul:

XXXIII

But these between a silver streamlet glides,
And scarce a name distinguisheth the brook,
Though rival kingdoms press its verdant sides,
Here leans the idle shepherd on his crook,
And vacant on the rippling waves doth look,
That peaceful still 'twixt bitterest foemen flow;
For proud each peasant as the noblest duke:
Well doth the Spanish hind the difference know
'Twixt him and Lusian slave, the lowest of the low.

XXXIV

But ere the mingling bounds have far been passed,
Dark Guadiana rolls his power along
In sullen billows, murmuring and vast,
So noted ancient roundelays among.
Whilome upon his banks did legions throng
Of Moor and Knight, in mailéd splendour drest:
Here ceased the swift their race, here sunk the strong;
The Paynim turban and the Christian crest
Mixed on the bleeding stream, by floating hosts oppressed.

XXXV

Oh, lovely Spain! renowned, romantic Land!
Where is that Standard which Pelagio bore,
When Cava's traitor-sire first called the band
That dyed thy mountain streams with Gothic gore?
Where are those bloody Banners which of yore
Waved o'er thy sons, victorious to the gale,
And drove at last the spoilers to their shore?
Red gleamed the Cross, and waned the Crescent pale,
While Afric's echoes thrilled with Moorish matrons' wail.

XXXVI

Teems not each ditty with the glorious tale?
Ah! such, alas! the hero's amplest fate!
When granite moulders and when records fail,
A peasant's plaint prolongs his dubious date.
Pride! bend thine eye from Heaven to thine estate,
See how the Mighty shrink into a song!
Can Volume, Pillar, Pile preserve thee great?
Or must thou trust Tradition's simple tongue,
When Flattery sleeps with thee, and History does thee wrong?

XXXVII

Awake, ye Sons of Spain! awake! advance!
Lo! Chivalry, your ancient Goddess, cries,
But wields not, as of old, her thirsty lance,
Nor shakes her crimson plumage in the skies:
Now on the smoke of blazing bolts she flies,
And speaks in thunder through yon engine's roar:
In every peal she calls—"Awake! arise!"
Say, is her voice more feeble than of yore,
When her war-song was heard on Andalusia's shore?

XXXVIII

Hark!—heard you not those hoofs of dreadful note?
Sounds not the clang of conflict on the heath?
Saw ye not whom the reeking sabre smote,
Nor saved your brethren ere they sank beneath
Tyrants and Tyrants' slaves?—the fires of Death,
The Bale-fires flash on high:—from rock to rock
Each volley tells that thousands cease to breathe;
Death rides upon the sulphury Siroc,
Red Battle stamps his foot, and Nations feel the shock.

XXXIX

Lo! where the Giant on the mountain stands,
His blood-red tresses deepening in the Sun,
With death-shot glowing in his fiery hands,
And eye that scorcheth all it glares upon;

Restless it rolls, now fixed, and now anon
Flashing afar,—and at his iron feet
Destruction cowers, to mark what deeds are done;
For on this morn three potent Nations meet,
To shed before his Shrine the blood he deems most sweet

XL

By Heaven! it is a splendid sight to see
(For one who hath no friend, no brother there)
Their rival scarfs of mixed embroidery,
Their various arms that glitter in the air!
What gallant War-hounds rouse them from their lair,
And gnash their fangs, loud yelling for the prey!
All join the chase, but few the triumph share;
The Grave shall bear the chiefest prize away,
And Havoc scarce for joy can number their array.

XLI

Three hosts combine to offer sacrifice;
Three tongues prefer strange orisons on high;
Three gaudy standards flout the pale blue skies;
The shouts are France, Spain, Albion, Victory!
The Foe, the Victim, and the fond Ally
That fights for all, but ever fights in vain,
Are met—as if at home they could not die—
To feed the crow on Talavera's plain,
And fertilise the field that each pretends to gain.

XLII

There shall they rot—Ambition's honoured fools!
Yes, Honour decks the turf that wraps their clay!
Vain Sophistry! in these behold the tools,
The broken tools, that Tyrants cast away
By myriads, when they dare to pave their way
With human hearts—to what?—a dream alone.
Can Despots compass aught that hails their sway?
Or call with truth one span of earth their own,
Save that wherein at last they crumble bone by bone?

XLIII

Oh, Albuera! glorious field of grief!
As o'er thy plain the Pilgrim pricked his steed,
Who could foresee thee, in a space so brief,
A scene where mingling foes should boast and bleed!
Peace to the perished! may the warrior's meed
And tears of triumph their reward prolong!
Till others fall where other chieftains lead,
Thy name shall circle round the gaping throng,
And shine in worthless lays, the theme of transient song.

XLIV

Enough of Battle's minions! let them play
Their game of lives, and barter breath for fame:
Fame that will scarce reanimate their clay,
Though thousands fall to deck some single name.
In sooth 'twere sad to thwart their noble aim
Who strike, blest hirelings! for their country's good,
And die, that living might have proved her shame;
Perished, perchance, in some domestic feud,
Or in a narrower sphere wild Rapine's path pursued.

XLV

Full swiftly Harold wends his lonely way
Where proud Sevilla triumphs unsubdued:
Yet is she free? the Spoiler's wished-for prey!
Soon, soon shall Conquest's fiery foot intrude,
Blackening her lovely domes with traces rude.
Inevitable hour! 'Gainst fate to strive
Where Desolation plants her famished brood
Is vain, or Ilion, Tyre might yet survive,
And Virtue vanquish all, and Murder cease to thrive.

XLVI

But all unconscious of the coming doom,
The feast, the song, the revel here abounds;
Strange modes of merriment the hours consume,
Nor bleed these patriots with their country's wounds.

Nor here War's clarion, but Love's rebeck sounds;
Here Folly still his votaries inthralls;
And young-eyed Lewdness walks her midnight rounds:
Girt with the silent crimes of Capitals,
Still to the last kind Vice clings to the tott'ring walls.

XLVII

Not so the rustic—with his trembling mate
He lurks, nor casts his heavy eye afar,
Lest he should view his vineyard desolate,
Blasted below the dun hot breath of War.
No more beneath soft eve's consenting star
Fandango twirls his jocund castanet:
Ah, Monarchs! could ye taste the mirth ye mar,
Not in the toils of Glory would ye fret;
The hoarse dull drum would sleep, and Man be happy yet!

XLVIII

How carols now the lusty muleteer?
Of Love, Romance, Devotion is his lay,
As whilome he was wont the leagues to cheer,
His quick bells wildly jingling on the way?
No! as he speeds, he chants "Vivā el Rey!"
And checks his song to execrate Godoy,
The royal wittol Charles, and curse the day
When first Spain's queen beheld the black-eyed boy
And gore-faced Treason sprung from her adulterate joy.

XLIX

On yon long level plain, at distance crowned
With crags, whereon those Moorish turrets rest,
Wide-scattered hoof-marks dint the wounded ground;
And, scathed by fire, the greensward's darkened vest
Tells that the foe was Andalusia's guest:
Here was the camp, the watch-flame, and the host,
Here the bold peasant stormed the Dragon's nest;
Still does he mark it with triumphant boast,
And points to yonder cliffs, which oft were won and lost.

L

And whomsoe'er along the path you meet
Bears in his cap the badge of crimson hue,
Which tells you whom to shun and whom to greet:
Woe to the man that walks in public view
Without of loyalty this token true:
Sharp is the knife, and sudden is the stroke;
And sorely would the Gallic foeman rue,
If subtle poniards, wrapt beneath the cloke,
Could blunt the sabre's edge, or clear the cannon's smoke.

LI

At every turn Morena's dusky height
Sustains aloft the battery's iron load;
And, far as mortal eye can compass sight,
The mountain-howitzer, the broken road,
The bristling palisade, the fosse o'erflowed,
The stationed bands, the never-vacant watch,
The magazine in rocky durance stowed,
The holstered steed beneath the shed of thatch,
The ball-piled pyramid, the ever-blazing match,

LII

Portend the deeds to come:—but he whose nod
Has tumbled feebler despots from their sway,
A moment pauseth ere he lifts the rod;
A little moment deigneth to delay:
Soon will his legions sweep through these their way;
The West must own the Scourger of the world.
Ah! Spain! how sad will be thy reckoning-day,
When soars Gaul's Vulture, with his wings unfurled,
And thou shalt view thy sons in crowds to Hades hurled

LIII

And must they fall? the young, the proud, the brave,
To swell one bloated Chief's unwholesome reign?
No step between submission and a grave?
The rise of Rapine and the fall of Spain?

And doth the Power that man adores ordain
Their doom, nor heed the suppliant's appeal?
Is all that desperate Valour acts in vain?
And Counsel sage, and patriotic Zeal—
The Veteran's skill—Youth's fire—and Manhood's heart of steel?

LIV

Is it for this the Spanish maid, aroused,
Hangs on the willow her unstrung guitar,
And, all unsexed, the Anlace hath espoused,
Sung the loud song, and dared the deed of war?
And she, whom once the semblance of a scar
Appalled, an owlet's 'larum chilled with dread,
Now views the column-scattering bay'net jar,
The falchion flash, and o'er the yet warm dead
Stalks with Minerva's step where Mars might quake to tread.

LV

Ye who shall marvel when you hear her tale,
Oh! had you known her in her softer hour,
Marked her black eye that mocks her coal-black veil,
Heard her light, lively tones in Lady's bower,
Seen her long locks that foil the painter's power,
Her fairy form, with more than female grace,
Scarce would you deem that Saragoza's tower
Beheld her smile in Danger's Gorgon face,
Thin the closed ranks, and lead in Glory's fearful chase.

LVI

Her lover sinks—she sheds no ill-timed tear;
Her Chief is slain—she fills his fatal post;
Her fellows flee—she checks their base career;
The Foe retires—she heads the sallying host;
Who can appease like her a lover's ghost?
Who can avenge so well a leader's fall?
What maid retrieve when man's flushed hope is lost?
Who hang so fiercely on the flying Gaul,
Foiled by a woman's hand, before a battered wall?

LVII

Yet are Spain's maids no race of Amazons,
But formed for all the witching arts of love:
Though thus in arms they emulate her sons,
And in the horrid phalanx dare to move,
'Tis but the tender fierceness of the dove,
Pecking the hand that hovers o'er her mate:
In softness as in firmness far above
Remoter females, famed for sickening prate;
Her mind is nobler sure, her charms perchance as great.

LVIII

The seal Love's dimpling finger hath impressed
Denotes how soft that chin which bears his touch:
Her lips, whose kisses pout to leave their nest
Bid man be valiant ere he merit such:
Her glance how wildly beautiful! how much
Hath Phœbus wooed in vain to spoil her cheek
Which glows yet smoother from his amorous clutch!
Who round the North for paler dames would seek?
How poor their forms appear! how languid, wan, and weak!

LIX

Match me, ye climes! which poets love to laud;
Match me, ye harems of the land! where now
I strike my strain, far distant, to applaud
Beauties that ev'n a cynic must avow;
Match me those Houries, whom ye scarce allow
To taste the gale lest Love should ride the wind,
With Spain's dark-glancing daughters—deign to know.
There your wise Prophet's Paradise we find,
His black-eyed maids of Heaven, angelically kind.

LX

Oh, thou Parnassus! whom I now survey,
Not in the phrensy of a dreamer's eye,
Not in the fabled landscape of a lay,
But soaring snow-clad through thy native sky,

In the wild pomp of mountain-majesty!
What marvel if I thus essay to sing?
The humblest of thy pilgrims passing by
Would gladly woo thine Echoes with his string,
Though from thy heights no more one Muse will wave her wing

LXI

Oft have I dreamed of Thee! whose glorious name
Who knows not, knows not man's divinest lore:
And now I view thee—'tis, alas! with shame
That I in feeblest accents must adore.
When I recount thy worshippers of yore
I tremble, and can only bend the knee;
Nor raise my voice, nor vainly dare to soar,
But gaze beneath thy cloudy canopy
In silent joy to think at last I look on Thee!

LXII

Happier in this than mightiest Bards have been,
Whose Fate to distant homes confined their lot,
Shall I unmoved behold the hallowed scene,
Which others rave of, though they know it not?
Though here no more Apollo haunts his Grot,
And thou, the Muses' seat, art now their grave,
Some gentle Spirit still pervades the spot,
Sighs in the gale, keeps silence in the Cave,
And glides with glassy foot o'er yon melodious wave.

LXIII

Of thee hereafter. Ev'n amidst my strain
I turned aside to pay my homage here;
Forgot the land, the sons, the maids of Spain;
Her fate, to every freeborn bosom dear;
And hailed thee, not perchance without a tear.
Now to my theme—but from thy holy haunt
Let me some remnant, some memorial bear;
Yield me one leaf of Daphne's deathless plant,
Nor let thy votary's hope be deemed an idle vaunt.

LXIV

But ne'er didst thou, fair Mount! when Greece was young,
See round thy giant base a brighter choir,
Nor e'er did Delphi, when her Priestess sung
The Pythian hymn with more than mortal fire,
Behold a train more fitting to inspire
The song of love, than Andalusia's maids
Nurst in the glowing lap of soft Desire:
Ah! that to these were given such peaceful shades
As Greece can still bestow, though Glory fly her glades.

LXV

Fair is proud Seville; let her country boast
Her strength, her wealth, her site of ancient days;
But Cadiz, rising on the distant coast,
Calls forth a sweeter, though ignoble praise.
Ah, Vice! how soft are thy voluptuous ways!
While boyish blood is mantling, who can 'scape
The fascination of thy magic gaze?
A Cherub-Hydra round us dost thou gape,
And mould to every taste thy dear delusive shape.

LXVI

When Paphos fell by Time—accurséd Time!
The Queen who conquers all must yield to thee—
The Pleasures fled, but sought as warm a clime;
And Venus, constant to her native Sea,
To nought else constant, hither deigned to flee,
And fixed her shrine within these walls of white:
Though not to one dome circumscribeth She
Her worship, but, devoted to her rite,
A thousand Altars rise, for ever blazing bright.

LXVII

From morn till night, from night still startled Morn
Peeps blushing on the Revel's laughing crew,
The Song is heard, the rosy Garland worn;
Devices quaint, and Frolics ever new.

Tread on each other's kibes. A long adieu
He bids to sober joy that here sojourns:
Nought interrupts the riot, though in lieu
Of true devotion monkish incense burns,
And Love and Prayer unite, or rule the hour by turns.

LXVIII

The Sabbath comes, a day of blessèd rest:
What hallows it upon this Christian shore?
Lo! it is sacred to a solemn Feast:
Hark! heard you not the forest-monarch's roar?
Crashing the lance, he snuffs the spouting gore
Of man and steed, o'erthrown beneath his horn;
The thronged arena shakes with shouts for more;
Yells the mad crowd o'er entrails freshly torn,
Nor shrinks the female eye, nor ev'n affects to mourn.

LXIX

The seventh day this—the Jubilee of man!
London! right well thou know'st the day of prayer:
Then thy spruce citizen, washed artisan,
And smug apprentice gulp their weekly air:
Thy coach of hackney, whiskey, one-horse chair,
And humblest gig through sundry suburbs whirl,
To Hampstead, Brentford, Harrow make repair;
Till the tired jade the wheel forgets to hurl,
Provoking envious gibe from each pedestrian churl.

LXX

Some o'er thy Thamis row the ribboned fair,
Others along the safer turnpike fly;
Some Richmond-hill ascend, some scud to Ware,
And many to the steep of Highgate hie.
Ask ye, Bœotian Shades! the reason why?
'Tis to the worship of the solemn Horn,
Grasped in the holy hand of Mystery,
In whose dread name both men and maids are sworn,
And consecrate the oath with draught, and dance till morn

LXXI

All have their fooleries—not alike are thine,
Fair Cadiz, rising o'er the dark blue sea!
Soon as the Matin bell proclaimeth nine,
Thy Saint-adorers count the Rosary:
Much is the VIRGIN teased to shrive them free
(Well do I ween the only virgin there)
From crimes as numerous as her beadsmen be;
Then to the crowded circus forth they fare:
Young, old, high, low, at once the same diversion share.

LXXII

The lists are oped, the spacious area cleared,
Thousands on thousands piled are seated round;
Long ere the first loud trumpet's note is heard,
Ne vacant space for lated wight is found:
Here Dons, Grandees, but chiefly Dames abound,
Skilled in the ogle of a roguish eye,
Yet ever well inclined to heal the wound;
None through their cold disdain are doomed to die,
As moon-struck bards complain, by Love's sad archery.

LXXIII

Hushed is the din of tongues—on gallant steeds,
With milk-white crest, gold spur, and light-poised lance,
Four cavaliers prepare for venturous deeds
And lowly-bending to the lists advance;
Rich are their scarfs, their chargers featly prance:
If in the dangerous game they shine to-day,
The crowd's loud shout and ladies' lovely glance,
Best prize of better acts! they bear away;
And all that kings or chiefs e'er gain their toils repay.

LXXIV

In costly sheen and gaudy cloak arrayed,
But all afoot, the light-limbed Matadore
Stands in the centre, eager to invade
The lord of lowing herds; but not before

The ground, with cautious tread, is traversed o'er,
Lest aught unseen should lurk to thwart his speed:
His arms a dart, he fights aloof, nor more
Can Man achieve without the friendly steed—
Alas! too oft condemned for him to bear and bleed.

LXXV

Thrice sounds the Clarion; lo! the signal falls,
The den expands, and Expectation mute
Gapes round the silent circle's peopled walls:
Bounds with one lashing spring the mighty brute,
And, wildly staring, spurns, with sounding foot,
The sand, nor blindly rushes on his foe:
Here, there, he points his threatening front, to suit
His first attack, wide-waving to and fro
His angry tail; red rolls his eye's dilated glow.

LXXVI

Sudden he stops—his eye is fixed—away—
Away, thou heedless boy! prepare the spear;
Now is thy time, to perish, or display
The skill that yet may check his mad career!
With well-timed croupe the nimble coursers veer;
On foams the Bull, but not unscathed he goes;
Streams from his flank the crimson torrent clear:
He flies, he wheels, distracted with his throes;
Dart follows dart—lance, lance—loud bellowings speak his woes.

LXXVII

Again he comes; nor dart nor lance avail,
Nor the wild plunging of the tortured horse;
Though Man and Man's avenging arms assail,
Vain are his weapons, vainer is his force.
One gallant steed is stretched a mangled corse;
Another, hideous sight! unseamed appears,
His gory chest unveils life's panting source;
Though death-struck, still his feeble frame he rears;
Staggering, but stemming all, his Lord unharmed he bears

LXXVIII

Foiled, bleeding, breathless, furious to the last,
Full in the centre stands the Bull at bay,
'Mid wounds, and clinging darts, and lances brast,
And foes disabled in the brutal fray:
And now the Matadores around him play,
Shake the red cloak, and poise the ready brand:
Once more through all he bursts his thundering way—
Vain rage! the mantle quits the conynge hand,
Wraps his fierce eye—'tis past—he sinks upon the sand!

LXXIX

Where his vast neck just mingles with the spine,
Sheathed in his form the deadly weapon lies.
He stops—he starts—disdaining to decline:
Slowly he falls, amidst triumphant cries,
Without a groan, without a struggle dies.
The decorated car appears—on high
The corse is piled—sweet sight for vulgar eyes—
Four steeds that spurn the rein, as swift as shy,
Hurl the dark bulk along, scarce seen in dashing by.

LXXX

Such the ungentle sport that oft invites
The Spanish maid, and cheers the Spanish swain.
Nurtured in blood betimes, his heart delights
In vengeance, gloating on another's pain.
What private feuds the troubled village stain!
Though now one phalanxed host should meet the foe,
Enough, alas! in humble homes remain,
To mediate 'gainst friend the secret blow,
For some slight cause of wrath, whence Life's warm stream must
    flow.

LXXXI

But Jealousy has fled: his bars, his bolts,
His withered Centinel, Duenna sage!
And all whereat the generous soul revolts,
Which the stern dotard deemed he could encage,

Have passed to darkness with the vanished age.
Who late so free as Spanish girls were seen,
(Ere War uprose in his volcanic rage,)
With braided tresses bounding o'er the green,
While on the gay dance shone Night's lover-loving Queen?

LXXXII

Oh! many a time and oft, had Harold loved,
Or dreamed he loved, since Rapture is a dream;
But now his wayward bosom was unmoved,
For not yet had he drunk of Lethe's stream;
And lately had he learned with truth to deem
Love has no gift so grateful as his wings:
How fair, how young, how soft soe'er he seem,
Full from the fount of Joy's delicious springs
Some bitter o'er the flowers its bubbling venom flings.

LXXXIII

Yet to the beauteous form he was not blind,
Though now it moved him as it moves the wise;
Not that Philosophy on such a mind
E'er deigned to bend her chastely-awful eyes:
But Passion raves herself to rest, or flies;
And Vice, that digs her own voluptuous tomb,
Had buried long his hopes, no more to rise:
Pleasure's palled Victim! life-abhorring Gloom
Wrote on his faded brow curst Cain's unresting doom.

LXXXIV

Still he beheld, nor mingled with the throng;
But viewed them not with misanthropic hate:
Fain would he now have joined the dance, the song;
But who may smile that sinks beneath his fate?
Nought that he saw his sadness could abate:
Yet once he struggled 'gainst the Demon's sway,
And as in Beauty's bower he pensive sate,
Poured forth his unpremeditated lay,
To charms as fair as those that soothed his happier day.

TO INEZ

1

Nay, smile not at my sullen brow;
    Alas! I cannot smile again:
Yet Heaven avert that ever thou
    Shouldst weep, and haply weep in vain.

2

And dost thou ask what secret woe
    I bear, corroding Joy and Youth?
And wilt thou vainly seek to know
    A pang, ev'n thou must fail to soothe?

3

It is not love, it is not hate,
    Nor low Ambition's honours lost,
That bids me loathe my present state,
    And fly from all I prized the most:

4

It is that weariness which springs
    From all I meet, or hear, or see:
To me no pleasure Beauty brings;
    Thine eyes have scarce a charm for me.

5

It is that settled, ceaseless gloom
    The fabled Hebrew Wanderer bore;
That will not look beyond the tomb,
    But cannot hope for rest before.

6

What Exile from himself can flee?
    To zones though more and more remote.

Still, still pursues, where'er I be,
  The blight of Life—the Demon Thought.

7

Yet others rapt in pleasure seem,
  And taste of all that I forsake;
Oh! may they still of transport dream,
  And ne'er—at least like me—awake!

8

Through many a clime 'tis mine to go,
  With many a retrospection curst;
And all my solace is to know,
  Whate'er betides, I've known the worst.

9

What is that worst? Nay do not ask—
  In pity from the search forbear:
Smile on—nor venture to unmask
  Man's heart, and view the Hell that's there.
                              January 25, 1810.

LXXXV

Adieu, fair Cadiz! yea, a long adieu!
Who may forget how well thy walls have stood?
When all were changing thou alone wert true,
First to be free and last to be subdued:
And if amidst a scene, a shock so rude,
Some native blood was seen thy streets to dye,
A Traitor only fell beneath the feud:
Here all were noble, save Nobility;
None hugged a Conqueror's chain, save fallen Chivalry!

LXXXVI

Such be the sons of Spain, and strange her Fate!
They fight for Freedom who were never free,
A Kingless people for a nerveless state;

Her vassals combat when their Chieftains flee,
True to the veriest slaves of Treachery:
Fond of a land which gave them nought but life,
Pride points the path that leads to Liberty;
Back to the struggle, baffled in the strife,
War, war is still the cry, "War even to the knife!"

LXXXVII

Ye, who would more of Spain and Spaniards know,
Go, read whate'er is writ of bloodiest strife:
Whate'er keen Vengeance urged on foreign foe
Can act, is acting there against man's life:
From flashing scimitar to secret knife,
War mouldeth there each weapon to his need—
So may he guard the sister and the wife,
So may he make each curst oppressor bleed—
So may such foes deserve the most remorseless deed!

LXXXVIII

Flows there a tear of Pity for the dead?
Look o'er the ravage of the reeking plain;
Look on the hands with female slaughter red;
Then to the dogs resign the unburied slain,
Then to the vulture let each corse remain,
Albeit unworthy of the prey-bird's maw;
Let their bleached bones, and blood's unbleaching stain,
Long mark the battle-field with hideous awe:
Thus only may our sons conceive the scenes we saw!

LXXXIX

Nor yet, alas! the dreadful work is done;
Fresh legions pour adown the Pyrenees:
It deepens still, the work is scarce begun,
Nor mortal eye the distant end foresees.
Fall'n nations gaze on Spain; if freed, she frees
More than her fell Pizarros once enchained:
Strange retribution! now Columbia's ease
Repairs the wrongs that Quito's sons sustained,
While o'er the parent clime prowls Murder unrestrained.

XC

Not all the blood at Talavera shed,
Not all the marvels of Barossa's fight,
Not Albuera lavish of the dead,
Have won for Spain her well asserted right.
When shall her Olive-Branch be free from blight?
When shall she breathe her from the blushing toil?
How many a doubtful day shall sink in night,
Ere the Frank robber turn him from his spoil,
And Freedom's stranger-tree grow native of the soil!

XCI

And thou, my friend!—since unavailing woe
Bursts from my heart, and mingles with the strain—
Had the sword laid thee with the mighty low,
Pride might forbid e'en Friendship to complain:
But thus unlaurelled to descend in vain,
By all forgotten, save the lonely breast,
And mix unbleeding with the boasted slain,
While Glory crowns so many a meaner crest!
What hadst thou done to sink so peacefully to rest?

XCII

Oh, known the earliest, and esteemed the most!
Dear to a heart where nought was left so dear!
Though to my hopeless days for ever lost,
In dreams deny me not to see thee here!
And Morn in secret shall renew the tear
Of Consciousness awaking to her woes,
And Fancy hover o'er thy bloodless bier,
Till my frail frame return to whence it rose,
And mourned and mourner lie united in repose.

XCIII

Here is one fytte of Harold's pilgrimage:
Ye who of him may further seek to know,
Shall find some tidings in a future page,

If he that rhymeth now may scribble moe.
Is this too much? stern Critic! say not so:
Patience! and ye shall hear what he beheld
In other lands, where he was doomed to go:
Lands that contain the monuments of Eld,
Ere Greece and Grecian arts by barbarous hands were quelled.

CANTO THE SECOND

I

Come, blue-eyed Maid of Heaven!—but Thou, alas!
Didst never yet one mortal song inspire—
Goddess of Wisdom! here thy temple was,
And is, despite of War and wasting fire,
And years, that bade thy worship to expire:
But worse than steel, and flame, and ages slow,
Is the dread sceptre and dominion dire
Of men who never felt the sacred glow
That thoughts of thee and thine on polished breasts bestow.

II

Ancient of days! august Athena! where,
Where are thy men of might? thy grand in soul?
Gone—glimmering through the dream of things that were:
First in the race that led to Glory's goal,
They won, and passed away—is this the whole?
A schoolboy's tale, the wonder of an hour!
The Warrior's weapon and the Sophist's stole
Are sought in vain, and o'er each mouldering tower,
Dim with the mist of years, gray flits the shade of power.

III

Son of the Morning, rise! approach you here!
Come—but molest not yon defenceless Urn:
Look on this spot—a Nation's sepulchre!
Abode of Gods, whose shrines no longer burn.
Even Gods must yield—Religions take their turn:
Twas Jove's—'tis Mahomet's—and other Creeds

Will rise with other years, till Man shall learn
Vainly his incense soars, his victim bleeds;
Poor child of Doubt and Death, whose hope is built on reeds.

IV

Bound to the Earth, he lifts his eye to Heaven—
Is 't not enough, Unhappy Thing! to know
Thou art? Is this a boon so kindly given,
That being, thou would'st be again, and go,
Thou know'st not, reck'st not to what region, so
On Earth no more, but mingled with the skies?
Still wilt thou dream on future Joy and Woe?
Regard and weigh yon dust before it flies:
That little urn saith more than thousand Homilies.

V

Or burst the vanished Hero's lofty mound;
Far on the solitary shore he sleeps:
He fell, and falling nations mourned around;
But now not one of saddening thousands weeps,
Nor warlike worshipper his vigil keeps
Where demi-gods appeared, as records tell.
Remove yon skull from out the scattered heaps:
Is that a Temple where a God may dwell?
Why ev'n the Worm at last disdains her shattered cell!

VI

Look on its broken arch, its ruined wall,
Its chambers desolate, and portals foul:
Yes, this was once Ambition's airy hall,
The Dome of Thought, the Palace of the Soul:
Behold through each lack-lustre, eyeless hole,
The gay recess of Wisdom and of Wit
And Passion's host, that never brooked control:
Can all Saint, Sage, or Sophist ever writ,
People this lonely tower, this tenement refit?

VII

Well didst thou speak, Athena's wisest son!
"All that we know is, nothing can be known."
Why should we shrink from what we cannot shun?
Each hath its pang, but feeble sufferers groan
With brain-born dreams of Evil all their own.
Pursue what Chance or Fate proclaimeth best—
Peace waits us on the shores of Acheron:
There no forced banquet claims the sated guest,
But Silence spreads the couch of ever welcome Rest.

VIII

Yet if, as holiest men have deemed, there be
A land of Souls beyond that sable shore,
To shame the Doctrine of the Sadducee
And Sophists, madly vain of dubious lore;
How sweet it were in concert to adore
With those who made our mortal labours light!
To hear each voice we feared to hear no more!
Behold each mighty shade revealed to sight,
The Bactrian, Samian sage, and all who taught the Right!

IX

There, Thou!—whose Love and Life together fled,
Have left me here to love and live in vain—
Twined with my heart, and can I deem thee dead
When busy Memory flashes on my brain?
Well—I will dream that we may meet again,
And woo the vision to my vacant breast:
If aught of young Remembrance then remain,
Be as it may Futurity's behest,
For me 'twere bliss enough to know thy spirit blest!

X

Here let me sit upon this massy stone,
The marble column's yet unshaken base;
Here, son of Saturn! was thy favourite throne:
Mightiest of many such! Hence let me trace

The latent grandeur of thy dwelling-place.
It may not be: nor ev'n can Fancy's eye
Restore what Time hath laboured to deface:
Yet these proud Pillars claim no passing sigh;
Unmoved the Moslem sits, the light Greek carols by.

XI

But who, of all the plunderers of yon Fane
On high—where Pallas lingered, loth to flee
The latest relic of her ancient reign—
The last, the worst, dull spoiler, who was he?
Blush, Caledonia! such thy son could be!
England! I joy no child he was of thine:
Thy free-born men should spare what once was free;
Yet they could violate each saddening shrine,
And bear these altars o'er the long-reluctant brine.

XII

But most the modern Pict's ignoble boast,
To rive what Goth, and Turk, and Time hath spared:
Cold as the crags upon his native coast,
His mind as barren and his heart as hard,
Is he whose head conceived, whose hand prepared,
Aught to displace Athena's poor remains:
Her Sons too weak the sacred shrine to guard,
Yet felt some portion of their Mother's pains,
And never knew, till then, the weight of Despot's chains.

XIII

What! shall it e'er be said by British tongue,
Albion was happy in Athena's tears?
Though in thy name the slaves her bosom wrung,
Tell not the deed to blushing Europe's ears;
The Ocean Queen, the free Britannia, bears
The last poor plunder from a bleeding land:
Yes, she, whose generous aid her name endears,
Tore down those remnants with a Harpy's hand,
Which envious Eld forbore, and tyrants left to stand.

XIV

Where was thine Ægis, Pallas! that appalled
Stern Alaric and Havoc on their way?
Where Peleus' son? whom Hell in vain enthralled,
His shade from Hades upon that dread day
Bursting to light in terrible array!
What! could not Pluto spare the Chief once more,
To scare a second robber from his prey?
Idly he wandered on the Stygian shore,
Nor now preserved the walls he loved to shield before.

XV

Cold is the heart, fair Greece! that looks on Thee,
Nor feels as Lovers o'er the dust they loved;
Dull is the eye that will not weep to see
Thy walls defaced, thy mouldering shrines removed
By British hands, which it had best behoved
To guard those relics ne'er to be restored:—
Curst be the hour when from their isle they roved,
And once again thy hapless bosom gored,
And snatched thy shrinking Gods to Northern climes abhorred!

XVI

But where is Harold? shall I then forget
To urge the gloomy Wanderer o'er the wave?
Little recked he of all that Men regret;
No loved-one now in feigned lament could rave;
No friend the parting hand extended gave,
Ere the cold Stranger passed to other climes:
Hard is his heart whom charms may not enslave;
But Harold felt not as in other times,
And left without a sigh the land of War and Crimes.

XVII

He that has sailed upon the dark blue sea
Has viewed at times, I ween, a full fair sight,
When the fresh breeze is fair as breeze may be,
The white sail set, the gallant Frigate tight—

Masts, spires, and strand retiring to the right,
The glorious Main expanding o'er the bow,
The Convoy spread like wild swans in their flight,
The dullest sailer wearing bravely now—
So gaily curl the waves before each dashing prow.

XVIII

And oh, the little warlike world within!
The well-reeved guns, the netted canopy,
The hoarse command, the busy humming din,
When, at a word, the tops are manned on high:
Hark, to the Boatswain's call, the cheering cry!
While through the seaman's hand the tackle glides;
Or schoolboy Midshipman that, standing by,
Strains his shrill pipe as good or ill betides,
And well the docile crew that skilful Urchin guides.

XIX

White is the glassy deck, without a stain,
Where on the watch the staid Lieutenant walks:
Look on that part which sacred doth remain
For the lone Chieftain, who majestic stalks,
Silent and feared by all—not oft he talks
With aught beneath him, if he would preserve
That strict restraint, which broken, ever balks
Conquest and Fame: but Britons rarely swerve
From law, however stern, which tends their strength to nerve

XX

Blow! swiftly blow, thou keel-compelling gale!
Till the broad Sun withdraws his lessening ray;
Then must the Pennant-bearer slacken sail,
That lagging barks may make their lazy way.
Ah! grievance sore, and listless dull delay,
To waste on sluggish hulks the sweetest breeze!
What leagues are lost, before the dawn of day,
Thus loitering pensive on the willing seas,
The flapping sail hauled down to halt for logs like these!

XXI

The Moon is up; by Heaven, a lovely eve!
Long streams of light o'er dancing waves expand;
Now lads on shore may sigh, and maids believe:
Such be our fate when we return to land!
Meantime some rude Arion's restless hand
Wakes the brisk harmony that sailors love;
A circle there of merry listeners stand
Or to some well-known measure featly move,
Thoughtless, as if on shore they still were free to rove.

XXII

Through Calpe's straits survey the steepy shore;
Europe and Afric on each other gaze!
Lands of the dark-eyed Maid and dusky Moor
Alike beheld beneath pale Hecate's blaze:
How softly on the Spanish shore she plays!
Disclosing rock, and slope, and forest brown,
Distinct, though darkening with her waning phase;
But Mauritania's giant-shadows frown,
From mountain-cliff to coast descending sombre down.

XXIII

'Tis night, when Meditation bids us feel
We once have loved, though Love is at an end:
The Heart, lone mourner of its baffled zeal,
Though friendless now, will dream it had a friend.
Who with the weight of years would wish to bend,
When Youth itself survives young Love and Joy?
Alas! when mingling souls forget to blend,
Death hath but little left him to destroy!
Ah! happy years! once more who would not be a boy?

XXIV

Thus bending o'er the vessel's laving side,
To gaze on Dian's wave-reflected sphere,
The Soul forgets her schemes of Hope and Pride,
And flies unconscious o'er each backward year:

None are so desolate but something dear,
Dearer than self, possesses or possessed
A thought, and claims the homage of a tear;
A flashing pang! of which the weary breast
Would still, albeit in vain, the heavy heart divest.

XXV

To sit on rocks—to muse o'er flood and fell—
To slowly trace the forest's shady scene,
Where things that own not Man's dominion dwell,
And mortal foot hath ne'er or rarely been;
To climb the trackless mountain all unseen,
With the wild flock that never needs a fold;
Alone o'er steeps and foaming falls to lean;
This is not Solitude—'tis but to hold
Converse with Nature's charms, and view her stores unrolled

XXVI

But midst the crowd, the hum, the shock of men,
To hear, to see, to feel, and to possess,
And roam along, the World's tired denizen,
With none who bless us, none whom we can bless;
Minions of Splendour shrinking from distress!
None that, with kindred consciousness endued,
If we were not, would seem to smile the less,
Of all that flattered—followed—sought, and sued;
This is to be alone—This, This is Solitude!

XXVII

More blest the life of godly Eremite,
Such as on lonely Athos may be seen,
Watching at eve upon the Giant Height,
Which looks o'er waves so blue, skies so serene,
That he who there at such an hour hath been
Will wistful linger on that hallowed spot;
Then slowly tear him from the 'witching scene,
Sigh forth one wish that such had been his lot,
Then turn to hate a world he had almost forgot.

CANTO TWO

XXVIII

Pass we the long unvarying course, the track
Oft trod, that never leaves a trace behind;
Pass we the calm—the gale—the change—the tack,
And each well known caprice of wave and wind;
Pass we the joys and sorrows sailors find,
Cooped in their wingéd sea-girt citadel;
The foul—the fair—the contrary—the kind—
As breezes rise and fall and billows swell,
Till on some jocund morn—lo, Land! and All is well!

XXIX

But not in silence pass Calypso's isles,
The sister tenants of the middle deep;
There for the weary still a Haven smiles,
Though the fair Goddess long hath ceased to weep,
And o'er her cliffs a fruitless watch to keep
For him who dared prefer a mortal bride:
Here, too, his boy essayed the dreadful leap
Stern Mentor urged from high to yonder tide;
While thus of both bereft, the Nymph-Queen doubly sighed.

XXX

Her reign is past, her gentle glories gone:
But trust not this; too easy Youth, beware!
A mortal Sovereign holds her dangerous throne,
And thou may'st find a new Calypso there.
Sweet Florence! could another ever share
This wayward, loveless heart, it would be thine:
But checked by every tie, I may not dare
To cast a worthless offering at thy shrine,
Nor ask so dear a breast to feel one pang for *mine*.

XXXI

Thus Harold deemed, as on that Lady's eye
He looked, and met its beam without a thought,
Save Admiration glancing harmless by:
Love kept aloof, albeit not far remote,

Who knew his Votary often lost and caught,
But knew him as his Worshipper no more,
And ne'er again the Boy his bosom sought:
Since now he vainly urged him to adore,
Well deemed the little God his ancient sway was o'er.

XXXII

Fair Florence found, in sooth with some amaze,
One who, 'twas said, still sighed to all he saw,
Withstand, unmoved, the lustre of her gaze,
Which others hailed with real or mimic awe,
Their hope, their doom, their punishment, their law;
All that gay Beauty from her bondsmen claims:
And much she marvelled that a youth so raw
Nor felt, nor feigned at least, the oft-told flames,
Which, though sometimes they frown, yet rarely anger dames.

XXXIII

Little knew she that seeming marble heart,
Now masked in silence or withheld by Pride,
Was not unskilful in the spoiler's art,
And spread its snares licentious far and wide;
Nor from the base pursuit had turned aside,
As long as aught was worthy to pursue:
But Harold on such arts no more relied;
And had he doted on those eyes so blue,
Yet never would he join the lover's whining crew.

XXXIV

Not much he kens, I ween, of Woman's breast,
Who thinks that wanton thing is won by sighs;
What careth she for hearts when once possessed?
Do proper homage to thine Idol's eyes,
But not too humbly—or she will despise
Thee and thy suit, though told in moving tropes:
Disguise ev'n tenderness, if thou art wise;
Brisk Confidence still best with woman copes:
Pique her and soothe in turn—soon Passion crowns thy hopes.

XXXV

'Tis an old lesson—Time approves it true,
And those who know it best, deplore it most;
When all is won that all desire to woo,
The paltry prize is hardly worth the cost:
Youth wasted—Minds degraded—Honour lost—
These are thy fruits, successful Passion! these!
If, kindly cruel, early Hope is crost,
Still to the last it rankles, a disease,
Not to be cured when Love itself forgets to please.

XXXVI

Away! nor let me loiter in my song,
For we have many a mountain-path to tread,
And many a varied shore to sail along,
By pensive Sadness, not by Fiction, led—
Climes, fair withal as ever mortal head
Imagined in its little schemes of thought,
Or e'er in new Utopias were ared,
To teach Man what he might be, or he ought—
If that corrupted thing could ever such be taught.

XXXVII

Dear Nature is the kindest mother still!
Though always changing, in her aspect mild;
From her bare bosom let me take my fill,
Her never-weaned, though not her favoured child.
Oh! she is fairest in her features wild,
Where nothing polished dares pollute her path:
To me by day or night she ever smiled,
Though I have marked her when none other hath,
And sought her more and more, and loved her best in wrath.

XXXVIII

Land of Albania! where Iskander rose,
Theme of the young, and beacon of the wise,
And he his namesake, whose oft-baffled foes
Shrunk from his deeds of chivalrous emprize:

Land of Albania! let me bend mine eyes
On thee, thou rugged Nurse of savage men!
The Cross descends, thy Minarets arise,
And the pale Crescent sparkles in the glen,
Through many a cypress-grove within each city's ken.

XXXIX

Childe Harold sailed, and passed the barren spot,
Where sad Penelope o'erlooked the wave;
And onward viewed the mount, not yet forgot,
The Lover's refuge, and the Lesbian's grave.
Dark Sappho! could not Verse immortal save
That breast imbued with such immortal fire?
Could she not live who life eternal gave?
If life eternal may await the lyre,
That only Heaven to which Earth's children may aspire.

XL

'Twas on a Grecian autumn's gentle eve
Childe Harold hailed Leucadia's cape afar;
A spot he longed to see, nor cared to leave:
Oft did he mark the scenes of vanished war,
Actium—Lepanto—fatal Trafalgar;
Mark them unmoved, for he would not delight
(Born beneath some remote inglorious star)
In themes of bloody fray, or gallant fight,
But loathed the bravo's trade, and laughed at martial wight.

XLI

But when he saw the Evening star above
Leucadia's far-projecting rock of woe,
And hailed the last resort of fruitless love,
He felt, or deemed he felt, no common glow:
And as the stately vessel glided slow
Beneath the shadow of that ancient mount,
He watched the billows' melancholy flow,
And, sunk albeit in thought as he was wont,
More placid seemed his eye, and smooth his pallid front.

XLII

Morn dawns; and with it stern Albania's hills,
Dark Suli's rocks, and Pindus' inland peak,
Robed half in mist, bedewed with snowy rills,
Arrayed in many a dun and purple streak,
Arise; and, as the clouds along them break,
Disclose the dwelling of the mountaineer:
Here roams the wolf—the eagle whets his beak—
Birds—beasts of prey—and wilder men appear,
And gathering storms around convulse the closing year.

XLIII

Now Harold felt himself at length alone,
And bade to Christian tongues a long adieu;
Now he adventured on a shore unknown,
Which all admire, but many dread to view:
His breast was armed 'gainst fate, his wants were few;
Peril he sought not, but ne'er shrank to meet:
The scene was savage, but the scene was new;
This made the ceaseless toil of travel sweet,
Beat back keen Winter's blast, and welcomed Summer's heat.

XLIV

Here the red Cross, for still the Cross is here,
Though sadly scoffed at by the circumcised,
Forgets that Pride to pampered priesthood dear,—
Churchman and Votary alike despised.
Foul Superstition! howsoe'er disguised,
Idol—Saint—Virgin—Prophet—Crescent—Cross—
For whatsoever symbol thou art prized,
Thou sacerdotal gain, but general loss!
Who from true Worship's gold can separate thy dross?

XLV

Ambracia's gulf behold, where once was lost
A world for Woman, lovely, harmless thing!
In yonder rippling bay, their naval host
Did many a Roman chief and Asian King

To doubtful conflict, certain slaughter bring:
Look where the second Cæsar's trophies rose!
Now, like the hands that reared them, withering:
Imperial Anarchs, doubling human woes!
GOD! was thy globe ordained for such to win and lose?

XLVI

From the dark barriers of that rugged clime,
Ev'n to the centre of Illyria's vales,
Childe Harold passed o'er many a mount sublime,
Through lands scarce noticed in historic tales:
Yet in famed Attica such lovely dales
Are rarely seen; nor can fair Tempe boast
A charm they know not; loved Parnassus fails,
Though classic ground and consecrated most,
To match some spots that lurk within this lowering coast.

XLVII

He passed bleak Pindus, Acherusia's lake,
And left the primal city of the land,
And onwards did his further journey take
To greet Albania's Chief, whose dread command
Is lawless law; for with a bloody hand
He sways a nation, turbulent and bold:
Yet here and there some daring mountain-band
Disdain his power, and from their rocky hold
Hurl their defiance far, nor yield, unless to gold.

XLVIII

Monastic Zitza! from thy shady brow,
Thou small, but favoured spot of holy ground!
Where'er we gaze—around—above—below,—
What rainbow tints, what magic charms are found!
Rock, river, forest, mountain, all abound,
And bluest skies that harmonise the whole:
Beneath, the distant Torrent's rushing sound
Tells where the volumed Cataract doth roll
Between those hanging rocks, that shock yet please the soul.

XLIX

Amidst the grove that crowns yon tufted hill,
Which, were it not for many a mountain nigh
Rising in lofty ranks and loftier still,
Might well itself be deemed of dignity,
The Convent's white walls glisten fair on high:
Here dwells the caloyer, nor rude is he,
Nor niggard of his cheer; the passer by
Is welcome still; nor heedless will he flee
From hence, if he delight kind Nature's sheen to see.

L

Here in the sultriest season let him rest,
Fresh is the green beneath those agéd trees;
Here winds of gentlest wing will fan his breast,
From Heaven itself he may inhale the breeze:
The plain is far beneath—oh! let him seize
Pure pleasure while he can; the scorching ray
Here pierceth not, impregnate with disease:
Then let his length the loitering pilgrim lay,
And gaze, untired, the Morn—the Noon—the Eve away

LI

Dusky and huge, enlarging on the sight,
Nature's volcanic Amphitheatre,
Chimæra's Alps extend from left to right:
Beneath, a living valley seems to stir;
Flocks play trees wave, streams flow—the mountain-fir
Nodding above; behold black Acheron!
Once consecrated to the sepulchre.
Pluto! if this be Hell I look upon,
Close shamed Elysium's gates—my shade shall seek for none

LII

Ne city's towers pollute the lovely view;
Unseen is Yanina, though not remote,
Veiled by the screen of hills: here men are few,
Scanty the hamlet, rare the lonely cot:

But, peering down each precipice, the goat
Browseth; and, pensive o'er his scattered flock,
The little shepherd in his white capote
Doth lean his boyish form along the rock,
Or in his cave awaits the Tempest's short-lived shock.

LIII

Oh! where, Dodona! is thine agéd Grove,
Prophetic Fount, and Oracle divine?
What valley echoed the response of Jove?
What trace remaineth of the Thunderer's shrine?
All, all forgotten—and shall Man repine
That his frail bonds to fleeting life are broke?
Cease, Fool! the fate of Gods may well be thine:
Wouldst thou survive the marble or the oak?
When nations, tongues, and worlds must sink beneath the stroke.

LIV

Epirus' bounds recede, and mountains fail;
Tired of up-gazing still, the wearied eye
Reposes gladly on as smooth a vale
As ever Spring yclad in glassy dye:
Ev'n on a plain no humble beauties lie,
Where some bold river breaks the long expanse,
And woods along the banks are waving high,
Whose shadows in the glassy waters dance,
Or with the moonbeam sleep in Midnight's solemn trance.

LV

The Sun had sunk behind vast Tomerit,
And Laos wide and fierce came roaring by;
The shades of wonted night were gathering yet,
When, down the steep banks winding warily,
Childe Harold saw, like meteors in the sky,
The glittering minarets of Tepalen,
Whose walls o'erlook the stream; and drawing nigh,
He heard the busy hum of warrior-men
Swelling the breeze that sighed along the 'engthening glen.

LVI

He passed the sacred Haran's silent tower,
And underneath the wide o'erarching gate
Surveyed the dwelling of this Chief of power,
Where all around proclaimed his high estate.
Amidst no common pomp the Despot sate,
While busy preparation shook the court,
Slaves, eunuchs, soldiers, guests, and santons wait:—
Within, a palace, and without, a fort—
Here men of every clime appear to make resort.

LVII

Richly caparisoned, a ready row
Of arméd horse, and many a warlike store,
Circled the wide-extending court below;
Above, strange groups adorned the corridore;
And oft-times through the area's echoing door
Some high-capped Tartar spurred his steed away:
The Turk—the Greek—the Albanian—and the Moor,
Here mingled in their many-hued array,
While the deep war-drum's sound announced the close of day.

LVIII

The wild Albanian kirtled to his knee,
With shawl-girt head and ornamented gun,
And gold-embroidered garments, fair to see;
The crimson-scarféd men of Macedon;
The Delhi with his cap of terror on,
And crooked glaive—the lively, supple Greek,
And swarthy Nubia's mutilated son;
The bearded Turk that rarely deigns to speak,
Master of all around, too potent to be meek,

LIX

Are mixed conspicuous: some recline in groups,
Scanning the motley scene that varies round:
There some grave Moslem to devotion stoops,
And some that smoke, and some that play, are found;

Here the Albanian proudly treads the ground;
Half-whispering there the Greek is heard to prate;
Hark! from the Mosque the nightly solemn sound,
The Muezzin's call doth shake the minaret,
"There is no god but God!—to prayer—lo! God is great!"

LX

Just at this season Ramazani's fast
Through the long day its penance did maintain:
But when the lingering twilight hour was past,
Revel and feast assumed the rule again:
Now all was bustle, and the menial train
Prepared and spread the plenteous board within;
The vacant Gallery now seemed made in vain,
But from the chambers came the mingling din,
As page and slave anon were passing out and in.

LXI

Here woman's voice is never heard: apart,
And scarce permitted—guarded, veiled—to move,
She yields to one her person and her heart,
Tamed to her cage, nor feels a wish to rove:
For, not unhappy in her Master's love,
And joyful in a mother's gentlest cares,
Blest cares! all other feelings far above!
Herself more sweetly rears the babe she bears,
Who never quits the breast—no meaner passion shares

LXII

In marble-paved pavilion, where a spring
Of living water from the centre rose,
Whose bubbling did a genial freshness fling,
And soft voluptuous couches breathed repose,
ALI reclined, a man of war and woes:
Yet in his lineaments ye cannot trace,
While Gentleness her milder radiance throws
Along that agéd venerable face,
The deeds that lurk beneath, and stain him with disgrace.

LXIII

It is not that yon hoary lengthening beard
Ill suits the passions which belong to Youth;
Love conquers Age—so Hafiz hath averred,
So sings the Teian, and he sings in sooth—
But crimes that scorn the tender voice of ruth,
Beseeming all men ill, but most the man
In years, have marked him with a tiger's tooth;
Blood follows blood, and, through their mortal span,
In bloodier acts conclude those who with blood began.

LXIV

'Mid many things most new to ear and eye
The Pilgrim rested here his weary feet,
And gazed around on Moslem luxury,
Till quickly wearied with that spacious seat
Of Wealth and Wantonness, the choice retreat
Of sated Grandeur from the city's noise:
And were it humbler it in sooth were sweet;
But Peace abhorreth artificial joys,
And Pleasure, leagued with Pomp, the zest of both destroys.

LXV

Fierce are Albania's children, yet they lack
Not virtues, were those virtues more mature.
Where is the foe that ever saw their back?
Who can so well the toil of War endure?
Their native fastnesses not more secure
Than they in doubtful time of troublous need:
Their wrath how deadly! but their friendship sure,
When Gratitude or Valour bids them bleed—
Unshaken rushing on where'er their Chief may lead.

LXVI

Childe Harold saw them in their Chieftain's tower
Thronging to War in splendour and success;
And after viewed them, when, within their power,
Himself awhile the victim of distress;

That saddening hour when bad men hotlier press:
But these did shelter him beneath their roof,
When less barbarians would have cheered him less,
And fellow-countrymen have stood aloof—
In aught that tries the heart, how few withstand the proof!

LXVII

It chanced that adverse winds once drove his bark
Full on the coast of Suli's shaggy shore,
When all around was desolate and dark;
To land was perilous, to sojourn more;
Yet for awhile the mariners forbore,
Dubious to trust where Treachery might lurk:
At length they ventured forth, though doubting sore
That those who loathe alike the Frank and Turk
Might once again renew their ancient butcher work.

LXVIII

Vain fear! the Suliotes stretched the welcome hand,
Led them o'er rocks and past the dangerous swamp,
Kinder than polished slaves though not so bland,
And piled the hearth, and wrung their garments damp,
And filled the bowl, and trimmed the cheerful lamp,
And spread their fare—though homely, all they had:
Such conduct bears Philanthropy's rare stamp:
To rest the weary and to soothe the sad,
Doth lesson happier men, and shames at least the bad.

LXIX

It came to pass, that when he did address
Himself to quit at length this mountain-land,
Combined marauders half-way barred egress,
And wasted far and near with glaive and brand;
And therefore did he take a trusty band
To traverse Acarnania's forest wide,
In war well-seasoned, and with labours tanned,
Till he did greet white Achelous' tide,
And from his further bank Ætolia's wolds espied.

LXX

Where lone Utraikey forms its circling cove,
And weary waves retire to gleam at rest,
How brown the foliage of the green hill's grove,
Nodding at midnight o'er the calm bay's breast,
As winds come lightly whispering from the West,
Kissing, not ruffling, the blue deep's serene:—
Here Harold was received a welcome guest;
Nor did he pass unmoved the gentle scene,
For many a joy could he from Night's soft presence glean.

LXXI

On the smooth shore the night-fires brightly blazed,
The feast was done, the red wine circling fast,
And he that unawares had there ygazed
With gaping wonderment had stared aghast;
For ere night s midmost, stillest hour was past,
The native revels of the troop began;
Each Palikar his sabre from him cast,
And bounding hand in hand, man linked to man,
Yelling their uncouth dirge, long daunced the kirtled clan.

LXXII

Childe Harold at a little distance stood
And viewed, but not displeased, the revelrie
Nor hated harmless mirth, however rude:
In sooth, it was no vulgar sight to see
Their barbarous, yet their not indecent, glee;
And, as the flames along their faces gleamed,
Their gestures nimble, dark eyes flashing free,
The long wild locks that to their girdles streamed,
While thus in concert they this lay half sang, half screamed:—

1

TAMBOURGI! Tambourgi! thy 'larum afar
Gives hope to the valiant, and promise of war;
All the Sons of the mountains arise at the note,
Chimariot, Illyrian, and dark Suliote!

2

Oh! who is more brave than a dark Suliote,
In his snowy camese and his shaggy capote?
To the wolf and the vulture he leaves his wild flock,
And descends to the plain like the stream from the rock.

3

Shall the sons of Chimari, who never forgive
The fault of a friend, bid an enemy live?
Let those guns so unerring such vengeance forego?
What mark is so fair as the breast of a foe?

4

Macedonia sends forth her invincible race;
For a time they abandon the cave and the chase;
But those scarfs of blood-red shall be redder, before
The sabre is sheathed and the battle is o'er.

5

Then the Pirates of Parga that dwell by the waves,
And teach the pale Franks what it is to be slaves,
Shall leave on the beach the long galley and oar,
And track to his covert the captive on shore.

6

I ask not the pleasures that riches supply,
My sabre shall win what the feeble must buy;
Shall win the young bride with her long flowing hair,
And many a maid from her mother shall tear.

7

I love the fair face of the maid in her youth,
Her caresses shall lull me, her music shall soothe;
Let her bring from the chamber her many-toned lyre,
And sing us a song on the fall of her Sire.

8

Remember the moment when Previsa fell,
The shrieks of the conquered, the conquerors' yell;
The roofs that we fired, and the plunder we shared,
The wealthy we slaughtered, the lovely we spared.

9

I talk not of mercy, I talk not of fear;
He neither must know who would serve the Vizier:
Since the days of our Prophet the Crescent ne'er saw
A chief ever glorious like Ali Pashaw.

10

Dark Muchtar his son to the Danube is sped,
Let the yellow-haired Giaours view his horse-tail with dread;
When his Delhis come dashing in blood o'er the banks,
How few shall escape from the Muscovite ranks!

11

Selictar! unsheathe then our chief's Scimitār;
Tambourgi! thy 'larum gives promise of War.
Ye Mountains, that see us descend to the shore,
Shall view us as Victors, or view us no more!

LXXIII

Fair Greece! sad relic of departed Worth!
Immortal, though no more; though fallen, great!
Who now shall lead thy scattered children forth,
And long accustomed bondage uncreate?
Not such thy sons who whilome did await,
The hopeless warriors of a willing doom,
In bleak Thermopylæ's sepulchral strait—
Oh! who that gallant spirit shall resume,
Leap from Eurotas' banks, and call thee from the tomb?

LXXIV

Spirit of Freedom! when on Phyle's brow
'Thou sat'st with Thrasybulus and his train,
Couldst thou forebode the dismal hour which now
Dims the green beauties of thine Attic plain?
Not thirty tyrants now enforce the chain,
But every carle can lord it o'er thy land;
Nor rise thy sons, but idly rail in vain,
Trembling beneath the scourge of Turkish hand,
From birth till death enslaved—in word, in deed, unmanned.

LXXV

In all save form alone, how changed! and who
That marks the fire still sparkling in each eye,
Who but would deem their bosoms burned anew
With thy unquenchéd beam, lost Liberty!
And many dream withal the hour is nigh
That gives them back their fathers' heritage:
For foreign arms and aid they fondly sigh,
Nor solely dare encounter hostile rage,
Or tear their name defiled from Slavery's mournful page.

LXXVI

Hereditary Bondsmen! know ye not
Who would be free *themselves* must strike the blow?
By their right arms the conquest must be wrought?
Will Gaul or Muscovite redress ye? No!
True—they may lay your proud despoilers low,
But not for you will Freedom's Altars flame.
Shades of the Helots! triumph o'er your foe!
Greece! change thy lords, thy state is still the same;
Thy glorious day is o'er, but not thine years of shame.

LXXVII

The city won for Allah from the Giaour
The Giaour from Othman's race again may wrest;
And the Serai's impenetrable tower
Receive the fiery Frank, her former guest;

Or Wahab's rebel brood who dared divest
The Prophet's tomb of all its pious spoil,
May wind their path of blood along the West;
But ne'er will Freedom seek this fated soil,
But slave succeed to slave through years of endless toil.

LXXVIII

Yet mark their mirth—ere Lenten days begin,
That penance which their holy rites prepare
To shrive from Man his weight of mortal sin,
By daily abstinence and nightly prayer;
But ere his sackcloth garb Repentance wear,
Some days of joyaunce are decreed to all,
To take of pleasaunce each his secret share,
In motley robe to dance at masking ball,
And join the mimic train of merry Carnival.

LXXIX

And whose more rife with merriment than thine,
Oh Stamboul! once the Empress of their reign?
Though turbans now pollute Sophia's shrine,
And Greece her very altars eyes in vain:
(Alas! her woes will still pervade my strain!)
Gay were her minstrels once, for free her throng,
All felt the common joy they now must feign,
Nor oft I've seen such sight, nor heard such song,
As wooed the eye, and thrilled the Bosphorus along.

LXXX

Loud was the lightsome tumult on the shore;
Oft Music changed, but never ceased her tone,
And timely echoed back the measured oar,
And rippling waters made a pleasant moan:
The Queen of tides on high consenting shone.
And when a transient breeze swept o'er the wave,
'Twas, as if darting from her heavenly throne,
A brighter glance her form reflected gave,
Till sparkling billows seemed to light the banks they lave.

LXXXI

Glanced many a light Caique along the foam,
Danced on the shore the daughters of the land,
No thought had man or maid of rest or home,
While many a languid eye and thrilling hand
Exchanged the look few bosoms may withstand,
Or gently prest, returned the pressure still:
Oh Love! young Love! bound in thy rosy band,
Let sage or cynic prattle as he will,
These hours, and only these. redeem Life's years of ill!

LXXXII

But, midst the throng in merry masquerade,
Lurk there no hearts that throb with secret pain,
Even through the closest searment half betrayed?
To such the gentle murmurs of the main
Seem to re-echo all they mourn in vain;
To such the gladness of the gamesome crowd
Is source of wayward thought and stern disdain:
How do they loathe the laughter idly loud,
And long to change the robe of revel for the shroud!

LXXXIII

This must he feel, the true-born son of Greece,
If Greece one true-born patriot still can boast:
Not such as prate of War, but skulk in Peace,
The bondsman's peace, who sighs for all he lost,
Yet with smooth smile his Tyrant can accost,
And wield the slavish sickle, not the sword:
Ah! Greece! they love thee least who owe thee most—
Their birth, their blood, and that sublime record
Of hero Sires, who shame thy now degenerate horde!

LXXXIV

When riseth Lacedemon's Hardihood,
When Thebes Epaminondas rears again,
When Athens' children are with hearts endued,
When Grecian mothers shall give birth to men,

Then may st thou be restored; but not till then.
A thousand years scarce serve to form a state;
An hour may lay it in the dust: and when
Can Man its shattered splendour renovate,
Recall its virtues back, and vanquish Time and **Fate?**

LXXXV

And yet how lovely in thine age of woe,
Land of lost Gods and godlike men, art thou!
Thy vales of evergreen, thy hills of snow,
Proclaim thee Nature's varied favourite now:
Thy fanes, thy temples to thy surface bow,
Commingling slowly with heroic earth,
Broke by the share of every rustic plough:
So perish monuments of mortal birth,
So perish all in turn, save well-recorded *Worth:*

LXXXVI

Save where some solitary column mourns
Above its prostrate brethren of the cave;
Save where Tritonia's airy shrine adorns
Colonna's cliff, and gleams along the wave;
Save o'er some warrior's half-forgotten grave,
Where the gray stones and unmolested grass
Ages, but not Oblivion, feebly brave;
While strangers, only, not regardless pass,
Lingering like me, perchance, to gaze, and sigh "Alas!"

LXXXVII

Yet are thy skies as blue, thy crags as wild;
Sweet are thy groves, and verdant are thy fields,
Thine olive ripe as when Minerva smiled,
And still his honied wealth Hymettus yields;
There the blithe Bee his fragrant fortress builds,
The free-born wanderer of thy mountain-air;
Apollo still thy long, long summer gilds,
Still in his beam Mendeli's marbles glare:
Art, Glory, Freedom fail—but Nature still is fair.

Where'er we tread 'tis haunted, holy ground;
No earth of thine is lost in vulgar mould,
But one vast realm of Wonder spreads around,
And all the Muse's tales seem truly told,
Till the sense aches with gazing to behold
The scenes our earliest dreams have dwelt upon;
Each hill and dale, each deepening glen and wold
Defies the power which crushed thy temples gone:
Age shakes Athena's tower, but spares gray Maratho·

The Sun, the soil—but not the slave, the same;
Unchanged in all except its foreign Lord—
Preserves alike its bounds and boundless fame
The Battle-field, where Persia's victim horde
First bowed beneath the brunt of Hellas' sword,
As on the morn to distant Glory dear,
When Marathon became a magic word;
Which uttered, to the hearer's eye appear
The camp, the host, the fight, the Conqueror's careeı

The flying Mede, his shaftless broken bow—
The fiery Greek, his red pursuing spear;
Mountains above—Earth's, Ocean's plain below—
Death in the front, Destruction in the rear!
Such was the scene—what now remaineth here?
What sacred Trophy marks the hallowed ground,
Recording Freedom's smile and Asia's tear?
The rifled urn, the violated mound,
The dust thy courser's hoof, rude stranger! spurns around.

Yet to the remnants of thy Splendour past
Shall pilgrims, pensive, but unwearied, throng;
Long shall the voyager, with th' Ionian blast,
Hail the bright clime of Battle and of Song:

Long shall thine annals and immortal tongue
Fill with thy fame the youth of many a shore;
Boast of the agéd! lesson of the young!
Which Sages venerate and Bards adore,
As Pallas and the Muse unveil their awful lore.

XCII

The parted bosom clings to wonted home,
If aught that's kindred cheer the welcome hearth;
He that is lonely—hither let him roam,
And gaze complacent on congenial earth.
Greece is no lightsome land of social mirth:
But he whom Sadness sootheth may abide,
And scarce regret the region of his birth,
When wandering slow by Delphi's sacred side,
Or gazing o'er the plains where Greek and Persian died.

XCIII

Let such approach this consecrated Land,
And pass in peace along the magic waste;
But spare its relics—let no busy hand
Deface the scenes, already how defaced!
Not for such purpose were these altars placed:
Revere the remnants Nations once revered:
So may our Country's name be undisgraced,
So may'st thou prosper where thy youth was reared,
By every honest joy of Love and Life endeared!

XCIV

For thee, who thus in too protracted song
Hath soothed thine Idlesse with inglorious lays,
Soon shall thy voice be lost amid the throng
Of louder Minstrels in these later days:
To such resign the strife for fading Bays—
Ill may such contest now the spirit move
Which heeds nor keen Reproach nor partial Praise,
Since cold each kinder heart that might approve—
And none are left to please when none are left to love.

XCV

Thou too art gone, thou loved and lovely one!
Whom Youth and Youth's affections bound to me;
Who did for me what none beside have done,
Nor shrank from one albeit unworthy thee.
What is my Being! thou hast ceased to be!
Nor staid to welcome here thy wanderer home,
Who mourns o'er hours which we no more shall see—
Would they had never been, or were to come!
Would he had ne'er returned to find fresh cause to roam!

XCVI

Oh! ever loving, lovely, and beloved!
How selfish Sorrow ponders on the past,
And clings to thoughts now better far removed!
But Time shall tear thy shadow from me last.
All thou couldst have of mine, stern Death! thou hast;
The Parent, Friend, and now the more than friend:
Ne'er yet for one thine arrows flew so fast,
And grief with grief continuing still to blend,
Hath snatched the little joy that Life had yet to lend.

XCVII

Then must I plunge again into the crowd,
And follow all that Peace disdains to seek?
Where Revel calls, and Laughter, vainly loud,
False to the heart, distorts the hollow cheek,
To leave the flagging spirit doubly weak;
Still o'er the features, which perforce they cheer,
To feign the pleasure or conceal the pique:
Smiles form the channel of a future tear,
Or raise the writhing lip with ill-dissembled sneer.

XCVIII

What is the worst of woes that wait on Age?
What stamps the wrinkle deeper on the brow?
To view each loved one blotted from Life's page,
And be alone on earth, as I am now:

Before the Chastener humbly let me bow,
O'er Hearts divided and o'er Hopes destroyed:
Roll on, vain days! full reckless may ye flow,
Since Time hath reft whate'er my soul enjoyed,
And with the ills of Eld mine earlier years alloyed.

CANTO THE THIRD

"Afin que cette application vous forçât à penser à autre chose. Il n'y
a en vérité de remède que celui-la et le temps."—*Lettres du Roi de
Prusse et de M. D'Alembert.* [*Sept.* 7, 1776.]

I

Is thy face like thy mother's, my fair child!
ADA! sole daughter of my house and heart?
When last I saw thy young blue eyes they smiled,
And then we parted,—not as now we part,
But with a hope.—

          Awaking with a start,
The waters heave around me; and on high
The winds lift up their voices: I depart,
Whither I know not; but the hour's gone by,
When Albion's lessening shores could grieve or glad mine eye.

II

Once more upon the waters! yet once more!
And the waves bound beneath me as a steed
That knows his rider. Welcome to their roar!
Swift be their guidance, wheresoe'er it lead!
Though the strained mast should quiver as a reed,
And the rent canvass fluttering strew the gale,
Still must I on; for I am as a weed,
Flung from the rock, on Ocean's foam, to sail
Where'er the surge may sweep, the tempest's breath prevail.

III

In my youth's summer I did sing of One,
The wandering outlaw of his own dark mind;
Again I seize the theme, then but begun,

And bear it with me, as the rushing wind
Bears the cloud onwards: in that Tale I find
The furrows of long thought, and dried-up tears,
Which, ebbing, leave a sterile track behind,
O'er which all heavily the journeying years
Plod the last sands of life,—where not a flower appears.

IV

Since my young days of passion—joy or pain—
Perchance my heart and harp have lost a string—
And both may jar: it may be that in vain
I would essay, as I have sung, to sing:
Yet, though a dreary strain, to this I cling;
So that it wean me from the weary dream
Of selfish grief or gladness—so it fling
Forgetfulness around me—it shall seem
To me, though to none else, a not ungrateful theme.

V

He, who grown agéd in this world of woe,
In deeds, not years, piercing the depths of life,
So that no wonder waits him—nor below
Can Love or Sorrow, Fame, Ambition, Strife,
Cut to his heart again with the keen knife
Of silent, sharp endurance—he can tell
Why Thought seeks refuge in lone caves, yet rife
With airy images, and shapes which dwell
Still unimpaired, though old, in the Soul's haunted cell.

VI

'Tis to create, and in creating live
A being more intense, that we endow
With form our fancy, gaining as we give
The life we image, even as I do now—
What am I? Nothing: but not so art thou,
Soul of my thought! with whom I traverse earth,
Invisible but gazing, as I glow
Mixed with thy spirit, blended with thy birth,
And feeling still with thee in my crushed feelings' dearth.

VII

Yet must I think less wildly:—I *have* thought
Too long and darkly, till my brain became,
In its own eddy boiling and o'erwrought,
A whirling gulf of phantasy and flame:
And thus, untaught in youth my heart to tame,
My springs of life were poisoned. 'Tis too late!
Yet am I changed; though still enough the same
In strength to bear what Time can not abate,
And feed on bitter fruits without accusing Fate.

VIII

Something too much of this:—but now 'tis past,
And the spell closes with its silent seal:
Long absent HAROLD re-appears at last—
He of the breast which fain no more would feel,
Wrung with the wounds which kill not, but ne'er heal;
Yet Time, who changes all, had altered him
In soul and aspect as in age: years steal
Fire from the mind as vigour from the limb;
And Life's enchanted cup but sparkles near the brim.

IX

His had been quaffed too quickly, and he found
The dregs were wormwood; but he filled again,
And from a purer fount, on holier ground,
And deemed its spring perpetual—but in vain!
Still round him clung invisibly a chain
Which galled for ever, fettering though unseen,
And heavy though it clanked not; worn with pain,
Which pined although it spoke not, and grew keen,
Entering with every step he took through many a scene.

X

Secure in guarded coldness, he had mixed
Again in fancied safety with his kind,
And deemed his spirit now so firmly fixed
And sheathed with an invulnerable mind,

That, if no joy, no sorrow lurked behind;
And he, as one, might 'midst the many stand
Unheeded, searching through the crowd to find
Fit speculation—such as in strange land
He found in wonder-works of God and Nature's hand.

XI

But who can view the ripened rose, nor seek
To wear it? who can curiously behold
The smoothness and the sheen of Beauty's cheek,
Nor feel the heart can never all grow old?
Who can contemplate Fame through clouds unfold
The star which rises o'er her steep, nor climb?
Harold, once more within the vortex, rolled
On with the giddy circle, chasing Time,
Yet with a nobler aim than in his Youth's fond prime.

XII

But soon he knew himself the most unfit
Of men to herd with Man, with whom he held
Little in common; untaught to submit
His thoughts to others, though his soul was quelled
In youth by his own thoughts; still uncompelled,
He would not yield dominion of his mind
To Spirits against whom his own rebelled,
Proud though in desolation—which could find
A life within itself, to breathe without mankind.

XIII

Where rose the mountains, there to him were friends;
Where rolled the Ocean, thereon was his home;
Where a blue sky, and glowing clime, extends,
He had the passion and the power to roam;
The desert, forest, cavern, breaker's foam,
Were unto him companionship; they spake
A mutual language, clearer than the tome
Of his land's tongue, which he would oft forsake
For Nature's pages glassed by sunbeams on the lake.

XIV

Like the Chaldean, he could watch the stars,
Till he had peopled them with beings bright
As their own beams; and earth, and earthborn jars,
And human frailties, were forgotten quite:
Could he have kept his spirit to that flight
He had been happy; but this clay will sink
Its spark immortal, envying it the light
To which it mounts, as if to break the link
That keeps us from yon heaven which woos us to its brink.

XV

But in Man's dwellings he became a thing
Restless and worn, and stern and wearisome,
Drooped as a wild-born falcon with clipt wing,
To whom the boundless air alone were home:
Then came his fit again, which to o'ercome,
As eagerly the barred-up bird will beat
His breast and beak against his wiry dome
Till the blood tinge his plumage—so the heat
Of his impeded Soul would through his bosom eat.

XVI

Self-exiled Harold wanders forth again,
With nought of Hope left—but with less of gloom;
The very knowledge that he lived in vain,
That all was over on this side the tomb,
Had made Despair a smilingness assume,
Which, though 'twere wild,—as on the plundered wreck
When mariners would madly meet their doom
With draughts intemperate on the sinking deck,—
Did yet inspire a cheer, which he forbore to check.

XVII

Stop!—for thy tread is on an Empire's dust!
An Earthquake's spoil is sepulchred below!
Is the spot marked with no colossal bust?

Nor column trophied for triumphal show?
None; but *the moral's truth* tells simpler so.
As the ground was before, thus let it be;—
How that red rain hath made the harvest grow!
And is this all the world has gained by thee,
Thou first and last of Fields! king-making Victory?

XVIII

And Harold stands upon this place of skulls,
The grave of France, the deadly Waterloo!
How in an hour the Power which gave annuls
Its gifts, transferring fame as fleeting too!—
In "pride of place" here last the Eagle flew,
Then tore with bloody talon the rent plain,
Pierced by the shaft of banded nations through;
Ambition's life and labours all were vain—
He wears the shattered links of the World's broken chain.

XIX

Fit retribution! Gaul may champ the bit
And foam in fetters;—but is Earth more free?
Did nations combat to make *One* submit?
Or league to teach all Kings true Sovereignty?
What! shall reviving Thraldom again be
The patched-up Idol of enlightened days?
Shall we, who struck the Lion down, shall we
Pay the Wolf homage? proffering lowly gaze
And servile knees to Thrones? No! *prove* before ye praise?

XX

If not, o'er one fallen Despot boast no more!
In vain fair cheeks were furrowed with hot tears
For Europe's flowers long rooted up before
The trampler of her vineyards; in vain, years
Of death, depopulation, bondage, fears,
Have all been borne, and broken by the accord
Of roused-up millions: all that most endears
Glory, is when the myrtle wreathes a Sword—
Such as Harmodius drew on Athens' tyrant Lord.

XXI

There was a sound of revelry by night,
And Belgium's Capital had gathered then
Her Beauty and her Chivalry—and bright
The lamps shone o'er fair women and brave men;
A thousand hearts beat happily; and when
Music arose with its voluptuous swell,
Soft eyes looked love to eyes which spake again,
And all went merry as a marriage bell;
But hush! hark! a deep sound strikes like a rising knell!

XXII

Did ye not hear it?—No—'twas but the Wind,
Or the car rattling o'er the stony street;
On with the dance! let joy be unconfined;
No sleep till morn, when Youth and Pleasure meet
To chase the glowing Hours with flying feet—
But hark!—that heavy sound breaks in once more,
As if the clouds its echo would repeat;
And nearer—clearer—deadlier than before!
Arm! Arm! it is—it is—the cannon's opening roar!

XXIII

Within a windowed niche of that high hall
Sate Brunswick's fated Chieftain; he did hear
That sound the first amidst the festival,
And caught its tone with Death's prophetic ear;
And when they smiled because he deemed it near,
His heart more truly knew that peal too well
Which stretched his father on a bloody bier,
And roused the vengeance blood alone could quell;
He rushed into the field, and, foremost fighting, fell.

XXIV

Ah! then and there was hurrying to and fro—
And gathering tears, and tremblings of distress,
And cheeks all pale, which but an hour ago
Blushed at the praise of their own loveliness—

And there were sudden partings, such as press
The life from out young hearts, and choking sighs
Which ne'er might be repeated; who could guess
If ever more should meet those mutual eyes,
Since upon night so sweet such awful morn could rise!

XXV

And there was mounting in hot haste—the steed,
The mustering squadron, and the clattering car,
Went pouring forward with impetuous speed,
And swiftly forming in the ranks of war—
And the deep thunder peal on peal afar;
And near, the beat of the alarming drum
Roused up the soldier ere the Morning Star;
While thronged the citizens with terror dumb,
Or whispering, with white lips—"The foe! They come! they
        come!"

XXVI

And wild and high the "Cameron's Gathering" rose!
The war-note of Lochiel, which Albyn's hills
Have heard, and heard, too, have her Saxon foes:—
How in the noon of night that pibroch thrills,
Savage and shrill! But with the breath which fills
Their mountain pipe, so fill the mountaineers
With the fierce native daring which instils
The stirring memory of a thousand years,
And Evan's—Donald's—fame rings in each clansman's ears!

XXVII

And Ardennes waves above them her green leaves,
Dewy with Nature's tear-drops, as they pass—
Grieving, if aught inanimate e'er grieves,
Over the unreturning brave,—alas!
Ere evening to be trodden like the grass
Which *now* beneath them, but *above* shall grow
In its next verdure, when this fiery mass
Of living Valour, rolling on the foe
And burning with high Hope, shall moulder cold and low.

XXVIII

Last noon beheld them full of lusty life:—
Last eve in Beauty's circle proudly gay;
The Midnight brought the signal-sound of strife,
The Morn the marshalling in arms,—the Day
Battle's magnificently-stern array!
The thunder-clouds close o'er it, which when rent
The earth is covered thick with other clay
Which her own clay shall cover, heaped and pent,
Rider and horse,—friend,—foe—in one red burial blent!

XXIX

Their praise is hymned by loftier harps than mine;
Yet one I would select from that proud throng,
Partly because they blend me with his line,
And partly that I did his Sire some wrong,
And partly that bright names will hallow song;
And his was of the bravest, and when showered
The death-bolts deadliest the thinned files along,
Even where the thickest of War's tempest lowered,
They reached no nobler breast than thine, young, gallant
    Howard!

XXX

There have been tears and breaking hearts for thee,
And mine were nothing, had I such to give;
But when I stood beneath the fresh green tree,
Which living waves where thou didst cease to live,
And saw around me the wide field revive
With fruits and fertile promise, and the Spring
Come forth her work of gladness to contrive,
With all her reckless birds upon the wing,
I turned from all she brought to those she could not bring

XXXI

I turned to thee, to thousands, of whom each
And one as all a ghastly gap did make
In his own kind and kindred, whom to teach
Forgetfulness were mercy for their sake;

The Archangel's trump, not Glory's, must awake
Those whom they thirst for; though the sound of Fame
May for a moment soothe, it cannot slake
The fever of vain longing, and the name
So honoured but assumes a stronger, bitterer claim.

XXXII

They mourn, but smile at length—and, smiling, mourn:
The tree will wither long before it fall;
The hull drives on, though mast and sail be torn;
The roof-tree sinks, but moulders on the hall
In massy hoariness; the ruined wall
Stands when its wind-worn battlements are gone;
The bars survive the captive they enthral;
The day drags through though storms keep out the sun;
And thus the heart will break, yet brokenly live on:

XXXIII

Even as a broken Mirror, which the glass
In every fragment multiplies—and makes
A thousand images of one that was
The same—and still the more, the more it breaks;
And thus the heart will do which not forsakes,
Living in shattered guise; and still, and cold,
And bloodless, with its sleepless sorrow aches,
Yet withers on till all without is old,
Showing no visible sign, for such things are untold.

XXXIV

There is a very life in our despair,
Vitality of poison,—a quick root
Which feeds these deadly branches; for it were
As nothing did we die; but Life will suit
Itself to Sorrow's most detested fruit,
Like to the apples on the Dead Sea's shore,
All ashes to the taste: Did man compute
Existence by enjoyment, and count o'er
Such hours 'gainst years of life,—say, would he name threescore?

XXXV

The Psalmist numbered out the years of man:
They are enough; and if thy tale be *true*,
Thou, who didst grudge him even that fleeting span,
More than enough, thou fatal Waterloo!
Millions of tongues record thee, and anew
Their children's lips shall echo them, and say—
"Here, where the sword united nations drew,
Our countrymen were warring on that day!"
And this is much—and all—which will not pass away.

XXXVI

There sunk the greatest, nor the worst of men,
Whose Spirit, antithetically mixed,
One moment of the mightiest, and again
On little objects with like firmness fixed;
Extreme in all things! hadst thou been betwixt,
Thy throne had still been thine, or never been;
For Daring made thy rise as fall: thou seek'st
Even now to re-assume the imperial mien,
And shake again the world, the Thunderer of the scene!

XXXVII

Conqueror and Captive of the Earth art thou!
She trembles at thee still, and thy wild name
Was ne'er more bruited in men's minds than now
That thou art nothing, save the jest of Fame,
Who wooed thee once, thy Vassal, and became
The flatterer of thy fierceness—till thou wert
A God unto thyself; nor less the same
To the astounded kingdoms all inert,
Who deemed thee for a time whate'er thou didst assert.

XXXVIII

Oh, more or less than man—in high or low—
Battling with nations, flying from the field;
Now making monarchs' necks thy footstool, now
More than thy meanest soldier taught to yield;

An Empire thou couldst crush, command, rebuild,
But govern not thy pettiest passion, nor,
However deeply in men's spirits skilled,
Look through thine own, nor curb the lust of War,
Nor learn that tempted Fate will leave the loftiest Star.

XXXIX

Yet well thy soul hath brooked the turning tide
With that untaught innate philosophy,
Which, be it Wisdom, Coldness, or deep Pride,
Is gall and wormwood to an enemy.
When the whole host of hatred stood hard by,
To watch and mock thee shrinking, thou hast smiled
With a sedate and all-enduring eye;—
When Fortune fled her spoiled and favourite child,
He stood unbowed beneath the ills upon him piled.

XL

Sager than in thy fortunes; for in them
Ambition steeled thee on too far to show
That just habitual scorn, which could contemn
Men and their thoughts; 'twas wise to feel, not so
To wear it ever on thy lip and brow,
And spurn the instruments thou wert to use
Till they were turned unto thine overthrow:
'Tis but a worthless world to win or lose;
So hath it proved to thee, and all such lot who choose.

XLI

If, like a tower upon a headlong rock,
Thou hadst been made to stand or fall alone,
Such scorn of man had helped to brave the shock;
But men's thoughts were the steps which paved thy throne,
Their admiration thy best weapon shone;
The part of Philip's son was thine—not then
(Unless aside thy Purple had been thrown)
Like stern Diogenes to mock at men:
For sceptred Cynics Earth were far too wide a den.

XLII

But Quiet to quick bosoms is a Hell,
And *there* hath been thy bane; there is a fire
And motion of the Soul which will not dwell
In its own narrow being, but aspire
Beyond the fitting medium of desire;
And, but once kindled, quenchless evermore,
Preys upon high adventure, nor can tire
Of aught but rest; a fever at the core,
Fatal to him who bears, to all who ever bore.

XLIII

This makes the madmen who have made men mad
By their contagion; Conquerors and Kings,
Founders of sects and systems, to whom add
Sophists, Bards, Statesmen, all unquiet things
Which stir too strongly the soul's secret springs,
And are themselves the fools to those they fool;
Envied, yet how unenviable! what stings
Are theirs! One breast laid open were a school
Which would unteach Mankind the lust to shine or rule:

XLIV

Their breath is agitation, and their life
A storm whereon they ride, to sink at last,
And yet so nursed and bigoted to strife,
That should their days, surviving perils past,
Melt to calm twilight, they feel overcast
With sorrow and supineness, and so die;
Even as a flame unfed, which runs to waste
With its own flickering, or a sword laid by,
Which eats into itself, and rusts ingloriously.

XLV

He who ascends to mountain tops, shall find
The loftiest peaks most wrapt in clouds and snow;
He who surpasses or subdues mankind,
Must look down on the hate of those below.

Though high *above* the Sun of Glory glow,
And far *beneath* the Earth and Ocean spread,
Round him are icy rocks, and loudly blow
Contending tempests on his naked head,
And thus reward the toils which to those summits led.

XLVI

Away with these! true Wisdom's world will be
Within its own creation, or in thine,
Maternal Nature! for who teems like thee,
Thus on the banks of thy majestic Rhine?
There Harold gazes on a work divine,
A blending of all beauties; streams and dells,
Fruit, foliage, crag, wood, cornfield, mountain, vine,
And chiefless castles breathing stern farewells
From gray but leafy walls, where Ruin greenly dwells.

XLVII

And there they stand, as stands a lofty mind,
Worn, but unstooping to the baser crowd,
All tenantless, save to the crannying Wind,
Or holding dark communion with the Cloud.
There was a day when they were young and proud;
Banners on high, and battles passed below;
But they who fought are in a bloody shroud,
And those which waved are shredless dust ere now,
And the bleak battlements shall bear no future blow.

XLVIII

Beneath these battlements, within those walls,
Power dwelt amidst her passions; in proud state
Each robber chief upheld his arméd halls,
Doing his evil will, nor less elate
Than mightier heroes of a longer date.
What want these outlaws conquerors should have,
But History's purchased page to call them great?
A wider space—an ornamented grave?
Their hopes were not less warm, their souls were full as brave.

XLIX

In their baronial feuds and single fields,
What deeds of prowess unrecorded died!
And Love, which lent a blazon to their shields,
With emblems well devised by amorous pride,
Through all the mail of iron hearts would glide;
But still their flame was fierceness, and drew on
Keen contest and destruction near allied,
And many a tower for some fair mischief won,
Saw the discoloured Rhine beneath its ruin run.

L

But Thou, exulting and abounding river!
Making thy waves a blessing as they flow
Through banks whose beauty would endure for ever
Could man but leave thy bright creation so,
Nor its fair promise from the surface mow
With the sharp scythe of conflict,—then to see
Thy valley of sweet waters, were to know
Earth paved like Heaven—and to seem such to me,
Even now what wants thy stream?—that it should Lethe be

LI

A thousand battles have assailed thy banks
But these and half their fame have passed away,
And Slaughter heaped on high his weltering ranks:
Their very graves are gone, and what are they?
Thy tide washed down the blood of yesterday,
And all was stainless, and on thy clear stream
Glassed, with its dancing light, the sunny ray;
But o'er the blackened Memory's blighting dream
Thy waves would vainly roll, all sweeping as they seem

LII

Thus Harold inly said, and passed along,
Yet not insensible to all which here
Awoke the jocund birds to early song
In glens which might have made even exile dear:

Though on his brow were graven lines austere,
And tranquil sternness, which had ta'en the place
Of feelings fierier far but less severe—
Joy was not always absent from his face,
But o'er it in such scenes would steal with transient trace.

LIII

Nor was all Love shut from him, though his days
Of passion had consumed themselves to dust.
It is in vain that we would coldly gaze
On such as smile upon us; the heart must
Leap kindly back to kindness, though Disgust
Hath weaned it from all worldlings: thus he felt,
For there was soft Remembrance, and sweet Trust
In one fond breast, to which his own would melt,
And in its tenderer hour on that his bosom dwelt.

LIV

And he had learned to love,—I know not why,
For this in such as him seems strange of mood,—
The helpless looks of blooming Infancy,
Even in its earliest nurture; what subdued,
To change like this, a mind so far imbued
With scorn of man, it little boots to know;
But thus it was; and though in solitude
Small power the nipped affections have to grow,
In him this glowed when all beside had ceased to glow.

LV

And there was one soft breast, as hath been said,
Which unto his was bound by stronger ties
Than the church links withal; and,—though unwed,
That love was pure—and, far above disguise,
Had stood the test of mortal enmities,
Still undivided, and cemented more
By peril, dreaded most in female eyes;
But this was firm, and from a foreign shore
Well to that heart might his these absent greetings pour!

1

The castled Crag of Drachenfels
Frowns o'er the wide and winding Rhine,
Whose breast of waters broadly swells
Between the banks which bear the vine;
And hills all rich with blossomed trees,
And fields which promise corn and wine,
And scattered cities crowning these,
Whose far white walls along them shine,
Have strewed a scene, which I should see
With double joy wert *thou* with me.

2

And peasant girls, with deep blue eyes,
And hands which offer early flowers,
Walk smiling o'er this Paradise;
Above, the frequent feudal towers
Through green leaves lift their walls of gray;
And many a rock which steeply lowers,
And noble arch in proud decay,
Look o'er this vale of vintage-bowers;
But one thing want these banks of Rhine,—
Thy gentle hand to clasp in mine!

3

I send the lilies given to me—
Though long before thy hand they touch,
I know that they must withered be,
But yet reject them not as such;
For I have cherished them as dear,
Because they yet may meet thine eye,
And guide thy soul to mine even here,—
When thou behold'st them drooping nigh,
And know'st them gathered by the Rhine,
And offered from my heart to thine!

4

The river nobly foams and flows—
The charm of this enchanted ground,
And all its thousand turns disclose
Some fresher beauty's varying round:
The haughtiest breast its wish might bound
Through life to dwell delighted here;
Nor could on earth a spot be found
To Nature and to me so dear—
Could thy dear eyes in following mine
Still sweeten more these banks of Rhine!

LVI

By Coblentz, on a rise of gentle ground,
There is a small and simple Pyramid,
Crowning the summit of the verdant mound;
Beneath its base are Heroes' ashes hid—
Our enemy's—but let not that forbid
Honour to Marceau! o'er whose early tomb
Tears, big tears, gushed from the rough soldier's lid,
Lamenting and yet envying such a doom,
Falling for France, whose rights he battled to resume.

LVII

Brief, brave, and glorious was his young career,—
His mourners were two hosts, his friends and foes;
And fitly may the stranger lingering here
Pray for his gallant Spirit's bright repose;—
For he was Freedom's Champion, one of those,
The few in number, who had not o'erstept
The charter to chastise which she bestows
On such as wield her weapons; he had kept
The whiteness of his soul—and thus men o'er him wept.

LVIII

Here Ehrenbreitstein, with her shattered wall
Black with the miner's blast, upon her height
Yet shows of what she was, when shell and ball

Rebounding idly on her strength did light:—
A Tower of Victory! from whence the flight
Of baffled foes was watched along the plain:
But Peace destroyed what War could never blight,
And laid those proud roofs bare to Summer's rain—
On which the iron shower for years had poured in vain.

LIX

Adieu to thee, fair Rhine! How long delighted
The stranger fain would linger on his way!
Thine is a scene alike where souls united,
Or lonely Contemplation thus might stray;
And could the ceaseless vultures cease to prey
On self-condemning bosoms, it were here,
Where Nature, nor too sombre nor too gay,
Wild but not rude, awful yet not austere,
Is to the mellow Earth as Autumn to the year.

LX

Adieu to thee again! a vain adieu!
There can be no farewell to scene like thine;
The mind is coloured by thy every hue;
And if reluctantly the eyes resign
Their cherished gaze upon thee, lovely Rhine!
'Tis with the thankful glance of parting praise;
More mighty spots may rise—more glaring shine,
But none unite, in one attaching maze,
The brilliant, fair, and soft,—the glories of old days.

LXI

The negligently grand, the fruitful bloom
Of coming ripeness, the white city's sheen,
The rolling stream, the precipice's gloom,
The forest's growth, and Gothic walls between,—
The wild rocks shaped, as they had turrets been,
In mockery of man's art; and these withal
A race of faces happy as the scene,
Whose fertile bounties here extend to all,
Still springing o'er thy banks, though Empires near them fall

LXII

But these recede. Above me are the Alps,
The Palaces of Nature, whose vast walls
Have pinnacled in clouds their snowy scalps,
And throned Eternity in icy halls
Of cold Sublimity, where forms and falls
The Avalanche—the thunderbolt of snow!
All that expands the spirit, yet appals,
Gather around these summits, as to show
How Earth may pierce to Heaven, yet leave vain man below.

LXIII

But ere these matchless heights I dare to scan,
There is a spot should not be passed in vain,—
Morat! the proud, the patriot field! where man
May gaze on ghastly trophies of the slain,
Nor blush for those who conquered on that plain;
Here Burgundy bequeathed his tombless host,
A bony heap, through ages to remain,
Themselves their monument;—the Stygian coast
Unsepulchred they roamed, and shrieked each wandering ghost.

LXIV

While Waterloo with Cannæ's carnage vies,
Morat and Marathon twin names shall stand;
They were true Glory's stainless victories,
Won by the unambitious heart and hand
Of a proud, brotherly, and civic band,
All unbought champions in no princely cause
Of vice-entailed Corruption; they no land
Doomed to bewail the blasphemy of laws
Making Kings' rights divine, by some Draconic clause.

LXV

By a lone wall a lonelier column rears
A gray and grief-worn aspect of old days;
'Tis the last remnant of the wreck of years,
And looks as with the wild-bewildered gaze

Of one to stone converted by amaze,
Yet still with consciousness; and there it stands
Making a marvel that it not decays,
When the coeval pride of human hands,
Levelled Aventicum, hath strewed her subject lands.

LXVI

And there—oh! sweet and sacred be the name!
Julia—the daughter—the devoted—gave
Her youth to Heaven; her heart, beneath a claim
Nearest to Heaven's, broke o'er a father's grave.
Justice is sworn 'gainst tears, and hers would crave
The life she lived in—but the Judge was just—
And then she died on him she could not save.
Their tomb was simple, and without a bust,
And held within their urn one mind—one heart—one dust.

LXVII

But these are deeds which should not pass away,
And names that must not wither, though the Earth
Forgets her empires with a just decay,
The enslavers and the enslaved—their death and birth;
The high, the mountain-majesty of Worth
Should be—and shall, survivor of its woe,
And from its immortality, look forth
In the Sun's face, like yonder Alpine snow,
Imperishably pure beyond all things below.

LXVIII

Lake Leman woos me with its crystal face,
The mirror where the stars and mountains view
The stillness of their aspect in each trace
Its clear depth yields of their far height and hue:
There is too much of Man here, to look through
With a fit mind the might which I behold;
But soon in me shall Loneliness renew
Thoughts hid, but not less cherished than of old,
Ere mingling with the herd had penned me in their fold.

To fly from, need not be to hate, mankind:
All are not fit with them to stir and toil,
Nor is it discontent to keep the mind
Deep in its fountain, lest it overboil
In the hot throng, where we become the spoil
Of our infection, till, too late and long,
We may deplore and struggle with the coil,
In wretched interchange of wrong for wrong
Midst a contentious world, striving where none are strong.

LXX

There, in a moment, we may plunge our years
In fatal penitence, and in the blight
Of our own Soul turn all our blood to tears,
And colour things to come with hues of Night;
The race of life becomes a hopeless flight
To those that walk in darkness: on the sea
The boldest steer but where their ports invite—
But there are wanderers o'er Eternity,
Whose bark drives on and on, and anchored ne'er shall be.

LXXI

Is it not better, then, to be alone,
And love Earth only for its earthly sake?
By the blue rushing of the arrowy Rhone,
Or the pure bosom of its nursing Lake,
Which feeds it as a mother who doth make
A fair but froward infant her own care,
Kissing its cries away as these awake;—
Is it not better thus our lives to wear,
Than join the crushing crowd, doomed to inflict or bear?

LXXII

I live not in myself, but I become
Portion of that around me; and to me
High mountains are a feeling, but the hum
Of human cities torture: I can see

Nothing to loathe in Nature, save to be
A link reluctant in a fleshly chain,
Classed among creatures, when the soul can flee,
And with the sky—the peak—the heaving plain
Of ocean, or the stars, mingle—and not in vain.

LXXIII

And thus I am absorbed, and this is life:—
I look upon the peopled desert past,
As on a place of agony and strife,
Where, for some sin, to Sorrow I was cast,
To act and suffer, but remount at last
With a fresh pinion; which I feel to spring,
Though young, yet waxing vigorous as the Blast
Which it would cope with, on delighted wing,
Spurning the clay-cold bonds which round our being cling.

LXXIV

And when, at length, the mind shall be all free
From what it hates in this degraded form,
Reft of its carnal life, save what shall be
Existent happier in the fly and worm,—
When Elements to Elements conform,
And dust is as it should be, shall I not
Feel all I see less dazzling but more warm?
The bodiless thought? the Spirit of each spot?
Of which, even now, I share at times the immortal lot?

LXXV

Are not the mountains, waves, and skies, a part
Of me and of my Soul, as I of them?
Is not the love of these deep in my heart
With a pure passion? should I not contemn
All objects, if compared with these? and stem
A tide of suffering, rather than forego
Such feelings for the hard and worldly phlegm
Of those whose eyes are only turned below,
Gazing upon the ground, with thoughts which dare not glow?

LXXVI

But this is not my theme; and I return
To that which is immediate, and require
Those who find contemplation in the urn,
To look on One, whose dust was once all fire,—
A native of the land where I respire
The clear air for a while—a passing guest,
Where he became a being,—whose desire
Was to be glorious; 'twas a foolish quest,
The which to gain and keep, he sacrificed all rest.

LXXVII

Here the self-torturing sophist, wild Rousseau,
The apostle of Affliction, he who threw
Enchantment over Passion, and from Woe
Wrung overwhelming eloquence, first drew
The breath which made him wretched; yet he knew
How to make Madness beautiful, and cast
O'er erring deeds and thoughts, a heavenly hue
Of words, like sunbeams, dazzling as they past
The eyes, which o'er them shed tears feelingly and fast.

LXXVIII

His love was Passion's essence—as a tree
On fire by lightning; with ethereal flame
Kindled he was, and blasted; for to be
Thus and enamoured, were in him the same.
But his was not the love of living dame,
Nor of the dead who rise upon our dreams,
But of ideal Beauty, which became
In him existence, and o'erflowing teems
Along his burning page, distempered though it seems.

LXXIX

This breathed itself to life in Julie, *this*
Invested her with all that's wild and sweet;
This hallowed, too, the memorable kiss
Which every morn his fevered lip would greet,

From hers, who but with friendship his would meet;
But to that gentle touch, through brain and breast
Flashed the thrilled Spirit's love-devouring heat;
In that absorbing sigh perchance more blest
Than vulgar minds may be with all they seek possest.

LXXX

His life was one long war with self-sought foes,
Or friends by him self-banished; for his mind
Had grown Suspicion's sanctuary, and chose,
For its own cruel sacrifice, the kind,
'Gainst whom he raged with fury strange and blind.
But he was phrensied,—wherefore, who may know?
Since cause might be which Skill could never find;
But he was phrensied by disease or woe,
To that worst pitch of all, which wears a reasoning show.

LXXXI

For then he was inspired, and from him came,
As from the Pythian's mystic cave of yore,
Those oracles which set the world in flame,
Nor ceased to burn till kingdoms were no more:
Did he not this for France? which lay, before,
Bowed to the inborn tyranny of years,
Broken and trembling to the yoke she bore,
Till by the voice of him and his compeers,
Roused up to too much wrath which follows o'ergrown fears?

LXXXII

They made themselves a fearful monument!
The wreck of old opinions—things which grew,
Breathed from the birth of Time: the veil they rent,
And what behind it lay, all earth shall view;
But good with ill they also overthrew,
Leaving but ruins, wherewith to rebuild
Upon the same foundation, and renew
Dungeons and thrones, which the same hour refilled,
As heretofore, because Ambition was self-willed.

But this will not endure, nor be endured!
Mankind have felt their strength, and made it felt.
They might have used it better, but, allured
By their new vigour, sternly have they dealt
On one another; Pity ceased to melt
With her once natural charities. But they,
Who in Oppression's darkness caved had dwelt,
They were not eagles, nourished with the day;
What marvel then, at times, if they mistook their prey?

LXXXIV

What deep wounds ever closed without a scar?
The heart's bleed longest, and but heal to wear
That which disfigures it; and they who war
With their own hopes, and have been vanquished, bear
Silence, but not submission: in his lair
Fixed Passion holds his breath, until the hour
Which shall atone for years; none need despair:
It came—it cometh—and will come,—the power
To punish or forgive—in *one* we shall be slower.

LXXXV

Clear, placid Leman! thy contrasted lake,
With the wild world I dwelt in, is a thing
Which warns me, with its stillness, to forsake
Earth's troubled waters for a purer spring.
This quiet sail is as a noiseless wing
To waft me from distraction; once I loved
Torn Ocean's roar, but thy soft murmuring
Sounds sweet as if a Sister's voice reproved,
That I with stern delights should e'er have been so moved.

LXXXVI

It is the hush of night, and all between
Thy margin and the mountains, dusk, yet clear,
Mellowed and mingling, yet distinctly seen,
Save darkened Jura, whose capt heights appear

Precipitously steep; and drawing near,
There breathes a living fragrance from the shore,
Of flowers yet fresh with childhood; on the ear
Drops the light drip of the suspended oar,
Or chirps the grasshopper one good-night carol more.

LXXXVII

He is an evening reveller, who makes
His life an infancy, and sings his fill;
At intervals, some bird from out the brakes
Starts into voice a moment, then is still.
There seems a floating whisper on the hill,
But that is fancy—for the Starlight dews
All silently their tears of Love instil,
Weeping themselves away, till they infuse
Deep into Nature's breast the spirit of her hues.

LXXXVIII

Ye Stars! which are the poetry of Heaven!
If in your bright leaves we would read the fate
Of men and empires,—'tis to be forgiven,
That in our aspirations to be great,
Our destinies o'erleap their mortal state,
And claim a kindred with you; for ye are
A Beauty and a Mystery, and create
In us such love and reverence from afar,
That Fortune,—Fame,—Power,—Life, have named themselves
a Star.

LXXXIX

All Heaven and Earth are still—though not in sleep,
But breathless, as we grow when feeling most;
And silent, as we stand in thoughts too deep:—
All Heaven and Earth are still: From the high host
Of stars, to the lulled lake and mountain-coast,
All is concentrated in a life intense,
Where not a beam, nor air, nor leaf is lost,
But hath a part of Being, and a sense
Of that which is of all Creator and Defence.

XC

Then stirs the feeling infinite, so felt
In solitude, where we are *least* alone;
A truth, which through our being then doth melt,
And purifies from self: it is a tone,
The soul and source of Music, which makes known
Eternal harmony, and sheds a charm
Like to the fabled Cytherea's zone,
Binding all things with beauty;—'twould disarm
The spectre Death, had he substantial power to harm.

XCI

Not vainly did the early Persian make
His altar the high places, and the peak
Of earth-o'ergazing mountains, and thus take
A fit and unwalled temple, there to seek
The Spirit, in whose honour shrines are weak,
Upreared of human hands. Come, and compare
Columns and idol-dwellings—Goth or Greek—
With Nature's realms of worship, earth and air—
Nor fix on fond abodes to circumscribe thy prayer!

XCII

The sky is changed!—and such a change! Oh Night,
And Storm, and Darkness, ye are wondrous strong,
Yet lovely in your strength, as is the light
Of a dark eye in Woman! Far along,
From peak to peak, the rattling crags among
Leaps the live thunder! Not from one lone cloud,
But every mountain now hath found a tongue,
And Jura answers, through her misty shroud,
Back to the joyous Alps, who call to her aloud!

XCIII

And this is in the Night:—Most glorious Night!
Thou wert not sent for slumber! let me be
A sharer in thy fierce and far delight,—
A portion of the tempest and of thee!

How the lit lake shines, a phosphoric sea,
And the big rain comes dancing to the earth!
And now again 'tis black,—and now, the glee
Of the loud hills shakes with its mountain-mirth,
As if they did rejoice o'er a young Earthquake's birth.

XCIV

Now, where the swift Rhone cleaves his way between
Heights which appear as lovers who have parted
In hate, whose mining depths so intervene,
That they can meet no more, though brokenhearted:
Though in their souls, which thus each other thwarted,
Love was the very root of the fond rage
Which blighted their life's bloom, and then departed:—
Itself expired, but leaving them an age
Of years all winters,—war within themselves to wage:

XCV

Now, where the quick Rhone thus hath cleft his way,
The mightiest of the storms hath ta'en his stand:
For here, not one, but many, make their play
And fling their thunder-bolts from hand to hand,
Flashing and cast around: of all the band,
The brightest through these parted hills hath forked
His lightnings,—as if he did understand,
That in such gaps as Desolation worked,
There the hot shaft should blast whatever therein lurked.

XCVI

Sky—Mountains—River—Winds—Lake—Lightnings! ye!
With night, and clouds, and thunder—and a Soul
To make these felt and feeling, well may be
Things that have made me watchful; the far roll
Of your departing voices, is the knoll
Of what in me is sleepless,—if I rest.
But where of ye, O Tempests! is the goal?
Are ye like those within the human breast?
Or do ye find, at length, like eagles, some high nest?

XCVII

Could I embody and unbosom now
That which is most within me,—could I wreak
My thoughts upon expression, and thus throw
Soul—heart—mind—passions—feelings—strong or weak—
All that I would have sought, and all I seek,
Bear, know, feel—and yet breathe—into *one* word,
And that one word were Lightning, I would speak;
But as it is, I live and die unheard,
With a most voiceless thought, sheathing it as a sword.

XCVIII

The Morn is up again, the dewy Morn,
With breath all incense, and with cheek all bloom—
Laughing the clouds away with playful scorn,
And living as if earth contained no tomb,—
And glowing into day: we may resume
The march of our existence: and thus I,
Still on thy shores, fair Leman! may find room
And food for meditation, nor pass by
Much, that may give us pause, if pondered fittingly.

XCIX

Clarens! sweet Clarens, birthplace of deep Love!
Thine air is the young breath of passionate Thought;
Thy trees take root in Love; the snows above,
The very Glaciers have his colours caught,
And Sun-set into rose-hues sees them wrought
By rays which sleep there lovingly: the rocks,
The permanent crags, tell here of Love, who sought
In them a refuge from the wordly shocks,
"Which stir and sting the Soul with Hope that woos, then mocks.

C

Clarens! by heavenly feet thy paths are trod,—
Undying Love's, who here ascends a throne
To which the steps are mountains; where the God
Is a pervading Life and Light,—so shown

Not on those summits solely, nor alone
In the still cave and forest; o'er the flower
His eye is sparkling, and his breath hath blown,
His soft and summer breath, whose tender power
Passes the strength of storms in their most desolate hour.

CI

All things are here of *Him;* from the black pines,
Which are his shade on high, and the loud roar
Of torrents, where he listeneth, to the vines
Which slope his green path downward to the shore,
Where the bowed Waters meet him, and adore,
Kissing his feet with murmurs; and the Wood,
The covert of old trees, with trunks all hoar,
But light leaves, young as joy, stands where it stood,
Offering to him, and his, a populous solitude.

CII

A populous solitude of bees and birds,
And fairy-formed and many-coloured things,
Who worship him with notes more sweet than words,
And innocently open their glad wings,
Fearless and full of life: the gush of springs,
And fall of lofty fountains, and the bend
Of stirring branches, and the bud which brings
The swiftest thought of Beauty, here extend
Mingling—and made by Love—unto one mighty end.

CIII

He who hath loved not, here would learn that lore,
And make his heart a spirit; he who knows
That tender mystery, will love the more;
For this is Love's recess, where vain men's woes,
And the world's waste, have driven him far from those,
For 'tis his nature to advance or die;
He stands not still, but or decays, or grows
Into a boundless blessing, which may vie
With the immortal lights in its eternity!

CIV

'Twas not for fiction chose Rousseau the spot,
Peopling it with affections; but he found
It was the scene which Passion must allot
To the Mind's purified beings; 'twas the ground
Where early Love his Psyche's zone unbound,
And hallowed it with loveliness: 'tis lone,
And wonderful, and deep, and hath a sound,
And sense, and sight of sweetness; here the Rhone
Hath spread himself a couch, the Alps have reared a throne.

CV

Lausanne! and Ferney! ye have been the abodes
Of Names which unto you bequeathed a name;
Mortals, who sought and found, by dangerous roads,
A path to perpetuity of Fame:
They were gigantic minds, and their steep aim
Was, Titan-like, on daring doubts to pile
Thoughts which should call down thunder, and the flame
Of Heaven again assailed—if Heaven, the while,
On man and man's research could deign do more than smile.

CVI

The one was fire and fickleness, a child
Most mutable in wishes, but in mind
A wit as various,—gay, grave, sage, or wild,—
Historian, bard, philosopher, combined;
He multiplied himself among mankind,
The Proteus of their talents: But his own
Breathed most in ridicule,—which, as the wind,
Blew where it listed, laying all things prone,—
Now to o'erthrow a fool, and now to shake a throne.

CVII

The other, deep and slow, exhausting thought,
And hiving wisdom with each studious year,
In meditation dwelt—with learning wrought,
And shaped his weapon with an edge severe,

Sapping a solemn creed with solemn sneer;
The lord of irony,—that master spell,
Which stung his foes to wrath, which grew from fear,
And doomed him to the zealot's ready Hell,
Which answers to all doubts so eloquently well.

CVIII

Yet, peace be with their ashes,—for by them
If merited, the penalty is paid;
It is not ours to judge,—far less condemn;
The hour must come when such things shall be made
Known unto all,—or hope and dread allayed
By slumber, on one pillow, in the dust,
Which, thus much we are sure, must lie decayed;
And when it shall revive, as is our trust,
'Twill be to be forgiven—or suffer what is just.

CIX

But let me quit Man's works, again to read
His Maker's, spread around me, and suspend
This page, which from my reveries I feed,
Until it seems prolonging without end.
The clouds above me to the white Alps tend,
And I must pierce them, and survey whate'er
May be permitted, as my steps I bend
To their most great and growing region, where
The earth to her embrace compels the powers of air.

CX

Italia, too! Italia! looking on thee,
Full flashes on the Soul the light of ages,
Since the fierce Carthaginian almost won thee,
To the last halo of the Chiefs and Sages
Who glorify thy consecrated pages;
Thou wert the throne and grave of empires—still,
The fount at which the panting Mind assuages
Her thirst of knowledge, quaffing there her fill,
Flows from the eternal source of Rome's imperial hill

CXI

Thus far have I proceeded in a theme
Renewed with no kind auspices:—to feel
We are not what we have been, and to deem
We are not what we should be,—and to steel
The heart against itself; and to conceal,
With a proud caution, love, or hate, or aught,—
Passion or feeling, purpose, grief, or zeal,
Which is the tyrant Spirit of our thought,—
Is a stern task of soul:—No matter,—it is taught.

CXII

And for these words, thus woven into song,
It may be that they are a harmless wile,—
The colouring of the scenes which fleet along,
Which I would seize, in passing, to beguile
My breast, or that of others, for a while.
Fame is the thirst of youth,—but I am not
So young as to regard men's frown or smile,
As loss or guerdon of a glorious lot;—
I stood and stand alone,—remembered or forgot.

CXIII

I have not loved the World, nor the World me;
I have not flattered its rank breath, nor bowed
To its idolatries a patient knee,
Nor coined my cheek to smiles,—nor cried aloud
In worship of an echo: in the crowd
They could not deem me one of such—I stood
Among them, but not of them—in a shroud
Of thoughts which were not their thoughts, and still could,
Had I not filed my mind, which thus itself subdued.

CXIV

I have not loved the World, nor the World me,—
But let us part fair foes; I do believe,
Though I have found them not, that there may be
Words which are things,—Hopes which will not deceive,

And Virtues which are merciful, nor weave
Snares for the failing: I would also deem
O'er others' griefs that some sincerely grieve—
That two, or one, are almost what they seem,—
That Goodness is no name—and Happiness no dream.

CXV

My daughter! with thy name this song begun!
My daughter! with thy name thus much shall end!—
I see thee not—I hear thee not—but none
Can be so wrapt in thee; Thou art the Friend
To whom the shadows of far years extend:
Albeit my brow thou never should'st behold,
My voice shall with thy future visions blend,
And reach into thy heart,—when mine is cold,—
A token and a tone, even from thy father's mould.

CXVI

To aid thy mind's development,—to watch
Thy dawn of little joys,—to sit and see
Almost thy very growth,—to view thee catch
Knowledge of objects,—wonders yet to thee!
To hold thee lightly on a gentle knee,
And print on thy soft cheek a parent's kiss,—
This, it should seem, was not reserved for me—
Yet this was in my nature:—as it is,
I know not what is there, yet something like to this.

CXVII

Yet, though dull Hate as duty should be taught,
I know that thou wilt love me,—though my name
Should be shut from thee, as a spell still fraught
With desolation, and a broken claim:
Though the grave closed between us,—'twere the same—
I know that thou wilt love me—though to drain
My blood from out thy being were an aim,
And an attainment,—all would be in vain,—
Still thou would'st love me, still that more than life retain.

CXVIII

The child of Love! though born in bitterness,
And nurtured in Convulsion! Of thy sire
These were the elements,—and thine no less.
As yet such are around thee,—but thy fire
Shall be more tempered, and thy hope far higher.
Sweet be thy cradled slumbers! O'er the sea
And from the mountains where I now respire,
Fain would I waft such blessing upon thee,
As—with a sigh—I deem thou might'st have been to me!

CANTO THE FOURTH

"Visto ho Toscana, Lombardia, Romagna,
Quel monte che divide, e quel che serra
Italia, e un mare e l' altro, che la bagna."
Ariosto, Satira iv. lines 59-61.

TO

JOHN HOBHOUSE, Esq., A.M.,

F.R.S., &c., &c., &c.

VENICE, January 2, 1818.

MY DEAR HOBHOUSE,

AFTER an interval of eight years between the composition of
the first and last cantos of *Childe Harold,* the conclusion of the
poem is about to be submitted to the public. In parting with
so old a friend, it is not extraordinary that I should recur to one
still older and better,—to one who has beheld the birth and death
of the other, and to whom I am far more indebted for the social
advantages of an enlightened friendship, than—though not ungrateful—I can, or could be, to *Childe Harold,* for any public
favour reflected through the poem on the poet,—to one, whom
I have known long, and accompanied far, whom I have found
wakeful over my sickness and kind in my sorrow, glad in my
prosperity and firm in my adversity, true in counsel and trusty
in peril,—to a friend often tried and never found wanting;—to
yourself.

In so doing, I recur from fiction to truth; and in dedicating to
you in its complete, or at least concluded state, a poetical work

which is the longest, the most thoughtful and comprehensive of my compositions, I wish to do honour to myself by the record of many years' intimacy with a man of learning, of talent, of steadiness, and of honour. It is not for minds like ours to give or to receive flattery; yet the praises of sincerity have ever been permitted to the voice of friendship; and it is not for you, nor even for others, but to relieve a heart which has not elsewhere, or lately, been so much accustomed to the encounter of good-will as to withstand the shock firmly, that I thus attempt to commemorate your good qualities, or rather the advantages which I have derived from their exertion. Even the recurrence of the date of this letter, the anniversary of the most unfortunate day of my past existence, but which cannot poison my future while I retain the resource of your friendship, and of my own faculties, will henceforth have a more agreeable recollection for both, inasmuch as it will remind us of this my attempt to thank you for an indefatigable regard, such as few men have experienced, and no one could experience without thinking better of his species and of himself.

It has been our fortune to traverse together, at various periods, the countries of chivalry, history, and fable—Spain, Greece, Asia Minor, and Italy; and what Athens and Constantinople were to us a few years ago, Venice and Rome have been more recently. The poem also, or the pilgrim, or both, have accompanied me from first to last; and perhaps it may be a pardonable vanity which induces me to reflect with complacency on a composition which in some degree connects me with the spot where it was produced, and the objects it would fain describe; and however unworthy it may be deemed of those magical and memorable abodes, however short it may fall of our distant conceptions and immediate impressions, yet as a mark of respect for what is venerable, and of feeling for what is glorious, it has been to me a source of pleasure in the production, and I part with it with a kind of regret, which I hardly suspected that events could have left me for imaginary objects.

With regard to the conduct of the last canto, there will be found less of the pilgrim than in any of the preceding, and that little slightly, if at all, separated from the author speaking in his own person. The fact is, that I had become weary of drawing a line which every one seemed determined not to perceive: like the Chinese in Goldsmith's *Citizen of the World*, whom nobody would believe to be a Chinese, it was in vain that I asserted, and imagined that I had drawn, a distinction between the author and the pilgrim; and the very anxiety to preserve this difference, and disappointment at finding it unavailing, so far crushed my efforts in the composition, that I determined to abandon it altogether—and have done so. The opinions which have been, or may be, formed on that subject are *now* a matter of indifference: the work is to depend on itself, and not on the writer; and the author, who has no resources in his own mind beyond the reputation, transient or permanent, which is to arise from his literary efforts, deserves the fate of authors.

In the course of the following canto it was my intention, either in the text or in the notes, to have touched upon the present state of Italian literature, and perhaps of manners. But the text, within the limits I proposed, I soon found hardly sufficient for the labyrinth of external objects, and the consequent reflections: and for the whole of the notes, excepting a few of the shortest, I am indebted to yourself, and these were necessarily limited to the elucidation of the text.

It is also a delicate, and no very grateful task, to dissert upon the literature and manners of a nation so dissimilar; and requires an attention and impartiality which would induce us,—though perhaps no inattentive observers, nor ignorant of the language or customs of the people amongst whom we have recently abode—to distrust, or at least defer our judgment, and more narrowly examine our information. The state of literary, as well as political party, appears to run, or to *have* run, so high, that for a stranger to steer impartially between them, is next to impossible. It may be enough, then, at least for my purpose, to quote from their own beautiful language—"Mi pare che in un paese tutto poetico, che vanta la lingua la più nobile ed insieme la più dolce, tutte tutte le vie diverse si possono tentare, e che sinche la patria di Alfieri e di Monti non ha perduto l'antico valore, in tutte essa dovrebbe essere la prima." Italy has great names still—Canova, Monti, Ugo Foscolo, Pindemonte, Visconti, Morelli, Cicognara, Albrizzi, Mezzofanti, Mai, Mustoxidi, Aglietti, and Vacca, will secure to the present generation an honourable place in most of the departments of Art, Science, and Belles Lettres; and in some the very highest—Europe—the World—has but one Canova.

It has been somewhere said by Alfieri, that "La pianta uomo nasce più robusta in Italia che in qualunque altra terra—e che gli stessi atroci delitti che vi si commettono ne sono una prova." Without subscribing to the latter part of his proposition, a dangerous doctrine, the truth of which may be disputed on better grounds, namely, that the Italians are in no respect more ferocious than their neighbours, that man must be wilfully blind, or ignorantly heedless, who is not struck with the extraordinary capacity of this people, or, if such a word be admissible, their *capabilities,* the facility of their acquisitions, the rapidity of their conceptions, the fire of their genius, their sense of beauty, and, amidst all the disadvantages of repeated revolutions, the desolation of battles, and the despair of ages, their still unquenched "longing after immortality,"—the immortality of independence. And when we ourselves, in riding round the walls of Rome, heard the simple lament of the labourers' chorus, "Roma! Roma! Roma! Roma non è più come era prima!" it was difficult not to contrast this melancholy dirge with the bacchanal roar of the songs of exultation still yelled from the London taverns, over the carnage of Mont St. Jean, and the betrayal of Genoa, of Italy, of France, and of the world, by men whose conduct you yourself have exposed in a work worthy of the better days of our history. For me,—

> "Non movero mai corda
> Ove la turba di sue ciance assorda."

What Italy has gained by the late transfer of nations, it were useless for Englishmen to enquire, till it becomes ascertained that England has acquired something more than a permanent army and a suspended Habeas Corpus; it is enough for them to look at home. For what they have done abroad, and especially in the South, "Verily they *will have* their reward," and at no very distant period.

Wishing you, my dear Hobhouse, a safe and agreeable return to that country whose real welfare can be dearer to none than to yourself, I dedicate to you this poem in its completed state; and repeat once more how truly I am ever

Your obliged

And affectionate friend,

BYRON.

I

I STOOD in Venice, on the "Bridge of Sighs";
A Palace and a prison on each hand:
I saw from out the wave her structures rise
As from the stroke of the Enchanter's wand:
A thousand Years their cloudy wings expand
Around me, and a dying Glory smiles
O'er the far times, when many a subject land

Looked to the wingéd Lion's marble piles,
Where Venice sate in state, throned on her hundred isles!

II

She looks a sea Cybele, fresh from Ocean,
Rising with her tiara of proud towers
At airy distance, with majestic motion,
A Ruler of the waters and their powers:
And such she was;—her daughters had their dowers
From spoils of nations, and the exhaustless East
Poured in her lap all gems in sparkling showers:
In purple was she robed, and of her feast
Monarchs partook, and deemed their dignity increased.

III

In Venice Tasso's echoes are no more,
And silent rows the songless Gondolier;
Her palaces are crumbling to the shore,
And Music meets not always now the ear:
Those days are gone—but Beauty still is here.
States fall—Arts fade—but Nature doth not die,
Nor yet forget how Venice once was dear,
The pleasant place of all festivity,
The Revel of the earth—the Masque of Italy!

IV

But unto us she hath a spell beyond
Her name in story, and her long array
Of mighty shadows, whose dim forms despond
Above the Dogeless city's vanished sway;
Ours is a trophy which will not decay
With the Rialto; Shylock and the Moor,
And Pierre, can not be swept or worn away—
The keystones of the Arch! though all were o'er,
For us repeopled were the solitary shore.

V

The Beings of the Mind are not of clay:
Essentially immortal, they create

And multiply in us a brighter ray
And more beloved existence: that which Fate
Prohibits to dull life in this our state
Of mortal bondage, by these Spirits supplied,
First exiles, then replaces what we hate;
Watering the heart whose early flowers have died,
And with a fresher growth replenishing the void.

VI

Such is the refuge of our youth and age—
The first from Hope, the last from Vacancy;
And this wan feeling peoples many a page—
And, may be, that which grows beneath mine eye:
Yet there are things whose strong reality
Outshines our fairy-land; in shape and hues
More beautiful than our fantastic sky,
And the strange constellations which the Muse
O'er her wild universe is skilful to diffuse:

VII

I saw or dreamed of such,—but let them go,—
They came like Truth—and disappeared like dreams;
And whatsoe'er they were—are now but so:
I could replace them if I would; still teems
My mind with many a form which aptly seems
Such as I sought for, and at moments found;
Let these too go—for waking Reason deems
Such over-weening phantasies unsound,
And other voices speak, and other sights surround.

VIII

I've taught me other tongues—and in strange eyes
Have made me not a stranger; to the mind
Which is itself, no changes bring surprise;
Nor is it harsh to make, nor hard to find
A country with—aye, or without mankind;
Yet was I born where men are proud to be,—
Not without cause; and should I leave behind
The inviolate Island of the sage and free,
And seek me out a home by a remoter sea,

IX

Perhaps I loved it well; and should I lay
My ashes in a soil which is not mine,
My Spirit shall resume it—if we may
Unbodied choose a sanctuary. I twine
My hopes of being remembered in my line
With my land's language: if too fond and far
These aspirations in their scope incline,—
If my Fame should be, as my fortunes are,
Of hasty growth and blight, and dull Oblivion bar

X

My name from out the temple where the dead
Are honoured by the Nations—let it be—
And light the Laurels on a loftier head!
And be the Spartan's epitaph on me—
"Sparta hath many a worthier son than he."
Meantime I seek no sympathies, nor need—
The thorns which I have reaped are of the tree
I planted,—they have torn me,—and I bleed:
I should have known what fruit would spring from such a seed.

XI

The spouseless Adriatic mourns her Lord,
And annual marriage now no more renewed—
The Bucentaur lies rotting unrestored,
Neglected garment of her widowhood!
St. Mark yet sees his Lion where he stood
Stand, but in mockery of his withered power,
Over the proud Place where an Emperor sued,
And monarchs gazed and envied in the hour
When Venice was a Queen with an unequalled dower.

XII

The Suabian sued, and now the Austrian reigns—
An Emperor tramples where an Emperor knelt;
Kingdoms are shrunk to provinces, and chains

Clank over sceptred cities; Nations melt
From Power's high pinnacle, when they have felt
The sunshine for a while, and downward go
Like Lauwine loosened from the mountain's belt;
Oh for one hour of blind old Dandolo!
Th' octogenarian chief, Byzantium's conquering foe.

XIII

Before St. Mark still glow his Steeds of brass,
Their gilded collars glittering in the sun;
But is not Doria's menace come to pass?
Are they not bridled?—Venice, lost and won,
Her thirteen hundred years of freedom done,
Sinks, like a sea-weed, unto whence she rose!
Better be whelmed beneath the waves, and shun,
Even in Destruction's depth, her foreign foes,
From whom Submission wrings an infamous repose.

XIV

In youth She was all glory,—a new Tyre,—
Her very by-word sprung from Victory,
The "Planter of the Lion," which through fire
And blood she bore o'er subject Earth and Sea;
Though making many slaves, Herself still free,
And Europe's bulwark 'gainst the Ottomite;
Witness Troy's rival, Candia! Vouch it, ye
Immortal waves that saw Lepanto's fight!
For ye are names no Time nor Tyranny can blight.

XV

Statues of glass—all shivered—the long file
Of her dead Doges are declined to dust;
But where they dwelt, the vast and sumptuous pile
Bespeaks the pageant of their splendid trust;
Their sceptre broken, and their sword in rust,
Have yielded to the stranger: empty halls,
Thin streets, and foreign aspects, such as must
Too oft remind her who and what enthrals,
Have flung a desolate cloud o'er Venice' lovely walls.

XVI

When Athens' armies fell at Syracuse,
And fettered thousands bore the yoke of war,
Redemption rose up in the Attic Muse,
Her voice their only ransom from afar:
See! as they chant the tragic hymn, the car
Of the o'ermastered Victor stops—the reins
Fall from his hands—his idle scimitar
Starts from its belt—he rends his captive's chains,
And bids him thank the Bard for Freedom and his strains.

XVII

Thus, Venice! if no stronger claim were thine,
Were all thy proud historic deeds forgot—
Thy choral memory of the Bard divine,
Thy love of Tasso, should have cut the knot
Which ties thee to thy tyrants; and thy lot
Is shameful to the nations,—most of all,
Albion! to thee: the Ocean queen should not
Abandon Ocean's children; in the fall
Of Venice think of thine, despite thy watery wall.

XVIII

I loved her from my boyhood—she to me
Was as a fairy city of the heart,
Rising like water-columns from the sea—
Of Joy the sojourn, and of Wealth the mart;
And Otway, Radcliffe, Schiller, Shakespeare's art,
Had stamped her image in me, and even so,
Although I found her thus, we did not part;
Perchance even dearer in her day of woe,
Than when she was a boast, a marvel, and a show.

XIX

I can repeople with the past—and of
The present there is still for eye and thought,
And meditation chastened down, enough;
And more, it may be, than I hoped or sought;

And of the happiest moments which were wrought
Within the web of my existence, some
From thee, fair Venice! have their colours caught:
There are some feelings Time can not benumb,
Nor Torture shake, or mine would now be cold and dumb.

XX

But, from their nature, will the Tannen grow
Loftiest on loftiest and least sheltered rocks,
Rooted in barrenness, where nought below
Of soil supports them 'gainst the Alpine shocks
Of eddying storms; yet springs the trunk, and mocks
The howling tempest, till its height and frame
Are worthy of the mountains from whose blocks
Of bleak, gray granite into life it came,
And grew a giant tree;—the Mind may grow the same.

XXI

Existence may be borne, and the deep root
Of life and sufferance make its firm abode
In bare and desolated bosoms: mute
The camel labours with the heaviest load,
And the wolf dies in silence,—not bestowed
In vain should such example be; if they,
Things of ignoble or of savage mood,
Endure and shrink not, we of nobler clay
May temper it to bear,—it is but for a day.

XXII

All suffering doth destroy, or is destroyed,
Even by the sufferer—and, in each event,
Ends:—Some, with hope replenished and rebuoyed,
Return to whence they came—with like intent,
And weave their web again; some, bowed and bent,
Wax gray and ghastly, withering ere their time,
And perish with the reed on which they leant;
Some seek devotion—toil—war—good or crime,
According as their souls were formed to sink or climb.

XXIII

But ever and anon of griefs subdued
There comes a token like a Scorpion's sting,
Scarce seen, but with fresh bitterness imbued;
And slight withal may be the things which bring
Back on the heart the weight which it would fling
Aside for ever: it may be a sound—
A tone of music—summer's eve—or spring—
A flower—the wind—the Ocean—which shall wound,
Striking the electric chain wherewith we are darkly bound;

XXIV

And how and why we know not, nor can trace
Home to its cloud this lightning of the mind,
But feel the shock renewed, nor can efface
The blight and blackening which it leaves behind,
Which out of things familiar, undesigned,
When least we deem of such, calls up to view
The Spectres whom no exorcism can bind,
The cold—the changed—perchance the dead, anew—
The mourned—the loved—the lost—too many! yet how few!

XXV

But my Soul wanders; I demand it back
To meditate amongst decay, and stand
A ruin amidst ruins; there to track
Fall'n states and buried greatness, o'er a land
Which *was* the mightiest in its old command,
And *is* the loveliest, and must ever be
The master-mould of Nature's heavenly hand;
Wherein were cast the heroic and the free,—
The beautiful—the brave—the Lords of earth and sea,

XXVI

The Commonwealth of Kings—the Men of Rome!
And even since, and now, fair Italy!
Thou art the Garden of the World, the Home
Of all Art yields. and Nature can decree;

Even in thy desert, what is like to thee?
Thy very weeds are beautiful—thy waste
More rich than other climes' fertility;
Thy wreck a glory—and thy ruin graced
With an immaculate charm which cannot be defaced.

XXVII

The Moon is up, and yet it is not night—
Sunset divides the sky with her—a sea
Of glory streams along the Alpine height
Of blue Friuli's mountains; Heaven is free
From clouds, but all colours seems to be,—
Melted to one vast Iris of the West,—
Where the Day joins the past Eternity;
While, on the other hand, meek Dian's crest
Floats through the azure air—an island of the blest!

XXVIII

A single star is at her side, and reigns
With her o'er half the lovely heaven; but still
Yon sunny Sea heaves brightly, and remains
Rolled o'er the peak of the far Rhætian hill,
As Day and Night contending were, until
Nature reclaimed her order:—gently flows
The deep-dyed Brenta, where their hues instil
The odorous purple of a new-born rose,
Which streams upon her stream, and glassed within it glows.

XXIX

Filled with the face of heaven, which, from afar,
Comes down upon the waters! all its hues,
From the rich sunset to the rising star,
Their magical variety diffuse:
And now they change—a paler Shadow strews
Its mantle o'er the mountains; parting Day
Dies like the Dolphin, whom each pang imbues
With a new colour as it gasps away—
The last still loveliest, till—'tis gone—and all is gray.

XXX

There is a tomb in Arqua;—reared in air,
Pillared in their sarcophagus, repose
The bones of Laura's lover: here repair
Many familiar with his well-sung woes,
The Pilgrims of his Genius. He arose
To raise a language, and his land reclaim
From the dull yoke of her barbaric foes:
Watering the tree which bears his Lady's name
With his melodious tears, he gave himself to Fame.

XXXI

They keep his dust in Arqua, where he died—
The mountain-village where his latter days
Went down the vale of years; and 'tis their pride—
An honest pride—and let it be their praise,
To offer to the passing stranger's gaze
His mansion and his sepulchre—both plain
And venerably simple—such as raise
A feeling more accordant with his strain
Than if a Pyramid formed his monumental fane.

XXXII

And the soft quiet hamlet where he dwelt
Is one of that complexion which seems made
For those who their mortality have felt,
And sought a refuge from their hopes decayed
In the deep umbrage of a green hill's shade,
Which shows a distant prospect far away
Of busy cities, now in vain displayed,
For they can lure no further; and the ray
Of a bright Sun can make sufficient holiday.

XXXIII

Developing the mountains, leaves, and flowers,
And shining in the brawling brook, where-by,
Clear as its current, glide the sauntering hours
With a calm languor, which, though to the eye

Idlesse it seem, hath its morality.
If from society we learn to live,
'Tis Solitude should teach us how to die;
It hath no flatterers—Vanity can give
No hollow aid; alone—man with his God must strive:

XXXIV

Or, it may be, with Demons, who impair
The strength of better thoughts, and seek their prey
In melancholy bosoms—such as were
Of moody texture from their earliest day,
And loved to dwell in darkness and dismay,
Deeming themselves predestined to a doom
Which is not of the pangs that pass away;
Making the Sun like blood, the Earth a tomb,
The tomb a hell—and Hell itself a murkier gloom.

XXXV

Ferrara! in thy wide and grass-grown streets,
Whose symmetry was not for solitude,
There seems as 'twere a curse upon the Seats
Of former Sovereigns, and the antique brood
Of Este, which for many an age made good
Its strength within thy walls, and was of yore
Patron or Tyrant, as the changing mood
Of petty power impelled, of those who wore
The wreath which Dante's brow alone had worn before.

XXXVI

And Tasso is their glory and their shame—
Hark to his strain! and then survey his cell!
And see how dearly earned Torquato's fame,
And where Alfonso bade his poet dwell:
The miserable Despot could not quell
The insulted mind he sought to quench, and blend
With the surrounding maniacs, in the hell
Where he had plunged it. Glory without end
Scattered the clouds away—and on that name attend

XXXVII

The tears and praises of all time, while thine
Would rot in its oblivion—in the sink
Of worthless dust, which from thy boasted line
Is shaken into nothing—but the link
Thou formest in his fortunes bids us think
Of thy poor malice, naming thee with scorn:
Alfonso! how thy ducal pageants shrink
From thee! if in another station born,
Scarce fit to be the slave of him thou mad'st to mourn:

XXXVIII

Thou! formed to eat, and be despised, and die,
Even as the beasts that perish—save that thou
Hadst a more splendid trough and wider sty:
He! with a glory round his furrowed brow,
Which emanated then, and dazzles now,
In face of all his foes, the Cruscan quire,
And Boileau, whose rash envy could allow
No strain which shamed his country's creaking lyre,
That whetstone of the teeth—Monotony in wire!

XXXIX

Peace to Torquato's injured shade! 'twas his
In life and death to be the mark where Wrong
Aimed with her poisoned arrows,—but to miss.
Oh, Victor unsurpassed in modern song!
Each year brings forth its millions—but how long
The tide of Generations shall roll on,
And not the whole combined and countless throng
Compose a mind like thine? though all in one
Condensed their scattered rays—they would not form a Sun.

XL

Great as thou art, yet paralleled by those,
Thy countrymen, before thee born to shine,
The Bards of Hell and Chivalry: first rose
The Tuscan Father's Comedy Divine;

Then, not unequal to the Florentine,
The southern Scott, the minstrel who called forth
A new creation with his magic line,
And, like the Ariosto of the North,
Sang Ladye-love and War, Romance and Knightly Worth.

XLI

The lightning rent from Ariosto's bust
The iron crown of laurel's mimicked leaves;
Nor was the ominous element unjust,
For the true laurel-wreath which Glory weaves
Is of the tree no bolt of thunder cleaves,
And the false semblance but disgraced his brow;
Yet still, if fondly Superstition grieves,
Know, that the lightning sanctifies below
Whate'er it strikes;—yon head is doubly sacred now.

XLII

Italia! oh, Italia! thou who hast
The fatal gift of Beauty, which became
A funeral dower of present woes and past—
On thy sweet brow is sorrow ploughed by shame,
And annals graved in characters of flame.
Oh, God! that thou wert in thy nakedness
Less lovely or more powerful, and couldst claim
Thy right, and awe the robbers back, who press
To shed thy blood, and drink the tears of thy distress;

XLIII

Then might'st thou more appal—or, less desired,
Be homely and be peaceful, undeplored
For thy destructive charms; then, still untired,
Would not be seen the arméd torrents poured
Down the deep Alps; nor would the hostile horde
Of many-nationed spoilers from the Po
Quaff blood and water; nor the stranger's sword
Be thy sad weapon of defence—and so,
Victor or vanquished, thou the slave of friend or foe.

XLIV

Wandering in youth, I traced the path of him,
The Roman friend of Rome's least-mortal mind,
The friend of Tully: as my bark did skim
The bright blue waters with a fanning wind,
Came Megara before me, and behind
Ægina lay—Piræus on the right,
And Corinth on the left; I lay reclined
Along the prow, and saw all these unite
In ruin—even as he had seen the desolate sight;

XLV

For Time hath not rebuilt them, but upreared
Barbaric dwellings on their shattered site,
Which only make more mourned and more endeared
The few last rays of their far-scattered light,
And the crushed relics of their vanished might.
The Roman saw these tombs in his own age,
These sepulchres of cities, which excite
Sad wonder, and his yet surviving page
The moral lesson bears, drawn from such pilgrimage.

XLVI

That page is now before me, and on mine
His Country's ruin added to the mass
Of perished states he mourned in their decline,
And I in desolation: all that was
Of then destruction is; and now, alas!
Rome—Rome imperial, bows her to the storm,
In the same dust and blackness, and we pass
The skeleton of her Titanic form,
Wrecks of another world, whose ashes still are warm.

XLVII

Yet, Italy! through every other land
Thy wrongs should ring—and shall—from side to side;
Mother of Arts! as once of Arms! thy hand
Was then our Guardian, and is still our Guide;

Parent of our Religion! whom the wide
Nations have knelt to for the keys of Heaven!
Europe, repentant of her parricide,
Shall yet redeem thee, and, all backward driven,
Roll the barbarian tide, and sue to be forgiven.

XLVIII

But Arno wins us to the fair white walls,
Where the Etrurian Athens claims and keeps
A softer feeling for her fairy halls:
Girt by her theatre of hills, she reaps
Her corn, and wine, and oil—and Plenty leaps
To laughing life, with her redundant Horn.
Along the banks where smiling Arno sweeps
Was modern Luxury of Commerce born,
And buried Learning rose, redeemed to a new Morn,

XLIX

There, too, the Goddess loves in stone, and fills
The air around with Beauty—we inhale
The ambrosial aspect, which, beheld, instils
Part of its immortality—the veil
Of heaven is half undrawn—within the pale
We stand, and in that form and face behold
What Mind can make, when Nature's self would fail;
And to the fond Idolaters of old
Envy the innate flash which such a Soul could mould:

L

We gaze and turn away, and know not where,
Dazzled and drunk with Beauty, till the heart
Reels with its fulness; there—for ever there—
Chained to the chariot of triumphal Art,
We stand as captives, and would not depart.
Away!—there need no words, nor terms precise,
The paltry jargon of the marble mart,
Where Pedantry gulls Folly—we have eyes:
Blood—pulse—and breast confirm the Dardan Shepherd's prize.

LI

Appear'dst thou not to Paris in this guise?
Or to more deeply blest Anchises? or,
In all thy perfect Goddess-ship, when lies
Before thee thy own vanquished Lord of War?
And gazing in thy face as toward a star,
Laid on thy lap, his eyes to thee upturn,
Feeding on thy sweet cheek! while thy lips are
With lava kisses melting while they burn,
Showered on his eyelids, brow, and mouth, as from an urn!

LII

Glowing, and circumfused in speechless love—
Their full divinity inadequate
That feeling to express, or to improve—
The Gods become as mortals—and man's fate
Has moments like their brightest; but the weight
Of earth recoils upon us;—let it go!
We can recall such visions, and create,
From what has been, or might be, things which grow
Into thy statue's form, and look like gods below.

LIII

I leave to learnéd fingers, and wise hands,
The Artist and his Ape, to teach and tell
How well his Connoisseurship understands
The graceful bend, and the voluptuous swell:
Let these describe the undescribable:
I would not their vile breath should crisp the stream
Wherein that Image shall for ever dwell—
The unruffled mirror of the loveliest dream
That ever left the sky on the deep soul to beam.

LIV

In Santa Croce's holy precincts lie
Ashes which make it holier, dust which is
Even in itself an immortality,
Though there were nothing save the past, and this,

The particle of those sublimities
Which have relapsed to chaos:—here repose
Angelo's—Alfieri's bones—and his,
The starry Galileo, with his woes;
Here Machiavelli's earth returned to whence it rose.

LV

These are four minds, which, like the elements,
Might furnish forth creation:—Italy!
Time, which hath wronged thee with ten thousand rents
Of thine imperial garment, shall deny
And hath denied, to every other sky,
Spirits which soar from ruin:—thy Decay
Is still impregnate with divinity,
Which gilds it with revivifying ray;
Such as the great of yore, Canova is to-day.

LVI

But where repose the all Etruscan three—
Dante, and Petrarch, and, scarce less than they,
The Bard of Prose, creative Spirit! he
Of the Hundred Tales of Love—where did they lay
Their bones, distinguished from our common clay
In death as life? Are they resolved to dust,
And have their Country's Marbles nought to say?
Could not her quarries furnish forth one bust?
Did they not to her breast their filial earth entrust?

LVII

Ungrateful Florence! Dante sleeps afar,
Like Scipio, buried by the upbraiding shore:
Thy factions, in their worse than civil war,
Proscribed the Bard whose name for evermore
Their children's children would in vain adore
With the remorse of ages; and the crown
Which Petrarch's laureate brow supremely wore,
Upon a far and foreign soil had grown—
His life, his Fame—his Grave, though rifled—not thine own.

LVIII

Boccaccio to his parent earth bequeathed
His dust,—and lies it not her Great among,
With many a sweet and solemn requiem breathed
O'er him who formed the Tuscan's siren tongue?
That music in itself, whose sounds are song,
The poetry of speech? No;—even his tomb
Uptorn, must bear the hyæna bigot's wrong,
No more amidst the meaner dead find room,
Nor claim a passing sigh, because it told for *whom!*

LIX

And Santa Croce wants their mighty dust;
Yet for this want more noted, as of yore
The Cæsar's pageant, shorn of Brutus' bust,
Did but of Rome's best Son remind her more:
Happier Ravenna! on thy hoary shore,
Fortress of falling Empire! honoured sleeps
The immortal Exile;—Arqua, too, her store
Of tuneful relics proudly claims and keeps,
While Florence vainly begs her banished dead and weeps.

LX

What is her Pyramid of precious stones?
Of porphyry, jasper, agate, and all hues
Of gem and marble, to encrust the bones
Of merchant-dukes? the momentary dews
Which, sparkling to the twilight stars, infuse
Freshness in the green turf that wraps the dead,
Whose names are Mausoleums of the Muse,
Are gently prest with far more reverent tread
Than ever paced the slab which paves the princely head.

LXI

There be more things to greet the heart and eyes
In Arno's dome of Art's most princely shrine,
Where Sculpture with her rainbow Sister vies;
There be more marvels yet—but not for mine;

For I have been accustomed to entwine
My thoughts with Nature, rather, in the fields,
Than Art in galleries: though a work divine
Calls for my Spirit's homage, yet it yields
Less than it feels, because the weapon which it wields

LXII

Is of another temper, and I roam
By Thrasimene's lake, in the defiles
Fatal to Roman rashness, more at home;
For there the Carthaginian's warlike wiles
Come back before me, as his skill beguiles
The host between the mountains and the shore,
Where Courage falls in her despairing files,
And torrents, swoll'n to rivers with their gore,
Reek through the sultry plain, with legions scattered o'er,

LXIII

Like to a forest felled by mountain winds:
And such the storm of battle on this day,
And such the frenzy, whose convulsion blinds
To all save Carnage, that, beneath the fray,
An Earthquake reeled unheededly away!
None felt stern Nature rocking at his feet,
And yawning forth a grave for those who lay
Upon their bucklers for a winding sheet—
Such is the absorbing hate when warring nations meet!

LXIV

The Earth to them was as a rolling bark
Which bore them to Eternity—they saw
The Ocean round, but had no time to mark
The motions of their vessel; Nature's law,
In them suspended, recked not of the awe
Which reigns when mountains tremble, and the birds
Plunge in the clouds for refuge, and withdraw
From their down-toppling nests; and bellowing herds
Stumble o'er heaving plains—and Man's dread hath no words.

LXV

Far other scene is Thrasimene now;
Her lake a sheet of silver, and her plain
Rent by no ravage save the gentle plough;
Her agéd trees rise thick as once the slain
Lay where their roots are; but a brook hath ta'en—
A little rill of scanty stream and bed—
A name of blood from that day's sanguine rain;
And Sanguinetto tells ye where the dead
Made the earth wet, and turned the unwilling waters red.

LXVI

But thou, Clitumnus! in thy sweetest wave
Of the most living crystal that was e'er
The haunt of river-Nymph, to gaze and lave
Her limbs where nothing hid them, thou dost rear
Thy grassy banks whereon the milk-white steer
Grazes—the purest God of gentle waters!
And most serene of aspect, and most clear;
Surely that stream was unprofaned by slaughters—
A mirror and a bath for Beauty's youngest daughters!

LXVII

And on thy happy shore a Temple still,
Of small and delicate proportion, keeps,
Upon a mild declivity of hill,
Its memory of thee; beneath it sweeps
Thy current's calmness; oft from out it leaps
The finny darter with the glittering scales,
Who dwells and revels in thy glassy deeps;
While, chance, some scattered water-lily sails
Down where the shallower wave still tells its bubbling tales.

LXVIII

Pass not unblest the Genius of the place!
If through the air a Zephyr more serene
Win to the brow, 'tis his; and if ye trace
Along his margin a more eloquent green,

If on the heart the freshness of the scene
Sprinkle its coolness, and from the dry dust
Of weary life a moment lave it clean
With Nature's baptism,—'tis to him ye must
Pay orisons for this suspension of disgust.

LXIX

The roar of waters!—from the headlong height
Velino cleaves the wave-worn precipice;
The fall of waters! rapid as the light
The flashing mass foams shaking the abyss;
The Hell of Waters! where they howl and hiss,
And boil in endless torture; while the sweat
Of their great agony, wrung out from this
Their Phlegethon, curls round the rocks of jet
That gird the gulf around, in pitiless horror set,

LXX

And mounts in spray the skies, and thence again
Returns in an unceasing shower, which round,
With its unemptied cloud of gentle rain,
Is an eternal April to the ground,
Making it all one emerald:—how profound
The gulf! and how the Giant Element
From rock to rock leaps with delirious bound,
Crushing the cliffs, which, downward worn and rent
With his fierce footsteps, yield in chasms a fearful vent

LXXI

To the broad column which rolls on, and shows
More like the fountain of an infant sea
Torn from the womb of mountains by the throes
Of a new world, than only thus to be
Parent of rivers, which flow gushingly,
With many windings, through the vale:—Look back!
Lo! where it comes like an Eternity,
As if to sweep down all things in its track,
Charming the eye with dread,—a matchless cataract,

LXXII

Horribly beautiful! but on the verge,
From side to side, beneath the glittering morn,
An Iris sits, amidst the infernal surge,
Like Hope upon a death-bed, and, unworn
Its steady dyes, while all around is torn
By the distracted waters, bears serene
Its brilliant hues with all their beams unshorn:
Resembling, 'mid the torture of the scene,
Love watching Madness with unalterable mien.

LXXIII

Once more upon the woody Apennine—
The infant Alps, which—had I not before
Gazed on their mightier Parents, where the pine
Sits on more shaggy summits, and where roar
The thundering Lauwine—might be worshipped more:
But I have seen the soaring Jungfrau rear
Her never-trodden snow, and seen the hoar
Glaciers of bleak Mont Blanc both far and near—
And in Chimari heard the Thunder-Hills of fear,

LXXIV

Th' Acroceraunian mountains of old name;
And on Parnassus seen the Eagles fly
Like Spirits of the spot, as 'twere for fame,
For still they soared unutterably high:
I've looked on Ida with a Trojan's eye;
Athos—Olympus—Ætna—Atlas—made
These hills seem things of lesser dignity;
All, save the lone Soracte's height, displayed
Not *now* in snow, which asks the lyric Roman's aid

LXXV

For our remembrance, and from out the plain
Heaves like a long-swept wave about to break,
And on the curl hangs pausing: not in vain
May he, who will, his recollections rake,

And quote in classic raptures, and awake
The hills with Latin echoes—I abhorred
Too much, to conquer for the Poet's sake,
The drilled dull lesson, forced down word by word
In my repugnant youth, with pleasure to record

LXXVI

Aught that recalls the daily drug which turned
My sickening memory; and, though Time hath taught
My mind to meditate what then it learned,
Yet such the fixed inveteracy wrought
By the impatience of my early thought,
That, with the freshness wearing out before
My mind could relish what it might have sought,
If free to choose, I cannot now restore
Its health—but what it then detested, still abhor.

LXXVII

Then farewell, Horace—whom I hated so,
Not for thy faults, but mine: it is a curse
To understand, not feel thy lyric flow,
To comprehend, but never love thy verse;
Although no deeper Moralist rehearse
Our little life, nor Bard prescribe his art,
Nor livelier Satirist the conscience pierce,
Awakening without wounding the touched heart,
Yet fare thee well—upon Soracte's ridge we part.

LXXVIII

Oh, Rome! my Country! City of the Soul!
The orphans of the heart must turn to thee,
Lone Mother of dead Empires! and control
In their shut breasts their petty misery.
What are our woes and sufferance? Come and see
The cypress—hear the owl—and plod your way
O'er steps of broken thrones and temples—Yet
Whose agonies are evils of a day—
A world is at our feet as fragile as our clay.

LXXIX

The Niobe of nations! there she stands,
Childless and crownless, in her voiceless woe;
An empty urn within her withered hands,
Whose holy dust was scattered long ago;
The Scipios' tomb contains no ashes now;
The very sepulchres lie tenantless
Of their heroic dwellers: dost thou flow,
Old Tiber! through a marble wilderness?
Rise, with thy yellow waves, and mantle her distress.

LXXX

The Goth, the Christian—Time—War—Flood, and Fire,
Have dealt upon the seven-hilled City's pride;
She saw her glories star by star expire,
And up the steep barbarian Monarchs ride,
Where the car climbed the Capitol; far and wide
Temple and tower went down, nor left a site:—
Chaos of ruins! who shall trace the void,
O'er the dim fragments cast a lunar light,
And say, "here was, or is," where all is doubly night?

LXXXI

The double night of ages, and of her,
Night's daughter, Ignorance, hath wrapt and wrap
All round us; we but feel our way to err:
The Ocean hath his chart, the Stars their map,
And Knowledge spreads them on her ample lap;
But Rome is as the desert—where we steer
Stumbling o'er recollections; now we clap
Our hands, and cry "Eureka!" "it is clear"—
When but some false Mirage of ruin rises near.

LXXXII

Alas! the lofty city! and, alas,
The trebly hundred triumphs! and the day
When Brutus made the dagger's edge surpass
The Conqueror's sword in bearing fame away!

Alas, for Tully's voice, and Virgil's lay,
And Livy's pictured page!—but these shall be
Her resurrection; all beside—decay.
Alas, for Earth, for never shall we see
That brightness in her eye she bore when Rome was free!

LXXXIII

Oh, thou, whose chariot rolled on Fortune's wheel,
Triumphant Sylla! Thou, who didst subdue
Thy country's foes ere thou wouldst pause to feel
The wrath of thy own wrongs, or reap the due
Of hoarded vengeance till thine Eagles flew
O'er prostrate Asia;—thou, who with thy frown
Annihilated senates;—Roman, too,
With all thy vices—for thou didst lay down
With an atoning smile a more than earthly crown,

LXXXIV

Thy dictatorial wreath—couldst thou divine
To what would one day dwindle that which made
Thee more than mortal? and that so supine,
By aught than Romans, Rome should thus be laid?—
She who was named Eternal, and arrayed
Her warriors but to conquer—she who veiled
Earth with her haughty shadow, and displayed,
Until the o'er-canopied horizon failed,
Her rushing wings—Oh! she who was Almighty hailed!

LXXXV

Sylla was first of victors; but our own,
The sagest of usurpers, Cromwell!—he
Too swept off senates while he hewed the throne
Down to a block—immortal rebel! See
What crimes it costs to be a moment free,
And famous through all ages! but beneath
His fate the moral lurks of destiny;
His day of double victory and death
Beheld him win two realms, and happier yield his breath.

LXXXVI

The third of the same Moon whose former course
Had all but crowned him, on the selfsame day
Deposed him gently from his throne of force,
And laid him with the Earth's preceding clay.
And showed not Fortune thus how fame and sway,
And all we deem delightful, and consume
Our souls to compass through each arduous way,
Are in her eyes less happy than the tomb?
Were they but so in Man's, how different were his doom!

LXXXVII

And thou, dread Statue! yet existent in
The austerest form of naked majesty—
Thou who beheldest, 'mid the assassins' din,
At thy bathed base the bloody Cæsar lie,
Folding his robe in dying dignity—
An offering to thine altar from the Queen
Of gods and men, great Nemesis! did he die,
And thou, too, perish, Pompey? have ye been
Victors of countless kings, or puppets of a scene?

LXXXVIII

And thou, the thunder-stricken nurse of Rome!
She-wolf! whose brazen-imaged dugs impart
The milk of conquest yet within the dome
Where, as a monument of antique art,
Thou standest:—Mother of the mighty heart,
Which the great Founder sucked from thy wild teat,
Scorched by the Roman Jove's ethereal dart,
And thy limbs black with lightning—dost thou yet
Guard thine immortal cubs, nor thy fond charge forget?

LXXXIX

Thou dost;—but all thy foster-babes are dead—
The men of iron—and the World hath reared
Cities from out their sepulchres: men bled
In imitation of the things they feared,

And fought and conquered, and the same course steered,
At apish distance; but as yet none have,
Nor could, the same supremacy have neared,
Save one vain Man, who is not in the grave—
But, vanquished by himself, to his own slaves a slave—

XC

The fool of false dominion—and a kind
Of bastard Cæsar, following him of old
With steps unequal; for the Roman's mind
Was modelled in a less terrestrial mould,
With passions fiercer, yet a judgment cold,
And an immortal instinct which redeemed
The frailties of a heart so soft, yet bold—
Alcides with the distaff now he seemed
At Cleopatra's feet,—and now himself he beamed,

XCI

And came—and saw—and conquered! But the man
Who would have tamed his Eagles down to flee,
Like a trained falcon, in the Gallic van,
Which he, in sooth, long led to Victory,
With a deaf heart which never seemed to be
A listener to itself, was strangely framed;
With but one weakest weakness—Vanity—
Coquettish in ambition—still he aimed—
At what? can he avouch, or answer what he claimed?

XCII

And would be all or nothing—nor could wait
For the sure grave to level him; few years
Had fixed him with the Cæsars in his fate,
On whom we tread: For *this* the conqueror rears
The Arch of Triumph! and for this the tears
And blood of earth flow on as they have flowed,
An universal Deluge, which appears
Without an Ark for wretched Man's abode,
And ebbs but to reflow!—Renew thy rainbow, God!

XCIII

What from this barren being do we reap?
Our senses narrow, and our reason frail,
Life short, and truth a gem which loves the deep,
And all things weighed in Custom's falsest scale;
Opinion an Omnipotence,—whose veil
Mantles the earth with darkness, until right
And wrong are accidents, and Men grow pale
Lest their own judgments should become too bright,
And their free thoughts be crimes, and Earth have too much light.

XCIV

And thus they plod in sluggish misery,
Rotting from sire to son, and age to age,
Proud of their trampled nature, and so die,
Bequeathing their hereditary rage
To the new race of inborn slaves, who wage
War for their chains, and rather than be free,
Bleed gladiator-like, and still engage
Within the same Arena where they see
Their fellows fall before, like leaves of the same tree.

XCV

I speak not of men's creeds—they rest between
Man and his maker—but of things allowed,
Averred, and known, and daily, hourly seen—
The yoke that is upon us doubly bowed,
And the intent of Tyranny avowed,
The edict of Earth's rulers, who are grown
The apes of him who humbled once the proud,
And shook them from their slumbers on the throne;
Too glorious, were this all his mighty arm had done.

XCVI

Can tyrants but by tyrants conquered be,
And Freedom find no Champion and no Child,
Such as Columbia saw arise when she
Sprung forth a Pallas, armed and undefiled?

Or must such minds be nourished in the wild,
Deep in the unpruned forest, 'midst the roar
Of cataracts, where nursing Nature smiled
On infant Washington? Has Earth no more
Such seeds within her breast, or Europe no such shore?

XCVII

But France got drunk with blood to vomit crime;
And fatal have her Saturnalia been
To Freedom's cause, in every age and clime;
Because the deadly days which we have seen,
And vile Ambition, that built up between
Man and his hopes an adamantine wall,
And the base pageant last upon the scene,
Are grown the pretext for the eternal thrall
Which nips Life's tree, and dooms man's worst—his second fall

XCVIII

Yet, Freedom! yet thy banner, torn but flying,
Streams like the thunder-storm *against* the wind!
Thy trumpet voice, though broken now and dying,
The loudest still the Tempest leaves behind;
Thy tree hath lost its blossoms, and the rind,
Chopped by the axe, looks rough and little worth,
But the sap lasts,—and still the seed we find
Sown deep, even in the bosom of the North;
So shall a better spring less bitter fruit bring forth.

XCIX

There is a stern round tower of other days,
Firm as a fortress, with its fence of stone,
Such as an army's baffled strength delays,
Standing with half its battlements alone,
And with two thousand years of ivy grown,
The garland of Eternity, where wave
The green leaves over all by Time o'erthrown;—
What was this tower of strength? within its cave
What treasure lay so locked, so hid?—A woman's grave.

C

But who was she, the Lady of the dead,
Tombed in a palace? Was she chaste and fair?
Worthy a king's—or more—a Roman's bed?
What race of Chiefs and Heroes did she bear?
What daughter of her beauties was the heir?
How lived—how loved—how died she? Was she not
So honoured—and conspicuously there,
Where meaner relics must not dare to rot,
Placed to commemorate a more than mortal lot?

CI

Was she as those who love their lords, or they
Who love the lords of others? such have been
Even in the olden time, Rome's annals say.
Was she a matron of Cornelia's mien,
Or the light air of Egypt's graceful Queen,
Profuse of joy—or 'gainst it did she war,
Inveterate in virtue? Did she lean
To the soft side of the heart, or wisely bar
Love from amongst her griefs?—for such the affections are

CII

Perchance she died in youth—it may be, bowed
With woes far heavier than the ponderous tomb
That weighed upon her gentle dust: a cloud
Might gather o'er her beauty, and a gloom
In her dark eye, prophetic of the doom
Heaven gives its favourites—early death—yet shed
A sunset charm around her, and illume
With hectic light, the Hesperus of the dead,
Of her consuming cheek the autumnal leaflike red.

CIII

Perchance she died in age—surviving all,
Charms—kindred—children—with the silver gray
On her long tresses, which might yet recall
It may be, still a something of the day

When they were braided, and her proud array
And lovely form were envied, praised, and eyed
By Rome—But whither would Conjecture stray?
Thus much alone we know—Metella died,
The wealthiest Roman's wife: Behold his love or pride!

CIV

I know not why—but standing thus by thee
It seems as if I had thine inmate known,
Thou Tomb! and other days come back on me
With recollected music, though the tone
Is changed and solemn, like the cloudy groan
Of dying thunder on the distant wind;
Yet, could I seat me by this ivied stone
Till I had bodied, forth the heated mind,
Forms from the floating wreck which Ruin leaves behind;

CV

And from the planks, far shattered o'er the rocks,
Built me a little bark of hope, once more
To battle with the Ocean and the shocks
Of the loud breakers, and the ceaseless roar
Which rushes on the solitary shore
Where all lies foundered that was ever dear:
But could I gather from the wave-worn store
Enough for my rude boat,—where should I steer?
There woos no home, nor hope, nor life, save what is here

CVI

Then let the Winds howl on! their harmony
Shall henceforth be my music, and the Night
The sound shall temper with the owlets' cry,
As I now hear them, in the fading light
Dim o'er the bird of darkness' native site,
Answering each other on the Palatine,
With their large eyes, all glistening gray and bright,
And sailing pinions.—Upon such a shrine
What are our petty griefs?—let me not number mine.

CVII

Cypress and ivy, weed and wallflower grown
Matted and massed together—hillocks heaped
On what were chambers—arch crushed, column strown
In fragments—choked up vaults, and frescos steeped
In subterranean damps, where the owl peeped,
Deeming it midnight:—Temples—Baths—or Halls?
Pronounce who can: for all that Learning reaped
From her research hath been, that these are walls—
Behold the Imperial Mount! 'tis thus the Mighty falls.

CVIII

There is the moral of all human tales;
'Tis but the same rehearsal of the past,
First Freedom, and then Glory—when that fails,
Wealth—Vice—Corruption,—Barbarism at last:—
And History, with all her volumes vast,
Hath but *one* page,—'tis better written here,
Where gorgeous Tyranny hath thus amassed
All treasures, all delights, that Eye or Ear,
Heart, Soul could seek—Tongue ask—Away with words! draw
    near

CIX

Admire—exult—despise—laugh—weep,—for here
There is such matter for all feeling:—Man!
Thou pendulum betwixt a smile and tear,
Ages and Realms are crowded in this span,
This mountain, whose obliterated plan
The pyramid of Empires pinnacled,
Of Glory's gewgaws shining in the van
Till the Sun's rays with added flame were filled!
Where are its golden roofs? where those who dared to build?

CX

Tully was not so eloquent as thou,
Thou nameless column with the buried base!
What are the laurels of the Cæsar's brow?
Crown me with ivy from his dwelling-place.

Whose arch or pillar meets me in the face,
Titus' or Trajan's? No—'tis that of Time:
Triumph, arch, pillar, all he doth displace
Scoffing; and apostolic statues climb
To crush the Imperial urn, whose ashes slept sublime,

CXI

Buried in air, the deep blue sky of Rome,
And looking to the stars: they had contained
A Spirit which with these would find a home,
The last of those who o'er the whole earth reigned,
The Roman Globe—for, after, none sustained,
But yielded back his conquests:—he was more
Than a mere Alexander, and, unstained
With household blood and wine, serenely wore
His sovereign virtues—still we Trajan's name adore.

CXII

Where is the rock of Triumph, the high place
Where Rome embraced her heroes?—where the steep
Tarpeian?—fittest goal of Treason's race,
The Promontory whence the Traitor's Leap
Cured all ambition? Did the conquerors heap
Their spoils here? Yes; and in yon field below,
A thousand years of silenced factions sleep—
The Forum, where the immortal accents glow,
And still the eloquent air breathes—burns with Cicero!

CXIII

The field of Freedom—Faction—Fame—and Blood:
Here a proud people's passions were exhaled,
From the first hour of Empire in the bud
To that when further worlds to conquer failed;
But long before had Freedom's face been veiled,
And Anarchy assumed her attributes;
Till every lawless soldier, who assailed,
Trod on the trembling Senate's slavish mutes,
Or raised the venal voice of baser prostitutes.

CXIV

Then turn we to her latest Tribune's name,
From her ten thousand tyrants turn to thee,
Redeemer of dark centuries of shame—
The friend of Petrarch—hope of Italy—
Rienzi! last of Romans! While the tree
Of Freedom's withered trunk puts forth a leaf,
Even for thy tomb a garland let it be—
The Forum's champion, and the people's chief—
Her new-born Numa thou—with reign, alas! too brief.

CXV

Egeria! sweet creation of some heart
Which found no mortal resting-place so fair
As thine ideal breast; whate'er thou art
Or wert,—a young Aurora of the air,
The nympholepsy of some fond despair—
Or—it might be—a Beauty of the earth,
Who found a more than common Votary there
Too much adoring—whatsoe'er thy birth,
Thou wert a beautiful Thought, and softly bodied forth.

CXVI

The mosses of thy Fountain still are sprinkled
With thine Elysian water-drops; the face
Of thy cave-guarded Spring, with years unwrinkled,
Reflects the meek-eyed Genius of the place,
Whose green, wild margin now no more erase
Art's works; nor must the delicate waters sleep
Prisoned in marble—bubbling from the base
Of the cleft statue, with a gentle leap
The rill runs o'er—and, round—fern, flowers, and ivy, creep

CXVII

Fantastically tangled: the green hills
Are clothed with early blossoms—through the grass
The quick-eyed lizard rustles—and the bills
Of summer-birds sing welcome as ye pass;

Flowers fresh in hue, and many in their class,
Implore the pausing step, and with their dyes
Dance in the soft breeze in a fairy mass;
The sweetness of the Violet's deep blue eyes,
Kissed by the breath of heaven, seems coloured by its skies.

CXVIII

Here didst thou dwell, in this enchanted cover,
Egeria! thy all heavenly bosom beating
For the far footsteps of thy mortal lover;
The purple Midnight veiled that mystic meeting
With her most starry canopy—and seating
Thyself by thine adorer. what befel?
This cave was surely shaped out for the greeting
Of an enamoured Goddess, and the cell
Haunted by holy Love—the earliest Oracle!

CXIX

And didst thou not, thy breast to his replying,
Blend a celestial with a human heart;
And Love, which dies as it was born, in sighing,
Share with immortal transports? could thine art
Make them indeed immortal, and impart
The purity of Heaven to earthly joys,
Expel the venom and not blunt the dart—
The dull satiety which all destroys—
And root from out the soul the deadly weed which cloys?

CXX

Alas! our young affections run to waste,
Or water but the desert! whence arise
But weeds of dark luxuriance, tares of haste,
Rank at the core, though tempting to the eyes,
Flowers whose wild odours breathe but agonies,
And trees whose gums are poison; such the plants
Which spring beneath her steps as Passion flies
O'er the World's wilderness, and vainly pants
For some celestial fruit forbidden to our wants.

CXXI

Oh, Love! no habitant of earth thou art—
An unseen Seraph, we believe in thee,—
A faith whose martyrs are the broken heart,—
But never yet hath seen, nor e'er shall see
The naked eye, thy form, as it should be;
The mind hath made thee, as it peopled Heaven,
Even with its own desiring phantasy,
And to a thought such shape and image given,
As haunts the unquenched soul—parched—wearied—wrung—
    and riven.

CXXII

Of its own beauty is the mind diseased,
And fevers into false creation:—where,
Where are the forms the sculptor's soul hath seized?
In him alone. Can Nature show so fair?
Where are the charms and virtues which we dare
Conceive in boyhood and pursue as men,
The unreached Paradise of our despair,
Which o'er-informs the pencil and the pen,
And overpowers the page where it would bloom again?

CXXIII

Who loves, raves—'tis youth's frenzy—but the cure
Is bitterer still, as charm by charm unwinds
Which robed our idols, and we see too sure
Nor Worth nor Beauty dwells from out the mind's
Ideal shape of such; yet still it binds—
The fatal spell, and still it draws us on,
Reaping the whirlwind from the oft-sown winds;
The stubborn heart, its alchemy begun,
Seems ever near the prize—wealthiest when most undone.

CXXIV

We wither from our youth, we gasp away—
Sick—sick; unfound the boon—unslaked the thirst.
Though to the last, in verge of our decay,
Some phantom lures, such as we sought at first—

But all too late,—so are we doubly curst.
Love, Fame, Ambition, Avarice—'tis the same,
Each idle—and all ill—and none the worst—
For all are meteors with a different name,
And Death the sable smoke where vanishes the flame.

CXXV

Few—none—find what they love or could have loved,
Though accident, blind contact, and the strong
Necessity of loving, have removed
Antipathies—but to recur, ere long,
Envenomed with irrevocable wrong;
And Circumstance, that unspiritual God
And Miscreator, makes and helps along
Our coming evils with a crutch-like rod,
Whose touch turns Hope to dust,—the dust we all have trod.

CXXVI

Our life is a false nature—'tis not in
The harmony of things,—this hard decree,
This uneradicable taint of Sin,
This boundless Upas, this all-blasting tree,
Whose root is Earth—whose leaves and branches be
The skies which rain their plagues on men like dew—
Disease, death, bondage—all the woes we see,
And worse, the woes we see not—which throb through
The immedicable soul, with heart-aches ever new.

CXXVII

Yet let us ponder boldly—'tis a base
Abandonment of reason to resign
Our right of thought—our last and only place
Of refuge; this, at least, shall still be mine:
Though from our birth the faculty divine
Is chained and tortured—cabined, cribbed, confined,
And bred in darkness, lest the Truth should shine
Too brightly on the unpreparéd mind,
The beam pours in—for Time and Skill will couch the blind.

CXXVIII

Arches on arches! as it were that Rome,
Collecting the chief trophies of her line,
Would build up all her triumphs in one dome,
Her Coliseum stands; the moonbeams shine
As 'twere its natural torches—for divine
Should be the light which streams here,—to illume
This long-explored but still exhaustless mine
Of Contemplation; and the azure gloom
Of an Italian night, where the deep skies assume

CXXIX

Hues which have words and speak to ye of Heaven,
Floats o'er this vast and wondrous monument,
And shadows forth its glory. There is given
Unto the things of earth, which Time hath bent,
A Spirit's feeling, and where he hath leant
His band, but broke his scythe, there is a power
And magic in the ruined battlement,
For which the Palace of the present hour
Must yield its pomp, and wait till Ages are its dower.

CXXX

Oh, Time! the Beautifier of the dead,
Adorner of the ruin—Comforter
And only Healer when the heart hath bled;—
Time! the Corrector where our judgments err,
The test of Truth, Love—sole philosopher,
For all beside are sophists—from thy thrift,
Which never loses though it doth defer—
Time, the Avenger! unto thee I lift
My hands, and eyes, and heart, and crave of thee a gift:

CXXXI

Amidst this wreck, where thou hast made a shrine
And temple more divinely desolate—
Among thy mightier offerings here are mine,
Ruins of years—though few, yet full of fate:—

If thou hast ever seen me too elate,
Hear me not; but if calmly I have borne
Good, and reserved my pride against the hate
Which shall not whelm me, let me not have worn
This iron in my soul in vain—shall *they* not mourn?

CXXXII

And Thou, who never yet of human wrong
Left the unbalanced scale, great Nemesis!
Here, where the ancient paid thee homage long—
Thou, who didst call the Furies from the abyss,
And round Orestes bade them howl and hiss
For that unnatural retribution—just,
Had it but been from hands less near—in this
Thy former realm, I call thee from the dust!
Dost thou not hear my heart?—Awake! thou shalt, and must.

CXXXIII

It is not that I may not have incurred,
For my ancestral faults or mine, the wound
I bleed withal; and, had it been conferred
With a just weapon, it had flowed unbound;
But now my blood shall not sink in the ground—
To thee I do devote it—*Thou* shalt take
The vengeance, which shall yet be sought and found—
Which if *I* have not taken for the sake——
But let that pass—I sleep—but Thou shalt yet awake.

CXXXIV

And if my voice break forth, 'tis not that now
I shrink from what is suffered: let him speak
Who hath beheld decline, upon my brow,
Or seen my mind's convulsion leave it weak;
But in this page a record will I seek.
Not in the air shall these my words disperse,
Though I be ashes; a far hour shall wreak
The deep prophetic fulness of this verse,
And pile on human heads the mountain of my curse!

CXXXV

That curse shall be Forgiveness.—Have I not—
Hear me, my mother Earth! behold it, Heaven!—
Have I not had to wrestle with my lot?
Have I not suffered things to be forgiven?
Have I not had my brain seared, my heart riven,
Hopes sapped, name blighted, Life's life lied away?
And only not to desperation driven,
Because not altogether of such clay
As rots into the souls of those whom I survey.

CXXXVI

From mighty wrongs to petty perfidy
Have I not seen what human things could do?
From the loud roar of foaming calumny
To the small whisper of the as paltry few—
And subtler venom of the reptile crew,
The Janus glance of whose significant eye,
Learning to lie with silence, would *seem* true—
And without utterance, save the shrug or sigh,
Deal round to happy fools its speechless obloquy.

CXXXVII

But I have lived, and have not lived in vain:
My mind may lose its force, my blood its fire,
And my frame perish even in conquering pain;
But there is that within me which shall tire
Torture and Time, and breathe when I expire;
Something unearthly, which they deem not of,
Like the remembered tone of a mute lyre,
Shall on their softened spirits sink, and move
In hearts all rocky now the late remorse of Love.

CXXXVIII

The seal is set.—Now welcome, thou dread Power
Nameless, yet thus omnipotent, which here
Walk'st in the shadow of the midnight hour
With a deep awe, yet all distinct from fear;

Thy haunts are ever where the dead walls rear
Their ivy mantles, and the solemn scene
Derives from thee a sense so deep and clear
That we become a part of what has been,
And grow upon the spot—all-seeing but unseen.

CXXXIX

And here the buzz of eager nations ran,
In murmured pity, or loud-roared applause,
As man was slaughtered by his fellow man.
And wherefore slaughtered? wherefore, but because
Such were the bloody Circus' genial laws,
And the imperial pleasure.—Wherefore not?
What matters where we fall to fill the maws
Of worms—on battle-plains or listed spot?
Both are but theatres—where the chief actors rot.

CXL

I see before me the Gladiator lie:
He leans upon his hand—his manly brow
Consents to death, but conquers agony,
And his drooped head sinks gradually low—
And through his side the last drops, ebbing slow
From the red gash, fall heavy, one by one,
Like the first of a thunder-shower; and now
The arena swims around him—he is gone,
Ere ceased the inhuman shout which hailed the wretch who won.

CXLI

He heard it, but he heeded not—his eyes
Were with his heart—and that was far away;
He recked not of the life he lost nor prize,
But where his rude hut by the Danube lay—
There were his young barbarians all at play,
There was their Dacian mother—he, their sire,
Butchered to make a Roman holiday—
All this rushed with his blood—Shall he expire
And unavenged?—Arise! ye Goths, and glut your ire!

CXLII

But here, where Murder breathed her bloody steam;—
And here, where buzzing nations choked the ways,
And roared or murmured like a mountain stream
Dashing or winding as its torrent strays;
Here, where the Roman million's blame or praise
Was Death or Life—the playthings of a crowd—
My voice sounds much—and fall the stars' faint rays
On the arena void—seats crushed—walls bowed—
And galleries, where my steps seem echoes strangely loud.

CXLIII

A Ruin—yet what Ruin! from its mass
Walls—palaces—half-cities, have been reared;
Yet oft the enormous skeleton ye pass,
And marvel where the spoil could have appeared.
Hath it indeed been plundered, or but cleared?
Alas! developed, opens the decay,
When the colossal fabric's form is neared:
It will not bear the brightness of the day,
Which streams too much on all—years—man—have reft away.

CXLIV

But when the rising moon begins to climb
Its topmost arch, and gently pauses there—
When the stars twinkle through the loops of Time,
And the low night-breeze waves along the air
The garland-forest, which the gray walls wear,
Like laurels on the bald first Cæsar's head—
When the light shines serene but doth not glare—
Then in this magic circle raise the dead;—
Heroes have trod this spot—'tis on their dust ye tread.

CXLV

"While stands the Coliseum, Rome shall stand:
When falls the Coliseum, Rome shall fall;
And when Rome falls—the World." From our own land
Thus spake the pilgrims o'er this mighty wall

In Saxon times, which we are wont to call
Ancient; and these three mortal things are still
On their foundations, and unaltered all—
Rome and her Ruin past Redemption's skill—
The World—the same wide den—of thieves, or what ye will.

CXLVI

Simple, erect, severe, austere, sublime—
Shrine of all saints and temple of all Gods,
From Jove to Jesus—spared and blest by Time—
Looking tranquillity, while falls or nods
Arch—empire—each thing round thee—and Man plods
His way through thorns to ashes—glorious Dome!
Shalt thou not last? Time's scythe and Tyrants' rods
Shiver upon thee—sanctuary and home
Of Art and Piety—Pantheon!—pride of Rome!

CXLVII

Relic of nobler days, and noblest arts!
Despoiled yet perfect! with thy circle spreads
A holiness appealing to all hearts;
To Art a model—and to him who treads
Rome for the sake of ages, Glory sheds
Her light through thy sole aperture; to those
Who worship, here are altars for their beads—
And they who feel for Genius may repose
Their eyes on honoured forms, whose busts around them close.

CXLVIII

There is a dungeon, in whose dim drear light
What do I gaze on? Nothing—Look again!
Two forms are slowly shadowed on my sight—
Two insulated phantoms of the brain:
It is not so—I see them full and plain—
An old man, and a female young and fair,
Fresh as a nursing mother, in whose vein
The blood is nectar:—but what doth she there,
With her unmantled neck, and bosom white and bare?

CXLIX

Full swells the deep pure fountain of young life,
Where *on* the heart and *from* the heart we took
Our first and sweetest nurture—when the wife.
Blest into mother, in the innocent look,
Or even the piping cry of lips that brook
No pain and small suspense, a joy perceives
Man knows not—when from out its cradled nook
She sees her little bud put forth its leaves—
What may the fruit be yet?—I know not—Cain was Eve's.

CL

But here Youth offers to Old Age the food,
The milk of his own gift: it is her Sire
To whom she renders back the debt of blood
Born with her birth:—No—he shall not expire
While in those warm and lovely veins the fire
Of health and holy feeling can provide
Great Nature's Nile, whose deep stream rises higher
Than Egypt's river:—from that gentle side
Drink—drink, and live—Old Man! Heaven's realm holds no such
    tide.

CLI

The starry fable of the Milky Way
Has not thy story's purity; it is
A constellation of a sweeter ray,
And sacred Nature triumphs more in this
Reverse of her decree, than in the abyss
Where sparkle distant worlds:—Oh, holiest Nurse!
No drop of that clear stream its way shall miss
To thy Sire's heart, replenishing its source
With life, as our freed souls rejoin the Universe.

CLII

Turn to the Mole which Hadrian reared on high,
Imperial mimic of old Egypt's piles,
Colossal copyist of deformity—
Whose travelled phantasy from the far Nile's

Enormous model, doomed the artist's toils
To build for Giants, and for his vain earth,
His shrunken ashes, raise this Dome: How smiles
The gazer's eye with philosophic mirth,
To view the huge design which sprung from such a birth!

CLIII

But lo! the Dome—the vast and wondrous Dome,
To which Diana's marvel was a cell—
Christ's mighty shrine above His martyr's tomb!
I have beheld the Ephesian's miracle—
Its columns strew the wilderness, and dwell
The hyæna and the jackal in their shade;
I have beheld Sophia's bright roofs swell
There glittering mass i' the Sun, and have surveyed
Its sanctuary the while the usurping Moslem prayed;

CLIV

But thou, of temples old, or altars new,
Standest alone—with nothing like to thee—
Worthiest of God, the Holy and the True!
Since Zion's desolation, when that He
Forsook his former city, what could be,
Of earthly structures, in His honour piled,
Of a sublimer aspect? Majesty—
Power—Glory—Strength—and Beauty all are aisled
In this eternal Ark of worship undefiled.

CLV

Enter: its grandeur overwhelms thee not;
And why? it is not lessened—but thy mind,
Expanded by the Genius of the spot,
Has grown colossal, and can only find
A fit abode wherein appear enshrined
Thy hopes of Immortality—and thou
Shalt one day, if found worthy, so defined
See thy God face to face, as thou dost now
His Holy of Holies—nor be blasted by his brow.

CLVI

Thou movest—but increasing with the advance,
Like climbing some great Alp, which still doth rise,
Deceived by its gigantic elegance—
Vastness which grows but grows to harmonize—
All musical in its immensities;
Rich marbles, richer painting—shrines where flame
The lamps of gold—and haughty dome which vies
In air with Earth's chief structures, though their frame
Sits on the firm-set ground—and this the clouds must claim.

CLVII

Thou seest not all—but piecemeal thou must break,
To separate contemplation, the great whole;
And as the Ocean many bays will make
That ask the eye—so here condense thy soul
To more immediate objects, and control
Thy thoughts until thy mind hath got by heart
Its eloquent proportions, and unroll
In mighty graduations, part by part,
The Glory which at once upon thee did not dart.

CLVIII

Not by its fault—but thine: Our outward sense
Is but of gradual grasp—and as it is
That what we have of feeling most intense
Outstrips our faint expression; even so this
Outshining and o'erwhelming edifice
Fools our fond gaze, and greatest of the great
Defies at first our Nature's littleness,
Till, growing with its growth, we thus dilate
Our Spirits to the size of that they contemplate.

CLIX

Then pause and be enlightened; there is more
In such a survey than the sating gaze
Of wonder pleased, or awe which would adore
The worship of the place, or the mere praise

Of Art and its great Masters, who could raise
What former time, nor skill, nor thought could plan:
The fountain of Sublimity displays
Its depth, and thence may draw the mind of Man
Its golden sands, and learn what great Conceptions can.

CLX

Or, turning to the Vatican, go see
Laocoön's torture dignifying pain—
A Father's love and Mortal's agony
With an Immortal's patience blending:—Vain
The struggle—vain, against the coiling strain
And gripe, and deepening of the dragon's grasp,
The Old Man's clench; the long envenomed chain
Rivets the living links,—the enormous Asp
Enforces pang on pang, and stifles gasp on gasp.

CLXI

Or view the Lord of the unerring bow,
The God of Life, and Poesy, and Light—
The Sun in human limbs arrayed, and brow
All radiant from his triumph in the fight;
The shaft hath just been shot—the arrow bright
With an Immortal's vengeance—in his eye
And nostril beautiful Disdain, and Might
And Majesty, flash their full lightnings by,
Developing in that one glance the Deity.

CLXII

But in his delicate form—a dream of Love,
Shaped by some solitary Nymph, whose breast
Longed for a deathless lover from above,
And maddened in that vision—are exprest
All that ideal Beauty ever blessed
The mind with in its most unearthly mood,
When each conception was a heavenly Guest—
A ray of Immortality—and stood,
Starlike, around, until they gathered to a God!

CLXIII

And if it be Prometheus stole from Heaven
The fire which we endure—it was repaid
By him to whom the energy was given
Which this poetic marble hath arrayed
With an eternal Glory—which, if made
By human hands, is not of human thought—
And Time himself hath hallowed it, nor laid
One ringlet in the dust—nor hath it caught
A tinge of years, but breathes the flame with which 'twas
    wrought.

CLXIV

But where is he, the Pilgrim of my Song,
The Being who upheld it through the past?
Methinks he cometh late and tarries long.
He is no more—these breathings are his last—
His wanderings done—his visions ebbing fast,
And he himself as nothing:—if he was
Aught but a phantasy, and could be classed
With forms which live and suffer—let that pass—
His shadow fades away into Destruction's mass,

CLXV

Which gathers shadow—substance—life, and all
That we inherit in its mortal shroud—
And spreads the dim and universal pall
Through which all things grow phantoms; and the cloud
Between us sinks and all which ever glowed,
Till Glory's self is twilight, and displays
A melancholy halo scarce allowed
To hover on the verge of darkness—rays
Sadder than saddest night, for they distract the gaze,

CLXVI

And send us prying into the abyss,
To gather what we shall be when the frame
Shall be resolved to something less than this—
Its wretched essence; and to dream of fame,

And wipe the dust from off the idle name
We never more shall hear,—but never more,
Oh, happier thought! can we be made the same:—
It is enough in sooth that *once* we bore
These fardels of the heart—the heart whose sweat was gore.

CLXVII

Hark! forth from the abyss a voice proceeds,
A long low distant murmur of dread sound,
Such as arises when a nation bleeds
With some deep and immedicable wound;—
Through storm and darkness yawns the rending ground—
The gulf is thick with phantoms, but the Chief
Seems royal still, though with her head discrowned,
And pale, but lovely, with maternal grief
She clasps a babe, to whom her breast yields no relief.

CLXVIII

Scion of Chiefs and Monarchs, where art thou?
Fond Hope of many nations, art thou dead?
Could not the Grave forget thee, and lay low
Some less majestic, less belovéd head?
In the sad midnight, while thy heart still bled,
The mother of a moment, o'er thy boy,
Death hushed that pang for ever: with thee fled
The present happiness and promised joy
Which filled the Imperial Isles so full it seemed to cloy.

CLXIX

Peasants bring forth in safety.—Can it be,
Oh thou that wert so happy, so adored!
Those who weep not for Kings shall weep for thee,
And Freedom's heart, grown heavy, cease to hoard
Her many griefs, for *one?*—for she had poured
Her orisons for thee, and o'er thy head
Beheld her Iris.—Thou, too, lonely Lord,
And desolate Consort—vainly wert thou wed!
The husband of a year! the father of the dead!

Of sackcloth was thy wedding garment made;
Thy bridal's fruit is ashes: in the dust
The fair-haired Daughter of the Isles is laid,
The love of millions! How we did entrust
Futurity to her! and, though it must
Darken above our bones, yet fondly deemed
Our children should obey her child, and blessed
Her and her hoped-for seed, whose promise seemed
Like stars to shepherds' eyes:—'twas but a meteor beamed.

Woe unto us—not her—for she sleeps well:
The fickle reek of popular breath, the tongue
Of hollow counsel, the false oracle,
Which from the birth of Monarchy hath rung
Its knell in princely ears, till the o'erstung
Nations have armed in madness—the strange fate
Which tumbles mightiest sovereigns, and hath flung
Against their blind omnipotence a weight
Within the opposing scale, which crushes soon or late,—

These might have been her destiny—but no—
Our hearts deny it: and so young, so fair,
Good without effort, great without a foe;
But now a Bride and Mother—and now *there!*
How many ties did that stern moment tear!
From thy Sire's to his humblest subject's breast
Is linked the electric chain of that despair,
Whose shock was as an Earthquake's, and opprest
The land which loved thee so that none could love thee best.

Lo, Nemi! navelled in the woody hills
So far, that the uprooting Wind which tears
The oak from his foundation, and which spills
The Ocean o'er its boundary, and bears

its foam against the skies, reluctant spares
The oval mirror of thy glassy lake;
And calm as cherished hate, its surface wears
A deep cold settled aspect nought can shake,
All coiled into itself and round, as sleeps the snake.

CLXXIV

And near, Albano's scarce divided waves
Shine from a sister valley;—and afar
The Tiber winds, and the broad Ocean laves
The Latian coast where sprung the Epic war,
"Arms and the Man," whose re-ascending star
Rose o'er an empire:—but beneath thy right
Tully reposed from Rome;—and where yon bar
Of girdling mountains intercepts the sight
The Sabine farm was tilled, the weary Bard's delight.

CLXXV

But I forget.—My Pilgrim's shrine is won,
And he and I must part,—so let it be,—
His task and mine alike are nearly done;
Yet once more let us look upon the Sea;
The Midland Ocean breaks on him and me,
And from the Alban Mount we now behold
Our friend of youth, that Ocean, which when we
Beheld it last by Calpe's rock unfold
Those waves, we followed on till the dark Euxine rolled

CLXXVI

Upon the blue Symplegades: long years—
Long, though not very many—since have done
Their work on both; some suffering and some tears
Have left us nearly where we had begun:
Yet not in vain our mortal race hath run—
We have had our reward—and it is here,
That we can yet feel gladdened by the Sun,
And reap from Earth—Sea—joy almost as dear
As if there were no Man to trouble what is clear.

Oh! that the Desert were my dwelling-place,
With one fair Spirit for my minister,
That I might all forget the human race,
And, hating no one, love but only her!
Ye elements!—in whose ennobling stir
I feel myself exalted—Can ye not
Accord me such a Being? Do I err
In deeming such inhabit many a spot?
Though with them to converse can rarely be our lot.

There is a pleasure in the pathless woods,
There is a rapture on the lonely shore,
There is society, where none intrudes,
By the deep Sea, and Music in its roar:
I love not Man the less, but Nature more,
From these our interviews, in which I steal
From all I may be, or have been before,
To mingle with the Universe, and feel
What I can ne'er express—yet can not all conceal.

Roll on, thou deep and dark blue Ocean—roll!
Ten thousand fleets sweep over thee in vain;
Man marks the earth with ruin—his control
Stops with the shore;—upon the watery plain
The wrecks are all thy deed, nor doth remain
A shadow of man's ravage, save his own,
When, for a moment, like a drop of rain,
He sinks into thy depths with bubbling groan—
Without a grave—unknelled, uncoffined, and unknown.

His steps are not upon thy paths,—thy fields
Are not a spoil for him,—thou dost arise
And shake him from thee; the vile strength he wields
For Earth's destruction thou dost all despise.

Spurning him from thy bosom to the skies—
And send'st him, shivering in thy playful spray
And howling, to his Gods, where haply lies
His petty hope in some near port or bay,
And dashest him again to Earth:—there let him lay.

CLXXXI

The armaments which thunderstrike the walls
Of rock-built cities, bidding nations quake,
And Monarchs tremble in their Capitals,
The oak Leviathans, whose huge ribs make
Their clay creator the vain title take
Of Lord of thee, and Arbiter of War—
These are thy toys, and, as the snowy flake,
They melt into thy yeast of waves, which mar
Alike the Armada's pride, or spoils of Trafalgar.

CLXXXII

Thy shores are empires, changed in all save thee—
Assyria—Greece—Rome—Carthage—what are they?
Thy waters washed them power while they were free,
And many a tyrant since; their shores obey
The stranger, slave, or savage; their decay
Has dried up realms to deserts:—not so thou,
Unchangeable save to thy wild waves' play;
Time writes no wrinkle on thine azure brow—
Such as Creation's dawn beheld, thou rollest now.

CLXXXIII

Thou glorious mirror, where the Almighty's form
Glasses itself in tempests; in all time,
Calm or convulsed—in breeze, or gale, or storm—
Icing the Pole, or in the torrid clime
Dark-heaving—boundless, endless, and sublime—
The image of Eternity—the throne
Of the Invisible; even from out thy slime
The monsters of the deep are made—each Zone
Obeys thee—thou goest forth, dread, fathomless, alone.

And I have loved thee, Ocean! and my joy
Of youthful sports was on thy breast to be
Borne, like thy bubbles, onward: from a boy
I wantoned with thy breakers—they to me
Were a delight; and if the freshening sea
Made them a terror—'twas a pleasing fear,
For I was as it were a Child of thee,
And trusted to thy billows far and near,
And laid my hand upon thy mane—as I do here.

My task is done—my song hath ceased—my theme
Has died into an echo; it is fit
The spell should break of this protracted dream.
The torch shall be extinguished which hath lit
My midnight lamp—and what is writ, is writ,—
Would it were worthier! but I am not now
That which I have been—and my visions flit
Less palpably before me—and the glow
Which in my Spirit dwelt is fluttering, faint, and low.

Farewell! a word that must be, and hath been—
A sound which makes us linger;—yet—farewell!
Ye! who have traced the Pilgrim to the scene
Which is his last—if in your memories dwell
A thought which once was his—if on ye swell
A single recollection—not in vain
He wore his sandal-shoon, and scallop-shell;
Farewell! with *him* alone may rest the pain,
If such there were—with *you*, the Moral of his Strain

SHORTER POEMS

From HOURS OF IDLENESS

ON THE DEATH OF A YOUNG LADY

COUSIN TO THE AUTHOR, AND VERY DEAR TO HIM

[Byron calls this his "first dash into poetry," composed when
he was fourteen. "It was the ebullition of a passion for my first
Cousin Margaret Parker . . . one of the most beautiful of evanescent beings." *Detached Thoughts,* 1821.]

1

Hush'd are the winds, and still the evening gloom,
    Not e'en a zephyr wanders through the grove,
Whilst I return to view my Margaret's tomb,
    And scatter flowers on the dust I love.

2

Within this narrow cell reclines her clay,
    That clay, where once such animation beam'd;
The King of Terrors seiz'd her as his prey;
    Not worth, nor beauty, have her life redeem'd.

3

Oh! could that King of Terrors pity feel,
    Or Heaven reverse the dread decree of fate,
Not here the mourner would his grief reveal,
    Not here the Muse her virtues would relate.

4

But wherefore weep? Her matchless spirit soars
  Beyond where splendid shines the orb of day;
And weeping angels lead her to those bowers,
  Where endless pleasures virtuous deeds repay.

5

And shall presumptuous mortals Heaven arraign!
  And, madly, Godlike Providence accuse!
Ah! no, far fly from me attempts so vain;—
  I'll ne'er submission to my God refuse.

6

Yet is remembrance of those virtues dear,
  Yet fresh the memory of that beauteous face;
Still they call forth my warm affection's tear,
  Still in my heart retain their wonted place.

                                        1802.
              [*First publ., December, 1806.*]

ON LEAVING NEWSTEAD ABBEY

"Why dost thou build the hall, Son of the winged days? Thou look-
est from thy tower to-day: yet a few years, and the blast of the des-
art comes: it howls in thy empty court."—OSSIAN.

1

THROUGH thy battlements, Newstead, the hollow winds whistle:
  Thou, the hall of my Fathers, art gone to decay;
In thy once smiling garden, the hemlock and thistle
  Have choak'd up the rose which late bloom'd in the way.

2

Of the mail-cover'd Barons, who, proudly, to battle,
  Led their vassals from Europe to Palestine's plain,

The escutcheon and shield, which with ev'ry blast rattle,
　Are the only sad vestiges now that remain.

3

No more doth old Robert, with harp-stringing numbers,
　Raise a flame, in the breast, for the war-laurell'd wreath;
Near Askalon's towers, John of Horistan slumbers,
　Unnerv'd is the hand of his minstrel, by death.

4

Paul and Hubert too sleep in the valley of Cressy;
　For the safety of Edward and England they fell:
My Fathers! the tears of your country redress ye:
　How you fought! how you died! still her annals can tell.

5

On Marston, with Rupert, 'gainst traitors contending,
　Four brothers enrich'd, with their blood, the bleak field;
For the rights of a monarch their country defending,
　Till death their attachment to royalty seal'd.

6

Shades of heroes, farewell! your descendant departing
　From the seat of his ancestors, bids you adieu!
Abroad, or at home, your remembrance imparting
　New courage, he'll think upon glory and you.

7

Though a tear dim his eye at this sad separation,
　'Tis nature, not fear, that excites his regret;
Far distant he goes, with the same emulation,
　The fame of his fathers he ne'er can forget.

8

That fame, and that memory, still will he cherish;
　He vows that he ne'er will disgrace your renown:

Like you will he live, or like you will he perish;
When decay'd, may he mingle his dust with your own!

1803.

[First publ., December, 1806.]

THE FIRST KISS OF LOVE

'Α βάρβιτος δὲ χορδαῖς
"Ερωτα μοῦνον ἠχεῖ.
—ANACREON

1

AWAY with your fictions of flimsy romance,
    Those tissues of falsehood which Folly has wove;
Give me the mild beam of the soul-breathing glance,
    Or the rapture which dwells on the first kiss of love.

2

Ye rhymers, whose bosoms with fantasy glow,
    Whose pastoral passions are made for the grove;
From what blest inspiration your sonnets would flow,
    Could you ever have tasted the first kiss of love!

3

If Apollo should e'er his assistance refuse,
    Or the Nine be dispos'd from your service to rove,
Invoke them no more, bid adieu to the Muse,
    And try the effect, of the first kiss of love.

4

I hate you, ye cold compositions of art,
    Though prudes may condemn me, and bigots reprove;
I court the effusions that spring from the heart,
    Which throbs, with delight, to the first kiss of love.

5

Your shepherds, your flocks, those fantastical themes,
  Perhaps may amuse, yet they never can move:
Arcadia displays but a region of dreams;
  What are visions like these, to the first kiss of love?

6

Oh! cease to affirm that man, since his birth,
  From Adam, till now, has with wretchedness strove;
Some portion of Paradise still is on earth,
  And Eden revives, in the first kiss of love.

7

When age chills the blood, when our pleasures are past—
  For years fleet away with the wings of the dove—
The dearest remembrance will still be the last,
  Our sweetest memorial, the first kiss of love.

December 23, 1806.
[First publ., January, 1807.]

TO WOMAN

Woman! experience might have told me
That all must love thee, who behold thee:
Surely experience might have taught
Thy firmest promises are nought;
But, plac'd in all thy charms before me,
All I forget, but to adore thee.
Oh memory! thou choicest blessing,
When join'd with hope, when still possessing;
But how much curst by every lover
When hope is fled, and passion's over.
Woman, that fair and fond deceiver,
How prompt are striplings to believe her!
How throbs the pulse, when first we view
The eye that rolls in glossy blue,
Or sparkles black, or mildly throws

A beam from under hazel brows!
How quick we credit every oath,
And hear her plight the willing troth!
Fondly we hope 'twill last for aye,
When, lo! she changes in a day.
This record will for ever stand,
"Woman, thy vows are trac'd in sand."
                    [*First publ., December, 1806.*]

LOVE'S LAST ADIEU

'Aεὶ δ' αεί με φεύγει.—ANACREON.

1

THE roses of Love glad the garden of life,
    Though nurtur'd 'mid weeds dropping pestilent dew,
Till Time crops the leaves with unmerciful knife,
    Or prunes them for ever, in Love's last adieu!

2

In vain, with endearments we soothe the sad heart,
    In vain do we vow for an age to be true;
The chance of an hour may command us to part,
    Or Death disunite us, in Love's last adieu!

3

Still Hope, breathing peace through the grief-swollen breas'
    Will whisper, "Our meeting we yet may renew:"
With this dream of deceit half our sorrow's represt,
    Nor taste we the poison, of Love's last adieu!

4

Oh! mark you yon pair: in the sunshine of youth
    Love twin'd round their childhood his flowers as they grew;
They flourish awhile in the season of truth,
    Till chill'd by the winter of Love's last adieu!

5

Sweet lady! why thus doth a tear steal its way
 Down a cheek which outrivals thy bosom in hue?
Yet why do I ask?—to distraction a prey,
 Thy reason has perish'd, with Love's last adieu!

6

Oh! who is yon Misanthrope, shunning mankind?
 From cities to caves of the forest he flew:
There, raving, he howls his complaint to the wind;
 The mountains reverberate Love's last adieu!

7

Now Hate rules a heart which in Love's easy chains
 Once Passion's tumultuous blandishments knew;
Despair now inflames the dark tide of his veins;
 He ponders, in frenzy, on Love's last adieu!

8

How he envies the wretch with a soul wrapt in steel!
 His pleasures are scarce, yet his troubles are few,
Who laughs at the pang that he never can feel,
 And dreads not the anguish of Love's last adieu!

9

Youth flies, life decays, even hope is o'ercast;
 No more, with Love's former devotion, we sue:
He spreads his young wing, he retires with the blast;
 The shroud of affection is Love's last adieu!

10

In this life of probation, for rapture divine,
 Astrea declares that some penance is due;
From him, who has worshipp'd at Love's gentle **shrine,**
 The atonement is ample, in Love's last adieu!

11

Who kneels to the God, on his altar of light
    Must myrtle and cypress alternately strew:
His myrtle, an emblem of purest delight—
    His cypress, the garland of Love's last adieu!

[*First publ., January, 1807.*]

REPLY TO SOME VERSES OF J. M. B. PIGOT, Esq.,

ON THE CRUELTY OF HIS MISTRESS

1

WHY, Pigot, complain
    Of this damsel's disdain,
Why thus in despair do you fret?
    For months you may try,
    Yet, believe me, a *sigh*
Will never obtain a *coquette*.

2

Would you teach her to love?
    For a time seem to rove;
At first she may *frown* in a *pet*;
    But leave her awhile,
    She shortly will smile,
And then you may *kiss* your *coquette*.

3

For such are the airs
    Of these fanciful fairs,
They think all our *homage* a *debt:*
    Yet a partial neglect
    Soon takes an effect,
And humbles the proudest *coquette*.

4

Dissemble your pain,
And lengthen your chain,
And seem her *hauteur* to *regret;*
If again you shall sigh,
She no more will deny,
That *yours* is the rosy *coquette.*

5

If still, from false pride,
Your pangs she deride,
This whimsical virgin forget;
Some *other* admire,
Who will *melt* with your *fire,*
And laugh at the *little coquette.*

6

For *me,* I adore
Some *twenty* or more,
And love them most dearly; but yet,
Though my heart they enthral,
I'd abandon them all,
Did they act like your blooming *coquette.*

7

No longer repine,
Adopt this design,
And break through her slight-woven net!
Away with despair,
No longer forbear
To fly from the captious *coquette.*

8

Then quit her, my friend!
Your bosom defend,
Ere quite with her snares you're beset:
Lest your deep-wounded heart,

When incens'd by the smart
Should lead you to *curse* the *coquette.*
October 27, 1806.
[*First publ., December, 1806.*]

TO THE SIGHING STREPHON

1

Your pardon, my friend,
If my rhymes did offend,
Your pardon, a thousand times o'er;
From friendship I strove,
Your pangs to remove,
But, I swear, I will do so no more.

2

Since your *beautiful* maid,
Your flame has repaid,
No more I your folly regret;
She's now most divine,
And I bow at the shrine,
Of this quickly reformèd coquette.

3

Yet still, I must own,
I should never have known
From *your verses*, what else she deserv'd;
Your pain seem'd so great,
I pitied your fate,
As your fair was so dev'lish reserv'd.

4

Since the balm-breathing kiss
Of this magical Miss,
Can such wonderful transports produce;
Since the "*world you forget,
When your lips once have met,*"
My counsel will get but abuse.

5

You say, "When I rove,
I know nothing of love;"
'Tis true, I am given to range;
If I rightly remember,
I've lov'd a good number;
Yet there's pleasure, at least, in a change.

6

I will not advance,
By the rules of romance,
To humour a whimsical fair;
Though a smile may delight,
Yet a *frown* will *affright,*
Or drive me to dreadful despair.

7

While my blood is thus warm,
I ne'er shall reform,
To mix in the Platonists' school;
Of this I am sure,
Was my Passion so pure,
Thy *Mistress* would think me a fool.

8

And if I should shun,
Every *woman* for *one,*
Whose *image* must fill my whole breast;
Whom I must *prefer,*
And *sigh* but for *her,*
What an *insult* 'twould be to the *rest!*

9

Now Strephon, good-bye;
I cannot deny,
Your *passion* appears most *absurd;*
Such *love* as you plead,

Is *pure* love, indeed,
For it *only* consists in the *word.*
[*First publ., December, 1806.*]

TO ELIZA

[Addressed to Elizabeth Pigot, Byron's friend and neighbor at
Southwell, near Nottingham, where he spent his holidays from
Harrow.]

1

ELIZA! what fools are the Mussulman sect,
  Who, to woman, deny the soul's future existence;
Could they see thee, Eliza! they'd own their defect,
  And this doctrine would meet with a general resistance.

2

Had their Prophet possess'd half an atom of sense,
  He ne'er would have *woman* from Paradise driven;
Instead of his *Houris,* a flimsy pretence,
  With *woman alone* he had peopled his Heaven.

3

Yet, still, to increase your calamities more,
  Not content with depriving your bodies of spirit,
He allots one poor husband to share amongst four!—
  With *souls* you'd dispense; but, this last, who could bear it?

4

His religion to please neither *party* is made;
  On *husbands* 'tis *hard,* to the wives most uncivil;
Still I can't contradict, what so oft has been said,
  "Though women are angels, yet wedlock's the devil."

5

This terrible truth, even Scripture has told.
  Ye Benedicks! hear me, and listen with rapture;

If a glimpse of redemption you wish to behold,
   Of St. Matt.—read the second and twentieth chapter.

6

'Tis surely enough upon earth to be vex'd,
   With wives who eternal confusion are spreading;
"But in Heaven," (so runs the Evangelist's Text,)
   "We neither have giving in marriage, or wedding."

7

From this we suppose, (as indeed well we may,)
   That should Saints after death, with their spouses put up more,
And wives, as in life, aim at absolute sway,
   All Heaven would ring with the conjugal uproar.

8

Distraction and Discord would follow in course,
   Nor Matthew, nor Mark, nor St. Paul, can deny it,
The only expedient is general divorce,
   To prevent universal disturbance and riot.

9

But though husband and wife shall at length be disjoin'd,
   Yet woman and man ne'er were meant to dissever,
Our chains once dissolv'd, and our hearts unconfin'd,
   We'll love without bonds, but we'll love you for ever.

10

Though souls are denied you by fools and by rakes,
   Should you own it yourselves, I would even then doubt you,
Your nature so much of *celestial* partakes,
   The Garden of Eden would wither without you.

                    Southwell, October 9, 1806.
                    [*First publ., December, 1806.*]

LACHIN Y GAIR

1

Away, ye gay landscapes, ye gardens of roses!
   In you let the minions of luxury rove;
Restore me the rocks, where the snow-flake reposes,
   Though still they are sacred to freedom and love:
Yet, Caledonia, belov'd are thy mountains,
   Round their white summits though elements war;
Though cataracts foam 'stead of smooth-flowing fountains,
   I sigh for the valley of dark Loch na Garr.

2

Ah! there my young footsteps in infancy wander'd:
   My cap was the bonnet, my cloak was the plaid;
On chieftains, long perish'd, my memory ponder'd,
   As daily I strode through the pine-cover'd glade;
I sought not my home, till the day's dying glory
   Gave place to the rays of the bright polar star;
For fancy was cheer'd by traditional story,
   Disclos'd by the natives of dark Loch na Garr.

3

"Shades of the dead! have I not heard your voices
   Rise on the night-rolling breath of the gale?"
Surely, the soul of the hero rejoices,
   And rides on the wind, o'er his own Highland vale!
Round Loch na Garr, while the stormy mist gathers,
   Winter presides in his cold icy car:
Clouds, there, encircle the forms of my Fathers;
   They dwell in the tempests of dark Loch na Garr.

4

"Ill starr'd, though brave, did no visions foreboding
   Tell you that fate had forsaken your cause?"
Ah! were you destin'd to die at Culloden

Victory crown'd not your fall with applause:
Still were you happy, in Death's earthy slumber,
    You rest with your clan, in the caves of Braemar;
The Pibroch resounds, to the piper's loud number,
    Your deeds, on the echoes of dark Loch na Garr.

5

'Years have roll'd on, Loch na Garr, since I left you,
    Years must elapse, ere I tread you again:
Nature of verdure and flowers has bereft you,
    Yet still are you dearer than Albion's plain:
England! thy beauties are tame and domestic,
    To one who has rov'd on the mountains afar:
Oh! for the crags that are wild and majestic,
    The steep, frowning glories of dark Loch na Garr.
                              [*First publ., June, 1807.*]

TO ROMANCE

1

PARENT of golden dreams, Romance!
    Auspicious Queen of childish joys,
Who lead'st along, in airy dance,
    Thy votive train of girls and boys;
At length, in spells no longer bound,
    I break the fetters of my youth;
No more I tread thy mystic round,
    But leave thy realms for those of Truth.

2

And yet 'tis hard to quit the dreams
    Which haunt the unsuspicious soul,
Where every nymph a goddess seems,
    Whose eyes through rays immortal roll;
While Fancy holds her boundless reign,
    And all assume a varied hue;
When Virgins seem no longer vain,
    And even Woman's smiles are true.

3

And must we own thee, but a name,
   And from thy hall of clouds descend?
Nor find a Sylph in every dame,
   A Pylades in every friend?
But leave, at once, thy realms of air
   To mingling bands of fairy elves;
Confess that Woman's false as fair,
   And friends have feeling for—themselves?

4

With shame, I own, I've felt thy sway;
   Repentant, now thy reign is o'er;
No more thy precepts I obey,
   No more on fancied pinions soar;
Fond fool! to love a sparkling eye,
   And think that eye to truth was dear;
To trust a passing wanton's sigh,
   And melt beneath a wanton's tear!

5

Romance! disgusted with deceit,
   Far from thy motley court I fly,
Where Affectation holds her seat,
   And sickly Sensibility;
Whose silly tears can never flow
   For any pangs excepting thine;
Who turns aside from real woe,
   To steep in dew thy gaudy shrine.

6

Now join with sable Sympathy,
   With cypress crown'd, array'd in weeds,
Who heaves with thee her simple sigh,
   Whose breast for every bosom bleeds;
And call thy sylvan female choir,
   To mourn a Swain for ever gone,

Who once could glow with equal fire,
  But bends not now before thy throne.

7

Ye genial Nymphs, whose ready tears
  On all occasions swiftly flow;
Whose bosoms heave with fancied fears,
  With fancied flames and phrenzy glow;
Say, will you mourn my absent name,
  Apostate from your gentle train?
An infant Bard, at least, may claim
  From you a sympathetic strain.

8

Adieu, fond race! a long adieu!
  The hour of fate is hovering nigh;
E'en now the gulf appears in view,
  Where unlamented you must lie:
Oblivion's blackening lake is seen,
  Convuls'd by gales you cannot weather,
Where you, and eke your gentle queen,
  Alas! must perish altogether.
                    [*First publ., June, 1807.*]

ANSWER TO SOME ELEGANT VERSES

SENT BY A FRIEND TO THE AUTHOR, COMPLAINING THAT ONE OF
HIS DESCRIPTIONS WAS RATHER TOO WARMLY DRAWN

"But if any old Lady, Knight, Priest, or Physician,
Should condemn me for printing a second edition;
If good Madam Squintum my work should abuse,
May I venture to give her a smack of my muse?"
            —ANSTEY's *New Bath Guide,* p. 169.

CANDOUR compels me, BECHER! * to commend
The verse, which blends the censor with the friend;

---

* The Rev. John Becher of Southwell encouraged Byron in his early
attempts at poetry, but it was his objection to Byron's poem "To Mary"
in his first volume, *Fugitive Pieces,* which caused Byron to destroy

Your strong yet just reproof extorts applause
From me, the heedless and imprudent cause;
For this wild error, which pervades my strain,
I sue for pardon,—must I sue in vain?
The wise sometimes from Wisdom's ways depart;
Can youth then hush the dictates of the heart?
Precepts of prudence curb, but can't conroul,
The fierce emotions of the flowing soul.   10
When Love's delirium haunts the glowing mind,
Limping Decorum lingers far behind;
Vainly the dotard mends her prudish pace,
Outstript and vanquish'd in the mental chase.
The young, the old, have worn the chains of love;
Let those, they ne'er confin'd, my lay reprove;
Let those, whose soul contemn the pleasing power,
Their censures on the hapless victim shower.
Oh! how I hate the nerveless, frigid song,
The ceaseless echo of the rhyming throng,   20
Whose labour'd lines, in chilling numbers flow,
To paint a pang the author ne'er can know!
The artless Helicon, I boast, is youth;—
My Lyre, the Heart—my Muse, the simple Truth.
Far be't from me the "virgin's mind" to "taint";
Seduction's dread is here no slight restraint.
The maid whose virgin breast is void of guile,
Whose wishes dimple in a modest smile,
Whose downcast eye disdains the wanton leer,
Firm in her virtue's strength, yet not severe;   30
She, whom a conscious grace shall thus refine,
Will ne'er be "tainted" by a strain of mine.
But, for the nymph whose premature desires
Torment her bosom with unholy fires,
No net to snare her willing heart is spread;
She would have fallen, though she ne'er had read.
For me, I fain would please the chosen few,
Whose souls, to feeling and to nature true,
Will spare the childish verse, and not destroy
The light effusions of a heedless boy.   40
I seek not glory from the senseless crowd;

the whole edition. Of the four copies now extant, one was Becher's
own copy, which he did not destroy. The offending poem was never
again published among Byron's works.

Of fancied laurels, I shall ne'er be proud;
Their warmest plaudits I would scarcely prize,
Their sneers or censures, I alike despise.
                            November 26, 1806.
                    [*First publ., January, 1807.*]

ELEGY ON NEWSTEAD ABBEY

"It is the voice of years, that are gone! they roll before me with all
their deeds."—OSSIAN.

1

NEWSTEAD! fast-falling, once-resplendent dome!
    Religion's shrine! repentant HENRY's pride!
Of Warriors, Monks, and Dames the cloister'd tomb,
    Whose pensive shades around thy ruins glide,

2

Hail to thy pile! more honour'd in thy fall,
    Than modern mansions, in their pillar'd state;
Proudly majestic frowns thy vaulted hall,
    Scowling defiance on the blasts of fate.

3

No mail-clad Serfs, obedient to their Lord,
    In grim array, the crimson cross demand;
Or gay assemble round the festive board,
    Their chief's retainers, an immortal band.

4

Else might inspiring Fancy's magic eye
    Retrace their progress, through the lapse of time;
Marking each ardent youth, ordain'd to die,
    A votive pilgrim, in Judea's clime.

5

But not from thee, dark pile! departs the Chief;
    His feudal realm in other regions lay:

In thee the wounded conscience courts relief,
    Retiring from the garish blaze of day.

6

Yes, in thy gloomy cells and shades profound,
    The monk abjur'd a world, he ne'er could view;
Or blood-stain'd Guilt, repenting, solace found,
    Or Innocence from stern Oppression flew.

7

A monarch bade thee, from that wild, arise,
    Where Sherwood's outlaws, once, were wont to prowl;
And Superstition's crimes of various dyes,
    Sought shelter in the priest's protecting cowl.

8

Where, now, the grass exhales a murky dew,
    The humid pall of life-extinguish'd clay,
In sainted fame the sacred fathers grew,
    Nor raised their pious voices, but to pray.

9

Where, now, the bats their wavering wings extend,
    Soon as the gloaming spreads her waning shade;
The choir did, oft, their mingling vespers blend,
    Or matin orisons to Mary paid.

10

Years roll on years; to ages, ages yield;
    Abbots to Abbots, in a line, succeed:
Religion's charter their protecting shield,
    Till royal sacrilege their doom decreed.

11

One holy HENRY rear'd the Gothic walls,
    And bade the pious inmates rest in peace;

Another HENRY the kind gift recalls,
   And bids Devotion's hallow'd echoes cease.

12

Vain is each threat, or supplicating prayer;
   He drives them exiles from their blest abode,
To roam a dreary world in deep despair—
   No friend, no home, no refuge, but their God.

13

Hark! how the hall, resounding to the strain,
   Shakes with the martial music's novel din!
The heralds of a warrior's haughty reign,
   High crested banners wave thy walls within.

14

Of changing sentinels the distant hum,
   The mirth of feasts, the clang of burnish'd arms,
The braying trumpet, and the hoarser drum,
   Unite in concert with increas'd alarms.

15

An abbey once, a regal fortress now,
   Encircled by insulting rebel powers;
War's dread machines o'erhang thy threat'ning brow,
   And dart destruction, in sulphureous showers.

16

Ah! vain defence! the hostile traitor's siege,
   Though oft repuls'd, by guile o'ercomes the brave;
His thronging foes oppress the faithful Liege,
   Rebellion's reeking standards o'er him wave.

17

Not unaveng'd the raging Baron yields;
   The blood of traitors smears the purple plain;

Unconquer'd still, his falchion there he wields,
  And days of glory yet for him remain.

18

Still, in that hour, the warrior wish'd to strew
  Self-gathered laurels on a self-sought grave;
But Charles' protecting genius hither flew,
  The monarch's friend, the monarch's hope, to save.

19

Trembling, she snatch'd him from th' unequal strife,
  In other fields the torrent to repel;
For nobler combats, here reserv'd his life,
  To lead the band, where godlike FALKLAND fell.

20

From thee, poor pile! to lawless plunder given,
  While dying groans their painful requiem sound,
Far different incense, now, ascends to Heaven,
  Such victims wallow on the gory ground.

21

There many a pale and ruthless Robber's corse,
  Noisome and ghast, defiles thy sacred sod;
O'er mingling man, and horse commix'd with horse,
  Corruption's heap, the savage spoilers trod.

22

Graves, long with rank and sighing weeds o'erspread,
  Ransack'd resign, perforce, their mortal mould:
From ruffian fangs, escape not e'en the dead,
  Raked from repose, in search for buried gold.

23

Hush'd is the harp, unstrung the warlike lyre,
  The minstrel's palsied hand reclines in death;

No more he strikes the quivering chords with fire,
    Or sings the glories of the martial wreath.

24

At length the sated murderers, gorged with prey,
    Retire: the clamour of the fight is o'er;
Silence again resumes her awful sway,
    And sable Horror guards the massy door.

25

Here, Desolation holds her dreary court:
    What satellites declare her dismal reign!
Shrieking their dirge, ill-omen'd birds resort,
    To flit their vigils, in the hoary fane.

26

Soon a new Morn's restoring beams dispel
    The clouds of Anarchy from Britain's skies;
The fierce Usurper seeks his native hell,
    And Nature triumphs, as the Tyrant dies.

27

With storms she welcomes his expiring groans;
    Whirlwinds, responsive, greet his labouring breath;
Earth shudders, as her caves receive his bones,
    Loathing the offering of so dark a death.

28

The legal Ruler now resumes the helm,
    He guides through gentle seas, the prow of state;
Hope cheers, with wonted smiles, the peaceful realm,
    And heals the bleeding wounds of wearied Hate.

29

The gloomy tenants, Newstead! of thy cells,
    Howling, resign their violated nest;

Again, the Master on his tenure dwells,
  Enjoy'd, from absence, with enraptur'd zest.

30

Vassals, within thy hospitable pale,
  Loudly carousing, bless their Lord's return;
Culture, again, adorns the gladdening vale,
  And matrons, once lamenting, cease to mourn.

31

A thousand songs, on tuneful echo, float,
  Unwonted foliage mantles o'er the trees;
And, hark! the horns proclaim a mellow note,
  The hunters' cry hangs lengthening on the breeze.

32

Beneath their coursers' hoofs the valleys shake;
  What fears! what anxious hopes! attend the chase!
The dying stag seeks refuge in the lake;
  Exulting shouts announce the finish'd race.

33

Ah happy days! too happy to endure!
  Such simple sports our plain forefathers knew:
No splendid vices glitter'd to allure;
  Their joys were many, as their cares were few.

34

From these descending, Sons to Sires succeed;
  Time steals along, and Death uprears his dart;
Another Chief impels the foaming steed,
  Another Crowd pursue the panting hart.

35

Newstead! what saddening change of scene is thine!
  Thy yawning arch betokens slow decay;

The last and youngest of a noble line,
   Now holds thy mouldering turrets in his sway.

36

Deserted now, he scans thy grey worn towers;
   Thy vaults, where dead of feudal ages sleep;
Thy cloisters, pervious to the wintry showers;
   These, these he views, and views them but to weep.

37

Yet are his tears no emblem of regret:
   Cherish'd Affection only bids them flow;
Pride, Hope, and Love, forbid him to forget,
   But warm his bosom with impassion'd glow.

38

Yet he prefers thee to the gilded domes,
   Or gewgaw grottos, of the vainly great;
Yet lingers 'mid thy damp and mossy tombs,
   Nor breathes a murmur 'gainst the will of Fate.

39

Haply thy sun, emerging yet may shine,
   Thee to irradiate with meridian ray;
Hours, splendid as the past, may still be thine,
   And bless thy future as thy former day.
                    [*First publ., January, 1807.*]

LINES

ADDRESSED TO THE REV. J. T. BECHER, ON HIS ADVISING THE
AUTHOR TO MIX MORE WITH SOCIETY

1

DEAR Becher, you tell me to mix with mankind;
   I cannot deny such a precept is wise;

But retirement accords with the tone of my mind:
I will not descend to a world I despise.

2

Did the Senate or Camp my exertions require,
    Ambition might prompt me, at once, to go forth;
When Infancy's years of probation expire,
    Perchance, I may strive to distinguish my birth.

3

The fire, in the cavern of Etna, conceal'd,
    Still mantles unseen in its secret recess;
At length, in a volume terrific, reveal'd,
    No torrent can quench it, no bounds can repress.

4

Oh! thus, the desire, in my bosom, for fame
    Bids me live, but to hope for posterity's praise.
Could I soar with the phœnix on pinions of flame,
    With him I would wish to expire in the blaze.

5

For the life of a Fox, of a Chatham the death,
    What censure, what danger, what woe would I brave!
Their lives did not end, when they yielded their breath;
    Their glory illumines the gloom of their grave.

6

Yet why should I mingle in Fashion's full herd?
    Why crouch to her leaders, or cringe to her rules?
Why bend to the proud, or applaud the absurd?
    Why search for delight, in the friendship of fools?

7

I have tasted the sweets, and the bitters, of love:
    In friendship I early was taught to believe;

My passion the matrons of prudence reprove,
   I have found that a friend may profess, yet deceive.

8

Το me what is wealth?—it may pass in an hour,
   If Tyrants prevail, or if Fortune should frown:
To me what is title?—the phantom of power;
   To me what is fashion?—I seek but renown.

9

Deceit is a stranger, as yet, to my soul:
   I, still, am unpractised to varnish the truth:
Then, why should I live in a hateful controul?
   Why waste, upon folly, the days of my youth?

1806.
[First publ., January, 1807.]

TO EDWARD NOEL LONG, Esq.

[Long was one of Byron's close friends at Harrow who accompanied him to Cambridge. Long entered the Guards and was
drowned on a transport in 1809. Byron had more in common with
him than with most of his Harrow friends. They engaged in
various escapades, were both remarkable swimmers, and their
correspondence shows that they shared skeptical and iconoclastic
opinions.]

"Nil ego contulerim jucundo sanus amico."—HORACE.

DEAR Long, in this sequester'd scene,
   While all around in slumber lie,
The joyous days, which ours have been,
   Come rolling fresh on Fancy's eye;
Thus, if, amidst the gathering storm,
While clouds the darken'd noon deform,
Yon heaven assumes a varied glow,
I hail the sky's celestial bow,
Which spreads the sign of future peace,
And bids the war of tempests cease.   **10**

Ah! though the present brings but pain,
I think those days may come again;
Or if, in melancholy mood,
Some lurking envious fear intrude,
To check my bosom's fondest thought,
    And interrupt the golden dream,
I crush the fiend with malice fraught,
    And, still, indulge my wonted theme.
Although we ne'er again can trace,
    In Granta's vale, the pedant's lore,   20
Nor through the groves of Ida chase
    Our raptured visions, as before;
Though Youth has flown on rosy pinion,
And Manhood claims his stern dominion,
Age will not every hope destroy,
But yield some hours of sober joy.

    Yes, I will hope that Time's broad wing
Will shed around some dews of spring:
But, if his scythe must sweep the flowers
Which bloom among the fairy bowers,   3(
Where smiling Youth delights to dwell,
And hearts with early rapture swell;
If frowning Age, with cold controul,
Confines the current of the soul,
Congeals the tear of Pity's eye,
Or checks the sympathetic sigh,
Or hears, unmov'd, Misfortune's groan,
And bids me feel for self alone;
Oh! may my bosom never learn
    To soothe its wonted heedless flow;   40
Still, still, despise the censor stern,
    But ne'er forget another's woe.
Yes, as you knew me in the days,
O'er which Remembrance yet delays,
Still may I rove untutor'd, wild,
And, even in age, at heart a child.

Though, now, on airy visions borne,
    To you my soul is still the same,—
Oft has it been my fate to mourn,
    And all my former joys are tame: 5(
But, hence! ye hours of sable hue!

Your frowns are gone, my sorrows o'er:
By every bliss my childhood knew,
   I'll think upon your shade no more.
Thus, when the whirlwind's rage is past,
   And caves their sullen roar enclose,
We heed no more the wintry blast,
   When lull'd by zephyr to repose.

Full often has my infant Muse,
   Attun'd to love her languid lyre;   60
But, now, without a theme to choose,
   The strains in stolen sighs expire.
My youthful nymphs, alas! are flown;
   E—— is a wife, and C—— a mother,
And Carolina sighs alone,
   And Mary's given to another;
And Cora's eye, which roll'd on me,
   Can now no more my love recall—
In truth, dear LONG, 'twas time to flee—
   For Cora's eye will shine on all.   70
And though the Sun, with genial rays,
His beams alike to all displays,
And every lady's eye's a *sun,*
These last should be confin'd to one.
The soul's meridian don't become her,
Whose Sun displays a general *summer!*
Thus faint is every former flame,
And Passion's self is now a name;
As, when the ebbing flames are low,
   The aid which once improv'd their light,   80
And bade them burn with fiercer glow,
   Now quenches all their sparks in night;
Thus has it been with Passion's fires,
   As many a boy and girl remembers,
While all the force of love expires,
   Extinguish'd with the dying embers.

But now, dear LONG, 'tis midnight's noon,
And clouds obscure the watery moon,
Whose beauties I shall not rehearse,
Describ'd in every stripling's verse;   90
For why should I the path go o'er
Which every bard has trod before?

Yet ere yon silver lamp of night
   Has thrice perform'd her stated round,
Has thrice retrac'd her path of light,
   And chas'd away the gloom profound,
I trust, that we, my gentle Friend,
Shall see her rolling orbit wend,
Above the dear-lov'd peaceful seat,
Which once contain'd our youth's retreat;   100
And, then, with those our childhood knew,
We'll mingle in the festive crew;
While many a tale of former day
Shall wing the laughing hours away;
And all the flow of souls shall pour
The sacred intellectual shower,
Nor cease, till Luna's waning horn,
Scarce glimmers through the mist of Morn.
          [First publ., June, 1807.]

TO A LADY

[Addressed to Mrs. Chaworth Musters, the "Mary" who was
the great love of Byron's adolescence.]

1

Oh! had my Fate been join'd with thine,
   As once this pledge appear'd a token,
These follies had not, then, been mine,
   For, then, my peace had not been broken.

2

To thee, these early faults I owe,
   To thee, the wise and old reproving:
They know my sins, but do not know
   'Twas thine to break the bonds of loving.

3

For once my soul, like thine, was pure,
   And all its rising fires could smother;

But, now, thy vows no more endure,
  Bestow'd by thee upon another.

4

Perhaps, his peace I could destroy,
  And spoil the blisses that await him;
Yet let my Rival smile in joy,
  For thy dear sake, I cannot hate him.

5

Ah! since thy angel form is gone,
  My heart no more can rest with any;
But what it sought in thee alone,
  Attempts, alas! to find in many.

6

Then, fare thee well, deceitful Maid!
  'Twere vain and fruitless to regret thee;
Nor Hope, nor Memory yield their aid,
  But Pride may teach me to forget thee.

7

Yet all this giddy waste of years,
  This tiresome round of palling pleasures;
These varied loves, these matrons' fears,
  These thoughtless strains to Passion's measures—

8

If thou wert mine, had all been hush'd:—
  This cheek, now pale from early riot,
With Passion's hectic ne'er had flush'd,
  But bloom'd in calm domestic quiet.

9

Yes, once the rural Scene was sweet,
  For Nature seem'd to smile before thee;

And once my Breast abhorr'd deceit,—
    For then it beat but to adore thee.

10

But, now, I seek for other joys—
    To think, would drive my soul to madness;
In thoughtless throngs, and empty noise,
    I conquer half my Bosom's sadness.

11

Yet, even in these, a thought will steal,
    In spite of every vain endeavour;
And fiends might pity what I feel—
    To know that thou art lost for ever.
                        [*First publ., June, 1807.*]

I WOULD I WERE A CARELESS CHILD

1

I WOULD I were a careless child,
    Still dwelling in my Highland cave,
Or roaming through the dusky wild,
    Or bounding o'er the dark blue wave;
The cumbrous pomp of Saxon pride,
    Accords not with the freeborn soul,
Which loves the mountain's craggy side,
    And seeks the rocks where billows roll.

2

Fortune! take back these cultur'd lands,
    Take back this name of splendid sound!
I hate the touch of servile hands,
    I hate the slaves that cringe around:
Place me among the rocks I love,
    Which sound to Ocean's wildest roar;
I ask but this—again to rove
    Through scenes my youth hath known before,

3

Few are my years, and yet I feel
    The World was ne'er design'd for me:
Ah! why do dark'ning shades conceal
    The hour when man must cease to be?
Once I beheld a splendid dream,
    A visionary scene of bliss:
Truth!—wherefore did thy hated beam
    Awake me to a world like this?

4

I lov'd—but those I lov'd are gone;
    Had friends—my early friends are fled.
How cheerless feels the heart alone,
    When all its former hopes are dead!
Though gay companions, o'er the bowl
    Dispel awhile the sense of ill;
Though Pleasure stirs the maddening soul,
    The heart—the heart—is lonely still.

5

How dull! to hear the voice of those
    Whom Rank or Chance, whom Wealth or Power,
Have made, though neither friends nor foes,
    Associates of the festive hour.
Give me again a faithful few,
    In years and feelings still the same,
And I will fly the midnight crew,
    Where boist'rous Joy is but a name.

6

And Woman, lovely Woman! thou,
    My hope, my comforter, my all!
How cold must be my bosom now,
    When e'en thy smiles begin to pall!
Without a sigh would I resign,
    This busy scene of splendid Woe,

To make that calm contentment mine,
　　Which Virtue knows, or seems to know.

7

Fain would I fly the haunts of men—
　　I seek to shun, not hate mankind;
My breast requires the sullen glen,
　　Whose gloom may suit a darken'd mind.
Oh! that to me the wings were given,
　　Which bear the turtle to her nest!
Then would I cleave the vault of Heaven,
　　To flee away, and be at rest.

　　　　　　　　　　[*First publ., 1808.*]

WHEN I ROVED A YOUNG HIGHLANDER

1

WHEN I rov'd a young Highlander o'er the dark heath,
　　And climb'd thy steep summit, oh Morven of snow!
To gaze on the torrent that thunder'd beneath,
　　Or the mist of the tempest that gather'd below;
Untutor'd by science, a stranger to fear,
　　And rude as the rocks, where my infancy grew,
No feeling, save one, to my bosom was dear;
　　Need I say, my sweet Mary, 'twas centered in you?

2

Yet it could not be Love, for I knew not the name,—
　　What passion can dwell in the heart of a child?
But, still, I perceive an emotion the same
　　As I felt, when a boy, on the crag-cover'd wild:
One image, alone, on my bosom impress'd,
　　I lov'd my bleak regions, nor panted for new;
And few were my wants, for my wishes were bless'd,
　　And pure were my thoughts, for my soul was with you.

3

I arose with the dawn, with my dog as my guide,
  From mountain to mountain I bounded along;
I breasted the billows of Dee's rushing tide,
  And heard at a distance the Highlander's song:
At eve, on my heath-cover'd couch of repose,
  No dreams, save of Mary, were spread to my view;
\nd warm to the skies my devotions arose,
  For the first of my prayers was a blessing on you.

4

I left my bleak home, and my visions are gone;
  The mountains are vanish'd, my youth is no more;
As the last of my race, I must wither alone,
  And delight but in days, I have witness'd before:
Ah! splendour has rais'd, but embitter'd my lot;
  More dear were the scenes which my infancy knew:
Though my hopes may have fail'd, yet they are not forgot,
  Though cold is my heart, still it lingers with you.

5

When I see some dark hill point its crest to the sky,
  I think of the rocks that o'ershadow Colbleen;
When I see the soft blue of a love-speaking eye,
  I think of those eyes that endear'd the rude scene;
When, haply, some light-waving locks I behold,
  That faintly resemble my Mary's in hue,
I think on the long flowing ringlets of gold,
  The locks that were sacred to beauty, and you.

6

Yet the day may arrive, when the mountains once more
  Shall rise to my sight, in their mantles of snow;
But while these soar above me, unchang'd as before,
  Will Mary be there to receive me?—ah, no!
Adieu, then, ye hills, where my childhood was bred!
  Thou sweet flowing Dee, to thy waters adieu!

No home in the forest shall shelter my head,—
Ah! Mary, what home could be mine, but with you?
[*First publ., 1808.*]

LINES WRITTEN BENEATH AN ELM IN THE CHURCHYARD OF HARROW

SPOT of my youth! whose hoary branches sigh,
Swept by the breeze that fans thy cloudless sky;
Where now alone I muse, who oft have trod,
With those I lov'd, thy soft and verdant sod;
With those who, scatter'd far, perchance deplore,
Like me, the happy scenes they knew before:
Oh! as I trace again thy winding hill,
Mine eyes admire, my heart adores thee still,
Thou drooping Elm! beneath whose boughs I lay,
And frequent mus'd the twilight hours away;   10
Where, as they once were wont, my limbs recline,
But, ah! without the thoughts which then were mine:
How do thy branches, moaning to the blast,
Invite the bosom to recall the past,
And seem to whisper, as they gently swell,
"Take, while thou canst, a lingering, last farewell!"

When Fate shall chill, at length, this fever'd breast,
And calm its cares and passions into rest,
Oft have I thought, 'twould soothe my dying hour,—
If aught may soothe, when Life resigns her power,—   20
To know some humbler grave, some narrow cell,
Would hide my bosom where it lov'd to dwell;
With this fond dream, methinks 'twere sweet to die—
And here it linger'd, here my heart might lie;
Here might I sleep where all my hopes arose,
Scene of my youth, and couch of my repose;
For ever stretch'd beneath this mantling shade,
Press'd by the turf where once my childhood play'd;
Wrapt by the soil that veils the spot I lov'd,
Mix'd with the earth o'er which my footsteps mov'd; 30
Blest by the tongues that charm'd my youthful ear,
Mourn'd by the few my soul acknowledged here;

Deplor'd by those in early days allied,
And unremember'd by the world beside.

September 2, 1807.
[*First publ., 1808.*]

MISCELLANEOUS AND OCCASIONAL POEMS

FRAGMENT

WRITTEN SHORTLY AFTER THE MARRIAGE OF MISS CHAWORTH

[Byron spent much of his time in 1803 and 1804 at Annesley
Hall courting his cousin Mary Chaworth, who married John Musters in August, 1805.]

1

HILLS of Annesley, Bleak and Barren,
    Where my thoughtless Childhood stray'd,
How the northern Tempests, warring,
    Howl above thy tufted Shade!

2

Now no more, the Hours beguiling,
    Former favourite Haunts I see;
Now no more my Mary smiling,
    Makes ye seem a Heaven to Me.

1805.
[*First publ., 1830.*]

TO A KNOT OF UNGENEROUS CRITICS

[Probably written in reply to criticisms of his *Fugitive Pieces*
by certain ladies of Southwell.]

RAIL on, Rail on, ye heartless crew!
My strains were never meant for you;
Remorseless Rancour still reveal,

And damn the verse you cannot feel.
Invoke those kindred passions' aid,
Whose baleful stings your breasts pervade;
Crush, if you can, the hopes of youth,
Trampling regardless on the Truth:
Truth's Records you consult in vain,
She will not blast her native strain;   10
She will assist her votary's cause,
His will at least be her applause,
Your prayer the gentle Power will spurn.
To Fiction's motley altar turn,
Who joyful in the fond address
Her favour'd worshippers will bless:
And lo! she holds a magic glass,
Where Images reflected pass;
Bent on your knees the Boon receive—
This will assist you to deceive—   20
The glittering gift was made for you,
Now hold it up to public view;
Lest evil unforeseen betide,
A Mask each canker'd brow shall hide,
(Whilst Truth my sole desire is nigh,
Prepar'd the danger to defy,)
"There is the Maid's perverted name,
"And there the Poet's guilty Flame,
"Gloaming a deep phosphoric fire,
"Threatening—but, ere it spreads, retire."   30
Says Truth, "Up Virgins, do not fear!
"The Comet rolls its Influence here;
" 'Tis Scandal's Mirror you perceive,
"These dazzling Meteors but deceive—
"Approach and touch—Nay, do not turn
"It blazes there, but will not burn."—
At once the shivering Mirror flies,
Teeming no more with varnished Lies;
The baffled Friends of Fiction start,
Too late desiring to depart—   40
Truth poising high Ithuriel's spear
Bids every Fiend unmask'd appear,
The vizard tears from every face,
And dooms them to a dire disgrace.
For e'er they compass their escape,
Each takes perforce a native shape—

The Leader of the wrathful Band,
Behold a portly Female stand!
She raves, impell'd by private pique,
This mean unjust revenge to seek;   50
From vice to save this virtuous Age,
Thus does she vent indecent rage!
What child has she of promise fair,
Who claims a fostering mother's care?
Whose Innocence requires defence,
Or forms at least a smooth pretence,
Thus to disturb a harmless Boy,
His humble hope, and peace annoy?
She need not fear the amorous rhyme,
Love will not tempt her future time,   60
For her his wings have ceas'd to spread,
No more he flutters round her head;
Her day's Meridian now is past,
The clouds of Age her Sun o'ercast;
To her the strain was never sent,
For feeling Souls alone 'twas meant—
The verse she seiz'd, unask'd, unbade,
And damn'd, ere yet the whole was read!
Yes! for one single erring verse,
Pronounc'd an unrelenting Curse;   70
Yes! at a first and transient view,
Condemn'd a heart she never knew.—
Can such a verdict then decide,
Which springs from disappointed pride?
Without a wondrous share of Wit,
To judge is such a Matron fit?
The rest of the censorious throng
Who to this zealous Band belong,
To her a general homage pay,
And right or wrong her wish obey: 80
Why should I point my pen of steel
To break "such flies upon the wheel?"
With minds to Truth and Sense unknown,
Who dare not call their words their own.
Rail on, Rail on, ye heartless Crew!
Your Leader's grand design pursue:
Secure behind her ample shield,
Yours is the harvest of the field.—
My path with thorns you cannot strew,

Nay more, my warmest thanks are due;   90
When such as you revile my Name,
Bright beams the rising Sun of Fame,
Chasing the shades of envious night,
Outshining every critic Light.—
Such, such as you will serve to show
Each radiant tint with higher glow.
Vain is the feeble cheerless toil,
Your efforts on yourselves recoil;
Then Glory still for me you raise,
Yours is the Censure, mine the Praise.   100
            —BYRON,
                December 1, 1806.
                [*First publ., 1898.*]

SOLILOQUY OF A BARD IN THE COUNTRY

'TWAS now the noon of night, and all was still,
Except a hapless Rhymer and his quill.
In vain he calls each Muse in order down,
Like other females, these will sometimes frown;
He frets, he fumes, and ceasing to invoke
The Nine, in anguish'd accents thus he spoke:
Ah, what avails it thus to waste my time,
To roll in Epic, or to rave in Rhyme?
What worth is some few partial readers' praise,
If ancient Virgins croaking *censures* raise!   10
Where few attend, 'tis useless to indite;
Where few can read, 'tis folly sure to write;
Where none but girls and striplings dare admire,
And Critics rise in every country Squire—
But yet this last my candid Muse admits,
When Peers are Poets, Squires may well be Wits;
When schoolboys vent their amorous flames in verse,
Matrons may sure their characters asperse;
And if a little parson joins the train,
And echoes back his Patron's voice again—   20
Though not delighted, yet I must forgive,
Parsons as well as other folks must live:—
From rage he rails not, rather say from dread.
He does not speak for Virtue, but for bread:

And this we know is in his Patron's giving,
For Parsons cannot eat without a *Living*.
The Matron knows I love the Sex too well,
Even unprovoked aggression to repel.
What though from private pique her anger grew,
And bade her blast a heart she never knew?   30
What though, she said, for one light heedless line,
That Wilmot's verse was far more pure than mine!
In wars like these, I neither fight nor fly,
When *dames* accuse 'tis bootless to deny;
Hers be the harvest of the martial field,
I can't attack, where Beauty forms the shield.
But when a pert Physician loudly cries,
Who hunts for scandal, and who lives by lies,
A walking register of daily news,
Train'd to invent, and skilful to abuse—   40
For arts like these at bounteous tables fed,
When S—— condemns a book he never read,
Declaring with a coxcomb's native air,
The *moral's* shocking, though the *rhymes* are fair.
Ah! must he rise unpunish'd from the feast,
Nor lash'd by vengeance into truth at least?
Such lenity were more than Man's indeed!
Those who condemn, should surely deign to read.
Yet must I spare—nor thus my pen degrade,
I quite forgot that scandal was his trade.   50
For food and raiment thus the coxcomb rails,
For those who fear his physic, like his *tales*.
Why should his harmless censure seem offence?
Still let him eat, although at my expense,
And join the herd to Sense and Truth unknown,
Who dare not call their very thoughts their own,
And share with these applause, a godlike bribe,
In short, do anything, except *prescribe:*—
For though in garb of Galen he appears,
His practice is not equal to his years.   60
Without improvement since he first began,
A young Physician though an ancient Man—
Now let me cease—Physician, Parson, Dame,
Still urge your task, and if you can, defame.
The humble offerings of my Muse destroy,
And crush, oh! noble conquest! crush a Boy.
What though some silly girls have lov'd the strain,

And kindly bade me tune my Lyre again;
What though some feeling, or some partial few,
Nay, Men of Taste and Reputation too,   70
Have deign'd to praise the firstlings of my Muse—
If *you* your sanction to the theme refuse,
If *you* your great protection still withdraw,
Whose Praise is Glory, and whose Voice is law!
Soon must I fall an unresisting foe,
A hapless victim yielding to the blow.—
Thus Pope by Curl and Dennis was destroyed,
Thus Gray and Mason yield to furious Lloyd;
From Dryden, Milbourne tears the palm away,
And thus I fall, though meaner far than they: 80
As in the field of combat, side by side,
A Fabius and some noble Roman died.

December, 1806.
[*First publ., 1898.*]

L'AMITIÉ EST L'AMOUR SANS AILES

1

WHY should my anxious breast repine,
    Because my youth is fled?
Days of delight may still be mine;
    Affection is not dead.
In tracing back the years of youth,
One firm record, one lasting truth
    Celestial consolation brings;
Bear it, ye breezes, to the seat,
Where first my heart responsive beat,—
    "Friendship is Love without his wings!"

2

Through few, but deeply chequer'd years,
    What moments have been mine!
Now half obscured by clouds of tears,
    Now bright in rays divine;
Howe'er my future doom be cast,
My soul, enraptur'd with the past,
    To one idea fondly clings;

Friendship! that thought is all thine own,
Worth worlds of bliss, that thought alone—
    "Friendship is Love without his wings!"

3

Where yonder yew-trees lightly wave
    Their branches on the gale,
Unheeded heaves a simple grave,
    Which tells the common tale;
Round this unconscious schoolboys stray,
Till the dull knell of childish play
    From yonder studious mansion rings;
But here, whene'er my footsteps move,
My silent tears too plainly prove,
    "Friendship is Love without his wings!"

4

Oh, Love, before thy glowing shrine,
    My early vows were paid;
My hopes, my dreams, my heart was thine,
    But these are now decay'd;
For thine are pinions like the wind,
No trace of thee remains behind,
    Except, alas! thy jealous stings.
Away, away! delusive power,
Thou shalt not haunt my coming hour;
    Unless, indeed, without thy wings.

5

Seat of my youth! thy distant spire
    Recalls each scene of joy;
My bosom glows with former fire,—
    In mind again a boy.
Thy grove of elms, thy verdant hill,
Thy every path delights me still,
    Each flower a double fragrance flings;
Again, as once, in converse gay,
Each dear associate seems to say,
    "Friendship is Love without his wings!"

6

My Lycus! wherefore dost thou weep?
    Thy falling tears restrain;
Affection for a time may sleep,
    But, oh, 'twill wake again.
Think, think, my friend, when next we meet,
Our long-wish'd interview, how sweet!
    From this my hope of rapture springs;
While youthful hearts thus fondly swell,
Absence, my friend, can only tell,
    "Friendship is Love without his wings!"

7

In one, and one alone deceiv'd,
    Did I my error mourn?
No—from oppressive bonds reliev'd,
    I left the wretch to scorn.
I turn'd to those my childhood knew,
With feelings warm, with bosoms true,
    Twin'd with my heart's according strings;
And till those vital chords shall break,
For none but these my breast shall wake
    Friendship, the power deprived of wings!

8

Ye few! my soul, my life is yours,
    My memory and my hope;
Your worth a lasting love insures,
    Unfetter'd in its scope;
From smooth deceit and terror sprung,
With aspect fair and honey'd tongue.
    Let Adulation wait on kings;
With joy elate, by snares beset,
We, we, my friends, can ne'er forget,
    "Friendship is Love without his wings!"

9

Fictions and dreams inspire the bard,
  Who rolls the epic song;
Friendship and truth be my reward—
  To me no bays belong;
If laurell'd Fame but dwells with lies.
Me the Enchantress ever flies,
  Whose heart and not whose fancy sings;
Simple and young, i dare not feign;
Mine be the rude yet heartfelt strain,
  "Friendship is Love without his wings!"
            December 29, 1806.
            [*First publ., 1832.*]

THE PRAYER OF NATURE

1

FATHER of Light! great God of Heaven!
  Hear'st thou the accents of despair?
Can guilt like man's be e'er forgiven?
  Can vice atone for crimes by prayer?

2

Father of Light, on thee I call!
  Thou see'st my soul is dark within;
Thou, who canst mark the sparrow's fall,
  Avert from me the death of sin.

3

No shrine I seek, to sects unknown;
  Oh, point to me the path of truth!
Thy dread Omnipotence I own;
  Spare, yet amend, the faults of youth.

4

Let bigots rear a gloomy fane,
  Let Superstition hail the pile,

Let priests, to spread their sable reign,
  With tales of mystic rites beguile.

5

Shall man confine his Maker's sway
  To Gothic domes of mouldering stone?
Thy temple is the face of day;
  Earth, Ocean, Heaven thy boundless throne.

6

Shall man condemn his race to Hell,
  Unless they bend in pompous form?
Tell us that all, for one who fell,
  Must perish in the mingling storm?

7

Shall each pretend to reach the skies,
  Yet doom his brother to expire,
Whose soul a different hope supplies,
  Or doctrines less severe inspire?

8

Shall these, by creeds they can't expound,
  Prepare a fancied bliss or woe?
Shall reptiles, grovelling on the ground,
  Their great Creator's purpose know?

9

Shall those, who live for self alone,
  Whose years float on in daily crime—
Shall they, by Faith, for guilt atone,
  And live beyond the bounds of Time?

10

Father! no prophet's laws I seek,—
  Thy laws in Nature's works appear;—

I own myself corrupt and weak,
    Yet will I *pray*, for thou wilt hear!

11

Thou, who canst guide the wandering star,
    Through trackless realms of æther's space;
Who calm'st the elemental war,
    Whose hand from pole to pole I trace:

12

Thou, who in wisdom plac'd me here,
    Who, when thou wilt, canst take me hence,
Ah! whilst I tread this earthly sphere,
    Extend to me thy wide defence.

13

To Thee, my God, to Thee I call!
    Whatever weal or woe betide,
By thy command I rise or fall,
    In thy protection I confide.

14

If, when this dust to dust's restor'd,
    My soul shall float on airy wing,
How shall thy glorious Name ador'd
    Inspire her feeble voice to sing!

15

But, if this fleeting spirit share
    With clay the Grave's eternal bed,
While Life yet throbs I raise my prayer,
    Though doom'd no more to quit the dead.

16

To Thee I breathe my humble strain,
    Grateful for all thy mercies past,

And hope, my God, to thee again
This erring life may fly at last.
                    December 29, 1806.
                    [*First publ., 1830.*]

ON THE EYES OF MISS A—— H——

[Anne Houson, of Southwell.]

ANNE'S Eye is liken'd to the *Sun*,
    From it such Beams of Beauty fall;
And *this* can be denied by none,
    For like the *Sun*—it shines on *All*.

Then do not admiration smother,
    Or say these glances don't become her;
To *you*, or *I*, or *any other*,
    Her *Sun*, displays perpetual Summer.
                    January 14, 1807.
                    [*First publ., 1898.*]

EGOTISM. A LETTER TO J. T. BECHER

'Εαυτὸν Βύρων αἔιδει.

1

IF Fate should seal my Death to-morrow,
    (Though much *I* hope she will *postpone* it,)
I've held a share of *Joy* and *Sorrow*,
    Enough for *Ten;* and *here* I *own* it.

2

I've liv'd as many other men live,
    And yet, I think, with more enjoyment;
For could I through my days again live,
    I'd pass them in the *same* employment.

3

That *is* to say, with *some exception,*
   For though I will not make confession,
I've seen too much of man's deception
   Ever again to trust profession.

4

Some sage *Mammas* with gesture haughty,
   Pronounce me quite a youthful Sinner—
But *Daughters* say, "although he's naughty,
   You must not check a *Young Beginner!*"

5

I've lov'd, and many damsels know it—
   But whom I don't intend to mention,
As *certain stanzas* also show it,
   Some say *deserving Reprehension.*

6

Some ancient Dames, of virtue fiery,
   (Unless Report does much belie them,)
Have lately made a sharp Enquiry,
   And much it *grieves* me to *deny* them.

7

Two whom I lov'd had *eyes* of *Blue,*
   To which I hope you've no objection;
The *Rest* had eyes of *darker Hue*—
   Each Nymph, of course, was *all perfection.*

8

But here I'll close my *chaste* Description,
   Nor say the deeds of animosity;
For *silence* is the best prescription,
   To *physic* idle curiosity.

9

Of *Friends* I've known a *goodly Hundred*—
　　For finding *one* in each acquaintance,
By *some deceiv'd,* by others plunder'd,
　　Friendship, to me, was not *Repentance.*

10

At *School* I thought like other *Children;*
　　Instead of *Brains,* a fine Ingredient,
Romance, my *youthful Head bewildering,*
　　To *Sense* had made me disobedient.

11

A victim, *nearly* from affection,
　　To certain *very precious scheming,*
The still remaining recollection
　　Has *cured* my *boyish soul* of *Dreaming.*

12

By Heaven! I rather would forswear
　　The Earth, and all the joys reserv'd me,
Than dare again the *specious Snare,*
　　From which *my Fate* and *Heaven preserv'd* me.

13

Still I possess some Friends who love me—
　　In each a much-esteem'd and true one;
The Wealth of Worlds shall never move me
　　To quit their Friendship, for a new one.

14

But, Becher! you're a *reverend pastor,*
　　Now take it in consideration,
Whether for penance I should fast, or
　　Pray for my *sins* in expiation.

15

I own myself the child of *Folly,*
    But not so wicked as they make me—
I soon must die of melancholy,
    If *Female* smiles should e'er forsake me.

16

Philosophers have *never doubted,*
    That *Ladies' Lips* were made for *kisses!*
For *Love!* I could not live without it,
    For such a *curséd* place as *This is.*

17

Say, Becher, I shall be forgiven!
    If *you* don't warrant my salvation,
I must resign all *Hopes* of *Heaven!*
    For, *Faith,* I can't withstand Temptation.

P.S.—These were written between one and two, after *mid-night.* I have not *corrected,* or *revised.* Yours,

BYRON.
[*First publ., 1898.*]

QUERIES TO CASUISTS

THE Moralists tell us that Loving is Sinning,
    And always are prating about and about it,
But as Love of Existence itself's the beginning,
    Say, what would Existence itself be without it?
They argue the point with much furious Invective,
    Though perhaps 'twere no difficult task to confute it;
But if Venus and Hymen should once prove defective,
    Pray who would there be to defend or dispute it?

—BYRON.
[*First publ., 1898.*]

TO A VAIN LADY

[Anne Houson, of Southwell.]

1

Ah, heedless girl! why thus disclose
  What ne'er was meant for other ears;
Why thus destroy thine own repose,
  And dig the source of future tears?

2

Oh, thou wilt weep, imprudent maid,
  While lurking envious foes will smile,
For all the follies thou hast said
  Of those who spoke but to beguile.

3

Vain girl! thy ling'ring woes are nigh,
  If thou believ'st what striplings say:
Oh, from the deep temptation fly,
  Nor fall the specious spoiler's prey.

4

Dost thou repeat, in childish boast,
  The words man utters to deceive?
Thy peace, thy hope, thy all is lost,
  If thou canst venture to believe.

5

While now amongst thy female peers
  Thou tell'st again the soothing tale,
Canst thou not mark the rising sneers
  Duplicity in vain would veil?

6

These tales in secret silence hush,
  Nor make thyself the public gaze:
What modest maid without a blush
  Recounts a flattering coxcomb's praise?

7

Will not the laughing boy despise
  Her who relates each fond conceit—
Who, thinking Heaven is in her eyes,
  Yet cannot see the slight deceit?

8

For she who takes a soft delight
  These amorous nothings in revealing,
Must credit all we say or write,
  While vanity prevents concealing.

9

Cease, if you prize your Beauty's reign!
  No jealousy bids me reprove:
One, who is thus from nature vain,
  I pity, but I cannot love.
               January 15, 1807.
             [*First publ., 1832.*]

TO ANNE

[Anne Houson, of Southwell.]

1

OH, Anne, your offences to me have been grievous:
  I thought from my wrath no atonement could save you;
But Woman is made to command and deceive us—
  I look'd in your face, and I almost forgave you.

2

I vow'd I could ne'er for a moment respect you,
  Yet thought that a day's separation was long;
When we met, I determined again to suspect you—
  Your smile soon convinced me, *suspicion* was wrong.

3

I swore, in a transport of young indignation,
  With fervent contempt evermore to disdain you:
I saw you—my *anger* became *admiration;*
  And now, all my wish, all my hope's to regain you.

4

With beauty like yours, oh, how vain the contention!
  Thus lowly I sue for forgiveness before you;—
At once to conclude such a fruitless dissension,
  Be false, my sweet Anne, when I cease to adore you!

                              January 16, 1807.
                              [*First publ., 1832.*]

TO THE AUTHOR OF A SONNET

BEGINNING "'SAD IS MY VERSE,' YOU SAY, 'AND YET NO TEAR'"

1

Thy verse is "sad" enough, no doubt:
  A devilish deal more sad than witty!
Why we should weep I can't find out,
  Unless for *thee* we weep in pity.

2

Yet there is one I pity more;
  And much, alas! I think he needs it:
For he, I'm sure, will suffer sore,
  Who, to his own misfortune, reads it.

3

Thy rhymes, without the aid of magic,
  May *once* be read—but never after:
Yet their effect's by no means tragic,
  Although by far too dull for laughter.

4

But would you make our bosoms bleed,
  And of no common pang complain—
If you would make us weep indeed,
  Tell us, you'll read them o'er again.
                  March 8, 1807.
                  [*First publ., 1832.*]

TO AN OAK AT NEWSTEAD

1

Young Oak! when I planted thee deep in the ground,
  I hoped that thy days would be longer than mine;
That thy dark-waving branches would flourish around,
  And ivy thy trunk with its mantle entwine.

2

Such, such was my hope, when in Infancy's years,
  On the land of my Fathers I rear'd thee with pride;
They are past, and I water thy stem with my tears,—
  Thy decay, not the *weeds* that surround thee can hide

3

I left thee, my Oak, and, since that fatal hour,
  A stranger has dwelt in the hall of my Sire;
Till Manhood shall crown me, not mine is the power,
  But his, whose neglect may have bade thee expire.

4

Oh! hardy thou wert—even now little care
  Might revive thy young head, and thy wounds gently heal:
But thou wert not fated affection to share—
  For who could suppose that a Stranger would feel?

5

Ah, droop not, my Oak! lift thy head for a while;
  Ere twice round yon Glory this planet shall run,
The hand of thy Master will teach thee to smile,
  When Infancy's years of probation are done.

6

Oh, live then, my Oak! tow'r aloft from the weeds,
  That clog thy young growth, and assist thy decay,
For still in thy bosom are Life's early seeds,
  And still may thy branches their beauty display.

7

Oh! yet, if Maturity's years may be thine,
  Though *I* shall lie low in the cavern of Death,
On thy leaves yet the day-beam of ages may shine,
  Uninjur'd by Time, or the rude Winter's breath.

8

For centuries still may thy boughs lightly wave
  O'er the corse of thy Lord in thy canopy laid;
While the branches thus gratefully shelter his grave,
  The Chief who survives may recline in thy shade.

9

And as he, with his boys, shall revisit this spot,
  He will tell them in whispers more softly to tread.
Oh! surely, by these I shall ne'er be forgot;
  Remembrance still hallows the dust of the dead.

10

And here, will they say, when in Life's glowing prime,
   Perhaps he has pour'd forth his young simple lay,
And here must he sleep, till the moments of Time
   Are lost in the hours of Eternity's day.

1807.
[First publ., 1832.]

TO HARRIET

[Harriet Maltby, of Southwell.]

1

HARRIET! to see such Circumspection,
In Ladies I have no objection,
   Concerning what they read;
An ancient Maid's a sage adviser,
Like *her*, you will be much the wiser,
   In word, as well as Deed.

2

But Harriet, I don't wish to flatter,
And really think 'twould make the matter
   More perfect if not quite,
If other Ladies when they preach,
Would certain Damsels also teach
   More cautiously to write.

[First publ., 1898.]

FAREWELL! IF EVER FONDEST PRAYER

1

FAREWELL! if ever fondest prayer
   For other's weal availed on high,
Mine will not all be lost in air,

But waft thy name beyond the sky.
'Twere vain to speak—to weep—to sigh:
    Oh! more than tears of blood can tell,
When wrung from Guilt's expiring eye,
    Are in that word—Farewell!—·Farewell!

2

These lips are mute, these eyes are dry;
    But in my breast and in my brain,
Awake the pangs that pass not by,
    The thought that ne'er shall sleep again.
My soul nor deigns nor dares complain,
    Though Grief and Passion there rebel:
I only know we loved in vain—
    I only feel—Farewell!—Farewell!

1808.
[First publ., 1814.]

WHEN WE TWO PARTED

[Addressed to Lady Frances Webster, and not, as long believed, to Byron's half-sister Augusta Leigh. See "'When We Two Parted': A Byron Mystery Resolved" by John Gore, *Cornhill Magazine,* Jan., 1928, pp. 39-53.]

1

WHEN we two parted
    In silence and tears,
Half broken-hearted
    To sever for years,
Pale grew thy cheek and cold,
    Colder thy kiss;
Truly that hour foretold
    Sorrow to this.

2

The dew of the morning
    Sunk chill on my brow—
It felt like the warning

Of what I feel now.
'Thy vows are all broken,
  And light is thy fame:
I hear thy name spoken,
  And share in its shame.

3

They name thee before me,
  A knell to mine ear;
A shudder comes o'er me—
  Why wert thou so dear?
They know not I knew thee,
  Who knew thee too well:—
Long, long shall I rue thee,
  Too deeply to tell.

4

In secret we met—
  In silence I grieve,
That thy heart could forget,
  Thy spirit deceive.
If I should meet thee
  After long years,
How should I greet thee?—
  With silence and tears.
                    1808.
          [*First publ., 1816.*]

AND WILT THOU WEEP WHEN I AM LOW?

1

AND wilt thou weep when I am low?
  Sweet lady! speak those words again:
Yet if they grieve thee, say not so—
  I would not give that bosom pain.

2

My heart is sad, my hopes are gone,
    My blood runs coldly through my breast;
And when I perish, thou alone
    Wilt sigh above my place of rest.

3

And yet, methinks, a gleam of peace
    Doth through my cloud of anguish shine;
And for a while my sorrows cease,
    To know thy heart hath felt for mine.

4

O lady! blessèd be that tear—
    It falls for one who cannot weep;
Such precious drops are doubly dear
    To those whose eyes no tear may steep.

5

Sweet lady! once my heart was warm
    With every feeling soft as thine;
But Beauty's self hath ceas'd to charm
    A wretch created to repine.

6

Yet wilt thou weep when I am low?
    Sweet lady! speak those words again:
Yet if they grieve thee, say not so—
    I would not give that bosom pain.
                            August 12, 1808.
                        [First publ., 1809.]

REMIND ME NOT, REMIND ME NOT

1

REMIND me not, remind me not,
　Of those belov'd, those vanish'd hours,
　　When all my soul was given to thee;
Hours that may never be forgot,
　Till Time unnerves our vital powers,
　　And thou and I shall cease to be.

2

Can I forget—canst thou forget,
　When playing with thy golden hair,
　　How quick thy fluttering heart did move?
Oh! by my soul, I see thee yet,
　With eyes so languid, breast so fair,
　　And lips, though silent, breathing love.

3

When thus reclining on my breast,
　Those eyes threw back a glance so sweet,
　　As half reproach'd yet rais'd desire,
And still we near and nearer prest,
　And still our glowing lips would meet,
　　As if in kisses to expire.

4

And then those pensive eyes would close,
　And bid their lids each other seek,
　　Veiling the azure orbs below;
While their long lashes' darken'd gloss
　Seem'd stealing o'er thy brilliant cheek,
　　Like raven's plumage smooth'd on snow.

5

I dreamt last night our love return'd,
   And, sooth to say, that very dream
     Was sweeter in its phantasy,
Than if for other hearts I burn'd,
   For eyes that ne'er like thine could beam
     In Rapture's wild reality.

6

Then tell me not, remind me not,
   Of hours which, though for ever gone,
     Can still a pleasing dream restore,
Till thou and I shall be forgot,
   And senseless, as the mouldering stone
     Which tells that we shall be no more.

                      August 13, 1808.
                    [*First publ., 1809.*]

TO A YOUTHFUL FRIEND

1

FEW years have pass'd since thou and I
   Were firmest friends, at least in name
And Childhood's gay sincerity
   Preserv'd our feelings long the same.

2

But now, like me, too well thou know'st
   What trifles oft the heart recall;
And those who once have lov'd the most
   Too soon forget they lov'd at all.

3

And such the change the heart displays,
   So frail is early friendship's reign,

A month's brief lapse, perhaps a day's,
　Will view thy mind estrang'd again.

4

If so, it never shall be mine
　To mourn the loss of such a heart;
The fault was Nature's fault, not thine,
　Which made thee fickle as thou art.

5

As rolls the Ocean's changing tide,
　So human feelings ebb and flow;
And who would in a breast confide
　Where stormy passions ever glow?

6

It boots not that, together bred,
　Our childish days were days of joy:
My spring of life has quickly fled;
　Thou, too, hast ceas'd to be a boy.

7

And when we bid adieu to youth,
　Slaves to the specious World's controul,
We sigh a long farewell to truth;
　That World corrupts the noblest soul.

8

Ah! joyous season! when the mind
　Dares all things boldly but to lie;
When Thought ere spoke is unconfin'd,
　And sparkles in the placid eye.

9

Not so in Man's maturer years,
　When Man himself is but a tool;

When Interest sways our hopes and fears,
    And all must love and hate by rule.

10

With fools in kindred vice the same,
    We learn at length our faults to blend;
And those, and those alone, may claim
    The prostituted name of friend.

11

Such is the common lot of man:
    Can we then 'scape from folly free?
Can we reverse the general plan,
    Nor be what all in turn must be?

12

No; for myself, so dark my fate
    Through every turn of life hath been;
Man and the World so much I hate,
    I care not when I quit the scene.

13

But thou, with spirit frail and light,
    Wilt shine awhile, and pass away;
As glow-worms sparkle through the night,
    But dare not stand the test of day.

14

Alas! whenever Folly calls
    Where parasites and princes meet,
(For cherish'd first in royal halls
    The welcome vices kindly greet,)

15

Ev'n now thou'rt nightly seen to add
    One insect to the fluttering crowd;

And still thy trifling heart is glad
To join the vain and court the proud.

16

There dost thou glide from fair to fair,
Still simpering on with eager haste,
As flies, along the gay parterre,
That taint the flowers they scarcely taste.

17

But say, what nymph will prize the flame
Which seems, as marshy vapours move,
To flit along from dame to dame,
An ignis-fatuus gleam of love?

18

What friend for thee, howe'er inclin'd,
Will deign to own a kindred care?
Who will debase his manly mind
For friendship every fool may share?

19

In time forbear; amidst the throng
No more so base a thing be seen;
No more so idly pass along;
Be something, any thing, but—mean.
                    August 20, 1808.
                    [*First publ., 1809.*]

LINES INSCRIBED UPON A CUP FORMED
FROM A SKULL

[The skull was found in the garden of Newstead Abbey,
Byron's estate. "A strange fancy seized me," Byron told Thomas
Medwin, "of having it mounted as a drinking-cup. I accordingly
sent it to town, and it returned with a very high polish, and of a
mottled colour like tortoise-shell." Byron and his friends dressed

in monkish gowns, filled the cup with claret, and passed it around
amid much hilarity.]

1

START not—nor deem my spirit fled:
  In me behold the only skull,
From which, unlike a living head,
  Whatever flows is never dull.

2

I liv'd, I lov'd, I quaff'd, like thee:
  I died: let earth my bones resign;
Fill up—thou canst not injure me;
  The worm hath fouler lips than thine.

3

Better to hold the sparkling grape,
  Than nurse the earth-worm's slimy brood;
And circle in the goblet's shape
  The drink of Gods, than reptiles' food.

4

Where once my wit, perchance, hath shone,
  In aid of others' let me shine;
And when, alas! our brains are gone,
  What nobler substitute than wine?

5

Quaff while thou canst: another race,
  When thou and thine, like me, are sped,
May rescue thee from Earth's embrace,
  And rhyme and revel with the dead.

6

Why not? since through life's little day
  Our heads such sad effects produce;

Redeem'd from worms and wasting clay,
This chance is theirs, to be of use.
Newstead Abbey, 1808.
[*First publ., 1814.*]

INSCRIPTION ON THE MONUMENT OF A NEWFOUNDLAND DOG

[Byron's dog, "Boatswain," died November 18, 1808 and was buried in a vault in the garden at Newstead Abbey. In a will drawn up in 1811 (later changed), Byron expressed a wish to b͡ buried in the same vault.]

WHEN some proud son of man returns to earth,
Unknown to glory, but upheld by birth,
The sculptor's art exhausts the pomp of woe
And storied urns record who rest below:
When all is done, upon the tomb is seen,
Not what he was, but what he should have been:
But the poor dog, in life the firmest friend,
The first to welcome, foremost to defend,
Whose honest heart is still his master's own,
Who labours, fights, lives, breathes for him alone,
Unhonour'd falls unnotic'd all his worth—
Denied in heaven the soul he held on earth:
While Man, vain insect! hopes to be forgiven,
And claims himself a sole exclusive Heaven.
Oh Man! thou feeble tenant of an hour,
Debas'd by slavery, or corrupt by power,
Who knows thee well must quit thee with disgust,
Degraded mass of animated dust!
Thy love is lust, thy friendship all a cheat,
Thy smiles hypocrisy, thy words deceit!
By nature vile, ennobled but by name,
Each kindred brute might bid thee blush for shame.
Ye! who perchance behold its simple urn,
Pass on—it honours none you wish to mourn:
To mark a Friend's remains these stones arise;
I never knew but one—and here he lies.
Newstead Abbey, October 30, 1808.
[*First publ., 1809.*]

WELL! THOU ART HAPPY

[Byron dined at Annesley Hall with Mary Chaworth Musters and her husband and was much affected when her small daughter was brought into the room, for he had been greatly attached to Mary Chaworth before her marriage.]

1

WELL! thou art happy, and I feel
    That I should thus be happy too;
For still my heart regards thy weal
    Warmly, as it was wont to do.

2

Thy husband's blest—and 'twill impart
    Some pangs to view his happier lot:
But let them pass—Oh! how my heart
    Would hate him if he lov'd thee not!

3

When late I saw thy favourite child,
    I thought my jealous heart would break;
But when the unconscious infant smil'd,
    I kiss'd it for its mother's sake.

4

I kiss'd it,—and repress'd my sighs
    Its father in its face to see;
But then it had its mother's eyes,
    And they were all to love and me.

5

Mary, adieu! I must away:
    While thou art blest I'll not repine;
But near thee I can never stay;
    My heart would soon again be thine.

6

I deem'd that Time, I deem'd that Pride,
   Had quench'd at length my boyish flame;
Nor knew, till seated by thy side,
   My heart in all,—save hope,—the same.

7

Yet was I calm: I knew the time
   My breast would thrill before thy look;
But now to tremble were a crime—
   We met,—and not a nerve was shook.

8

I saw thee gaze upon my face,
   Yet meet with no confusion there:
One only feeling could'st thou trace;
   The sullen calmness of despair.

9

Away! away! my early dream,
   Remembrance never must awake:
Oh! where is Lethe's fabled stream?
   My foolish heart be still, or break.
           November 2, 1808.
           [*First publ., 1809.*]

TO A LADY

ON BEING ASKED MY REASON FOR QUITTING ENGLAND
IN THE SPRING

[To Mrs. Chaworth Musters.]

1

WHEN Man, expell'd from Eden's bowers,
   A moment linger'd near the gate,

Each scene recall'd the vanish'd hours,
    And bade him curse his future fate.

2

But, wandering on through distant climes,
    He learnt to bear his load of grief;
Just gave a sigh to other times,
    And found in busier scenes relief.

3

Thus, Lady! will it be with me,
    And I must view thy charms no more;
For, while I linger near to thee,
    I sigh for all I knew before.

4

In flight I shall be surely wise,
    Escaping from temptation's snare;
I cannot view my Paradise
    Without the wish of dwelling there.
               December 2, 1808.
               [*First publ.*, *1809.*]

STANZAS TO A LADY,

ON LEAVING ENGLAND

[To Mrs. Chaworth Musters.]

1

'Tis done—and shivering in the gale
The bark unfurls her snowy sail;
And whistling o'er the bending mast,
Loud sings on high the fresh'ning blast;
And I must from this land be gone,
Because I cannot love but one.

2

But could I be what I have been,
And could I see what I have seen—
Could I repose upon the breast
Which once my warmest wishes blest—
I should not seek another zone,
Because I cannot love but one.

3

'Tis long since I beheld that eye
Which gave me bliss or misery;
And I have striven, but in vain,
Never to think of it again:
For though I fly from Albion,
I still can only love but one.

4

As some lone bird, without a mate,
My weary heart is desolate;
I look around, and cannot trace
One friendly smile or welcome face,
And ev'n in crowds am still alone,
Because I cannot love but one.

5

And I will cross the whitening foam,
And I will seek a foreign home;
Till I forget a false fair face,
I ne'er shall find a resting-place;
My own dark thoughts I cannot shun,
But ever love, and love but one.

6

The poorest, veriest wretch on earth
Still finds some hospitable hearth,
Where Friendship's or Love's softer glow
May smile in joy or soothe in woe;

But friend or leman I have none,
Because I cannot love but one.

7

I go—but wheresoe'er I flee
There's not an eye will weep for me;
There's not a kind congenial heart,
Where I can claim the meanest part;
Nor thou, who hast my hopes undone,
Wilt sigh, although I love but one.

8

To think of every early scene,
Of what we are, and what we've been,
Would whelm some softer hearts with woe—
But mine, alas! has stood the blow;
Yet still beats on as it begun,
And never truly loves but one.

9

And who that dear lov'd one may be,
Is not for vulgar eyes to see;
And why that early love was cross'd,
Thou know'st the best, I feel the most;
But few that dwell beneath the sun
Have lov'd so long, and lov'd but one.

10

I've tried another's fetters too,
With charms perchance as fair to view:
And I would fain have lov'd as well,
But some unconquerable spell
Forbade my bleeding breast to own
A kindred care for aught but one.

11

'Twould soothe to take one lingering view,
And bless thee in my last adieu;

Yet wish I not those eyes to weep
For him that wanders o'er the deep;
His home, his hope, his youth are gone,
Yet still he loves, and loves but one.

1809.
[First publ., 1809.]

TO FLORENCE

[This and the two poems following were addressed to Mrs.
Spencer Smith, whom Byron met in Malta.]

1

OH LADY! when I left the shore,
    The distant shore which gave me birth,
I hardly thought to grieve once more,
    To quit another spot on earth:

2

Yet here, amidst this barren isle,
    Where panting Nature droops the head,
Where only thou art seen to smile,
    I view my parting hour with dread.

3

Though far from Albin's craggy shore,
    Divided by the dark-blue main;
A few, brief, rolling seasons o'er,
    Perchance I view her cliffs again:

4

But wheresoe'er I now may roam,
    Through scorching clime, and varied sea,
Though Time restore me to my home,
    I ne'er shall bend mine eyes on thee:

5

On thee, in whom at once conspire
    All charms which heedless hearts can move,
Whom but to see is to admire,
    And, oh! forgive the word—to love.

6

Forgive the word, in one who ne'er
    With such a word can more offend;
And since thy heart I cannot share,
    Believe me, what I am, thy friend.

7

And who so cold as look on thee,
    Thou lovely wand'rer, and be less?
Nor be, what man should ever be,
    The friend of Beauty in distress?

8

Ah! who would think that form had past
    Through Danger's most destructive path,
Had graved the death-winged tempest's blast,
    And 'scaped a Tyrant's fiercer wrath?

9

Lady! when I shall view the walls
    Where free Byzantium once arose,
And Stamboul's Oriental halls
    The Turkish tyrants now enclose;

10

Though mightiest in the lists of fame,
    That glorious city still shall be;
On me 'twill hold a dearer claim,
    As spot of thy nativity:

11

And though I bid thee now farewell,
　　When I behold that wondrous scene—
Since where thou art I may not dwell—
　　'Twill soothe to be where thou hast been.
　　　　　　　　September, 1809.
　　　　　　　　[*First publ., 1812.*]

STANZAS COMPOSED DURING A THUNDERSTORM

1

CHILL and mirk is the nightly blast,
　　Where Pindus' mountains rise,
And angry clouds are pouring fast
　　The vengeance of the skies.

2

Our guides are gone, our hope is lost,
　　And lightnings, as they play,
But show where rocks our path have crost,
　　Or gild the torrent's spray.

3

Is yon a cot I saw, though low?
　　When lightning broke the gloom—
How welcome were its shade!—ah, no!
　　'Tis but a Turkish tomb.

4

Through sounds of foaming waterfalls,
　　I hear a voice exclaim—
My way-worn countryman, who calls
　　On distant England's name.

5

A shot is fired—by foe or friend?
    Another—'tis to tell
The mountain-peasants to descend,
    And lead us where they dwell.

6

Oh! who in such a night will dare
    To tempt the wilderness?
And who mid thunder-peals can hear
    Our signal of distress?

7

And who that heard our shouts would rise
    To try the dubious road?
Nor rather deem from nightly cries
    That outlaws were abroad.

8

Clouds burst, skies flash, oh, dreadful hour!
    More fiercely pours the storm!
Yet here one thought has still the power
    To keep my bosom warm.

9

While wandering through each broken path
    O'er brake and craggy brow;
While elements exhaust their wrath,
    Sweet Florence, where art thou?

10

Not on the sea, not on the sea—
    Thy bark hath long been gone:
Oh, may the storm that pours on me,
    Bow down my head alone!

11

Full swiftly blew the swift Siroc,
  When last I pressed thy lip;
And long ere now, with foaming shock,
  Impelled thy gallant ship.

12

Now thou art safe; nay, long ere now
  Hast trod the shore of Spain;
'Twere hard if aught so fair as thou
  Should linger on the main.

13

And since I now remember thee
  In darkness and in dread,
As in those hours of revelry
  Which Mirth and Music sped;

14

Do thou, amid the fair white walls,
  If Cadiz yet be free,
At times from out her latticed halls
  Look o'er the dark blue sea;

15

Then think upon Calypso's isles,
  Endeared by days gone by;
To others give a thousand smiles,
  To me a single sigh.

16

And when the admiring circle mark
  The paleness of thy face,
A half-formed tear, a transient spark
  Of melancholy grace,

17

Again thou'lt smile, and blushing shun
  Some coxcomb's raillery;
Nor own for once thou thought'st on one,
  Who ever thinks on thee.

18

Though smile and sigh alike are vain,
  When severed hearts repine,
My spirit flies o'er Mount and Main,
  And mourns in search of *thine*.
           October 11, 1809.
          [*First publ., 1812.*]

STANZAS WRITTEN IN PASSING
THE AMBRACIAN GULF

1

THROUGH cloudless skies, in silvery sheen,
  Full beams the moon on Actium's coast:
And on these waves, for Egypt's queen,
  The ancient world was won and lost.

2

And now upon the scene I look,
  The azure grave of many a Roman;
Where stern Ambition once forsook
  His wavering crown to follow *Woman*

3

Florence! whom I will love as well
  (As ever yet was said or sung,
Since Orpheus sang his spouse from Hell)
  Whilst *thou* art *fair* and *I* am *young*;

4

Sweet Florence! those were pleasant times,
    When worlds were staked for Ladies' eyes:
Had bards as many realms as rhymes,
    Thy charms might raise new Antonies,

5

Though Fate forbids such things to be,
    Yet, by thine eyes and ringlets curled!
I cannot *lose* a *world* for thee,
    But would not lose *thee* for a World.
                    November 14, 1809.
                    [*First publ., 1812.*]

THE SPELL IS BROKE, THE CHARM IS FLOWN!

WRITTEN AT ATHENS, JANUARY 16, 1810

THE spell is broke, the charm is flown!
    Thus is it with Life's fitful fever:
We madly smile when we should groan;
    Delirium is our best deceiver.
Each lucid interval of thought
    Recalls the woes of Nature's charter;
And *He* that acts as *wise men ought,*
    But *lives*—as saints have died—a martyr
                    [*First publ., 1812.*]

THE GIRL OF CADIZ

[This poem, written during Byron's first pilgrimage, originally
was inserted in the manuscript of *Childe Harold,* Canto I. Byron
probably recognized that it was out of tone with that poem and
substituted the stanzas "To Inez."]

1

OH NEVER talk again to me
    Of northern climes and British ladies;
It has not been your lot to see,
    Like me, the lovely Girl of Cadiz.
Although her eye be not of blue,
    Nor fair her locks, like English lasses,
How far its own expressive hue
    The languid azure eye surpasses!

2

Prometheus-like from heaven she stole
    The fire that through those silken lashes
In darkest glances seems to roll,
    From eyes that cannot hide their flashes:
And as along her bosom steal
    In lengthened flow her raven tresses,
You'd swear each clustering lock could feel,
    And curled to give her neck caresses.

3

Our English maids are long to woo,
    And frigid even in possession;
And if their charms be fair to view,
    Their lips are slow at Love's confession;
But, born beneath a brighter sun,
    For love ordained the Spanish maid is,
And who,—when fondly, fairly won,—
    Enchants you like the Girl of Cadiz?

4

The Spanish maid is no coquette,
    Nor joys to see a lover tremble,
And if she love, or if she hate,
    Alike she knows not to dissemble.

Her heart can ne'er be bought or sold—
  Howe'er it beats, it beats sincerely;
And, though it will not bend to gold,
  'Twill love you long and love you dearly.

5

The Spanish girl that meets your love
  Ne'er taunts you with a mock denial,
For every thought is bent to prove
  Her passion in the hour of trial.
When thronging foemen menace Spain,
  She dares the deed and shares the danger;
And should her lover press the plain,
  She hurls the spear, her love's avenger.

6

And when, beneath the evening star,
  She mingles in the gay Bolero,
Or sings to her attuned guitar
  Of Christian knight or Moorish hero,
Or counts her beads with fairy hand
  Beneath the twinkling rays of Hesper,
Or joins Devotion's choral band,
  To chaunt the sweet and hallowed vesper;—

7

In each, her charms the heart must move
  Of all who venture to behold her;
Then let not maids less fair reprove
  Because her bosom is not colder:
Through many a clime 'tis mine to roam
  Where many a soft and melting maid is.
But none abroad, and few at home,
  May match the dark-eyed Girl of Cadiz.
                                    1809.
                            [First publ., 1832.]

WRITTEN AFTER SWIMMING FROM SESTOS
TO ABYDOS

[Byron swam across the Hellespont in an hour and ten minutes on May 3, 1810.]

1

IF, in the month of dark December,
 Leander, who was nightly wont
(What maid will not the tale remember?)
 To cross thy stream, broad Hellespont!

2

If, when the wintry tempest roared,
 He sped to Hero, nothing loth,
And thus of old thy current poured,
 Fair Venus! how I pity both!

3

For *me*, degenerate modern wretch,
 Though in the genial month of May
My dripping limbs I faintly stretch,
 And think I've done a feat to-day.

4

But since he crossed the rapid tide,
 According to the doubtful story,
To woo,—and—Lord knows what beside,
 And swam for Love, as I for Glory;

5

'Twere hard to say who fared the best:
 Sad mortals! thus the Gods still plague you!
He lost his labour, I my jest:
 For he was drowned, and I've the ague.

May 9, 1810.
[*First publ., 1812.*]

MAID OF ATHENS, ERE WE PART

Ζωή μου, σᾶς ἀγαπῶ.

[The original inspiration of this poem is supposed to be Theresa Macri, daughter of a former British Consul's widow from whom Byron rented rooms when he was in Athens in 1810. Theresa was then under thirteen.]

1

MAID of Athens, ere we part,
Give, oh give me back my heart!
Or, since that has left my breast,
Keep it now, and take the rest!
Hear my vow before I go,
Ζωή μου, σᾶς ἀγαπῶ.

2

By those tresses unconfined,
Wooed by each Ægean wind;
By those lids whose jetty fringe
Kiss thy soft cheeks' blooming tinge;
By those wild eyes like the roe,
Ζωή μου, σᾶς ἀγαπῶ.

3

By that lip I long to taste;
By that zone-encircled waist;
By all the token-flowers that tell
What words can never speak so well;
By Love's alternate joy and woe,
Ζωή μου, σᾶς ἀγαπῶ.

4

Maid of Athens! I am gone:
Think of me, sweet! when alone.
Though I fly to Istambol,

> Athens holds my heart and soul:
> Can I cease to love thee? No!
> Ζωή μου, σᾶς ἀγαπῶ.

Athens, 1810.
[*First publ.*, 1812.]

FAREWELL TO MALTA

Adieu, ye joys of La Valette!
Adieu, Sirocco, sun, and sweat!
Adieu, thou palace rarely entered!
Adieu, ye mansions where—I've ventured!
Adieu, ye curséd streets of stairs!
(How surely he who mounts them swears!)
Adieu, ye merchants often failing!
Adieu, thou mob for ever railing!
Adieu, ye packets—without letters!
Adieu, ye fools—who ape your betters! 10
Adieu, thou damned'st quarantine,
That gave me fever, and the spleen!
Adieu that stage which makes us yawn, Sirs,
Adieu his Excellency's dancers!
Adieu to Peter—whom no fault's in,
But could not teach a colonel waltzing;
Adieu, ye females fraught with graces!
Adieu red coats, and redder faces!
Adieu the supercilious air
Of all that strut *en militaire!* 20
I go—but God knows when, or why,
To smoky towns and cloudy sky,
To things (the honest truth to say)
As bad—but in a different way.

Farewell to these, but not adieu
Triumphant sons of truest blue!
While either Adriatic shore,
And fallen chiefs, and fleets no more,
And nightly smiles, and daily dinners,
Proclaim you war and women's winners. 30
Pardon my Muse, who apt to prate is,
And take my rhyme—because 'tis "gratis."

And now I've got to Mrs. Fraser,
Perhaps you think I mean to praise her—
And were I vain enough to think
My praise was worth this drop of ink,
A line—or two—were no hard matter,
As here, indeed, I need not flatter:
But she must be content to shine
In better praises than in mine, 40
With lively air, and open heart,
And fashion's ease, without its art;
Her hours can gaily glide along,
Nor ask the aid of idle song.

And now, O Malta! since thou'st got us,
Thou little military hot-house!
I'll not offend with words uncivil,
And wish thee rudely at the Devil,
But only stare from out my casement,
And ask, "for what is such a place meant?" 50
Then, in my solitary nook,
Return to scribbling, or a book,
Or take my physic while I'm able
(Two spoonfuls hourly, by this label),
Prefer my nightcap to my beaver,
And bless my stars I've got a fever.

May 26, 1811.
[*First publ., 1816.*]

NEWSTEAD ABBEY

1

IN THE dome of my Sires as the clear moonbeam falls
Through Silence and Shade o'er its desolate walls,
It shines from afar like the glories of old;
It gilds, but it warms not—'tis dazzling, but cold.

2

Let the Sunbeam be bright for the younger of days:
'Tis the light that should shine on a race that decays

When the Stars are on high and the dews on the ground,
And the long shadow lingers the ruin around.

3

And the step that o'erechoes the gray floor of stone
Falls sullenly now, for 'tis only my own;
And sunk are the voices that sounded in mirth,
And empty the goblet, and dreary the hearth.

4

And vain was each effort to raise and recall
The brightness of old to illumine our Hall;
And vain was the hope to avert our decline,
And the fate of my fathers had faded to mine.

5

And theirs was the wealth and the fulness of Fame,
And mine to inherit too haughty a name;
And theirs were the times and the triumphs of yore,
And mine to regret, but renew them no more.

6

And Ruin is fixed on my tower and my wall,
Too hoary to fade, and too massy to fall;
It tells not of Time's or the tempest's decay,
But the wreck of the line that have held it in sway.

August 26, 1811.
[*First publ., 1878.*]

EPISTLE TO A FRIEND

IN ANSWER TO SOME LINES EXHORTING THE AUTHOR TO BE CHEERFUL, AND TO "BANISH CARE"

[The friend was probably the Rev. Francis Hodgson, who had tried to cheer Byron and bring him out of his dark mood caused by the death of his mother and several close friends in succession.]

"OH! banish care"—such ever be
The motto of *thy* revelry!
Perchance of *mine,* when wassail nights
Renew those riotous delights,
Wherewith the children of Despair
Lull the lone heart, and "banish care."
But not in Morn's reflecting hour,
When present, past, and future lower,
When all I loved is changed or gone,
Mock with such taunts the woes of one,   10
Whose every thought—but let them pass—
Thou know'st I am not what I was.
But, above all, if thou wouldst hold
Place in a heart that ne'er was cold,
By all the powers that men revere,
By all unto thy bosom dear,
Thy joys below, thy hopes above,
Speak—speak of anything but Love.

'Twere long to tell, and vain to hear,
The tale of one who scorns a tear;   20
And there is little in that tale
Which better bosoms would bewail.
But mine has suffered more than well
'Twould suit philosophy to tell.
I've seen my bride another's bride,—
Have seen her seated by his side,—
Have seen the infant, which she bore,
Wear the sweet smile the mother wore,
When she and I in youth have smiled,
As fond and faultless as her child;—   30
Have seen her eyes, in cold disdain,
Ask if I felt no secret pain;
And *I* have acted well my part,
And made my cheek belie my heart,
Returned the freezing glance she gave,
Yet felt the while *that* woman's slave;—
Have kissed, as if without design,
The babe which ought to have been mine,
And showed, alas! in each caress
Time had not made me love the less.   40

But let this pass—I'll whine no more,
Nor seek again an eastern shore;
The world befits a busy brain,—
I'll hie me to its haunts again.
But if, in some succeeding year,
When Britain's "May is in the sere,"
Thou hear'st of one, whose deepening crimes
Suit with the sablest of the times,
Of one, whom love nor pity sways,
Nor hope of fame, nor good men's praise;　　　50
One, who in stern Ambition's pride,
Perchance not blood shall turn aside;
One ranked in some recording page
With the worst anarchs of the age,
Him wilt thou *know*—and *knowing* pause,
Nor with the *effect* forget the cause.

Newstead Abbey, October 11, 1811.
[*First publ., 1830.*]

TO THYRZA

[The identity of Thyrza, like that of Wordsworth's Lucy, remains a mystery. That she was a real person seems likely, for Byron never wrote so feelingly except from real experience. The two following poems are also addressed to Thyrza.]

WITHOUT a stone to mark the spot,
　And say, what Truth might well have said,
By all, save one, perchance forgot,
　Ah! wherefore art thou lowly laid?
By many a shore and many a sea
　Divided, yet beloved in vain;
The Past, the Future fled to thee,
　To bid us meet—no—ne'er again!
Could this have been—a word, a look,
　That softly said, "We part in peace,"　　　10
Had taught my bosom how to brook,
　With fainter sighs, thy soul's release.
And didst thou not—since Death for thee
　Prepared a light and pangless dart—
Once long for him thou ne'er shalt see,

Who held, and holds thee in his heart?
Oh! who like him had watched thee here?
  Or sadly marked thy glazing eye,
In that dread hour ere Death appear,
  When silent Sorrow fears to sigh,   20
Till all was past? But when no more
  'Twas thine to reck of human woe,
Affection's heart-drops, gushing o'er,
  Had flowed as fast—as now they flow.
Shall they not flow, when, many a day,
  In these, to me, deserted towers—
Ere called but for a time away—
  Affection's mingling tears were ours?
Ours too the glance none saw beside;
  The smile none else might understand;   30
The whispered thought of hearts allied,
  The pressure of the thrilling hand;
The kiss, so guiltless and refined,
  That Love each warmer wish forebore;
Those eyes proclaimed so pure a mind,
  Ev'n Passion blushed to plead for more—
The tone, that taught me to rejoice,
  When prone, unlike thee, to repine;
The song, celestial from thy voice,
  But sweet to me from none but thine;   40
The pledge we wore—I wear it still,
  But where is thine?—Ah! where art thou?
Oft have I borne the weight of ill,
  But never bent beneath till now!
Well hast thou left in Life's best bloom
  The cup of Woe for me to drain;
If rest alone be in the tomb,
  I would not wish thee here again:
But if in worlds more blest than this
  Thy virtues seek a fitter sphere,   50
Impart some portion of thy bliss,
  To wean me from mine anguish here.
Teach me—too early taught by thee!
  To bear, forgiving and forgiven:
On earth thy love was such to me;
  It fain would form my hope in Heaven!
                              October 11, 1811.
                              [*First publ., 1812.*]

AWAY, AWAY, YE NOTES OF WOE

1

AWAY, away, ye notes of Woe!
    Be silent, thou once soothing Strain,
Or I must flee from hence—for, oh!
    I dare not trust those sounds again.
To me they speak of brighter days—
    But lull the chords, for now, alas!
I must not think, I may not gaze,
    On what I *am*—on what I *was*.

2

The voice that made those sounds more sweet
    Is hushed, and all their charms are fled;
And now their softest notes repeat
    A dirge, an anthem o'er the dead!
Yes, Thyrza! yes, they breathe of thee,
    Belovéd dust! since dust thou art;
And all that once was Harmony
    Is worse than discord to my heart!

3

'Tis silent all!—but on my ear
    The well remembered Echoes thrill;
I hear a voice I would not hear,
    A voice that now might well be still:
Yet oft my doubting Soul 'twill shake;
    Ev'n Slumber owns its gentle tone,
Till Consciousness will vainly wake
    To listen, though the dream be flown.

4

Sweet Thyrza! waking as in sleep,
    Thou art but now a lovely dream;
A Star that trembled o'er the deep,
    Then turned from earth its tender beam.

But he who through Life's dreary way
　Must pass, when Heaven is veiled in wrath,
Will long lament the vanished ray
　That scattered gladness o'er his path.
December 8, 1811.
[First publ., 1812.]

ONE STRUGGLE MORE, AND I AM FREE

1

ONE struggle more, and I am free
　From pangs that rend my heart in twain;
One last long sigh to Love and thee,
　Then back to busy life again.
It suits me well to mingle now
　With things that never pleased before:
Though every joy is fled below,
　What future grief can touch me more?

2

Then bring me wine, the banquet bring;
　Man was not formed to live alone:
I'll be that light unmeaning thing
　That smiles with all, and weeps with none.
It was not thus in days more dear,
　It never would have been, but thou
Hast fled, and left me lonely here;
　Thou'rt nothing,—all are nothing now.

3

In vain my lyre would lightly breathe!
　The smile that Sorrow fain would wear
But mocks the woe that lurks beneath,
　Like roses o'er a sepulchre.
Though gay companions o'er the bowl
　Dispel awhile the sense of ill;
Though Pleasure fires the maddening soul,
　The Heart,—the Heart is lonely still!

4

On many a lone and lovely night
  It soothed to gaze upon the sky;
For then I deemed the heavenly light
  Shone sweetly on thy pensive eye:
And oft I thought at Cynthia's noon,
  When sailing o'er the Ægean wave,
"Now Thyrza gazes on that moon"—
  Alas, it gleamed upon her grave!

5

When stretched on Fever's sleepless bed,
  And sickness shrunk my throbbing veins,
" 'Tis comfort still," I faintly said,
  "That Thyrza cannot know my pains:"
Like freedom to the time-worn slave—
  A boon 'tis idle then to give—
Relenting Nature vainly gave
  My life, when Thyrza ceased to live!

6

My Thyrza's pledge in better days,
  When Love and Life alike were new!
How different now thou meet'st my gaze!
  How tinged by time with Sorrow's hue!
The heart that gave itself with thee
  Is silent—ah, were mine as still!
Though cold as e'en the dead can be,
  It feels, it sickens with the chill.

7

Thou bitter pledge! thou mournful token!
  Though painful, welcome to my breast!
Still, still, preserve that love unbroken,
  Or break the heart to which thou'rt pressed.
Time tempers Love, but not removes,
  More hallowed when its Hope is fled:

Oh! what are thousand living loves
　　To that which cannot quit the dead?
　　　　　　　[*First publ., 1812.*]

EUTHANASIA

1

WHEN Time, or soon or late, shall bring
　　The dreamless sleep that lulls the dead,
Oblivion! may thy languid wing
　　Wave gently o'er my dying bed!

2

No band of friends or heirs be there,
　　To weep, or wish, the coming blow:
No maiden, with dishevelled hair,
　　To feel, or feign, decorous woe.

3

But silent let me sink to Earth,
　　With no officious mourners near
I would not mar one hour of mirth,
　　Nor startle Friendship with a fear.

4

Yet Love, if Love in such an hour
　　Could nobly check its useless sighs,
Might then exert its latest power
　　In her who lives, and him who dies.

5

'Twere sweet, my Psyche! to the last
　　Thy features still serene to see:
Forgetful of its struggles past,
　　E'en Pain itself should smile on thee.

6

But vain the wish—for Beauty still
  Will shrink, as shrinks the ebbing breath;
And Woman's tears, produced at will,
  Deceive in life, unman in death.

7

Then lonely be my latest hour,
  Without regret, without a groan;
For thousands Death hath ceased to lower,
  And pain been transient or unknown.

8

"Aye, but to die, and go," alas!
  Where all have gone, and all must go!
To be the nothing that I was
  Ere born to life and living woe!

9

Count o'er the joys thine hours have seen,
  Count o'er thy days from anguish free,
And know, whatever thou hast been,
  'Tis something better not to be.

               [*First publ., 1812.*]

AND THOU ART DEAD, AS YOUNG AND FAIR

'Heu, quanto minus est cum reliquis versari quam tui meminisse!"

1

AND thou art dead, as young and fair
  As aught of mortal birth;
And form so soft, and charms so rare,
  Too soon returned to Earth!
Though Earth received them in her bed,
And o'er the spot the crowd may tread

In carelessness or mirth,
There is an eye which could not brook
A moment on that grave to look.

2

I will not ask where thou liest low,
  Nor gaze upon the spot;
There flowers or weeds at will may grow,
  So I behold them not:
It is enough for me to prove
That what I loved, and long must love,
  Like common earth can rot;
To me there needs no stone to tell,
'Tis Nothing that I loved so well.

3

Yet did I love thee to the last
  As fervently as thou,
Who didst not change through all the past,
  And canst not alter now.
The love where Death has set his seal,
Nor age can chill, nor rival steal,
  Nor falsehood disavow:
And, what were worse, thou canst not see
Or wrong, or change, or fault in me.

4

The better days of life were ours;
  The worst can be but mine:
The sun that cheers, the storm that lowers,
  Shall never more be thine.
The silence of that dreamless sleep
I envy now too much to weep;
  Nor need I to repine,
That all those charms have passed away
I might have watched through long decay.

5

The flower in ripened bloom unmatched
    Must fall the earliest prey;
Though by no hand untimely snatched,
    The leaves must drop away:
And yet it were a greater grief
To watch it withering, leaf by leaf,
    Than see it plucked to-day;
Since earthly eye but ill can bear
To trace the change to foul from fair.

6

I know not if I could have borne
    To see thy beauties fade;
The night that followed such a morn
    Had worn a deeper shade:
Thy day without a cloud hath passed,
And thou wert lovely to the last;
    Extinguished, not decayed;
As stars that shoot along the sky
Shine brightest as they fall from high.

7

As once I wept, if I could weep,
    My tears might well be shed,
To think I was not near to keep
    One vigil o'er thy bed;
To gaze, how fondly! on thy face,
To fold thee in a faint embrace,
    Uphold thy drooping head;
And show that love, however vain,
Nor thou nor I can feel again.

8

Yet how much less it were to gain,
    Though thou hast left me free,
The loveliest things that still remain,
    Than thus remember thee!

The all of thine that cannot die
Through dark and dread Eternity
  Returns again to me,
And more thy buried love endears
Than aught, except its living years.
February, 1812.
[First publ., 1812.]

LINES TO A LADY WEEPING

[First published in The Morning Chronicle, March 7, 1812.
anonymously. Byron refers to a famous incident at a banquet at
Carlton House, February 22, 1812, when the Princess Charlotte
wept because her father the Prince Regent had repudiated his
former political associates. There was a great furor when the
poem appeared in 1814 under Byron's name in the volume containing The Corsair.]

WEEP, daughter of a royal line,
  A Sire's disgrace, a realm's decay;
Ah! happy if each tear of thine
  Could wash a Father's fault away!
Weep—for thy tears are Virtue's tears—
  Auspicious to these suffering Isles;
And be each drop in future years
  Repaid thee by thy People's smiles!
March, 1812.

REMEMBER THEE! REMEMBER THEE!

[Addressed to Lady Caroline Lamb, who had written in one of
Byron's books in his absence, "Remember me!"]

1

REMEMBER thee! remember thee!
  Till Lethe quench Life's burning stream
Remorse and Shame shall cling to thee,
  And haunt thee like a feverish dream!

2

Remember thee! Aye, doubt it not.
  Thy husband too shall think of thee:
By neither shalt thou be forgot,
  Thou *false* to him, thou *fiend* to me!
      [*First publ., 1824.*]

THOU ART NOT FALSE, BUT THOU ART FICKLE

1

Thou are not false, but thou art fickle,
  To those thyself so fondly sought;
The tears that thou hast forced to trickle
  Are doubly bitter from that thought:
'Tis this which breaks the heart thou grievest,
Too well thou lov'st—*too soon* thou leavest.

2

The wholly false the *heart* despises,
  And spurns deceiver and deceit;
But she who not a thought disguises,
  Whose love is as sincere as sweet,—
When *she* can change who loved so truly,
It *feels* what mine has *felt* so newly.

3

To dream of joy and wake to sorrow
  Is doomed to all who love or live;
And if, when conscious on the morrow,
  We scarce our Fancy can forgive,
That cheated us in slumber only,
To leave the waking soul more lonely,

4

What must they feel whom no false vision
  But truest, tenderest Passion warmed?

Sincere, but swift in sad transition:
  As if a dream alone had charmed?
Ah! sure such *grief* is *Fancy's* scheming,
And all thy *Change* can be but *dreaming!*
          [*First publ., 1814.*]

ON BEING ASKED WHAT WAS
THE "ORIGIN OF LOVE"

THE "Origin of Love!"—Ah, why
  That cruel question ask of me,
When thou mayest read in many an eye
  He starts to life on seeing thee?
And shouldst thou seek his *end* to know:
  My heart forebodes, my fears foresee,
He'll linger long in silent woe;
  But live until—I cease to be.
          [*First publ., 1814.*]

SONNET

TO GENEVRA

THINE eyes' blue tenderness, thy long fair hair,
  And the wan lustre of thy features—caught,
  From contemplation—where serenely wrought,
Seems Sorrow's softness charmed from its despair—
Have thrown such speaking sadness in thine air,
  That—but I know thy blessèd bosom fraught
  With mines of unalloyed and stainless thought—
I should have deemed thee doomed to earthly care.
With such an aspect, by his colours blent,
  When from his beauty-breathing pencil born,
(Except that *thou* hast nothing to repent)
  The Magdalen of Guido saw the morn—
Such seem'st thou—but how much more excellent!
  With nought Remorse can claim—nor Virtue scorn.
          December 17, 1813.
          [*First publ., 1814.*]

SONNET

TO THE SAME

THY cheek is pale with thought, but not from woe,
　And yet so lovely, that if Mirth could flush
　Its rose of whiteness with the brightest blush,
My heart would wish away that ruder glow:
And dazzle not thy deep-blue eyes—but, oh!
　While gazing on them sterner eyes will gush,
　And into mine my mother's weakness rush,
Soft as the last drops round Heaven's airy bow.
For, through thy long dark lashes low depending,
　The soul of melancholy Gentleness
Gleams like a Seraph from the sky descending,
　Above all pain, yet pitying all distress;
At once such majesty with sweetness blending,
　I worship more, but cannot love thee less.

December 17, 1813.
[First publ., 1814.]

ODE TO NAPOLEON BUONAPARTE

"Expende Annibalem:—quot libras in duce summo Invenies?"
—JUVENAL, Sat. x. line 147.

"The Emperor Nepos was acknowledged by the *Senate*, by the *Italians*, and by the Provincials of *Gaul*; his moral virtues, and military talents, were loudly celebrated; and those who derived any private benefit from his government announced, in prophetic strains, the restoration of the public felicity. . . . By this shameful abdication, he protracted his life about five years, in a very ambiguous state, between an Emperor and an Exile, till ! ! !"—Gibbon's *Decline and Fall*, 1848, iv. 373, 374.

I

'TIS done—but yesterday a King!
　And armed with Kings to strive—
　And now thou art a nameless thing:

So abject—yet alive!
Is this the man of thousand thrones,
Who strewed our earth with hostile bones,
    And can he thus survive?
Since he, miscalled the Morning Star,
Nor man nor fiend hath fallen so far.

II

Ill-minded man! why scourge thy kind
    Who bowed so low the knee?
By gazing on thyself grown blind,
    Thou taught'st the rest to see.
With might unquestioned,—power to save,—
Thine only gift hath been the grave
    To those that worshipped thee;
Nor till thy fall could mortals guess
Ambition's less than littleness!

III

Thanks for that lesson—it will teach
    To after-warriors more
Than high Philosophy can preach,
    And vainly preached before.
That spell upon the minds of men
Breaks never to unite again,
    That led them to adore
Those Pagod things of sabre-sway,
With fronts of brass, and feet of clay.

IV

The triumph, and the vanity,
    The rapture of the strife—
The earthquake-voice of Victory,
    To thee the breath of life;
The sword, the sceptre, and that sway
Which man seemed made but to obey,
    Wherewith renown was rife—
All quelled!—Dark Spirit! what must be
The madness of thy memory!

V

The Desolator desolate!
  The Victor overthrown!
The Arbiter of others' fate
  A Suppliant for his own!
Is it some yet imperial hope
That with such change can calmly cope?
  Or dread of death alone?
To die a Prince—or live a slave—
Thy choice is most ignobly brave!

VI

He who of old would rend the oak,
  Dreamed not of the rebound;
Chained by the trunk he vainly broke—
  Alone—how looked he round?
Thou, in the sternness of thy strength,
An equal deed hast done at length,
  And darker fate hast found:
He fell, the forest prowlers' prey;
But thou must eat thy heart away!

VII

The Roman, when his burning heart
  Was slaked with blood of Rome,
Threw down the dagger—dared depart,
  In savage grandeur, home.—
He dared depart in utter scorn
Of men that such a yoke had borne,
  Yet left him such a doom!
His only glory was that hour
Of seif-upheld abandoned power.

VIII

The Spaniard, when the lust of sway
  Had lost its quickening spell,
Cast crowns for rosaries away,

An empire for a cell;
A strict accountant of his beads,
A subtle disputant on creeds,
  His dotage trifled well:
Yet better had he neither known—
A bigot's shrine, nor despot's throne.

IX

But thou—from thy reluctant hand
  The thunderbolt is wrung—
Too late thou leav'st the high command
  To which thy weakness clung;
All Evil Spirit as thou art,
It is enough to grieve the heart
  To see thine own unstrung;
To think that God's fair world hath been
The footstool of a thing so mean;

X

And Earth hath spilt her blood for him,
  Who thus can hoard his own!
And Monarchs bowed the trembling limb,
  And thanked him for a throne!
Fair Freedom! we may hold thee dear,
When thus thy mightiest foes their fear
  In humblest guise have shown.
Oh! ne'er may tyrant leave behind
A brighter name to lure mankind!

XI

Thine evil deeds are writ in gore,
  Nor written thus in vain—
Thy triumphs tell of fame no more,
  Or deepen every stain:
If thou hadst died as Honour dies,
Some new Napoleon might arise,
  To shame the world again—
But who would soar the solar height,
To set in such a starless night?

XII

Weighed in the balance, hero dust
  Is vile as vulgar clay;
Thy scales, Mortality! are just
  To all that pass away:
But yet, methought, the living great
Some higher sparks should animate,
  To dazzle and dismay:
Nor deemed Contempt could thus make mirth
Of these, the Conquerors of the earth.

XIII

And she, proud Austria's mournful flower,
  Thy still imperial bride;
How bears her breast the torturing hour?
  Still clings she to thy side?
Must she too bend, must she too share
Thy late repentance, long despair,
  Thou throneless Homicide?
If still she loves thee, hoard that gem,—
'Tis worth thy vanished diadem!

XIV

Then haste thee to thy sullen isle
  And gaze upon the sea;
That element may meet thy smile—
  It ne'er was ruled by thee!
Or trace with thine all idle hand,
In loitering mood upon the sand,
  That Earth is now as free!
That Corinth's pedagogue hath now
Transferred his by-word to thy brow.

XV

Thou Timour! in his captive's cage
  What thoughts will there be thine,
While brooding in thy prisoned rage?

But one—"The world *was* mine!"
Unless, like he of Babylon,
All sense is with thy sceptre gone,
    Life will not long confine
That spirit poured so widely forth—
So long obeyed—so little worth!

XVI

Or, like the thief of fire from heaven,
    Wilt thou withstand the shock?
And share with him, the unforgiven,
    His vulture and his rock!
Foredoomed by God—by man accurst,
And that last act, though not thy worst,
    The very Fiend's arch mock;
He in his fall preserved his pride,
And, if a mortal, had as proudly died!

XVII

There was a day—there was an hour,
    While earth was Gaul's—Gaul thine—
When that immeasurable power
    Unsated to resign
Had been an act of purer fame
Than gathers round Marengo's name,
    And gilded thy decline,
Through the long twilight of all time,
Despite some passing clouds of crime.

XVIII

But thou, forsooth, must be a King
    And don the purple vest,
As if that foolish robe could wring
    Remembrance from thy breast.
Where is that faded garment? where
The gewgaws thou wert fond to wear,
    The star, the string, the crest?
Vain forward child of Empire! say,
Are all thy playthings snatched away?

XIX

Where may the wearied eye repose
 When gazing on the Great;
Where neither guilty glory glows,
 Nor despicable state?
Yes—One—the first—the last—the best—
The Cincinnatus of the West,
 Whom Envy dared not hate,
Bequeathed the name of Washington,
To make man blush there was but one!
[First publ., April 16, 1814.]

STANZAS FOR MUSIC

1

I SPEAK not, I trace not, I breathe not thy name,
There is grief in the sound, there is guilt in the fame:
But the tear which now burns on my cheek may impart
The deep thoughts that dwell in that silence of heart.

2

Too brief for our passion, too long for our peace,
Were those hours—can their joy or their bitterness cease?
We repent, we abjure, we will break from our chain,—
We will part, we will fly to—unite it again!

3

Oh! thine be the gladness, and mine be the guilt!
Forgive me, adored one!—forsake, if thou wilt;—
But the heart which is thine shall expire undebased,
And *man* shall not break it—whatever *thou* mayst.

4

And stern to the haughty, but humble to thee.
This soul, in its bitterest blackness, shall be·

And our days seem as swift, and our moments more sweet,
With thee by my side, than with worlds at our feet.

5

One sigh of thy sorrow, one look of thy love,
Shall turn me or fix, shall reward or reprove;
And the heartless may wonder at all I resign—
Thy lip shall reply, not to them, but to *mine.*

May 4, 1814.
[*First publ., 1829.*]

STANZAS FOR MUSIC

"O Lachrymarum fons, tenero sacros
Ducentium ortus ex animo: quater
Felix! in imo qui scatentem
Pectore te, pia Nympha sensit."
—GRAY's Poemata.

[Written after he had received news of the death of his Harrow friend the Duke of Dorset.]

1

THERE's not a joy the world can give like that it takes away,
When the glow of early thought declines in Feeling's dull decay;
'Tis not on Youth's smooth cheek the blush alone, which fades so
    fast,
But the tender bloom of heart is gone, ere Youth itself be past.

2

Then the few whose spirits float above the wreck of happiness
Are driven o'er the shoals of guilt or ocean of excess:
The magnet of their course is gone, or only points in vain
The shore to which their shivered sail shall never stretch again.

3

Then the mortal coldness of the soul like Death itself comes
    down;

It cannot feel for others' woes, it dare not dream its own;
That heavy chill has frozen o'er the fountain of our tears,
And though the eye may sparkle still, 'tis where the ice appears.

4

Though wit may flash from fluent lips, and mirth distract the
        breast,
Through midnight hours that yield no more their former hope of
        rest;
'Tis but as ivy-leaves around the ruined turret wreath,
All green and wildly fresh without, but worn and grey beneath.

5

Oh, could I feel as I have felt,—or be what I have been,
Or weep as I could once have wept, o'er many a vanished scene;
As springs, in deserts found, seem sweet, all brackish though they
        be,
So, midst the withered waste of life, those tears would flow to me.

                                        March, 1815.
                                [*First publ., 1816.*]

STANZAS FOR MUSIC

1

THERE be none of Beauty's daughters
        With a magic like thee;
And like music on the waters
        Is thy sweet voice to me:
When, as if its sound were causing
The charmèd Ocean's pausing,
The waves lie still and gleaming,
And the lulled winds seem dreaming:

2

And the Midnight Moon is weaving
        Her bright chain o'er the deep;
Whose breast is gently heaving,
        As an infant's asleep:

So the spirit bows before thee,
To listen and adore thee;
With a full but soft emotion,
Like the swell of Summer's ocean.

March 28 [1816].
[First publ., 1816.]

DARKNESS

I HAD a dream, which was not all a dream.
The bright sun was extinguished, and the stars
Did wander darkling in the eternal space,
Rayless, and pathless, and the icy Earth
Swung blind and blackening in the moonless air;
Morn came and went—and came, and brought no day,
And men forgot their passions in the dread
Of this their desolation; and all hearts
Were chilled into a selfish prayer for light:
And they did live by watchfires—and the thrones,   10
The palaces of crownéd kings—the huts,
The habitations of all things which dwell,
Were burnt for beacons; cities were consumed,
And men were gathered round their blazing homes
To look once more into each other's face;
Happy were those who dwelt within the eye
Of the volcanoes, and their mountain-torch:
A fearful hope was all the World contained;
Forests were set on fire—but hour by hour
They fell and faded—and the crackling trunks   20
Extinguished with a crash—and all was black.
The brows of men by the despairing light
Wore an unearthly aspect, as by fits
The flashes fell upon them; some lay down
And hid their eyes and wept; and some did rest
Their chins upon their clenchéd hands, and smiled;
And others hurried to and fro, and fed
Their funeral piles with fuel, and looked up
With mad disquietude on the dull sky,
The pall of a past World; and then again   30
With curses cast them down upon the dust,
And gnashed their teeth and howled: the wild birds shrieked,

And, terrified, did flutter on the ground
And flap their useless wings; the wildest brutes
Came tame and tremulous; and vipers crawled
And twined themselves among the multitude,
Hissing, but stingless—they were slain for food:
And War, which for a moment was no more,
Did glut himself again:—a meal was bought
With blood, and each sate sullenly apart   40
Gorging himself in gloom: no Love was left;
All earth was but one thought—and that was Death,
Immediate and inglorious; and the pang
Of famine fed upon all entrails—men
Died, and their bones were tombless as their flesh;
The meagre by the meagre were devoured,
Even dogs assailed their masters, all save one,
And he was faithful to a corse, and kept
The birds and beasts and famished men at bay,
Till hunger clung them, or the dropping dead   50
Lured their lank jaws; himself sought out no food,
But with a piteous and perpetual moan,
And a quick desolate cry, licking the hand
Which answered not with a caress—he died.
The crowd was famished by degrees; but two
Of an enormous city did survive,
And they were enemies: they met beside
The dying embers of an altar-place
Where had been heaped a mass of holy things
For an unholy usage; they raked up,   60
And shivering scraped with their cold skeleton hands
The feeble ashes, and their feeble breath
Blew for a little life, and made a flame
Which was a mockery; then they lifted up
Their eyes as it grew lighter, and beheld
Each other's aspects—saw, and shrieked, and died—
Even of their mutual hideousness they died,
Unknowing who he was upon whose brow
Famine had written Fiend. The World was void,
The populous and the powerful was a lump,   70
Seasonless, herbless, treeless, manless, lifeless—
A lump of death—a chaos of hard clay.
The rivers, lakes, and ocean all stood still,
And nothing stirred within their silent depths;
Ships sailorless lay rotting on the sea,

And their masts fell down piecemeal: as they dropped
They slept on the abyss without a surge—
The waves were dead; the tides were in their grave,
The Moon, their mistress, had expired before;
The winds were withered in the stagnant air,   80
And the clouds perished; Darkness had no need
Of aid from them—She was the Universe.

Diodati, July, 1816.
[First publ., 1816.]

CHURCHILL'S GRAVE

A FACT LITERALLY RENDERED

[Charles Churchill (1731–1764), the satirical poet. Byron
visited his grave in Dover before sailing for Ostend, April 25,
1816.]

I STOOD beside the grave of him who blazed
    The Comet of a season, and I saw
The humblest of all sepulchres, and gazed
    With not the less of sorrow and of awe
On that neglected turf and quiet stone,
With name no clearer than the names unknown,
Which lay unread around it; and I asked
    The Gardener of that ground, why it might be
That for this plant strangers his memory tasked,
    Through the thick deaths of half a century;   10
And thus he answered—"Well, I do not know
Why frequent travellers turn to pilgrims so;
He died before my day of Sextonship,
    And I had not the digging of this grave."
And is this all? I thought,—and do we rip
    The veil of Immortality, and crave
I know not what of honour and of light
Through unborn ages, to endure this blight?
So soon, and so successless? As I said,
The Architect of all on which we tread,   20
For Earth is but a tombstone, did essay
To extricate remembrance from the clay,
Whose minglings might confuse a Newton's thought,
    Were it not that all life must end in one,

Of which we are but dreamers;—as he caught
  As 'twere the twilight of a former Sun,
Thus spoke he,—"I believe the man of whom
You wot, who lies in this selected tomb,
Was a most famous writer in his day,
And therefore travellers step from out their way   **80**
To pay him honour,—and myself whate'er
  Your honour pleases:"—then most pleased I shook
  From out my pocket's avaricious nook
Some certain coins of silver, which as 'twere
Perforce I gave this man, though I could spare
So much but inconveniently:—Ye smile,
I see ye, ye profane ones! all the while,
Because my homely phrase the truth would tell.
You are the fools, not I—for I did dwell
With a deep thought, and with a softened eye,   **40**
On that old Sexton's natural homily,
In which there was Obscurity and Fame,—
The Glory and the Nothing of a Name.

                    Diodati, 1816.
                [*First publ., 1816.*]

PROMETHEUS

I

Titan! to whose immortal eyes
  The sufferings of mortality,
  Seen in their sad reality,
Were not as things that gods despise;
What was thy pity's recompense?
A silent suffering, and intense;
The rock, the vulture, and the chain,
All that the proud can feel of pain,
The agony they do not show,
The suffocating sense of woe,
  Which speaks but in its loneliness,
And then is jealous lest the sky
Should have a listener, nor will sigh
  Until its voice is echoless.

II

Titan! to thee the strife was given
  Between the suffering and the will,
  Which torture where they cannot kill;
And the inexorable Heaven,
And the deaf tyranny of Fate,
The ruling principle of Hate,
Which for its pleasure doth create
The things it may annihilate,
Refused thee even the boon to die:
The wretched gift Eternity
Was thine—and thou hast borne it well.
All that the Thunderer wrung from thee
Was but the Menace which flung back
On him the torments of thy rack;
The fate thou didst so well foresee,
But would not to appease him tell;
And in thy Silence was his Sentence,
And in his Soul a vain repentance,
And evil dread so ill dissembled,
That in his hand the lightnings trembled.

III

Thy Godlike crime was to be kind,
  To render with thy precepts less
  The sum of human wretchedness,
And strengthen Man with his own mind;
But baffled as thou wert from high,
Still in thy patient energy,
In the endurance, and repulse
  Of thine impenetrable Spirit,
Which Earth and Heaven could not convulse,
  A mighty lesson we inherit:
Thou art a symbol and a sign
  To Mortals of their fate and force;
Like thee, Man is in part divine,
  A troubled stream from a pure source;
And Man in portions can foresee
His own funereal destiny;

His wretchedness, and his resistance,
And his sad unallied existence:
To which his Spirit may oppose
Itself—an equal to all woes—
    And a firm will, and a deep sense,
Which even in torture can descry
    Its own concentered recompense,
Triumphant where it dares defy,
And making Death a Victory.

> Diodati, July, 1816.
> [*First publ., 1816.*]

A FRAGMENT

COULD I remount the river of my years
To the first fountain of our smiles and tears,
I would not trace again the stream of hours
Between their outworn banks of withered flowers,
But bid it flow as now—until it glides
Into the number of the nameless tides.

.   .   .   .   .   .

What is this Death?—a quiet of the heart?
The whole of that of which we are a part?
For Life is but a vision—what I see
Of all which lives alone is Life to me,   10
And being so—the absent are the dead,
Who haunt us from tranquillity, and spread
A dreary shroud around us, and invest
With sad remembrancers our hours of rest.
    The absent are the dead—for they are cold,
And ne'er can be what once we did behold;
And they are changed, and cheerless,—or if yet
The unforgotten do not all forget,
Since thus divided—equal must it be
If the deep barrier be of earth, or sea;   20
It may be both—but one day end it must
In the dark union of insensate dust.
    The under-earth inhabitants—are they
But mingled millions decomposed to clay?

The ashes of a thousand ages spread
Wherever Man has trodden or shall tread?
Or do they in their silent cities dwell
Each in his incommunicative cell?
Or have they their own language? and a sense
Of breathless being?—darkened and intense   30
As Midnight in her solitude?—Oh Earth!
Where are the past?—and wherefore had they birth?
The dead are thy inheritors—and we
But bubbles on thy surface; and the key
Of thy profundity is in the Grave,
The ebon portal of thy peopled cave,
Where I would walk in spirit, and behold
Our elements resolved to things untold,
And fathom hidden wonders, and explore
The essence of great bosoms now no more.   40

. . . . . .

Diodati, July, 1816.
[*First publ.*, 1830.]

SONNET TO LAKE LEMAN

ROUSSEAU—Voltaire—our Gibbon—and De Staël—
    Leman! these names are worthy of thy shore,
    Thy shore of names like these! wert thou no more,
Their memory thy remembrance would recall:
To them thy banks were lovely as to all,
    But they have made them lovelier, for the lore
    Of mighty minds doth hallow in the core
Of human hearts the ruin of a wall
    Where dwelt the wise and wondrous; but by *thee*
How much more, Lake of Beauty! do we feel,
    In sweetly gliding o'er thy crystal sea,
The wild glow of that not ungentle zeal,
    Which of the Heirs of Immortality
Is proud, and makes the breath of Glory real!
                        Diodati, July, 1816.
                        [*First publ.*, 1816.]

MONODY ON THE DEATH
OF THE
RIGHT HON. R. B. SHERIDAN

SPOKEN AT DRURY-LANE THEATRE,
LONDON

[Sheridan died July 7, 1816. Byron received the news on July 17 at the Villa Diodati on the Lake of Geneva and immediately wrote the "Monody" at the request of his friend Douglas Kinnaird. It was spoken at Drury Lane Theatre, long under the proprietorship of Sheridan, on September 7 and published two days later. Byron had been closely associated with Sheridan during his last years.]

WHEN the last sunshine of expiring Day
In Summer's twilight weeps itself away,
Who hath not felt the softness of the hour
Sink on the heart, as dew along the flower?
With a pure feeling which absorbs and awes
While Nature makes that melancholy pause—
Her breathing moment on the bridge where Time
Of light and darkness forms an arch sublime—
Who hath not shared that calm, so still and deep,
The voiceless thought which would not speak but weep,   10
A holy concord, and a bright regret,
A glorious sympathy with suns that set?
'Tis not harsh sorrow, but a tenderer woe,
Nameless, but dear to gentle hearts below,
Felt without bitterness—but full and clear,
A sweet dejection—a transparent tear,
Unmixed with worldly grief or selfish stain—
Shed without shame, and secret without pain.
Even as the tenderness that hour instils
When Summer's day declines along the hills,   20
So feels the fulness of our heart and eyes
When all of Genius which can perish dies.
A mighty Spirit is eclipsed—a Power
Hath passed from day to darkness—to whose hour
Of light no likeness is bequeathed—no name,

Focus at once of all the rays of Fame!
The flash of Wit—the bright Intelligence,
The beam of Song—the blaze of Eloquence,
Set with their Sun, but still have left behind
The enduring produce of immortal Mind;   30
Fruits of a genial morn, and glorious noon,
A deathless part of him who died too soon.
But small that portion of the wondrous whole,
These sparkling segments of that circling Soul,
Which all embraced, and lightened over all,
To cheer—to pierce—to please—or to appal.
From the charmed council to the festive board,
Of human feelings the unbounded lord;
In whose acclaim the loftiest voices vied,
The praised—the proud—who made his praise their pride. 40
When the loud cry of trampled Hindostan
Arose to Heaven in her appeal from Man,
His was the thunder—his the avenging rod,
The wrath—the delegated voice of God!
Which shook the nations through his lips, and blazed
Till vanquished senates trembled as they praised.

And here, oh! here, where yet all young and warm,
The gay creations of his spirit charm,
The matchless dialogue—the deathless wit,
Which knew not what it was to intermit;   50
The glowing portraits, fresh from life, that bring
Home to our hearts the truth from which they spring;
These wondrous beings of his fancy, wrought
To fulness by the fiat of his thought,
Here in their first abode you still may meet,
Bright with the hues of his Promethean heat;
A Halo of the light of other days,
Which still the splendour of its orb betrays.
But should there be to whom the fatal blight
Of failing Wisdom yields a base delight,   60
Men who exult when minds of heavenly tone
Jar in the music which was born their own,
Still let them pause—ah! little do they know
That what to them seemed Vice might be but Woe.
Hard is his fate on whom the public gaze
Is fixed for ever to detract or praise;
Repose denies her requiem to his name,

And Folly loves the martyrdom of Fame.
The secret enemy whose sleepless eye
Stands sentinel—accuser—judge—and spy;   70
The foe, the fool, the jealous, and the vain,
The envious who but breathe in others' pain—
Behold the host! delighting to deprave,
Who track the steps of Glory to the grave,
Watch every fault that daring Genius owes
Half to the ardour which its birth bestows,
Distort the truth, accumulate the lie,
And pile the pyramid of Calumny!
These are his portion—but if joined to these
Gaunt Poverty should league with deep Disease,   80
If the high Spirit must forget to soar,
And stoop to strive with Misery at the door,
To soothe Indignity—and face to face
Meet sordid Rage, and wrestle with Disgrace,
To find in Hope but the renewed caress,
The serpent-fold of further Faithlessness:—
If such may be the Ills which men assail,
What marvel if at last the mightiest fail?
Breasts to whom all the strength of feeling given
Bear hearts electric—charged with fire from Heaven,   90
Black with the rude collision, inly torn,
By clouds surrounded, and on whirlwinds borne,
Driven o'er the lowering atmosphere that nurst
Thoughts which have turned to thunder—scorch, and burst.

But far from us and from our mimic scene
Such things should be—if such have ever been;
Ours be the gentler wish, the kinder task,
To give the tribute Glory need not ask,
To mourn the vanished beam, and add our mite
Of praise in payment of a long delight.   100
Ye Orators! whom yet our councils yield,
Mourn for the veteran Hero of your field!
The worthy rival of the wondrous *Three!*
Whose words were sparks of Immortality!
Ye Bards! to whom the Drama's Muse is dear,
He was your Master—emulate him *here!*
Ye men of wit and social eloquence!
He was your brother—bear his ashes hence!

While Powers of mind almost of boundless range,
Complete in kind, as various in their change,
While Eloquence—Wit—Poesy—and Mirth,
That humbler Harmonist of care on Earth,
Survive within our souls—while lives our sense
Of pride in Merit's proud pre-eminence,
Long shall we seek his likeness—long in vain.
And turn to all of him which may remain,
Sighing that Nature formed but one such man,
And broke the die—in moulding Sheridan!

ON SAM ROGERS

[Written in 1818 and not intended for publication. Byron admired the poetry of Rogers and was friendly with him while in London, but he suspected him of being a scandal-monger. The verses were first published in *Fraser's Magazine* in 1833 while Rogers was still living.]

QUESTION

Nose and Chin that make a knocker,
Wrinkles that would puzzle Cocker;
Mouth that marks the envious Scorner,
With a Scorpion in each corner
Curling up his tail to sting you,
In the place that most may wring you;
Eyes of lead-like hue and gummy,
Carcase stolen from some mummy,
Bowels—(but they were forgotten,
Save the Liver, and that's rotten),   10
Skin all sallow, flesh all sodden,
Form the Devil would frighten G—d in.
Is't a Corpse stuck up for show,
Galvanized at times to go?
With the Scripture has't connection,
New proof of the Resurrection?
Vampire, Ghost, or Goul (*sic*), what is it?
I would walk ten miles to miss it.

ANSWER

MANY passengers arrest one,
To demand the same free question.   20
Shorter's my reply and franker,—
That's the Bard, and Beau, and Banker:
Yet, if you could bring about
Just to turn him inside out,
Satan's self would seem less sooty,
And his present aspect—Beauty.
Mark that (as he masks the bilious)
Air so softly supercilious,
Chastened bow, and mock humility,
Almost sickened to Servility: 30
Hear his tone (which is to talking
That which creeping is to walking—
Now on all fours, now on tiptoe):
Hear the tales he lends his lip to—
Little hints of heavy scandals—
Every friend by turns he handles:
All that women or that men do
Glides forth in an innuendo (*sic*)—
Clothed in odds and ends of humour,
Herald of each paltry rumour—   40
From divorces down to dresses,
Woman's frailties, Man's excesses:
All that life presents of evil
Make for him a constant revel
You're his foe—for that he fears you,
And in absence blasts and sears you;
You're his friend—for that he hates you,
First obliges, and then baits you,
Darting on the opportunity
When to do it with impunity: 50
You are neither—then he'll flatter,
Till he finds some trait for satire;
Hunts your weak point out, then shows it,
Where it injures, to expose it
In the mode that's most insidious,
Adding every trait that's hideous—
From the bile, whose blackening river

Rushes through his Stygian liver.
Then he thinks himself a lover—
Why? I really can't discover,   60
In his mind, age, face, or figure;
Viper broth might give him vigour:
Let him keep the cauldron steady,
He the venom has already.

For his faults—he has but *one;*
'Tis but Envy, when all's done:
He but pays the pain he suffers,
Clipping, like a pair of Snuffers,
Light that ought to burn the brighter
For this temporary blighter.   70
He's the Cancer of his Species,
And will eat himself to pieces,—
Plague personified and Famine,—
Devil, whose delight is damning.
For his merits—don't you know 'em?
Once he wrote a pretty Poem.

                                    1818.

STANZAS TO THE PO

[These stanzas were conceived in April, 1819, while Byron was
in Venice and not on the Po. There has been much confusion concerning them, partly because the Countess Teresa Guiccioli, to
whom they were addressed, tried to confuse the issue after
Byron's death, for she didn't want it to be known that they referred to her. There seems little doubt, however, that they express
Byron's sincere feelings with regard to his involvement with
Teresa whom he had met in Venice in April, and whose husband
in carrying her back to Ravenna had stopped at an estate at the
mouth of the Po. The verses were actually written down on June
1, just before Byron left to join the Countess in Ravenna. On
June 8, 1820, Byron wrote to Hobhouse: "You say the Po verses
are fine; I thought so little of them, that they lay by me a year
uncopied, but they were written in *red-hot* earnest and that
makes them good." The poem was first published by Medwin in
1824. There is an unpublished manuscript version in Byron's
hand in the Berg Collection in the New York Public Library

which differs considerably from the published one, especially in
the last eight lines which read:

> *My heart is all meridian, were it not*
> *I had not suffered now, nor should I be*
> *Despite old tortures ne'er to be forgot*
> *The slave again—Oh! Love! at least of thee!*
> *'Tis vain to struggle, I have struggled long*
> *To love again no more as once I loved.*
> *Oh! Time! why leave this earliest Passion strong?*
> *To tear a heart which pants to be unmoved?*]

1

RIVER, that rollest by the ancient walls,
   Where dwells the Lady of my love, when she
Walks by thy brink, and there, perchance, recalls
   A faint and fleeting memory of me:

2

What if thy deep and ample stream should be
   A mirror of my heart, where she may read
The thousand thoughts I now betray to thee,
   Wild as thy wave, and headlong as thy speed!

3

What do I say—a mirror of my heart?
   Are not thy waters sweeping, dark, and strong?
Such as my feelings were and are, thou art·
   And such as thou art were my passions long.

4

Time may have somewhat tamed them,—not for ever;
   Thou overflow'st thy banks, and not for aye
Thy bosom overboils, congenial river!
   Thy floods subside, and mine have sunk away:

5

But left long wrecks behind, and now again,
   Borne in our old unchanged career, we move;
Thou tendest wildly onwards to the main,
   And I—to loving *one* I should not love.

6

The current I behold will sweep beneath
    Her native walls, and murmur at her feet;
Her eyes will look on thee, when she shall breathe
    The twilight air, unharmed by summer's heat.

7

She will look on thee,—I have looked on thee,
    Full of that thought: and, from that moment, ne'er
Thy waters could I dream of, name, or see,
    Without the inseparable sigh for her!

8

Her bright eyes will be imaged in thy stream,—
    Yes! they will meet the wave I gaze on now:
Mine cannot witness, even in a dream,
    That happy wave repass me in its flow!

9

The wave that bears my tears returns no more:
    Will she return by whom that wave shall sweep?—
Both tread thy banks, both wander on thy shore,
    I by thy source, she by the dark-blue deep.

10

But that which keepeth us apart is not
    Distance, nor depth of wave, nor space of earth,
But the distraction of a various lot,
    As various as the climates of our birth.

11

A stranger loves the Lady of the land,
    Born far beyond the mountains, but his blood
Is all meridian, as if never fanned
    By the black wind that chills the polar flood.

12

My blood is all meridian; were it not,
   I had not left my clime, nor should I be,
In spite of tortures, ne'er to be forgot,
   A slave again of love,—at least of thee.

13

'Tis vain to struggle—let me perish young—
   Live as I lived, and love as I have loved;
To dust if I return, from dust I sprung,
   And then, at least, my heart can ne'er be moved.

June, 1819.

STANZAS

[Written in Venice, December 1, 1819, when Byron was debating whether to return to England or to rejoin the Countess Guiccioli in Ravenna.]

1

COULD Love for ever
  Run like a river,
  And Time's endeavour
    Be tried in vain—
No other pleasure
With this could measure;
And like a treasure
    We'd hug the chain.
But since our sighing
Ends not in dying,
And, formed for flying,
    Love plumes his wing;
Then for this reason
  Let's love a season;
But let that season be only Spring.

2

When lovers parted
Feel broken-hearted,
And, all hopes thwarted,
   Expect to die;
A few years older,
Ah! how much colder
They might behold her
   For whom they sigh!
When linked together,
In every weather,
They pluck Love's feather
   From out his wing—
He'll stay forever,
But sadly shiver
Without his plumage, when past the Spring.

3

Like Chiefs of Faction,
His life is action—
A formal paction
   That curbs his reign,
Obscures his glory,
Despot no more, he
Such territory
   Quits with disdain.
Still, still advancing,
With banners glancing,
His power enhancing,
   He must move on—
Repose but cloys him,
Retreat destroys him,
Love brooks not a degraded throne.

4

Wait not, fond lover!
Till years are over,
And then recover
   As from a dream.

While each bewailing
The other's failing,
With wrath and railing,
   All hideous seem—
While first decreasing,
Yet not quite ceasing,
Wait not till teasing,
   All passion blight:
If once diminished
Love's reign is finished—
Then part in friendship,—and bid good-night.

5

So shall Affection
To recollection
The dear connection
   Bring back with joy:
You had not waited
Till, tired or hated,
Your passions sated
   Began to cloy.
Your last embraces
Leave no cold traces—
The same fond faces
   As through the past:
And eyes, the mirrors
Of your sweet errors,
Reflect but rapture—not least though last.

6

True, separations
Ask more than patience;
What desperations
   From such have risen!
But yet remaining,
What is't but chaining
Hearts which, once waning,
   Beat 'gainst their prison?
Time can but cloy love,

And use destroy love:
The wingéd boy, Love,
　　Is but for boys—
You'll find it torture
Though sharper, shorter,
To wean, and not wear out your joys.
December 1, 1819.
[First publ., 1832.]

STANZAS WRITTEN ON THE ROAD
BETWEEN FLORENCE AND PISA

1

OH TALK not to me of a name great in story—
The days of our Youth are the days of our glory;
And the myrtle and ivy of sweet two-and-twenty
Are worth all your laurels, though ever so plenty.

2

What are garlands and crowns to the brow that is wrinkled?
'Tis but as a dead flower with May-dew be-sprinkled:
Then away with all such from the head that is hoary,
What care I for the wreaths that can *only* give glory?

3

Oh FAME!—if I e'er took delight in thy praises,
'Twas less for the sake of thy high-sounding phrases,
Than to see the bright eyes of the dear One discover,
She thought that I was not unworthy to love her.

4

There chiefly I sought thee, *there* only I found thee;
Her Glance was the best of the rays that surround thee,

When it sparkled o'er aught that was bright in my story,
I knew it was Love, and I felt it was Glory.

November 6, 1821.
[*First publ., 1830.*]

TO THE COUNTESS OF BLESSINGTON

1

You have asked for a verse:—the request
    In a rhymer 'twere strange to deny;
But my Hippocrene was but my breast,
    And my feelings (its fountain) are dry.

2

Were I now as I was, I had sung
    What Lawrence has painted so well;
But the strain would expire on my tongue
    And the theme is too soft for my shell.

3

I am ashes where once I was fire,
    And the bard in my bosom is dead;
What I loved I now merely admire,
    And my heart is as grey as my head.

4

My life is not dated by years—
    There are *moments* which act as a plough,
And there is not a furrow appears
    But is deep in my soul as my brow.

5

Let the young and the brilliant aspire
    To sing what I gaze on in vain;

For Sorrow has torn from my lyre
　The string which was worthy the strain.
B.
[*First publ., 1830.*]

ARISTOMENES

CANTO FIRST

1

THE Gods of old are silent on their shore,
Since the great Pan expired, and through the roar
Of the Ionian waters broke a dread
Voice which proclaimed "the Mighty Pan is dead."
How much died with him! false or true—the dream
Was beautiful which peopled every stream
With more than finny tenants, and adorned
The woods and waters with coy nymphs that scorned
Pursuing Deities, or in the embrace
Of gods brought forth the high heroic race   **10**
Whose names are on the hills and o'er the seas.
Cephalonia, September 10, 1823.
[*First publ., 1903.*]

LAST WORDS ON GREECE

WHAT are to me those honours or renown
　Past or to come, a new-born people's cry?
Albeit for such I could despise a crown
　Of aught save laurel, or for such could die.
I am a fool of passion, and a frown
　Of thine to me is as an adder's eye
To the poor bird whose pinion fluttering down
　Wafts unto death the breast it bore so high:
Such is this maddening fascination grown,
　So strong thy magic or so weak am I.
[*First publ., February, 1887.*]

ON THIS DAY I COMPLETE MY THIRTY-SIXTH YEAR

1

'T is time this heart should be unmoved,
    Since others it hath ceased to move:
Yet, though I cannot be beloved,
        Still let me love!

2

My days are in the yellow leaf;
    The flowers and fruits of Love are gone;
The worm, the canker, and the grief
        Are mine alone!

3

The fire that on my bosom preys
    Is lone as some Volcanic isle;
No torch is kindled at its blaze—
        A funeral pile.

4

The hope, the fear, the zealous care,
    The exalted portion of the pain
And power of love, I cannot share,
        But wear the chain.

5

But 't is not *thus*—and 't is not *here*—
    Such thoughts should shake my soul, nor *now*
Where Glory decks the hero's bier,
        Or binds his brow.

6

The Sword, the Banner, and the Field,
  Glory and Greece, around me see!
The Spartan, borne upon his shield,
    Was not more free.

7

Awake! (not Greece—she *is* awake!)
  Awake, my spirit! Think through *whom*
Thy life-blood tracks its parent lake,
    And then strike home!

8

Tread those reviving passions down,
  Unworthy manhood!—unto thee
Indifferent should the smile or frown
    Of Beauty be.

9

If thou regret'st thy youth, *why live?*
  The land of honourable death
Is here:—up to the Field, and give
    Away thy breath!

10

Seek out—less often sought than found—
  A soldier's grave, for thee the best;
Then look around, and choose thy ground,
    And take thy Rest.
              Missolonghi, Jan. 22, 1824.
          [*First publ., October 29, 1824.*]

[LOVE AND DEATH]

[Probably the last poem Byron wrote, addressed to the Greek
boy Lukas, whom Byron took from Cephalonia to Missolonghi as
a page.]

1

I WATCHED thee when the foe was at our side,
  Ready to strike at him—or thee and me,
Were safety hopeless—rather than divide
  Aught with one loved save love and liberty.

2

I watched thee on the breakers, when the rock,
  Received our prow, and all was storm and fear,
And bade thee cling to me through every shock;
  This arm would be thy bark, or breast thy bier.

3

I watched thee when the fever glazed thine eyes,
  Yielding my couch and stretched me on the ground
When overworn with watching, ne'er to rise
  From thence if thou an early grave hadst found.

4

The earthquake came, and rocked the quivering wall,
  And men and nature reeled as if with wine.
Whom did I seek around the tottering hall?
  For thee. Whose safety first provide for? Thine.

5

And when convulsive throes denied my breath
  The faintest utterance to my fading thought,
To thee—to thee—e'en in the gasp of death
  My spirit turned, oh! oftener than it ought.

6

Thus much and more; and yet thou lov'st me not,
  And never wilt! Love dwells not in our will.
Nor can I blame thee, though it be my lot
  To strongly, wrongly, vainly love thee still.
    [*First publ., February, 1887.*]

HEBREW MELODIES

ADVERTISEMENT

The subsequent poems were written at the request of my friend, the Hon. Douglas Kinnaird, for a Selection of Hebrew Melodies and have been published, with the music, arranged by Mr. Braham and Mr. Nathan.

January, 1815.

SHE WALKS IN BEAUTY

[Written after returning from a ball at Lady Sitwell's where he had seen the beautiful Lady Wilmot Horton in mourning with numerous spangles on her dress. Published with the *Hebrew Melodies* but not properly one of them.]

I

SHE walks in Beauty, like the night
  Of cloudless climes and starry skies;
And all that's best of dark and bright
  Meet in her aspect and her eyes:
Thus mellowed to that tender light
  Which Heaven to gaudy day denies.

II

One shade the more, one ray the less,
  Had half impaired the nameless grace
Which waves in every raven tress,
  Or softly lightens o'er her face;
Where thoughts serenely sweet express,
  How pure, how dear their dwelling-place.

III

And on that cheek, and o'er that brow,
　　So soft, so calm, yet eloquent,
The smiles that win, the tints that glow,
　　But tell of days in goodness spent,
A mind at peace with all below,
A heart whose love is innocent!

June 12, 1814.

THE HARP THE MONARCH MINSTREL SWEPT

I

The Harp the Monarch Minstrel swept,
　　The King of men, the loved of Heaven!
Which Music hallowed while she wept
　　O'er tones her heart of hearts had given—
Redoubled be her tears, its chords are riven!
　　It softened men of iron mould,
　　It gave them virtues not their own;
No ear so dull, no soul so cold,
　　That felt not—fired not to the tone,
Till David's Lyre grew mightier than his Throne!

II

It told the triumphs of our King,
　　It wafted glory to our God;
It made our gladdened valleys ring,
　　The cedars bow, the mountains nod;
Its sound aspired to Heaven and there abode!
　　Since then, though heard on earth no more,
　　Devotion and her daughter Love
Still bid the bursting spirit soar
　　To sounds that seem as from above,
In dreams that day's broad light can not remove.

IF THAT HIGH WORLD

I

IF THAT high world, which lies beyond
　　Our own, surviving Love endears;
If there the cherished heart be fond,
　　The eye the same, except in tears—
How welcome those untrodden spheres!
　　How sweet this very hour to die!
To soar from earth and find all fears
　　Lost in thy light—Eternity!

II

It must be so: 'tis not for self
　　That we so tremble on the brink;
And striving to o'erleap the gulf,
　　Yet cling to Being's severing link.
Oh! in that future let us think
　　To hold, each heart, the heart that shares;
With them the immortal waters drink,
　　And, soul in soul, grow deathless theirs!

THE WILD GAZELLE

I

THE wild gazelle on Judah's hills
　　Exulting yet may bound,
And drink from all the living rills
　　That gush on holy ground;
Its airy step and glorious eye
May glance in tameless transport by:—

II

A step as fleet, an eye more bright,
　　Hath Judah witnessed there;
And o'er her scenes of lost delight

Inhabitants more fair.
The cedars wave on Lebanon,
But Judah's statelier maids are gone!

III

More blest each palm that shades those plains
    Than Israel's scattered race;
For, taking root, it there remains
    In solitary grace:
It cannot quit its place of birth,
It will not live in other earth.

IV

But we must wander witheringly,
    In other lands to die;
And where our fathers' ashes be,
    Our own may never lie:
Our temple hath not left a stone,
And Mockery sits on Salem's throne.

OH! WEEP FOR THOSE

I

Oh! weep for those that wept by Babel's stream,
Whose shrines are desolate, whose land a dream;
Weep for the harp of Judah's broken shell;
Mourn—where their God hath dwelt the godless dwell!

II

And where shall Israel lave her bleeding feet?
And when shall Zion's song again seem sweet?
And Judah's melody once more rejoice
The hearts that leaped before its heavenly voice?

III

Tribes of the wandering foot and weary breast,
How shall ye flee away and be at rest!

The wild-dove hath her nest, the fox his cave,
Mankind their country—Israel but the grave!

ON JORDAN'S BANKS

I

ON JORDAN's banks the Arab's camels stray,
On Sion's hill the False One's votaries pray,
The Baal-adorer bows on Sinai's steep—
Yet there—even there—Oh God! thy thunders sleep:

II

There—where thy finger scorched the tablet stone!
There—where thy shadow to thy people shone!
Thy glory shrouded in its garb of fire:
Thyself—none living see and not expire!

III

Oh! in the lightning let thy glance appear;
Sweep from his shivered hand the oppressor's spear!
How long by tyrants shall thy land be trod?
How long thy temple worshipless, Oh God?

JEPHTHA'S DAUGHTER

I

SINCE our Country, our God—Oh, my Sire!
Demand that thy Daughter expire;
Since thy triumph was bought by thy vow—
Strike the bosom that's bared for thee now!

II

And the voice of my mourning is o'er,
And the mountains behold me no more:
If the hand that I love lay me low,
There cannot be pain in the blow!

III

And of this, oh, my Father! be sure—
That the blood of thy child is as pure
As the blessing I beg ere it flow,
And the last thought that soothes me below.

IV

Though the virgins of Salem lament,
Be the judge and the hero unbent!
I have won the great battle for thee,
And my Father and Country are free!

V

When this blood of thy giving hath gushed,
When the voice that thou lovest is hushed,
Let my memory still be thy pride,
And forget not I smiled as I died!

OH! SNATCHED AWAY IN BEAUTY'S BLOOM

I

Oh! snatched away in Beauty's bloom,
On thee shall press no ponderous tomb;
   But on thy turf shall roses rear
   Their leaves, the earliest of the year;
And the wild cypress wave in tender gloom:

II

And oft by yon blue gushing stream
   Shall Sorrow lean her drooping head,
And feed deep thought with many a dream,
   And lingering pause and lightly tread;
Fond wretch! as if her step disturbed the dead!

III

Away! we know that tears are vain,
 That Death nor heeds nor hears distress:
Will this unteach us to complain?
 Or make one mourner weep the less?
And thou—who tell'st me to forget—
Thy looks are wan, thine eyes are wet.

MY SOUL IS DARK

I

MY SOUL is dark—Oh! quickly string
 The harp I yet can brook to hear;
And let thy gentle fingers fling
 Its melting murmurs o'er mine ear.
If in this heart a hope be dear,
 That sound shall charm it forth again:
If in these eyes there lurk a tear
 'Twill flow, and cease to burn my brain.

II

But bid the strain be wild and deep,
 Nor let thy notes of joy be first:
I tell thee, minstrel, I must weep,
 Or else this heavy heart will burst;
For it hath been by sorrow nursed,
 And ached in sleepless silence long;
And now 'tis doomed to know the worst,
 And break at once—or yield to song.

I SAW THEE WEEP

I

I SAW thee weep—the big bright tear
 Came o'er that eye of blue;
And then, methought, it did appear

A violet dropping dew:
I saw thee smile—the sapphire's blaze
  Beside thee ceased to shine;
It could not match the living rays
  That filled that glance of thine.

II

As clouds from yonder sun receive
  A deep and mellow dye,
Which scarce the shade of coming eve
  Can banish from the sky,
Those smiles unto the moodiest mind
  Their own pure joy impart;
Their sunshine leaves a glow behind
  That lightens o'er the heart.

THY DAYS ARE DONE

I

THY days are done, thy fame begun;
  Thy country's strains record
The triumphs of her chosen Son,
  The slaughters of his sword!
The deeds he did, the fields he won,
  The freedom he restored!

II

Though thou art fall'n, while we are free
  Thou shalt not taste of death!
The generous blood that flowed from thee
  Disdained to sink beneath:
Within our veins its currents be,
  Thy spirit on our breath!

III

Thy name, our charging hosts along,
  Shall be the battle-word!
Thy fall, the theme of choral song

From virgin voices poured!
To weep would do thy glory wrong:
Thou shalt not be deplored.

SONG OF SAUL BEFORE HIS LAST BATTLE

I

WARRIORS and Chiefs! should the shaft or the sword
Pierce me in leading the host of the Lord,
Heed not the corse, though a King's, in your path:
Bury your steel in the bosoms of Gath!

II

Thou who art bearing my buckler and bow,
Should the soldiers of Saul look away from the foe,
Stretch me that moment in blood at thy feet!
Mine be the doom which they dared not to meet.

III

Farewell to others, but never we part,
Heir to my Royalty—Son of my heart!
Bright is the diadem, boundless the sway,
Or kingly the death, which awaits us to-day!

Seaham, 1815.

SAUL

I

THOU whose spell can raise the dead,
Bid the Prophet's form appear:—
"Samuel, raise thy buried head!
King, behold the phantom Seer!"
Earth yawned; he stood the centre of a cloud:
Light changed its hue, retiring from his shroud.
Death stood all glassy in his fixéd eye;
His hand was withered, and his veins were dry;
His foot, in bony whiteness, glittered there,

Shrunken and sinewless, and ghastly bare;
From lips that moved not and unbreathing frame,
Like caverned winds, the hollow accents came.
Saul saw, and fell to earth, as falls the oak
At once, and blasted by the thunder-stroke.

II

"Why is my sleep disquieted?
Who is he that calls the dead?
Is it thou, O King? Behold,
Bloodless are these limbs, and cold:
Such are mine; and such shall be
Thine to-morrow, when with me:
Ere the coming day is done,
Such shalt thou be—such thy Son.
Fare thee well, but for a day,
Then we mix our mouldering clay.
Thou—thy race, lie pale and low,
Pierced by shafts of many a bow;
And the falchion by thy side
To thy heart thy hand shall guide:
Crownless—breathless—headless fall,
Son and Sire—the house of Saul!"

Seaham, February, 1815.

"ALL IS VANITY, SAITH THE PREACHER"

I

FAME, Wisdom, Love, and Power were mine,
    And Health and Youth possessed me;
My goblets blushed from every vine,
    And lovely forms caressed me;
I sunned my heart in Beauty's eyes,
    And felt my soul grow tender;
All Earth can give, or mortal prize,
    Was mine of regal splendour.

II

I strive to number o'er what days
  Remembrance can discover,
Which all that Life or Earth displays
  Would lure me to live over.
There rose no day, there rolled no hour
  Of pleasure unembittered;
And not a trapping decked my Power
  That galled not while it glittered.

III

The serpent of the field, by art
  And spells, is won from harming;
But that which coils around the heart,
  Oh! who hath power of charming?
It will not list to Wisdom's lore,
  Nor Music's voice can lure it;
But there it stings for evermore
  The soul that must endure it.
                    Seaham, 1815.

WHEN COLDNESS WRAPS THIS SUFFERING CLAY

I

When coldness wraps this suffering clay,
  Ah! whither strays the immortal mind?
It cannot die, it cannot stay,
  But leaves its darkened dust behind.
Then, unembodied, doth it trace
  By steps each planet's heavenly way?
Or fill at once the realms of space,
  A thing of eyes, that all survey?

II

Eternal—boundless,—undecayed,
  A thought unseen, but seeing all,
All, all in earth, or skies displayed,

Shall it survey, shall it recall:
Each fainter trace that Memory holds
  So darkly of departed years,
In one broad glance the Soul beholds,
  And all, that was, at once appears.

III

Before Creation peopled earth,
  Its eye shall roll through chaos back;
And where the farthest heaven had birth,
  The Spirit trace its rising track.
And where the future mars or makes,
  Its glance dilate o'er all to be,
While sun is quenched—or System breaks,
  Fixed in its own Eternity.

IV

Above or Love—Hope—Hate—or Fear,
  It lives all passionless and pure:
An age shall fleet like earthly year;
  Its years as moments shall endure.
Away—away—without a wing,
  O'er all—through all—its thought shall fly,
A nameless and eternal thing,
  Forgetting what it was to die.

                              Seaham, 1815.

VISION OF BELSHAZZAR

I

THE King was on his throne,
  The Satraps thronged the hall:
A thousand bright lamps shone
  O'er that high festival.
A thousand cups of gold,
  In Judah deemed divine—
Jehovah's vessels hold
  The godless Heathen's wine!

II

In that same hour and hall,
  The fingers of a hand
Came forth against the wall,
  And wrote as if on sand:
The fingers of a man;—
  A solitary hand
Along the letters ran,
  And traced them like a wand.

III

The monarch saw, and shook,
  And bade no more rejoice;
All bloodless waxed his look,
  And tremulous his voice.
"Let the men of lore appear,
  The wisest of the earth,
And expound the words of fear,
  Which mar our royal mirth."

IV

Chaldea's seers are good,
  But here they have no skill;
And the unknown letters stood
  Untold and awful still.
And Babel's men of age
  Are wise and deep in lore;
But now they were not sage,
  They saw—but knew no more.

V

A captive in the land,
  A stranger and a youth,
He heard the King's command,
  He saw that writing's truth.
The lamps around were bright,
  The prophecy in view;

He read it on that night,—
  The morrow proved it true.

VI

"Belshazzar's grave is made,
  His kingdom passed away,
He, in the balance weighed,
  Is light and worthless clay;
The shroud, his robe of state,
  His canopy the stone;
The Mede is at his gate!
  The Persian on his throne!"

SUN OF THE SLEEPLESS!

Sun of the sleepless! melancholy star!
Whose tearful beam glows tremulously far,
That show'st the darkness thou canst not dispel,
How like art thou to Joy remembered well!
So gleams the past, the light of other days,
Which shines, but warms not with its powerless rays:
A night-beam, Sorrow watcheth to behold,
Distinct, but distant—clear—but, oh how cold!

WERE MY BOSOM AS FALSE AS THOU
DEEM'ST IT TO BE

I

Were my bosom as false as thou deem'st it to be,
I need not have wandered from far Galilee;
It was but abjuring my creed to efface
The curse which, thou say'st, is the crime of my race.

II

If the bad never triumph, then God is with thee!
If the slave only sin—thou art spotless and free!

If the Exile on earth is an Outcast on high,
Live on in thy faith—but in mine I will die.

III

I have lost for that faith more than thou canst bestow
As the God who permits thee to prosper doth know;
In his hand is my heart and my hope—and in thine
The land and the life which for him I resign.

Seaham, 1815.

HEROD'S LAMENT FOR MARIAMNE

I

Oh, Mariamne! now for thee
    The heart for which thou bled'st is bleeding;
Revenge is lost in Agony
    And wild Remorse to rage succeeding.
Oh, Mariamne! where art thou?
    Thou canst not hear my bitter pleading:
Ah! could'st thou—thou would'st pardon now,
    Though Heaven were to my prayer unheeding.

II

And is she dead?—and did they dare
    Obey my Frenzy's jealous raving?
My Wrath but doomed my own despair:
    The sword that smote her 's o'er me waving—
But thou art cold, my murdered Love!
    And this dark heart is vainly craving
For her who soars alone above,
    And leaves my soul, unworthy saving.

III

She's gone, who shared my diadem;
    She sunk, with her my joys entombing;
I swept that flower from Judah's stem,
    Whose leaves for me alone were blooming;

And mine's the guilt, and mine the hell,
  This bosom's desolation dooming;
And I have earned those tortures well,
  Which unconsumed are still consuming!
                    January 15, 1815.

ON THE DAY OF THE DESTRUCTION
OF JERUSALEM BY TITUS

I

FROM the last hill that looks on thy once holy dome,
I beheld thee, oh Sion! when rendered to Rome:
'Twas thy last sun went down, and the flames of thy fall
Flashed back on the last glance I gave to thy wall.

II

I looked for thy temple—I looked for my home,
And forgot for a moment my bondage to come;
I beheld but the death-fire that fed on thy fane,
And the fast-fettered hands that made vengeance in vain.

III

On many an eve, the high spot whence I gazed
Had reflected the last beam of day as it blazed;
While I stood on the height, and beheld the decline
Of the rays from the mountain that shone on thy shrine.

IV

And now on that mountain I stood on that day,
But I marked not the twilight beam melting away;
Oh! would that the lightning had glared in its stead,
And the thunderbolt burst on the Conqueror's head!

V

But the Gods of the Pagan shall never profane
The shrine where Jehovah disdained not to reign;

And scattered and scorned as thy people may be,
Our worship, oh Father! is only for thee.

                                        1815.

BY THE RIVERS OF BABYLON
WE SAT DOWN AND WEPT

I

WE SATE down and wept by the waters
    Of Babel, and thought of the day
When our foe, in the hue of his slaughters,
    Made Salem's high places his prey;
And Ye, oh her desolate daughters!
    Were scattered all weeping away.

II

While sadly we gazed on the river
    Which rolled on in freedom below,
They demanded the song; but, oh never
    That triumph the Stranger shall know!
May this right hand be withered for ever,
    Ere it string our high harp for the foe!

III

On the willow that harp is suspended,
    Oh Salem! its sound should be free;
And the hour when thy glories were ended
    But left me that token of thee:
And ne'er shall its soft tones be blended
    With the voice of the Spoiler by me!

                            January 15, 1813.

THE DESTRUCTION OF SENNACHERIB

1

THE Assyrian came down like the wolf on the fold,
And his cohorts were gleaming in purple and gold;

And the sheen of their spears was like stars on the sea,
When the blue wave rolls nightly on deep Galilee.

II

Like the leaves of the forest when Summer is green,
That host with their banners at sunset were seen:
Like the leaves of the forest when Autumn hath blown,
That host on the morrow lay withered and strown.

III

For the angel of Death spread his wings on the blast,
And breathed in the face of the foe as he passed;
And the eyes of the sleepers waxed deadly and chill,
And their hearts but once heaved—and for ever grew still!

IV

And there lay the steed with his nostril all wide,
But through it there rolled not the breath of his pride;
And the foam of his gasping lay white on the turf,
And cold as the spray of the rock-beating surf.

V

And there lay the rider distorted and pale,
With the dew on his brow, and the rust on his mail:
And the tents were all silent—the banners alone—
The lances unlifted—the trumpet unblown.

VI

And the widows of Ashur are loud in their wail,
And the idols are broke in the temple of Baal;
And the might of the Gentile, unsmote by the sword,
Hath melted like snow in the glance of the Lord!

                        Seaham, February 17, 1815.

A SPIRIT PASSED BEFORE ME

FROM JOB

I

A Spirit passed before me: I beheld
The face of Immortality unveiled—
Deep Sleep came down on every eye save mine—
And there it stood,—all formless—but divine:
Along my bones the creeping flesh did quake;
And as my damp hair stiffened, thus it spake:

II

"Is man more just than God? Is man more pure
Than he who deems even Seraphs insecure?
Creatures of clay—vain dwellers in the dust!
The moth survives you, and are ye more just?
Things of a day! you wither ere the night,
Heedless and blind to Wisdom's wasted light!"

"BY THE WATERS OF BABYLON"

I

In the valley of waters we wept on the day
When the host of the Stranger made Salem his prey;
And our heads on our bosoms all droopingly lay,
And our hearts were so full of the land far away!

II

The song they demanded in vain—it lay still
In our souls as the wind that hath died on the hill—
They called for the harp—but our blood they shall spill
Ere our right hands shall teach them one tone of their skill.

III

All stringlessly hung in the willow's sad tree,
As dead as her dead-leaf, those mute harps must be:
Our hands may be fettered—our tears still are free
For our God—and our Glory—and Sion, Oh *Thee!*

1815.

[*First publ., 1829.*]

DOMESTIC PIECES

FARE THEE WELL

[Lady Byron left her husband on January 16, 1816, assigning
no reason, and the real causes of the separation are still unknown.
These verses were written March 18 without the intention of
publication, but Byron was foolish enough to have fifty copies
printed for private circulation on April 7. Of course copies got out
and on April 21 it was published by Leigh Hunt in the *Examiner*
and brought a good deal of execration on Byron's head.]

> "Alas! they had been friends in youth;
> But whispering tongues can poison truth:
> And Constancy lives in realms above;
> And Life is thorny; and youth is vain:
> And to be wroth with one we love,
> Doth work like madness in the brain;
>
>   .   .   .   .   .   .
>
> But never either found another
> To free the hollow heart from paining—
> They stood aloof, the scars remaining,
> Like cliffs which had been rent asunder;
> A dreary sea now flows between,
> But neither heat, nor frost, nor thunder,
> Shall wholly do away, I ween,
> The marks of that which once hath been."
>   —COLERIDGE's *Christabel.*

FARE thee well! and if for ever,
  Still for ever, fare *thee well:*

Even though unforgiving, never
  'Gainst thee shall my heart rebel.
Would that breast were bared before thee
  Where thy head so oft hath lain,
While that placid sleep came o'er thee
  Which thou ne'er canst know again:
Would that breast, by thee glanced over,
  Every inmost thought could show!   **10**
Then thou would'st at last discover
  'Twas not well to spurn it so.
Though the world for this commend thee—
  Though it smile upon the blow,
Even its praises must offend thee,
  Founded on another's woe:
Though my many faults defaced me,
  Could no other arm be found,
Than the one which once embraced me,
  To inflict a cureless wound?   **20**
Yet, oh yet, thyself deceive not—
  Love may sink by slow decay,
But by sudden wrench, believe not
  Hearts can thus be torn away:
Still thine own its life retaineth—
  Still must mine, though bleeding, beat;
And the undying thought which paineth
  Is—that we no more may meet.
These are words of deeper sorrow
  Than the wail above the dead;   **30**
Both shall live—but every morrow
  Wake us from a widowed bed.
And when thou would'st solace gather—
  When our child's first accents flow—
Wilt thou teach her to say "Father!"
  Though his care she must forego?
When her little hands shall press thee—
  When her lip to thine is pressed—
Think of him whose prayer shall bless thee—·
  Think of him thy love *had* blessed!   **40**
Should her lineaments resemble
  Those thou never more may'st see,
Then thy heart will softly tremble
  With a pulse yet true to me.
All my faults perchance thou knowest—

All my madness—none can know;
All my hopes—where'er thou goest—
  Wither—yet with *thee* they go.
Every feeling hath been shaken;
  Pride—which not a world could bow— 50
Bows to thee—by thee forsaken,
  Even my soul forsakes me now.
But 'tis done—all words are idle—
  Words from me are vainer still;
But the thoughts we cannot bridle
  Force their way without the will.
Fare thee well! thus disunited—
  Torn from every nearer tie—
Seared in heart—and lone—and blighted—
  More than this I scarce can die. 6C

A SKETCH

"Honest—honest Iago!
  If that thou be'st a devil, I cannot kill thee."
                    —SHAKESPEARE.

[Written with bitterness in the belief that Lady Byron's maid,
Mrs. Clermont, was largely responsible for the separation.]

BORN in the garret, in the kitchen bred,
Promoted thence to deck her mistress' head;
Next—for some gracious service unexpressed,
And from its wages only to be guessed—
Raised from the toilet to the table,—where
Her wondering betters wait behind her chair.
With eye unmoved, and forehead unabashed,
She dines from off the plate she lately washed.
Quick with the tale, and ready with the lie,
The genial confidante and general spy— 10
Who could, ye gods! her next employment guess—
An only infant's earliest governess!
She taught the child to read, and taught so well,
That she herself, by teaching, learned to spell.
An adept next in penmanship she grows,
As many a nameless slander deftly shows:
What she had made the pupil of her art,

None know—but that high Soul secured the heart,
And panted for the truth it could not hear,
With longing breast and undeluded ear.   20
Foiled was perversion by that youthful mind,
Which Flattery fooled not, Baseness could not blind,
Deceit infect not, near Contagion soil,
Indulgence weaken, nor Example spoil,
Nor mastered Science tempt her to look down
On humbler talents with a pitying frown,
Nor Genius swell, nor Beauty render vain,
Nor Envy ruffle to retaliate pain,
Nor Fortune change, Pride raise, nor Passion bow,
Nor Virtue teach austerity—till now.   30
Serenely purest of her sex that live,
But wanting one sweet weakness—to forgive;
Too shocked at faults her soul can never know,
She deems that all could be like her below:
Foe to all vice, yet hardly Virtue's friend—
For Virtue pardons those she would amend.

But to the theme, now laid aside too long,
The baleful burthen of this honest song,
Though all her former functions are no more,
She rules the circle which she served before.   40
If mothers—none know why—before her quake;
If daughters dread her for the mother's sake;
If early habits—those false links, which bind
At times the loftiest to the meanest mind—
Have given her power too deeply to instil
The angry essence of her deadly will;
If like a snake she steal within your walls,
Till the black slime betray her as she crawls;
If like a viper to the heart she wind,
And leave the venom there she did not find;   50
What marvel that this hag of hatred works
Eternal evil latent as she lurks,
To make a Pandemonium where she dwells,
And reign the Hecate of domestic hells?
Skilled by a touch to deepen Scandal's tints
With all the kind mendacity of hints,
While mingling truth with falsehood—sneers with smiles—
A thread of candour with a web of wiles;
A plain blunt show of briefly-spoken seeming,

To hide her bloodless heart's soul-hardened scheming;   60
A lip of lies; a face formed to conceal,
And, without feeling, mock at all who feel:
With a vile mask the Gorgon would disown,—
A cheek of parchment, and an eye of stone.
Mark, how the channels of her yellow blood
Ooze to her skin, and stagnate there to mud,
Cased like the centipede in saffron mail,
Or darker greenness of the scorpion's scale—
(For drawn from reptiles only may we trace
Congenial colours in that soul or face)—   70
Look on her features! and behold her mind
As in a mirror of itself defined:
Look on the picture! deem it not o'ercharged—
There is no trait which might not be enlarged:
Yet true to "Nature's journeymen," who made
This monster when their mistress left off trade—
This female dog-star of her little sky,
Where all beneath her influence droop or die.

Oh! wretch without a tear—without a thought,
Save joy above the ruin thou hast wrought—   80
The time shall come, nor long remote, when thou
Shalt feel far more than thou inflictest now;
Feel for thy vile self-loving self in vain,
And turn thee howling in unpitied pain.
May the strong curse of crushed affections light
Back on thy bosom with reflected blight!
And make thee in thy leprosy of mind
As loathsome to thyself as to mankind!
Till all thy self-thoughts curdle into hate,
Black—as thy will for others would create: 90
Till thy hard heart be calcined into dust,
And thy soul welter in its hideous crust.
Oh, may thy grave be sleepless as the bed,
The widowed couch of fire, that thou hast spread!
Then, when thou fain wouldst weary Heaven with prayer,
Look on thine earthly victims—and despair!
Down to the dust!—and, as thou rott'st away,
Even worms shall perish on thy poisonous clay.
But for the love I bore, and still must bear,
To her thy malice from all ties would tear—   100
Thy name—thy human name—to every eye

The climax of all scorn should hang on high,
Exalted o'er thy less abhorred compeers—
And festering in the infamy of years.

March 29, 1816.

STANZAS TO AUGUSTA

[This and the two following poems were addressed to Byron's
half sister Augusta Leigh.]

WHEN all around grew drear and dark,
   And Reason half withheld her ray—
And Hope but shed a dying spark
   Which more misled my lonely way;
In that deep midnight of the mind,
   And that internal strife of heart,
When dreading to be deemed too kind,
   The weak despair—the cold depart;
When Fortune changed—and Love fled far,
   And Hatred's shafts flew thick and fast,   10
Thou wert the solitary star
   Which rose and set not to the last.
Oh! blest be thine unbroken light!
   That watched me as a Seraph's eye,
And stood between me and the night,
   For ever shining sweetly nigh.
And when the cloud upon us came,
   Which strove to blacken o'er thy ray—
Then purer spread its gentle flame,
   And dashed the darkness all away.   20
Still may thy Spirit dwell on mine,
   And teach it what to brave or brook—
There's more in one soft word of thine
   Than in the world's defied rebuke.
Thou stood'st, as stands a lovely tree,
   That still unbroke, though gently bent,
Still waves with fond fidelity
   Its boughs above a monument.
The winds might rend—the skies might pour,
   But there thou wert—and still wouldst be   30
Devoted in the stormiest hour
   To shed thy weeping leaves o'er me.

But thou and thine shall know no blight,
 Whatever fate on me may fall;
For Heaven in sunshine will requite
 The kind—and thee the most of all.
Then let the ties of baffled love
 Be broken—thine will never break;
Thy heart can feel—but will not move;
 Thy soul, though soft, will never shake.   40
And these, when all was lost beside,
 Were found and still are fixed in thee;—
And bearing still a breast so tried,
 Earth is no desert—ev'n to me.

       [First publ., 1816.]

STANZAS TO AUGUSTA

I

THOUGH the day of my Destiny's over,
 And the star of my Fate hath declined,
Thy soft heart refused to discover
 The faults which so many could find;
Though thy Soul with my grief was acquainted,
 It shrunk not to share it with me,
And the Love which my Spirit hath painted
 It never hath found but in *Thee*.

II

Then when Nature around me is smiling,
 The last smile which answers to mine,
I do not believe it beguiling,
 Because it reminds me of thine;
And when winds are at war with the ocean,
 As the breasts I believed in with me,
If their billows excite an emotion,
 It is that they bear me from *Thee*.

III

Though the rock of my last Hope is shivered,
 And its fragments are sunk in the wave,

Though I feel that my soul is delivered
    To Pain—it shall not be its slave.
There is many a pang to pursue me:
    They may crush, but they shall not contemn—
They may torture, but shall not subdue me—
    'Tis of *Thee* that I think—not of them.

IV

Though human, thou didst not deceive me,
    Though woman, thou didst not forsake,
Though loved, thou forborest to grieve me,
    Though slandered, thou never couldst shake,—
Though trusted, thou didst not disclaim me,
    Though parted, it was not to fly,
Though watchful, 'twas not to defame me,
    Nor, mute, that the world might belie.

V

Yet I blame not the World, nor despise it,
    Nor the war of the many with one;
If my Soul was not fitted to prize it,
    'Twas folly not sooner to shun:
And if dearly that error hath cost me,
    And more than I once could foresee,
I have found that, whatever it lost me,
    It could not deprive me of *Thee*.

VI

From the wreck of the past, which hath perished,
    Thus much I at least may recall,
It hath taught me that what I most cherished
    Deserved to be dearest of all:
In the Desert a fountain is springing,
    In the wide waste there still is a tree,
And a bird in the solitude singing,
    Which speaks to my spirit of *Thee*.
                   July 24, 1816.
                 [*First publ., 1816.*]

EPISTLE TO AUGUSTA

I

My Sister! my sweet Sister! if a name
Dearer and purer were, it should be thine.
Mountains and seas divide us, but I claim
No tears, but tenderness to answer mine:
Go where I will, to me thou art the same—
A loved regret which I would not resign.
There yet are two things in my destiny,—
A world to roam through, and a home with thee.

II

The first were nothing—had I still the last,
It were the haven of my happiness;
But other claims and other ties thou hast,
And mine is not the wish to make them less.
A strange doom is thy father's son's, and past
Recalling, as it lies beyond redress;
Reversed for him our grandsire's fate of yore,—
He had no rest at sea, nor I on shore.

III

If my inheritance of storms hath been
In other elements, and on the rocks
Of perils, overlooked or unforeseen,
I have sustained my share of worldly shocks,
The fault was mine; nor do I seek to screen
My errors with defensive paradox;
I have been cunning in mine overthrow,
The careful pilot of my proper woe.

IV

Mine were my faults, and mine be their reward.
My whole life was a contest, since the day
That gave me being, gave me that which marred
The gift,—a fate, or will, that walked astray;

And I at times have found the struggle hard,
And thought of shaking off my bonds of clay:
But now I fain would for a time survive,
If but to see what next can well arrive.

V

Kingdoms and Empires in my little day
I have outlived, and yet I am not old;
And when I look on this, the petty spray
Of my own years of trouble, which have rolled
Like a wild bay of breakers, melts away:
Something—I know not what—does still uphold
A spirit of slight patience;—not in vain,
Even for its own sake, do we purchase Pain.

VI

Perhaps the workings of defiance stir
Within me—or, perhaps, a cold despair
Brought on when ills habitually recur,—
Perhaps a kinder clime, or purer air,
(For even to this may change of soul refer,
And with light armour we may learn to bear,)
Have taught me a strange quiet, which was not
The chief companion of a calmer lot.

VII

I feel almost at times as I have felt
In happy childhood; trees, and flowers, and brooks,
Which do remember me of where I dwelt,
Ere my young mind was sacrificed to books,
Come as of yore upon me, and can melt
My heart with recognition of their looks;
And even at moments I could think I see
Some living thing to love—but none like thee.

VIII

Here are the Alpine landscapes which create
A fund for contemplation;—to admire
Is a brief feeling of a trivial date;

But something worthier do such scenes inspire:
Here to be lonely is not desolate,
For much I view which I could most desire,
And, above all, a Lake I can behold
Lovelier, not dearer, than our own of old.

IX

Oh that thou wert but with me!—but I grow
The fool of my own wishes, and forget
The solitude which I have vaunted so
Has lost its praise in this but one regret;
There may be others which I less may show;—
I am not of the plaintive mood, and yet
I feel an ebb in my philosophy,
And the tide rising in my altered eye.

X

I did remind thee of our own dear Lake,
By the old Hall which may be mine no more.
Leman's is fair; but think not I forsake
The sweet remembrance of a dearer shore:
Sad havoc Time must with my memory make,
Ere that or thou can fade these eyes before;
Though, like all things which I have loved, they are
Resigned for ever, or divided far.

XI

The world is all before me; I but ask
Of Nature that with which she will comply—
It is but in her Summer's sun to bask,
To mingle with the quiet of her sky,
To see her gentle face without a mask,
And never gaze on it with apathy.
She was my early friend, and now shall be
My sister—till I look again on thee.

XII

I can reduce all feelings but this one,—
And that I would not;—for at length I see

Such scenes as those wherein my life begun—
The earliest—even the only paths for me—
Had I but sooner learnt the crowd to shun,
I had been better than I now can be;
The Passions which have torn me would have slept—
I had not suffered, and *thou* hadst not wept.

XIII

With false Ambition what had I to do?
Little with Love, and least of all with Fame;
And yet they came unsought, and with me grew,
And made me all which they can make—a Name.
Yet this was not the end I did pursue;
Surely I once beheld a nobler aim.
But all is over—I am one the more
To baffled millions which have gone before.

XIV

And for the future, this world's future may
From me demand but little of my care:
I have outlived myself by many a day,
Having survived so many things that were;
My years have been no slumber, but the prey
Of ceaseless vigils; for I had the share
Of life which might have filled a century,
Before its fourth in time had passed me by.

XV

And for the remnant which may be to come
I am content; and for the past I feel
Not thankless,—for within the crowded sum
Of struggles, Happiness at times would steal,
And, for the present, I would not benumb
My feelings farther.—Nor shall I conceal
That with all this I still can look around,
And worship Nature with a thought profound.

XVI

For thee, my own sweet sister, in thy heart
I know myself secure, as thou in mine;
We were and are—I am, even as thou art—
Beings who ne'er each other can resign;
It is the same, together or apart—
From Life's commencement to its slow decline
We are entwined—let Death come slow or fast,
The tie which bound the first endures the last!

[*First publ., 1830.*]

LINES ON HEARING THAT LADY BYRON WAS ILL

And thou wert sad—yet I was not with thee;
    And thou wert sick, and yet I was not near;
Methought that Joy and Health alone could be
    Where I was *not*—and pain and sorrow here!
And is it thus?—it is as I foretold,
    And shall be more so; for the mind recoils
Upon itself, and the wrecked heart lies cold,
    While Heaviness collects the shattered spoils.
It is not in the storm nor in the strife
    We feel benumbed, and wish to be no more,   10
    But in the after-silence on the shore,
When all is lost, except a little life.

I am too well avenged!—but 'twas my right;
    Whate'er my sins might be, *thou* wert not sent
To be the Nemesis who should requite—
    Nor did Heaven choose so near an instrument.
Mercy is for the merciful!—if thou
Hast been of such, 'twill be accorded now.
Thy nights are banished from the realms of sleep:—
    Yes! they may flatter thee, but thou shalt feel   20
    A hollow agony which will not heal,
For thou art pillowed on a curse too deep;
Thou hast sown in my sorrow, and must reap
    The bitter harvest in a woe as real!
I have had many foes, but none like thee;

For 'gainst the rest myself I could defend,
  And be avenged, or turn them into friend;
But thou in safe implacability
Hadst nought to dread—in thy own weakness shielded,
And in my love, which hath but too much yielded,   30
  And spared, for thy sake, some I should not spare;
And thus upon the world—trust in thy truth,
And the wild fame of my ungoverned youth—
  On things that were not, and on things that are—
Even upon such a basis hast thou built
A monument, whose cement hath been guilt,
  The moral Clytemnestra of thy lord!
  And hewed down, with an unsuspected sword,
Fame, peace, and hope—and all the better life
  Which, but for this cold treason of thy heart,   40
Might still have risen from out the grave of strife,
  And found a nobler duty than to part.
But of thy virtues didst thou make a vice,
  Trafficking with them in a purpose cold,
  For present anger, and for future gold—
And buying others' grief at any price.
And thus once entered into crooked ways,
The early truth, which was thy proper praise,
Did not still walk beside thee—but at times,
And with a breast unknowing its own crimes,   50
Deceit, averments incompatible,
Equivocations, and the thoughts which dwell
  In Janus-spirits—the significant eye
Which learns to lie with silence—the pretext
Of prudence, with advantages annexed—
The acquiescence in all things which tend,
No matter how, to the desired end—
  All found a place in thy philosophy.
The means were worthy, and the end is won—   60
I would not do by thee as thou hast done!

September, 1816.
[First publ., August, 1832.]

THE DREAM

I

OUR life is twofold: Sleep hath its own world,
A boundary between the things misnamed
Death and existence: Sleep hath its own world,
And a wide realm of wild reality,
And dreams in their development have breath,
And tears, and tortures, and the touch of Joy;
They leave a weight upon our waking thoughts,
They take a weight from off our waking toils,
They do divide our being; they become
A portion of ourselves as of our time,   10
And look like heralds of Eternity;
They pass like spirits of the past,—they speak
Like Sibyls of the future; they have power—
The tyranny of pleasure and of pain;
They make us what we were not—what they will,
And shake us with the vision that's gone by,
The dread of vanished shadows—Are they so?
Is not the past all shadow—What are they?
Creations of the mind?—The mind can make
Substance, and people planets of its own   20
With beings brighter than have been, and give
A breath to forms which can outlive all flesh.
I would recall a vision which I dreamed
Perchance in sleep—for, in itself, a thought,
A slumbering thought, is capable of years,
And curdles a long life into one hour.

II

I saw two beings in the hues of youth
Standing upon a hill, a gentle hill,
Green and of mild declivity, the last
As 'twere the cape of a long ridge of such,   30
Save that there was no sea to lave its base,
But a most living landscape, and the wave

Of woods and cornfields, and the abodes of men
Scattered at intervals, and wreathing smoke
Arising from such rustic roofs;—the hill
Was crowned with a peculiar diadem
Of trees, in circular array, so fixed,
Not by the sport of nature, but of man:
These two, a maiden and a youth, were there   40
Gazing—the one on all that was beneath
Fair as herself—but the Boy gazed on her;
And both were young, and one was beautiful:
And both were young—yet not alike in youth.
As the sweet moon on the horizon's verge,
The Maid was on the eve of Womanhood;
The Boy had fewer summers, but his heart
Had far outgrown his years, and to his eye
There was but one belovéd face on earth,
And that was shining on him: he had looked
Upon it till it could not pass away;   50
He had no breath, no being, but in hers;
She was his voice; he did not speak to her,
But trembled on her words; she was his sight,
For his eye followed hers, and saw with hers,
Which coloured all his objects:—he had ceased
To live within himself; she was his life,
The ocean to the river of his thoughts,
Which terminated all: upon a tone,
A touch of hers, his blood would ebb and flow,
And his cheek change tempestuously—his heart   60
Unknowing of its cause of agony.
But she in these fond feelings had no share:
Her sighs were not for him; to her he was
Even as a brother—but no more; 'twas much,
For brotherless she was, save in the name
Her infant friendship had bestowed on him;
Herself the solitary scion left
Of a time-honoured race.—It was a name
Which pleased him, and yet pleased him not—and why?
Time taught him a deep answer—when she loved   70
Another: even *now* she loved another,
And on the summit of that hill she stood
Looking afar if yet her lover's steed
Kept pace with her expectancy, and flew.

III

A change came o'er the spirit of my dream.
There was an ancient mansion, and before
Its walls there was a steed caparisoned:
Within an antique Oratory stood
The Boy of whom I spake;—he was alone,
And pale, and pacing to and fro: anon   80
He sate him down, and seized a pen, and traced
Words which I could not guess of; then he leaned
His bowed head on his hands, and shook as 'twere
With a convulsion—then arose again,
And with his teeth and quivering hands did tear
What he had written, but he shed no tears.
And he did calm himself, and fix his brow
Into a kind of quiet: as he paused,
The Lady of his love re-entered there;
She was serene and smiling then, and yet   90
She knew she was by him beloved—she knew,
For quickly comes such knowledge, that his heart
Was darkened with her shadow, and she saw
That he was wretched, but she saw not all.
He rose, and with a cold and gentle grasp
He took her hand; a moment o'er his face
A tablet of unutterable thoughts
Was traced, and then it faded, as it came;
He dropped the hand he held, and with slow steps
Retired, but not as bidding her adieu,   100
For they did part with mutual smiles; he passed
From out the massy gate of that old Hall,
And mounting on his steed he went his way;
And ne'er repassed that hoary threshold more.

IV

A change came o'er the spirit of my dream.
The Boy was sprung to manhood: in the wilds
Of fiery climes he made himself a home,
And his Soul drank their sunbeams: he was girt
With strange and dusky aspects; he was not
Himself like what he had been; on the sea   110
And on the shore he was a wanderer;

There was a mass of many images
Crowded like waves upon me, but he was
A part of all; and in the last he lay
Reposing from the noontide sultriness,
Couched among fallen columns, in the shade
Of ruined walls that had survived the names
Of those who reared them; by his sleeping side
Stood camels grazing, and some goodly steeds
Were fastened near a fountain; and a man   120
Clad in a flowing garb did watch the while,
While many of his tribe slumbered around:
And they were canopied by the blue sky,
So cloudless, clear, and purely beautiful,
That God alone was to be seen in Heaven.

v

A change came o'er the spirit of my dream.
The Lady of his love was wed with One
Who did not love her better:—in her home,
A thousand leagues from his,—her native home,
She dwelt, begirt with growing Infancy,   130
Daughters and sons of Beauty,—but behold!
Upon her face there was the tint of grief,
The settled shadow of an inward strife,
And an unquiet drooping of the eye,
As if its lid were charged with unshed tears.
What could her grief be?—she had all she loved,
And he who had so loved her was not there
To trouble with bad hopes, or evil wish,
Or ill-repressed affliction, her pure thoughts.
What could her grief be?—she had loved him not, 140
Nor given him cause to deem himself beloved,
Nor could he be a part of that which preyed
Upon her mind—a spectre of the past.

VI

A change came o'er the spirit of my dream.
The Wanderer was returned.—I saw him stand
Before an Altar—with a gentle bride;
Her face was fair, but was not that which made
The Starlight of his Boyhood;—as he stood

Even at the altar, o'er his brow there came
The self-same aspect, and the quivering shock 150
That in the antique Oratory shook
His bosom in its solitude; and then—
As in that hour—a moment o'er his face
The tablet of unutterable thoughts
Was traced,—and then it faded as it came,
And he stood calm and quiet, and he spoke
The fitting vows, but heard not his own words,
And all things reeled around him; he could see
Not that which was, nor that which should have been—
But the old mansion, and the accustomed hall, 160
And the remembered chambers, and the place,
The day, the hour, the sunshine, and the shade,
All things pertaining to that place and hour,
And her who was his destiny, came back
And thrust themselves between him and the light:
What business had they there at such a time?

VII

A change came o'er the spirit of my dream.
The Lady of his love;—Oh! she was changed
As by the sickness of the soul; her mind
Had wandered from its dwelling, and her eyes 170
They had not their own lustre, but the look
Which is not of the earth; she was become
The Queen of a fantastic realm; her thoughts
Were combinations of disjointed things;
And forms, impalpable and unperceived
Of others' sight, familiar were to hers.
And this the world calls frenzy; but the wise
Have a far deeper madness—and the glance
Of melancholy is a fearful gift;
What is it but the telescope of truth? 180
Which strips the distance of its fantasies,
And brings life near in utter nakedness,
Making the cold reality too real!

VIII

A change came o'er the spirit of my dream.
The Wanderer was alone as heretofore,

The beings which surrounded him were gone,
Or were at war with him; he was a mark
For blight and desolation, compassed round
With Hatred and Contention; Pain was mixed
In all which was served up to him, until,   190
Like to the Pontic monarch of old days,
He fed on poisons, and they had no power,
But were a kind of nutriment; he lived
Through that which had been death to many men,
And made him friends of mountains: with the stars
And the quick Spirit of the Universe
He held his dialogues; and they did teach
To him the magic of their mysteries;
To him the book of Night was opened wide,
And voices from the deep abyss revealed   200
A marvel and a secret—Be it so.

IX

My dream was past; it had no further change.
It was of a strange order, that the doom
Of these two creatures should be thus traced out
Almost like a reality—the one
To end in madness—both in misery.

July, 1816.
[*First publ., 1816.*]

JEUX D'ESPRIT AND EPHEMERAL VERSES

EPITAPH ON JOHN ADAMS, OF SOUTHWELL,

A CARRIER, WHO DIED OF DRUNKENNESS

JOHN ADAMS lies here, of the parish of Southwell,
A *Carrier* who *carried* his can to his mouth well;
He carried so much and he carried so fast,
He could carry no more—so was carried at last;
For the liquor he drank being too much for one,
He could not *carry* off;—so he's now *carri-on.*

September, 1807.
[*First publ., 1830.*]

LINES TO MR. HODGSON

WRITTEN ON BOARD THE LISBON PACKET

[Included in a letter to the Rev. Francis Hodgson on the eve
of Byron's departure on his first pilgrimage to the Near East.]

1

HUZZA! Hodgson, we are going,
　　Our embargo's off at last;
Favourable breezes blowing
　　Bend the canvas o'er the mast.
From aloft the signal's streaming,
　　Hark! the farewell gun is fired;
Women screeching, tars blaspheming,
　　Tell us that our time's expired.
　　　　Here's a rascal
　　　　Come to task all,
　　Prying from the Custom-house,
　　　　Trunks unpacking,
　　　　Cases cracking—
　　Not a corner for a mouse
'Scapes unsearched amid the racket,
Ere we sail on board the Packet.

2

Now our boatmen quit their mooring,
　　And all hands must ply the oar;
Baggage from the quay is lowering,
　　We're impatient, push from shore.
"Have a care! that case holds liquor—
　　Stop the boat—I'm sick—oh Lord!"
"Sick, Ma'am, damme, you'll be sicker,
　　Ere you've been an hour on board."
　　　　Thus are screaming
　　　　Men and women,
　　Gemmen, ladies, servants, Jacks;
　　　　Here entangling,

All are wrangling,
Stuck together close as wax.—
Such the general noise and racket,
Ere we reach the Lisbon Packet.

3

Now we've reached her, lo! the Captain,
    Gallant Kidd, commands the crew;
Passengers their berths are clapt in,
    Some to grumble, some to spew.
"Hey day! call you that a cabin?
    Why 'tis hardly three feet square:
Not enough to stow Queen Mab in—
    Who the deuce can harbour there?"
        "Who, sir? plenty—
        Nobles twenty
    Did at once my vessel fill."—
        "Did they? Jesus,
        How you squeeze us!
    Would to God they did so still:
Then I'd 'scape the heat and racket
Of the good ship, Lisbon Packet."

4

Fletcher! Murray! Bob! where are you?
    Stretched along the deck like logs—
Bear a hand, you jolly tar, you!
    Here's a rope's end for the dogs.
Hobhouse muttering fearful curses,
    As the hatchway down he rolls,
Now his breakfast, now his verses,
    Vomits forth—and damns our souls
        "Here's a stanza
        On Braganza—
    Help!"—"A couplet?"—"No, a cup
        Of warm water—"
        "What's the matter?"
    "Zounds! my liver's coming up;
I shall not survive the racket
Of this brutal Lisbon Packet."

5

Now at length we're off for Turkey,
  Lord knows when we shall come back!
Breezes foul and tempests murky
  May unship us in a crack.
But, since Life at most a jest is,
  As philosophers allow,
Still to laugh by far the best is,
  Then laugh on—as I do now.
        Laugh at all things,
        Great and small things,
  Sick or well, at sea or shore;
        While we're quaffing,
        Let's have laughing—
Who the devil cares for more?—
Some good wine! and who would lack it,
Ev'n on board the Lisbon Packet?
        Falmouth Roads, June 30, 1809.
                    [*First publ., 1830.*]

FAREWELL PETITION TO J. C. H., ESQ^RE.

[John Cam Hobhouse accompanied Byron on his trip to the Eastern Mediterranean in 1809, but returned to England after they had visited Constantinople, while Byron remained another year in Greece.]

O THOU yclep'd by vulgar sons of Men
Cam Hobhouse! but by wags Byzantian Ben!
Twin sacred titles, which combined appear
To grace thy volume's front, and gild its rear,
Since now thou put'st thyself and work to Sea,
And leav'st all Greece to *Fletcher* and to me,
Oh, hear my single muse our sorrows tell,
One song for *self* and Fletcher quite as well—

First to the *Castle* of that man of woes
Dispatch the letter which *I must* enclose,   10
And when his lone Penelope shall say,
"*Why, where,* and *wherefore* doth my William stay?"

Spare not to move her pity, or her pride—
By all that Hero suffered, or defied;
The *chicken's toughness,* and the *lack* of *ale,*
The *stoney mountain* and the *miry vale,*
The *Garlick* steams, which *half* his meals enrich,
The *impending vermin,* and the threatened *Itch*—
That *ever breaking* Bed, beyond repair!
The hat too *old,* the coat too *cold* to wear,   20
The Hunger, *which repulsed from Sally's door*
Pursues her grumbling half from shore to shore,—
Be these the themes to greet his faithful Rib,
So may thy pen be smooth, thy tongue be glib!

This duty done, let me in turn demand
Some friendly office in my native land,
Yet let me ponder well, before I ask,
And set thee swearing at the tedious task.

First the Miscellany!—to Southwell town
Per coach for Mrs. *Pigot* frank it down,   30
So may'st thou prosper in the paths of Sale,
And Longman smirk and critics cease to rail.

All hail to Matthews! wash his reverend feet,
And in my name the man of Method Greet,—
Tell him, my Guide, Philosopher, and Friend,
Who cannot love me, and who will not mend,
Tell him, that not in vain I shall assay
To tread and trace our "old Horatian way,"
And be (with prose supply my dearth of rhymes)
What better men have been in better times.   40

Here let me cease, for why should I prolong
My notes, and vex a *Singer* with a *Song?*
Oh thou with pen perpetual in thy fist!
Dubbed for thy sins a stark Miscellanist,
So pleased the printer's orders to perform
For Messrs. *Longman, Hurst* and *Rees* and *Orme.*
Go—Get thee hence to Paternoster Row,
Thy patrons wave a duodecimo!
(Best form for *letters* from a distant land,
It fits the pocket, nor fatigues the hand.)   50
Then go, once more the joyous work commence

With stores of anecdote, and grains of sense;
Oh may Mammas relent, and Sires forgive!
And scribbling Sons grow dutiful and live!
                    Constantinople, June 7, 1810.
                        [*First publ., 1887.*]

TRANSLATION OF THE NURSE'S DOLE IN THE *MEDEA* OF EURIPIDES

[A parody translation of some lines of the *Medea* of Euripides,
included in a letter to Henry Drury, June 17, 1810.]

OH HOW I wish that an embargo
Had kept in port the good ship Argo!
Who, still unlaunched from Grecian docks,
Had never passed the Azure rocks;
But now I fear her trip will be a
Damned business for my Miss Medea, etc.
                        June, 1810.
                    [*First publ., 1830.*]

AN ODE TO THE FRAMERS OF THE FRAME BILL

[Byron's first speech in the House of Lords had been an eloquent attack upon the brutal "Frame Bill."]

1

OH WELL done Lord E——n! and better done R——r!
    Britannia must prosper with councils like yours;
Hawkesbury, Harrowby, help you to guide her,
    Whose remedy only must *kill* ere it cures:
Those villains, the Weavers, are all grown refractory,
    Asking some succour for Charity's sake—
So hang them in clusters round each Manufactory,
    That will at once put an end to *mistake.*

2

The rascals, perhaps, may betake them to robbing,
    The dogs to be sure have got nothing to eat—

So if we can hang them for breaking a bobbin,
　'T will save all the Government's money and meat:
Men are more easily made than machinery—
　Stockings fetch better prices than lives—
Gibbets on Sherwood will heighten the scenery,
　Shewing how Commerce, how Liberty thrives!

3

Justice is now in pursuit of the wretches,
　Grenadiers, Volunteers, Bow-street Police,
Twenty-two Regiments, a score of Jack Ketches,
　Three of the Quorum and two of the Peace;
Some Lords, to be sure, would have summoned the Judges
　To take their opinion, but that they ne'er shall,
For LIVERPOOL such a concession begrudges,
　So now they're condemned by *no Judges* at all.

4

Some folks for certain have thought it was shocking,
　When Famine appeals and when Poverty groans,
That Life should be valued at less than a stocking,
　And breaking of frames lead to breaking of bones.
If it should prove so, I trust, by this token,
　(And who will refuse to partake in the hope?)
That the frames of the fools may be first to be *broken,*
　Who, when asked for a *remedy,* sent down a *rope.*
　　　　　　　　　　[*First publ., March 2, 1812.*]

WINDSOR POETICS

LINES COMPOSED ON THE OCCASION OF HIS ROYAL HIGHNESS THE
PRINCE REGENT BEING SEEN STANDING BETWEEN THE COFFINS
OF HENRY VIII AND CHARLES I, IN THE ROYAL VAULT AT WINDSOR

FAMED for contemptuous breach of sacred ties,
By headless Charles see heartless Henry lies;
Between them stands another sceptred thing—
It moves, it reigns—in all but name, a king·

Charles to his people, Henry to his wife,
—In him the double tyrant starts to life:
Justice and Death have mixed their dust in vain,
Each royal Vampire wakes to life again.
Ah, what can tombs avail!—since these disgorge
The blood and dust of both—to mould a George.
[*First publ., 1819.*]

ON THE BUST OF HELEN BY CANOVA

["The *Helen* of Canova (a bust which is in the house of Madame the Countess d'Albrizzi, whom I know) is, without exception, to my mind, the most perfectly beautiful of human conceptions, and far beyond my ideas of human execution." Byron to John Murray, November 25, 1816.]

IN THIS belovèd marble view
    Above the works and thoughts of Man,
What Nature *could* but *would not* do,
    And Beauty and Canova *can!*
Beyond Imagination's power,
    Beyond the Bard's defeated art,
With Immortality her dower,
    Behold the *Helen* of the heart.
[*First publ., 1830.*]

SONG FOR THE LUDDITES

[In a letter to Thomas Moore, December 24, 1816. The reference is to the Luddite riots of 1811.]

1

As the Liberty lads o'er the sea
Bought their freedom, and cheaply, with blood,
        So we, boys, we
    Will *die* fighting, or *live* free,
And down with all kings but King Ludd!

2

When the web that we weave is complete,
And the shuttle exchanged for the sword,
   We will fling the winding sheet
   O'er the despot at our feet,
And dye it deep in the gore he has poured.

3

Though black as his heart its hue,
Since his veins are corrupted to mud,
   Yet this is the dew
   Which the tree shall renew
Of Liberty, planted by Ludd!
              December 24, 1816.
              [*First publ., 1830.*]

SO WE'LL GO NO MORE A-ROVING

[To Thomas Moore, February 28, 1817. Byron says that he
had been up late too many nights at the Carnival in Venice.]

1

So WE'LL go no more a-roving
   So late into the night,
Though the heart be still as loving,
   And the moon be still as bright.

2

For the sword outwears its sheath,
   And the soul wears out the breast,
And the heart must pause to breathe,
   And Love itself have rest.

3

Though the night was made for loving,
   And the day returns too soon,

Yet we'll go no more a-roving
By the light of the moon.
[*First publ., 1830.*]

VERSICLES

[To Thomas Moore, March 25, 1817. *The Missionary of the Andes* is by W. L. Bowles; *Ilderim,* by H. Gally Knight; *Margaret of Anjou* by Margaret Holford; *Waterloo and other Poems,* by Byron's friend, J. Wedderburn Webster; *Glenarvon, a Novel,* by Lady Caroline Lamb, who pictured Byron in the book, quoting one of his devastating letters to her after their *liaison* had broken up.]

I READ the "Christabel";
    Very well:
I read the "Missionary";
    Pretty—very:
I tried at "Ilderim";
    Ahem!
I read a sheet of "Marg'ret of *Anjou*";
    Can you?
I turned a page of Webster's "Waterloo";
    Pooh! pooh!
I looked at Wordsworth's milk-white "Rylstone Doe";
    Hillo!
I read "Glenarvon," too, by Caro Lamb;
    God damn!
[*First publ., 1830.*]

TO MR. MURRAY

[To John Murray, March 25, 1817. See note to previous poem.]

To HOOK the Reader, you, John Murray,
    Have published "Anjou's Margaret,"
Which won't be sold off in a hurry
    (At least, it has not been as yet);
And then, still further to bewilder him,

Without remorse, you set up "Ilderim";
  So mind you don't get into debt,—
Because—as how—if you should fail,
These books would be but baddish bail.
And mind you do *not* let escape
  These rhymes to *Morning Post* or Perry,
Which would be *very* treacherous—*very*,
And get me into such a scrape!
  For, firstly, I should have to sally,
  All in my little boat, against a *Galley*;
And, should I chance to slay the Assyrian wight,
Have next to combat with the female Knight:
And pricked to death expire upon her needle,
A sort of end which I should take indeed ill!
                              [*First publ.,* 1830.]

TO THOMAS MOORE

[To Thomas Moore, July 10, 1817.]

1

My BOAT is on the shore,
  And my bark is on the sea;
But, before I go, Tom Moore,
  Here's a double health to thee!

2

Here's a sigh to those who love me,
  And a smile to those who hate;
And, whatever sky's above me,
  Here's a heart for every fate.

3

Though the Ocean roar around me,
  Yet it still shall bear me on;
Though a desert should surround me,
  It hath springs that may be won.

4

Were 't the last drop in the well,
    As I gasped upon the brink,
Ere my fainting spirit fell,
    'Tis to thee that I would drink.

5

With that water, as this wine,
    The libation I would pour
Should be—peace with thine and mine,
    And a health to thee, Tom Moore.
            [*First publ., January 8, 1821.*]

EPISTLE FROM MR. MURRAY TO DR. POLIDORI

[To John Murray, August 21, 1817. Murray had asked Byron
to write him a "delicate declension" of the play sent him by the
touchy and vain Dr. John Polidori, who had been Byron's physician when he left England in April, 1816.]

DEAR Doctor, I have read your play,
Which is a good one in its way,—
Purges the eyes, and moves the bowels,
And drenches handkerchiefs like towels
With tears, that, in a flux of grief,
Afford hysterical relief
To shattered nerves and quickened pulses,
Which your catastrophe convulses.
    I like your moral and machinery;
Your plot, too, has such scope for Scenery!   10
Your dialogue is apt and smart;
The play's concoction full of art;
Your hero raves, your heroine cries,
All stab, and every body dies.
In short, your tragedy would be
The very thing to hear and see:
And for a piece of publication,
If I decline on this occasion,

It is not that I am not sensible
To merits in themselves ostensible,   20
But—and I grieve to speak it—plays
Are drugs—mere drugs, Sir—now-a-days.
I had a heavy loss by *Manuel*—
Too lucky if it prove not annual,—
And Sotheby, with his *Orestes,*
(Which, by the way, the old Bore's best is),
Has lain so very long on hand,
That I despair of all demand;
I've advertised, but see my books,
Or only watch my Shopman's looks;—   30
Still *Ivan, Ina,* and such lumber,
My back-shop glut, my shelves encumber.
    There's Byron, too, who once did better,
Has sent me, folded in a letter,
A sort of—it's no more a drama
Than *Darnley, Ivan,* or *Kehama;*
So altered since last year his pen is,
I think he's lost his wits at Venice.

    .   .   .   .   .   °
    .   .   .   .   .   .

In short, Sir, what with one and t'other,
I dare not venture on another.   40
I write in haste; excuse each blunder;
The Coaches through the street so thunder!
My room's so full—we've Gifford here
Reading MS., with Hookham Frere,
Pronouncing on the nouns and particles,
Of some of our forthcoming Articles.
    The *Quarterly*—Ah, Sir, if you
Had but the genius to review!—
A smart Critique upon St. Helena,
Or if you only would but tell in a   50
Short compass what——but to resume;
As I was saying, Sir, the Room—
The Room's so full of wits and bards,
Crabbes, Campbells, Crokers, Freres, and Wards
And others, neither bards nor wits:
My humble tenement admits
All persons in the dress of Gent.,

From Mr. Hammond to Dog Dent.
  A party dines with me to-day,
All clever men, who make their way: 60
Crabbe, Malcolm, Hamilton, and Chantrey,
Are all partakers of my pantry.
They're at this moment in discussion
On poor De Staël's late dissolution.
Her book, they say, was in advance—
Pray Heaven, she tell the truth of France!
'Tis said she certainly was married
To Rocca, and had twice miscarried,
No—not miscarried, I opine,—
But brought to bed at forty-nine.   70
Some say she died a Papist; some
Are of opinion that's a Hum;
I don't know that—the fellows Schlegel,
Are very likely to inveigle
A dying person in compunction
To try th' extremity of Unction.
But peace be with her! for a woman
Her talents surely were uncommon,
Her Publisher (and Public too)
The hour of her demise may rue—   80
For never more within his shop he—
Pray—was not she interred at Coppet?
Thus run our time and tongues away;—
But, to return, Sir, to your play:
Sorry, Sir, but I cannot deal,
Unless 'twere acted by O'Neill.
My hands are full—my head so busy,
I'm almost dead—and always dizzy;
And so, with endless truth and hurry,
Dear Doctor, I am yours,   90

             JOHN MURRAY.
             August 21, 1817.
       [First publ., 1830. Lines 67–82
         first publ., 1900.]

EPISTLE TO MR. MURRAY

[To John Murray, January 8, 1818. Byron was sending the
fourth canto of *Childe Harold* by his friend Hobhouse.]

1

My dear Mr. Murray,
You're in a damned hurry
    To set up this ultimate Canto;
But (if they don't rob us)
You'll see Mr. Hobhouse
    Will bring it safe in his portmanteau.

2

For the Journal you hint of,
As ready to print off,
    No doubt you do right to commend it;
But as yet I have writ off
The devil a bit of
    Our "Beppo":—when copied, I'll send it.

3

In the mean time you've "Galley"
Whose verses all tally,
    Perhaps you may say he's a Ninny,
But if you abashed are
because of *Alashtar*,
    He'll piddle another *Phrosine*.

4

Then you've Sotheby's Tour,—
No great things, to be sure,—
    You could hardly begin with a less work;
For the pompous rascallion,
Who don't speak Italian
    Nor French, must have scribbled by guesswork.

5

No doubt he's a rare man
Without knowing German
    Translating his way up Parnassus.
And now, still absurder.

He meditates Murder,
   As you'll see in the trash he calls *Tasso's*.

6

But you've others, his betters,
The real men of letters,
   Your Orators—Critics—and Wits—
And I'll bet that your Journal
(Pray is it diurnal?)
   Will pay with your luckiest hits.

7

You can make any loss up
With "Spence" and his gossip,
   A work which must surely succeed;
Then Queen Mary's Epistle-craft,
With the new "Fytte" of "Whistlecraft,"
   Must make people purchase and read.

8

Then you've General Gordon,
Who girded his sword on,
   To serve with a Muscovite Master,
And help him to polish
A nation so owlish,
   They thought shaving their beards a disaster.

9

For the man, *"poor and shrewd,"*
With whom you'd conclude
   A compact without more delay,
Perhaps some such pen is
Still extant in Venice;
   But please, Sir, to mention *your pay*.

10

Now tell me some news
Of your friends and the Muse,

Of the Bar, or the Gown, or the House,
From Canning, the tall wit,
To Wilmot, the small wit,
    Ward's creeping Companion and *Louse,*

11

Who's so damnably bit
With fashion and Wit,
    That he crawls on the surface like Vermin,
But an Insect in both,—
By his Intellect's growth,
    Of what size you may quickly determine.
                    Venice, January 8, 1818.
[*First publ., 1830. Stanzas 3, 5, 6, 10, 11,
    first publ., 1900.*]

[E NIHILO NIHIL;
OR
AN EPIGRAM BEWITCHED]

OF RHYMES I printed seven volumes—
The list concludes John Murray's columns:
Of these there have been few translations
For Gallic or Italian nations;
And one or two perhaps in German—
But in this last I can't determine.
But then I only sung of passions
That do not suit with modern fashions;
Of Incest and such like diversions
Permitted only to the Persians,   10
Or Greeks to bring upon their stages—
But that was in the earlier ages;
Besides my style is the romantic,
Which some call fine, and some call frantic;
While others are or would seem *as* sick
Of repetitions nicknamed Classic.
For my part all men must allow
Whatever I was, I'm classic now.
I saw and left my fault in time,
And chose a topic all sublime—   20

Wondrous as antient war or hero—
Then played and sung away like Nero,
Who sang of Rome, and I of Rizzo:
The subject has improved my wit so,
The first four lines the poet sees
Start forth in fourteen languages!
Though of seven volumes none before
Could ever reach the fame of four,
Henceforth I sacrifice all Glory
To the Rinaldo of my Story: 30
I've sung his health and appetite;
(The last word's not translated right—
He's turned it, God knows how, to vigour)
I'll sing them in a book that's bigger.
Oh! Muse prepare for thy Ascension!
And generous Rizzo! thou my pension.

February, 1818.
[First publ., 1903.]

BALLAD

TO THE TUNE OF "SALLY IN OUR ALLEY"

[This and the following poem were included in a letter to
John Murray, April 11, 1818. "Gally" is H. Gally Knight.]

1

OF ALL the twice ten thousand bards
    That ever penned a canto,
Whom pudding or whom Praise rewards
    For lining a portmanteau;
Of all the poets ever known,
    From Grub-street to Fop's Alley,
The Muse may boast—the World must own
    There's none like pretty Gally!

2

He writes as well as any Miss,
    Has published many a poem;
The shame is yours, the gain is his,

In case you should not know 'em.
He has ten thousand pounds a year—
I do not mean to vally—
His songs at sixpence would be dear,
   So give them gratis, Gally!

3

And if this statement should seem queer,
   Or set down in a hurry,
Go, ask (if he will be sincere)
   His bookseller—John Murray.
Come, say, how many have been sold,
   And don't stand shilly-shally,
Of bound and lettered, red and gold,
   Well printed works of Gally.

4

For Astley's circus Upton writes,
   And also for the Surrey; (*sic*)
Fitzgerald weekly still recites,
   Though grinning Critics worry:
Miss Holford's Peg, and Sotheby's Saul,
   In fame exactly tally;
From Stationer's Hall to Grocer's Stall
   They go—and so does Gally.

5

He rode upon a Camel's hump
   Through Araby the sandy,
Which surely must have hurt the rump
   Of this poetic dandy.
His rhymes are of the costive kind,
   And barren as each valley
In deserts which he left behind
   Has been the Muse of Gally.

6

He has a Seat in Parliament,
   Is fat and passing wealthy;

And surely he should be content
  With these and being healthy:
But Great Ambition will misrule
  Men at all risks to sally,—
Now makes a poet—now a fool,
  And *we* know *which*—of Gally.

7

Some in the playhouse like to row,
  Some with the Watch to battle,
Exchanging many a midnight blow
  To Music of the Rattle.
Some folks like rowing on the Thames,
  Some rowing in an Alley,
But all the Row my fancy claims
  Is *rowing* of my *Gally*.

[*First publ., 1903.*]

TO MR. MURRAY

1

STRAHAN, Tonson, Lintot of the times,
Patron and publisher of rhymes,
For thee the bard up Pindus climbs,
                    My Murray.

2

To thee, with hope and terror dumb,
The unfledged MS. authors come;
Thou printest all—and sellest some—
                    My Murray.

3

Upon thy table's baize so green
The last new Quarterly is seen,—
But where is thy new Magazine,
                    My Murray?

4

Along thy sprucest bookshelves shine
The works thou deemest most divine—
The Art of Cookery, and mine,
                    My Murray.

5

Tours, travels, Essays, too, I wist,
And Sermons, to thy mill bring grist;
And then thou hast the *Navy List*,
                    My Murray.

6

And Heaven forbid I should conclude,
Without "the Board of Longitude,"
Although this narrow paper would,
                    My Murray.
            Venice, April 11, 1818.
            [*First publ., 1830.*]

EPIGRAM

FROM THE FRENCH OF RULHIÈRES

[To John Murray, August 12, 1819. Byron says the stanzas
were written on some Frenchwoman. He gives a translation.]

If FOR silver, or for gold,
    You could melt ten thousand pimples
    Into half a dozen dimples,
Then your face we might behold,
    Looking, doubtless, much more snugly,
    Yet even *then* 'twould be damned ugly.
            [*First publ., 1830.*]

EPILOGUE

1

THERE's something in a stupid ass,
   And something in a heavy dunce;
But never since I went to school
   I heard or saw so damned a fool
As William Wordsworth is for once.

2

And now I've seen so great a fool
   As William Wordsworth is for once;
I really wish that Peter Bell
   And he who wrote it were in hell,
For writing nonsense for the nonce.

3

It saw the "light in ninety-eight,"
   Sweet babe of one and twenty years!
And then he gives it to the nation
   And deems himself of Shakespeare's peers!

4

He gives the perfect work to light!
   Will Wordsworth, if I might advise,
Content you with the praise you get
   From Sir George Beaumont, Baronet,
And with your place in the Excise!
                    1819.
         [First published, 1888.]

ON MY WEDDING-DAY

[To Thomas Moore, January 2, 1820, the anniversary of Byron's wedding.]

HERE's a happy New Year! but with reason
I beg you'll permit me to say—
Wish me *many* returns of the *Season*,
But as *few* as you please of the *Day*.
[*First publ., 1830.*]

MY BOY HOBBIE O

[This song, sent to John Murray, March 23, 1820, almost caused a breach in Byron's friendship with John Cam Hobhouse, who had been committed to Newgate Prison for several weeks for a parliamentary "breach of privilege."]

New Song to the tune of

"Whare hae ye been a' day,
My boy Tammy O?
Courting o' a young thing
Just come frae her Mammie O."

1

How came you in Hob's pound to cool,
My boy Hobbie O?
Because I bade the people pull
The House into the Lobby O.

2

What did the House upon this call,
My boy Hobbie O?
They voted me to Newgate all,
Which is an awkward Jobby O.

3

Who are now the people's men,
　　My boy Hobbie O?
There's I and Burdett—Gentlemen,
　　And blackguard Hunt and Cobby O.

4

You hate the house—*why* canvass, then?
　　My boy Hobbie O?
Because I would reform the den
　　As member for the Mobby O.

5

Wheretore do you hate the Whigs,
　　My boy Hobbie O?
Because they want to run their rigs,
　　As under Walpole Bobby O.

6

But when we at Cambridge were
　　My boy Hobbie O,
If my memory don't err
　　You founded a Whig Clubbie O.

7

When to the mob you make a speech,
　　My boy Hobbie O,
How do you keep without their reach
　　The watch within your fobby O?

8

But never mind such petty things,
　　My boy Hobbie O;
God save the people—damn all Kings,

So let us Crown the Mobby O!
Yours truly,
(Signed) *INFIDUS SCURRA.*
[*First publ., March, 1887.*]

LINES

ADDRESSED BY LORD BYRON TO MR. HOBHOUSE
ON HIS ELECTION FOR WESTMINSTER

[To John Murray, April 9, 1820. Byron's friend Hobhouse, after serving time in Newgate Prison for a breach of parliamentary privilege, was returned to the House of Commons from Westminster, having gained prestige by his fearless espousal of radical and popular causes.]

> Would you go to the house by the true gate,
>   Much faster than ever Whig Charley went;
> Let Parliament send you to Newgate,
>   And Newgate will send you to Parliament.
>   [*First publ., 1821.*]

A VOLUME OF NONSENSE

[To John Murray, September 28, 1820. Byron frequently ridiculed the popular writer William Sotheby, calling him "Botherby." "Gally" is H. Gally Knight, and the "feminine He-Man" is Felicia Hemans.]

> Dear Murray,—
>   You ask for a *"Volume of Nonsense,"*
> Have all of your authors exhausted their store?
> I thought you had published a good deal not long since,
>   And doubtless the Squadron are ready with more.
> But on looking again, I perceive that the Species
> Of "Nonsense" you want must be purely *"facetious";*
> And, as that is the case, you had best put to press
>   Mr. Sotheby's tragedies now in MS.,
>   Some Syrian Sally
>   From common-place Gally,

Or, if you prefer the bookmaking of women,
Take a spick and span "Sketch" of your feminine *He-Man.*
                                                    [*First publ., 1900.*]

STANZAS

[To Thomas Moore, November 5, 1820.]

WHEN a man hath no freedom to fight for at home,
    Let him combat for that of his neighbours;
Let him think of the glories of Greece and of Rome,
    And get knocked on the head for his labours.

To do good to Mankind is the chivalrous plan,
    And is always as nobly requited;
Then battle for Freedom wherever you can,
    And, if not shot or hanged, you'll get knighted.
                                                    [*First publ., 1830.*]

TO PENELOPE

JANUARY 2, 1821

[Byron was married January 2, 1815, and was separated from
his wife a little over a year later.]

        THIS day, of all our days, has done
            The worst for me and you:—
        'T is just *six* years since we were *one,*
            And *five* since we were *two.*
                            November 5, 1820.
                            [*First publ., 1824.*]

ON MY THIRTY-THIRD BIRTHDAY

JANUARY 22, 1821

        THROUGH Life's dull road, so dim and dirty,
        I have dragged to three-and-thirty.

What have these years left to me?
Nothing—except thirty-three.
[*First publ., 1830.*]

EPIGRAM

ON THE BRAZIERS' ADDRESS TO BE PRESENTED
IN *ARMOUR* BY THE COMPANY TO QUEEN CAROLINE

[To Thomas Moore, January 22, 1821.]

IT SEEMS that the Braziers propose soon to pass
An Address and to bear it themselves all in brass;
A superfluous pageant, for by the Lord Harry!
They'll *find,* where they're going, much *more* than they carry.

Or—

THE Braziers, it seems, are determined to pass
An Address, and present it themselves all in brass;
A superfluous $\begin{Bmatrix} \text{pageant} \\ \text{trouble} \end{Bmatrix}$ for, by the Lord Harry!
They'll find, where they're going, much more than they carry.
[*First publ., 1830.*]

EPIGRAM

[To Thomas Moore, June 22, 1821.]

THE world is a bundle of hay,
    Mankind are the asses who pull;
Each tugs it a different way,—
    And the greatest of all is John Bull!
[*First publ., 1830.*]

JOHN KEATS

[To John Murray, July 30, 1821.]

WHO killed John Keats?
    "I," says the Quarterly,

So savage and Tartarly;
" 'T was one of my feats."

Who shot the arrow?
"The poet-priest Milman"
(So ready to kill man)
"Or Southey, or Barrow."
[*First publ., 1830.*]

FROM THE FRENCH

[To Thomas Moore, August 2, 1821.]

ÆGLE, beauty and poet, has two little crimes;
She makes her own face, and does not make her rhymes.
[*First publ., 1823.*]

TO MR. MURRAY

[To John Murray, August 23, 1821. Byron thought the £ 2000 offered for *Sardanapalus, The Two Foscari,* and Cantos III, IV, and V of *Don Juan,* too little in comparison with what Murray had paid to other less popular authors. Murray had published *Memoirs of the last Nine Years of the Reign of George II* by Horace Walpole (Orford) and *Memoirs of James Earl of Waldegrave.*]

1

For Orford and for Waldegrave
You give much more than me you *gave;*
Which is not fairly to behave,
                    My Murray!

2

Because if a live dog, 't is said,
Be worth a lion fairly sped,
A *live lord* must be worth *two* dead,
                    My Murray!

3

And if, as the opinion goes,
Verse hath a better sale than prose,—
Certes, I should have more than those,
                                My Murray!

4

But now this sheet is nearly crammed,
So, if *you will*, *I* shan't be shammed,
And if you *won't*—*you* may be damned,
                                My Murray!
                        [*First publ., 1830.*]

[NAPOLEON'S SNUFF-BOX]

[According to Medwin, Lord Carlisle had written some verses
urging Lady Holland not to accept the snuff-box bequeathed her
by Napoleon, to which Byron wrote this reply.]

LADY, accept the box a hero wore,
    In spite of all this elegiac stuff:
Let not seven stanzas written by a bore,
    Prevent your Ladyship from taking snuff!
                                1821.
                        [*First published, 1824.*]

JOURNAL IN CEPHALONIA

THE dead have been awakened—shall I sleep?
    The World's at war with tyrants—shall I crouch?
The harvest's ripe—and shall I pause to reap?
    I slumber not; the thorn is in my Couch;
Each day a trumpet soundeth in mine ear,
    Its echo in my heart——
                                June 19, 1823.
                        [*First publ., 1901.*]

SONG TO THE SULIOTES

1

Up to battle! Sons of Suli
Up, and do your duty duly!
There the wall—and there the Moat is:
Bouwah! Bouwah! Suliotes!
There is booty—there is Beauty,
Up my boys and do your duty.

2

By the sally and the rally
Which defied the arms of Ali;
By your own dear native Highlands,
By your children in the islands,
Up and charge, my Stratiotes,
Bouwah!—Bouwah!—Suliotes!

3

As our ploughshare is the Sabre:
Here 's the harvest of our labour;
For behind those battered breaches
Are our foes with all their riches:
There is Glory—there is plunder—
Then away despite of thunder!

[*First publ.*, 1903.]

SATIRES

ENGLISH BARDS
AND
SCOTCH REVIEWERS

A Satire

> "I had rather be a kitten, and cry, mew!
> Than one of these same metre ballad-mongers."
> —SHAKESPEARE.

> "Such shameless Bards we have; and yet 'tis true,
> There are as mad, abandon'd Critics, too."
> —POPE.

[As early as October, 1807, Byron had been at work on a satire on contemporary writers in the general style of Pope. It was to be called *British Bards*. Then after Lord Brougham had written a severe criticism of Byron's *Hours of Idleness* in the *Edinburgh Review* of January, 1808, Byron revised the satire and published it anonymously in March, 1809. Believing Francis Jeffrey, the editor of the *Edinburgh Review,* to be the author of the offending article, he added many lines abusing him. The first edition had 696 lines. The second edition, enlarged to 1050 lines, was prepared for the press before he left England in June and published in the same year during his absence with his name on the title page. Two more editions were published in 1810, but before a fifth edition could appear Byron suppressed the poem, having in the meantime made friends with Lord Holland, Thomas Moore, and many others whom he had ridiculed in the satire, and having regretted almost from the first publication many of his snap judgments and unfair assessments of his contemporaries. To his chagrin, however, pirated editions continued to be published throughout his life.]

PREFACE

ALL my friends, learned and unlearned, have urged me not to publish this Satire with my name. If I were to be "turned from the career of my humour by quibbles quick, and paper bullets of the brain," I should have complied with their counsel. But I am not to be terrified by abuse, or bullied by reviewers, with or without arms. I can safely say that I have attacked none *personally*, who did not commence on the offensive. An Author's works are public property: he who purchases may judge, and publish his opinion if he pleases; and the Authors I have endeavoured to commemorate may do by me as I have done by them. I dare say they will succeed better in condemning my scribblings, than in mending their own. But my object is not to prove that I can write well, but, if *possible,* to make others write better.

As the Poem has met with far more success than I expected, I have endeavoured in this Edition to make some additions and alterations, to render it more worthy of public perusal.

In the First Edition of this Satire, published anonymously, fourteen lines on the subject of Bowles's Pope were written by, and inserted at the request of, an ingenious friend of mine, who has now in the press a volume of Poetry. In the present Edition they are erased, and some of my own substituted in their stead; my only reason for this being that which I conceive would operate with any other person in the same manner,—a determination not to publish with my name any production, which was not entirely and exclusively my own composition.

With regard to the real talents of many of the poetical persons whose performances are mentioned or alluded to in the following pages, it is presumed by the Author that there can be little difference of opinion in the Public at large; though, like other sectaries, each has his separate tabernacle of proselytes, by whom his abilities are over-rated, his faults overlooked, and his metrical canons received without scruple and without consideration. But the unquestionable possession of considerable genius by several of the writers here censured renders their mental prostitution more to be regretted. Imbecility may be pitied, or, at worst, laughed at and forgotten; perverted powers demand the most decided reprehension. No one can wish more than the Author that some known and able writer had undertaken their exposure, but Mr *Gifford* has devoted himself to Massinger, and, in the absence of the regular physician, a country practitioner may, in cases of absolute necessity, be allowed to prescribe his nostrum to prevent the extension of so deplorable an epidemic, provided there be no quackery in his treatment of the malady. A caustic is here offered; as it is to be feared nothing short of actual cautery can recover the numerous patients afflicted with the present prevalent and distressing *rabies* for rhyming.—As to the *Edinburgh Reviewers,* it would indeed require an Hercules to crush the Hydra; but if the Author succeeds in merely "bruising one of the heads of the serpent," though his own hand should suffer in the encounter, he will be amply satisfied.

STILL must I hear?—shall hoarse FITZGERALD bawl
His creaking couplets in a tavern hall,
And I not sing, lest, haply, Scotch Reviews
Should dub me scribbler, and denounce my *Muse?*
Prepare for rhyme—I'll publish, right or wrong:
Fools are my theme, let Satire be my song.

Oh! Nature's noblest gift—my grey goose-quill!
Slave of my thoughts, obedient to my will,
Torn from thy parent bird to form a pen,
That mighty instrument of little men!   10
The pen! foredoomed to aid the mental throes
Of brains that labour, big with Verse or Prose;
Though Nymphs forsake, and Critics may deride,
The Lover's solace, and the Author's pride.
What Wits! what Poets dost thou daily raise!
How frequent is thy use, how small thy praise!
Condemned at length to be forgotten quite,
With all the pages which 'twas thine to write.
But thou, at least, mine own especial pen!
Once laid aside, but now assumed again,   20
Our task complete, like Hamet's shall be free;
Though spurned by others, yet beloved by me:
Then let us soar to-day; no common theme,
No Eastern vision, no distempered dream
Inspires—our path, though full of thorns, is plain;
Smooth be the verse, and easy be the strain.

When Vice triumphant holds her sov'reign sway,
Obeyed by all who nought beside obey;
When Folly, frequent harbinger of crime,
Bedecks her cap with bells of every Clime;   30

When knaves and fools combined o'er all prevail,
And weigh their Justice in a Golden Scale;
E'en then the boldest start from public sneers,
Afraid of Shame, unknown to other fears,
More darkly sin, by Satire kept in awe,
And shrink from Ridicule, though not from Law.

Such is the force of Wit! but not belong
To me the arrows of satiric song;
The royal vices of our age demand
A keener weapon, and a mightier hand.   40
Still there are follies, e'en for me to chase,
And yield at least amusement in the race:
Laugh when I laugh, I seek no other fame,
The cry is up, and scribblers are my game:
Speed, Pegasus!—ye strains of great and small,
Ode! Epic! Elegy!—have at you all!
I, too, can scrawl, and once upon a time
I poured along the town a flood of rhyme,
A schoolboy freak, unworthy praise or blame;
I printed—older children do the same.   50
'Tis pleasant, sure, to see one's name in print;
A Book's a Book, altho' there's nothing in't.
Not that a Title's sounding charm can save
Or scrawl or scribbler from an equal grave:
This LAMB must own, since his patrician name
Failed to preserve the spurious Farce from shame.
No matter, GEORGE continues still to write,
Tho' now the name is veiled from public sight.
Moved by the great example, I pursue
The self-same road, but make my own review: 60
Not seek great JEFFREY's, yet like him will be
Self-constituted Judge of Poesy.

A man must serve his time to every trade
Save Censure—Critics all are ready made.
Take hackneyed jokes from MILLER, got by rote,
With just enough of learning to misquote;
A mind well skilled to find, or forge a fault;
A turn for punning—call it Attic salt;
To JEFFREY go, be silent and discreet,
His pay is just ten sterling pounds per sheet: 70
Fear not to lie, 'twill seem a *sharper* hit;

Shrink not from blasphemy, 'twill pass for wit;
Care not for feeling—pass your proper jest,
And stand a Critic, hated yet caressed.

And shall we own such judgment? no—as soon
Seek roses in December—ice in June;
Hope constancy in wind, or corn in chaff,
Believe a woman or an epitaph,
Or any other thing that's false, before
You trust in Critics, who themselves are sore;   80
Or yield one single thought to be misled
By JEFFREY's heart, or LAMB's Bœotian head.
To these young tyrants, by themselves misplaced,
Combined usurpers on the Throne of Taste;
To these, when Authors bend in humble awe,
And hail their voice as Truth, their word as Law;
While these are Censors, 'twould be sin to spare;
While such are Critics, why should I forbear?
But yet, so near all modern worthies run,
'Tis doubtful whom to seek, or whom to shun;   90
Nor know we when to spare, or where to strike,
Our Bards and Censors are so much alike.

Then should you ask me, why I venture o'er
The path which POPE and GIFFORD trod before;
If not yet sickened, you can still proceed;
Go on; my rhyme will tell you as you read.
"But hold!" exclaims a friend,—"here's some neglect:
This—that—and t'other line seem incorrect."
What then? the self-same blunder Pope has got,
And careless Dryden—"Aye, but Pye has not:"—   100
Indeed!—'tis granted, faith!—but what care I?
Better to err with POPE, than shine with PYE.

Time was, ere yet in these degenerate days
Ignoble themes obtained mistaken praise,
When Sense and Wit with Poesy allied,
No fabled Graces, flourished side by side;
From the same tount their inspiration drew,
And, reared by Taste, bloomed fairer as they grew.
Then, in this happy Isle, a POPE's pure strain
Sought the rapt soul to charm, nor sought in vain;   110
A polished nation's praise aspired to claim,

And raised the people's, as the poet's fame.
Like him great DRYDEN poured the tide of song,
In stream less smooth, indeed, yet doubly strong.
Then CONGREVE's scenes could cheer, or OTWAY's melt;
For Nature then an English audience felt—
But why these names, or greater still, retrace,
When all to feebler Bards resign their place?
Yet to such times our lingering looks are cast,
When taste and reason with those times are past.   120
Now look around, and turn each trifling page,
Survey the precious works that please the age;
This truth at least let Satire's self allow,
No dearth of Bards can be complained of now.
The loaded Press beneath her labour groans,
And Printers' devils shake their weary bones;
While SOUTHEY's Epics cram the creaking shelves,
And LITTLE's Lyrics shine in hot-pressed twelves.
Thus saith the *Preacher:* "Nought beneath the sun
Is new," yet still from change to change we run.   130
What varied wonders tempt us as they pass!
The Cow-pox, Tractors, Galvanism, and Gas,
In turns appear, to make the vulgar stare,
Till the swoln bubble bursts—and all is air!
Nor less new schools of Poetry arise,
Where dull pretenders grapple for the prize:
O'er Taste awhile these Pseudo-bards prevail;
Each country Book-club bows the knee to Baal,
And, hurling lawful Genius from the throne,
Erects a shrine and idol of its own;   140
Some leaden calf—but whom it matters not,
From soaring SOUTHEY, down to groveling STOTT.

Behold! in various throngs the scribbling crew,
For notice eager, pass in long review:
Each spurs his jaded Pegasus apace,
And Rhyme and Blank maintain an equal race;
Sonnets on sonnets crowd, and ode on ode;
And Tales of Terror jostle on the road;
Immeasurable measures move along;
For simpering Folly loves a varied song,   150
To strange, mysterious Dulness still the friend,
Admires the strain she cannot comprehend.

Thus Lays of Minstrels—may they be the last!—
On half-strung harps whine mournful to the blast,
While mountain spirits prate to river sprites,
That dames may listen to the sound at nights;
And goblin brats, of Gilpin Horner's brood
Decoy young Border-nobles through the wood,
And skip at every step, Lord knows how high,
And frighten foolish babes, the Lord knows why;   160
While high-born ladies in their magic cell,
Forbidding Knights to read who cannot spell,
Despatch a courier to a wizard's grave,
And fight with honest men to shield a knave.

Next view in state, proud prancing on his roan,
The golden-crested haughty Marmion,
Now forging scrolls, now foremost in the fight,
Not quite a Felon, yet but half a Knight,
The gibbet or the field prepared to grace—
A mighty mixture of the great and base.   170
And think'st thou, SCOTT! by vain conceit perchance,
On public taste to foist thy stale romance,
Though MURRAY with his MILLER may combine
To yield thy muse just half-a-crown per line?
No! when the sons of song descend to trade,
Their bays are sear, their former laurels fade,
Let such forego the poet's sacred name,
Who rack their brains for lucre, not for fame:
Still for stern Mammon may they toil in vain!
And sadly gaze on gold they cannot gain!   180
Such be their meed, such still the just reward
Of prostituted Muse and hireling bard!
For this we spurn Apollo's venal son,
And bid a long "good night to Marmion."

These are the themes that claim our plaudits now;
These are the Bards to whom the Muse must bow;
While MILTON, DRYDEN, POPE, alike forgot,
Resign their hallowed Bays to WALTER SCOTT.

The time has been, when yet the Muse was young,
When HOMER swept the lyre, and MARO sung,   190
An Epic scarce ten centuries could claim,

While awe-struck nations hailed the magic name:
The work of each immortal Bard appears
The single wonder of a thousand years.
Empires have mouldered from the face of earth,
Tongues have expired with those who gave them birth,
Without the glory such a strain can give,
As even in ruin bids the language live.
Not so with us, though minor Bards content,
On one great work a life of labour spent: 200
With eagle pinion soaring to the skies,
Behold the Ballad-monger SOUTHEY rise!
To him let CAMOËNS, MILTON, TASSO yield,
Whose annual strains, like armies, take the field.
First in the ranks see Joan of Arc advance,
The scourge of England and the boast of France!
Though burnt by wicked BEDFORD for a witch,
Behold her statue placed in Glory's niche;
Her fetters burst, and just released from prison,
A virgin Phœnix from her ashes risen.   210
Next see tremendous Thalaba come on,
Arabia's monstrous, wild, and wond'rous son;
Domdaniel's dread destroyer, who o'erthrew
More mad magicians than the world e'er knew.
Immortal Hero! all thy foes o'ercome,
For ever reign—the rival of Tom Thumb!
Since startled Metre fled before thy face,
Well wert thou doomed the last of all thy race!
Well might triumphant Genii bear thee hence,
Illustrious conqueror of common sense!   220
Now, last and greatest, Madoc spreads his sails,
Cacique in Mexico, and Prince in Wales;
Tells us strange tales, as other travellers do,
More old than Mandeville's, and not so true.
Oh, SOUTHEY! SOUTHEY! cease thy varied song!
A bard may chaunt too often and too long:
As thou art strong in verse, in mercy spare!
A fourth, alas! were more than we could bear.
But if, in spite of all the world can say,
Thou still wilt verseward plod thy weary way;   230
If still in Berkeley-Ballads most uncivil,
Thou wilt devote old women to the devil,
The babe unborn thy dread intent may rue:
"God help thee," SOUTHEY, and thy readers too.

Next comes the dull disciple of thy school,
That mild apostate from poetic rule,
The simple WORDSWORTH, framer of a lay
As soft as evening in his favourite May,
Who warns his friend "to shake off toil and trouble,
And quit his books, for fear of growing double"; 240
Who, both by precept and example, shows
That prose is verse, and verse is merely prose;
Convincing all, by demonstration plain,
Poetic souls delight in prose insane;
And Christmas stories tortured into rhyme
Contain the essence of the true sublime.
Thus, when he tells the tale of Betty Foy,
The idiot mother of "an idiot Boy";
A moon-struck, silly lad, who lost his way,
And, like his bard, confounded night with day; 250
So close on each pathetic part he dwells,
And each adventure so sublimely tells,
That all who view the "idiot in his glory"
Conceive the Bard the hero of the story.

Shall gentle COLERIDGE pass unnoticed here,
To turgid ode and tumid stanza dear?
Though themes of innocence amuse him best,
Yet still Obscurity's a welcome guest.
If Inspiration should her aid refuse
To him who takes a Pixy for a muse, 260
Yet none in lofty numbers can surpass
The bard who soars to elegize an ass:
So well the subject suits his noble mind,
He brays, the Laureate of the long-eared kind.

Oh! wonder-working LEWIS! Monk, or Bard,
Who fain would make Parnassus a churchyard!
Lo! wreaths of yew, not laurel, bind thy brow,
Thy Muse a Sprite, Apollo's sexton thou!
Whether on ancient tombs thou tak'st thy stand,
By gibb'ring spectres hailed, thy kindred band; 270
Or tracest chaste descriptions on thy page,
To please the females of our modest age;
All hail, M.P.! from whose infernal brain
Thin-sheeted phantoms glide, a grisly train;
At whose command "grim women" throng in crowds,

And kings of fire, of water, and of clouds,
With "small grey men,"—"wild yagers," and what not,
To crown with honour thee and WALTER SCOTT:
Again, all hail! if tales like thine may please,
St Luke alone can vanquish the disease: 280
Even Satan's self with thee might dread to dwell,
And in thy skull discern a deeper Hell.

Who in soft guise, surrounded by a choir
Of virgins melting, not to Vesta's fire,
With sparkling eyes, and cheek by passion flushed
Strikes his wild lyre, whilst listening dames are hushed?
'Tis LITTLE! young Catullus of his day,
As sweet, but as immoral, in his Lay!
Grieved to condemn, the Muse must still be just,
Nor spare melodious advocates of lust.   290
Pure is the flame which o'er her altar burns;
From grosser incense with disgust she turns:
Yet, kind to youth, this expiation o'er,
She bids thee, "mend thy line, and sin no more."

For thee, translator of the tinsel song,
To whom such glittering ornaments belong,
Hibernian STRANGFORD! with thine eyes of blue,
And boasted locks of red or auburn hue,
Whose plaintive strain each love-sick Miss admires,
And o'er harmonious fustian half expires,   300
Learn, if thou canst, to yield thine author's sense,
Nor vend thy sonnets on a false pretence.
Think'st thou to gain thy verse a higher place,
By dressing Camoëns in a suit of lace?
Mend, STRANGFORD! mend thy morals and thy taste;
Be warm, but pure; be amorous, but be chaste:
Cease to deceive; thy pilfered harp restore,
Nor teach the Lusian Bard to copy MOORE.

Behold—Ye Tarts!—one moment spare the text!—
HAYLEY's last work, and worst—until his next;   310
Whether he spin poor couplets into plays,
Or damn the dead with purgatorial praise,
His style in youth or age is still the same,
For ever feeble and for ever tame.
Triumphant first see "Temper's Triumphs" shine!

At least I'm sure they triumphed over mine.
Of "Music's Triumphs," all who read may swear
That luckless Music never triumphed there.

Moravians, rise! bestow some meet reward
On dull devotion—Lo! the Sabbath Bard,   320
Sepulchral GRAHAME, pours his notes sublime
In mangled prose, nor e'en aspires to rhyme;
Breaks into blank the Gospel of St Luke,
And boldly pilfers from the Pentateuch;
And, undisturbed by conscientious qualms,
Perverts the Prophets, and purloins the Psalms.

Hail, Sympathy! thy soft idea brings
A thousand visions of a thousand things,
And shows, still whimpering through three-score of years,
The maudlin prince of mournful sonneteers.   330
And art thou not their prince, harmonious BOWLES!
Thou first, great oracle of tender souls?
Whether thou sing'st with equal ease, and grief,
The fall of empires, or a yellow leaf;
Whether thy muse most lamentably tells
What merry sounds proceed from Oxford bells,
Or, still in bells delighting, finds a friend
In every chime that jingled from Ostend;
Ah! how much juster were thy Muse's hap,
If to thy bells thou would'st but add a cap!   340
Delightful BOWLES! still blessing and still blest,
All love thy strain, but children like it best.
'Tis thine, with gentle LITTLE's moral song,
To soothe the mania of the amorous throng!
With thee our nursery damsels shed their tears,
Ere Miss as yet completes her infant years:
But in her teens thy whining powers are vain;
She quits poor BOWLES for LITTLE's purer strain.
Now to soft themes thou scornest to confine
The lofty numbers of a harp like thine;   350
"Awake a louder and a loftier strain,"
Such as none heard before, or will again!
Where all discoveries jumbled from the flood.
Since first the leaky ark reposed in mud,
By more or less, are sung in every book,
From Captain Noah down to Captain Cook.

Nor this alone—but, pausing on the road,
The Bard sighs forth a gentle episode,
And gravely tells—attend, each beauteous Miss!—
When first Madeira trembled to a kiss.   360
BOWLES! in thy memory let this precept dwell,
Stick to thy Sonnets, Man!—at least they sell.
But if some new-born whim, or larger bribe,
Prompt thy crude brain, and claim thee for a scribe:
If 'chance some bard, though once by dunces feared,
Now, prone in dust, can only be revered;
If POPE, whose fame and genius, from the first,
Have foiled the best of critics, needs the worst,
Do thou essay: each fault, each failing scan;
The first of poets was, alas! but man.   370
Rake from each ancient dunghill ev'ry pearl,
Consult Lord Fanny, and confide in CURLL;
Let all the scandals of a former age
Perch on thy pen, and flutter o'er thy page;
Affect a candour which thou canst not feel,
Clothe envy in the garb of honest zeal;
Write, as if St John's soul could still inspire,
And do from hate what MALLET did for hire.
Oh! hadst thou lived in that congenial time,
To rave with DENNIS, and with RALPH to rhyme—   380
Thronged with the rest around his living head,
Not raised thy hoof against the lion dead,
A meet reward had crowned thy glorious gains,
And linked thee to the Dunciad for thy pains.

    Another Epic! Who inflicts again
More books of blank upon the sons of men?
Bœotian COTTLE, rich Bristowa's boast,
Imports old stories from the Cambrian coast,
And sends his goods to market—all alive!
Lines forty thousand, Cantos twenty-five!   390
Fresh fish from Hippocrene! who'll buy? who'll buy?
The precious bargain's cheap—in faith, not I.
Your turtle-feeder's verse must needs be flat,
Though Bristol bloat him with the verdant fat;
If Commerce fills the purse, she clogs the brain,
And AMOS COTTLE strikes the Lyre in vain.
In him an author's luckless lot behold!
Condemned to make the books which once he sold.

Oh, AMOS COTTLE!—Phœbus! what a name
To fill the speaking-trump of future fame!—   400
Oh, AMOS COTTLE! for a moment think
What meagre profits spring from pen and ink!
When thus devoted to poetic dreams,
Who will peruse thy prostituted reams?
Oh! pen perverted! paper misapplied!
Had COTTLE still adorned the counter's side,
Bent o'er the desk, or, born to useful toils,
Been taught to make the paper which he soils,
Ploughed, delved, or plied the oar with lusty limb,
He had not sung of Wales, nor I of him.   410

As Sisyphus against the infernal steep
Rolls the huge rock whose motions ne'er may sleep,
So up thy hill, ambrosial Richmond! heaves
Dull MAURICE all his granite weight of leaves:
Smooth, solid monuments of mental pain!
The petrifactions of a plodding brain,
That, ere they reach the top, fall lumbering back again.

With broken lyre and cheek serenely pale,
Lo! sad Alcæus wanders down the vale;
Though fair they rose, and might have bloomed at last,   420
His hopes have perished by the northern blast:
Nipped in the bud by Caledonian gales,
His blossoms wither as the blast prevails!
O'er his lost works let *classic* SHEFFIELD weep;
May no rude hand disturb their early sleep!

Yet say! why should the Bard, at once, resign
His claim to favour from the sacred Nine?
For ever startled by the mingled howl
Of Northern Wolves, that still in darkness prowl;
A coward Brood, which mangle as they prey,   430
By hellish instinct, all that cross their way:
Agéd or young, the living or the dead,
No mercy find—these harpies must be fed.
Why do the injured unresisting yield
The calm possession of their native field?
Why tamely thus before their fangs retreat,
Nor hunt the blood-hounds back to Arthur's Seat?

Health to immortal JEFFREY! once, in name,
England could boast a judge almost the same;
In soul so like, so merciful, yet just,   440
Some think that Satan has resigned his trust,
And given the Spirit to the world again,
To sentence Letters, as he sentenced men.
With hand less mighty, but with heart as black,
With voice as willing to decree the rack;
Bred in the Courts betimes, though all that law
As yet have taught him is to find a flaw,—
Since well instructed in the patriot school
To rail at party, though a party tool—
Who knows? if chance his patrons should restore   450
Back to the sway they forfeited before,
His scribbling toils some recompense may meet,
And raise this Daniel to the Judgment-Seat.
Let JEFFREY's shade indulge the pious hope,
And greeting thus, present him with a rope:
"Heir to my virtues! man of equal mind!
Skilled to condemn as to traduce mankind,
This cord receive! for thee reserved with care,
To wield in judgment, and at length to wear."

Health to great JEFFREY! Heaven preserve his life, 460
To flourish on the fertile shores of Fife,
And guard it sacred in its future wars,
Since authors sometimes seek the field of Mars!
Can none remember that eventful day,
That ever-glorious, almost fatal fray,
When LITTLE's leadless pistol met his eye,
And Bow-street Myrmidons stood laughing by?
Oh, day disastrous! on her firm-set rock,
Dunedin's castle felt a secret shock;
Dark rolled the sympathetic waves of Forth,   470
Low groaned the startled whirlwinds of the north;
TWEED ruffled half his waves to form a tear,
The other half pursued his calm career;
ARTHUR's steep summit nodded to its base,
The surly Tolbooth scarcely kept her place.
The Tolbooth felt—for marble sometimes can,
On such occasions, feel as much as man—
The Tolbooth felt defrauded of his charms,
If JEFFREY died, except within her arms:

Nay last, not least, on that portentous morn,   480
The sixteenth story, where himself was born,
His patrimonial garret, fell to ground,
And pale Edina shuddered at the sound:
Strewed were the streets around with milk-white reams,
Flowed all the Canongate with inky streams;
This of his candour seemed the sable dew,
That of his valour showed the bloodless hue;
And all with justice deemed the two combined
The mingled emblems of his mighty mind.
But Caledonia's goddess hovered o'er   490
The field, and saved him from the wrath of Moore;
From either pistol snatched the vengeful lead,
And straight restored it to her favourite's head;
That head, with greater than magnetic power,
Caught it, as Danäe caught the golden shower,
And, though the thickening dross will scarce refine,
Augments its ore, and is itself a mine.
"My son," she cried, "ne'er thirst for gore again,
Resign the pistol and resume the pen;
O'er politics and poesy preside,   500
Boast of thy country, and Britannia's guide!
For long as Albion's heedless sons submit,
Or Scottish taste decides on English wit,
So long shall last thine unmolested reign,
Nor any dare to take thy name in vain.
Behold, a chosen band shall aid thy plan,
And own thee chieftain of the critic clan.
First in the oat-fed phalanx shall be seen
The travelled Thane, Athenian Aberdeen.
Herbert shall wield Thor's hammer, and sometimes,   510
In gratitude, thou'lt praise his rugged rhymes.
Smug Sydney, too, thy bitter page shall seek,
And classic Hallam, much renowned for Greek;
Scott may perchance his name and influence lend
And paltry Pillans shall traduce his friend;
While gay Thalia's luckless votary, Lamb,
Damned like the Devil—Devil-like will damn.
Known be thy name! unbounded be thy sway!
Thy Holland's banquets shall each toil repay!
While grateful Britain yields the praise she owes   520
To Holland's hirelings and to Learning's foes.
Yet mark one caution ere thy next Review

Spread its light wings of Saffron and of Blue,
Beware lest blundering BROUGHAM destroy the sale,
Turn Beef to Bannocks, Cauliflowers to Kail."
Thus having said, the kilted Goddess kissed
Her son, and vanished in a Scottish mist.

Then prosper, JEFFREY! pertest of the train
Whom Scotland pampers with her fiery grain!
Whatever blessing waits a genuine Scot,   530
In double portion swells thy glorious lot;
For thee Edina culls her evening sweets,
And showers their odours on thy candid sheets,
Whose Hue and Fragrance to thy work adhere—
This scents its pages, and that gilds its rear.
Lo! blushing Itch, coy nymph, enamoured grown,
Forsakes the rest, and cleaves to thee alone,
And, too unjust to other Pictish men,
Enjoys thy person, and inspires thy pen!

Illustrious HOLLAND! hard would be his lot,   540
His hirelings mentioned, and himself forgot!
HOLLAND, with HENRY PETTY at his back,
The whipper-in and huntsman of the pack.
Blest be the banquets spread at Holland House,
Where Scotchmen feed, and Critics may carouse!
Long, long beneath that hospitable roof
Shall Grub-street dine, while duns are kept aloof.
See honest HALLAM lay aside his fork,
Resume his pen, review his Lordship's work,
And, grateful for the dainties on his plate,   550
Declare his landlord can at least translate!
Dunedin! view thy children with delight,
They write for food—and feed because they write:
And lest, when heated with the unusual grape,
Some glowing thoughts should to the press escape,
And tinge with red the female reader's cheek.
My lady skims the cream of each critique;
Breathes o'er the page her purity of soul,
Reforms each error, and refines the whole.

Now to the Drama turn—Oh! motley sight!   560
What precious scenes the wondering eyes invite:
Puns, and a Prince within a barrel pent,

And DIBDIN's nonsense yield complete content.
Though now, thank Heaven! the Rosciomania's o'er,
And full-grown actors are endured once more;
Yet what avail their vain attempts to please,
While British critics suffer scenes like these;
While REYNOLDS vents his "*dammes!*" "poohs!" and "zounds!"
And common-place and common sense confounds?
While KENNEY's "World"—ah! where is KENNEY's wit?—   570
ires the sad gallery, lulls the listless Pit;
nd BEAUMONT's pilfered Caratach affords
A tragedy complete in all but words?
Who but must mourn, while these are all the rage,
The degradation of our vaunted stage?
Heavens! is all sense of shame and talent gone?
Have we no living Bard of merit?—none?
Awake, GEORGE COLMAN! CUMBERLAND, awake!
Ring the alarum bell! let folly quake!
Oh! SHERIDAN! if aught can move thy pen,   580
Let Comedy assume her throne again;
Abjure the mummery of German schools;
Leave new Pizarros to translating fools;
Give, as thy last memorial to the age,
One classic drama, and reform the stage.
Gods! o'er those boards shall Folly rear her head,
Where GARRICK trod, and SIDDONS lives to tread?
On those shall Farce display Buffoonery's mask,
And HOOK conceal his heroes in a cask?
Shall sapient managers new scenes produce   590
From CHERRY, SKEFFINGTON, and Mother GOOSE?
While SHAKESPEARE, OTWAY, MASSINGER, forgot,
On stalls must moulder, or in closets rot?
Lo! with what pomp the daily prints proclaim
The rival candidates for Attic fame!
In grim array though LEWIS' spectres rise,
Still SKEFFINGTON and GOOSE divide the prize.
And, sure, *great* SKEFFINGTON must claim our praise,
For skirtless coats and skeletons of plays
Renowned alike; whose genius ne'er confines   600
Her flight to garnish Greenwood's gay designs;
Nor sleeps with "Sleeping Beauties," but anon
In five facetious acts comes thundering on;
While poor John Bull, bewildered with the scene,
Stares, wond'ring what the devil it can mean;

But as some hands applaud, a venal few!
Rather than sleep, why, John applauds it too.

Such are we now. Ah! wherefore should we turn
To what our fathers were, unless to mourn?
Degenerate Britons! are ye dead to shame,   610
Or, kind to dulness, do you fear to blame?
Well may the nobles of our present race
Watch each distortion of a NALDI's face;
Well may they smile on Italy's buffoons,
And worship CATALANI's pantaloons,
Since their own Drama yields no fairer trace
Of wit than puns, of humour than grimace.

Then let Ausonia, skilled in every art
To soften manners, but corrupt the heart,
Pour her exotic follies o'er the town,   620
To sanction Vice, and hunt Decorum down:
Let wedded strumpets languish o'er DESHAYES,
And bless the promise which his form displays;
While Gayton bounds before th' enraptured looks
Of hoary Marquises, and stripling Dukes:
Let high-born lechers eye the lively Presle
Twirl her light limbs, that spurn the needless veil;
Let Angiolini bare her breast of snow,
Wave the white arm, and point the pliant toe;
Collini trill her love-inspiring song,   630
Strain her fair neck, and charm the listening throng!
Whet not your scythe, Suppressors of our Vice!
Reforming Saints! too delicately nice!
By whose decrees, our sinful souls to save,
No Sunday tankards foam, no barbers shave;
And beer undrawn, and beards unmown, display
Your holy reverence for the Sabbath-day.

Or hail at once the patron and the pile
Of vice and folly, Greville and Argyle!
Where yon proud palace, Fashion's hallowed fane,   640
Spreads wide her portals for the motley train,
Behold the new Petronius of the day,
Our arbiter of pleasure and of play!
There the hired eunuch, the Hesperian choir,

The melting lute, the soft lascivious lyre,
The song from Italy, the step from France,
The midnight orgy, and the mazy dance,
The smile of beauty, and the flush of wine,
For fops, fools, gamesters, knaves, and Lords combine:
Each to his humour—Comus all allows;   650
Champagne, dice, music—or your neighbour's spouse.
Talk not to us, ye starving sons of trade!
Of piteous ruin, which ourselves have made;
In Plenty's sunshine Fortune's minions bask,
Nor think of Poverty, except "en masque,"
When for the night some lately titled ass
Appears the beggar which his grandsire was.
The curtain dropped, the gay Burletta o'er,
The audience take their turn upon the floor:
Now round the room the circling dow'gers sweep,   660
Now in loose waltz the thin-clad daughters leap;
The first in lengthened line majestic swim,
The last display the free unfettered limb!
Those for Hibernia's lusty sons repair
With art the charms which Nature could not spare;
These after husbands wing their eager flight,
Nor leave much mystery for the nuptial night.

Oh! blest retreats of infamy and ease,
Where, all forgotten but the power to please,
Each maid may give a loose to genial thought,   674
Each swain may teach new systems, or be taught:
There the blithe youngster, just returned from Spain,
Cuts the light pack, or calls the rattling main;
The jovial Caster's set, and seven's the Nick,
Or—done!—a thousand on the coming trick!
If, mad with loss, existence 'gins to tire,
And all your hope or wish is to expire,
Here's POWELL's pistol ready for your life,
And, kinder still, two PAGETS for your wife:
Fit consummation of an earthly race   680
Begun in folly, ended in disgrace,
While none but menials o'er the bed of death,
Wash thy red wounds, or watch thy wavering breath:
Traduced by liars, and forgot by all,
The mangled victim of a drunken brawl,
To live like CLODIUS, and like FALKLAND fall.

Truth! rouse some genuine Bard, and guide his hand
To drive this pestilence from out the land.
E'en I—least thinking of a thoughtless throng,
Just skilled to know the right and choose the wrong,   690
Freed at that age when Reason's shield is lost,
To fight my course through Passion's countless host,
Whom every path of Pleasure's flow'ry way
Has lured in turn, and all have led astray—
E'en I must raise my voice, e'en I must feel
Such scenes, such men, destroy the public weal:
Altho' some kind, censorious friend will say,
"What art thou better, meddling fool, than they?"
And every Brother Rake will smile to see
That miracle, a Moralist in me.   700
No matter—when some Bard in virtue strong,
GIFFORD perchance, shall raise the chastening song,
Then sleep my pen for ever! and my voice
Be only heard to hail him, and rejoice,
Rejoice, and yield my feeble praise, though I
May feel the lash that Virtue must apply.

As for the smaller fry, who swarm in shoals
From silly HAFIZ up to simple BOWLES,
Why should we call them from their dark abode,
In broad St Gile's or in Tottenham-Road?   710
Or (since some men of fashion nobly dare
To scrawl in verse) from Bond-street or the Square?
If things of Ton their harmless lays indite,
Most wisely doomed to shun the public sight,
What harm? in spite of every critic elf,
Sir T. may read his stanzas to himself;
MILES ANDREWS still his strength in couplets try,
And live in prologues, though his dramas die.
Lords too are Bards: such things at times befall,
And 'tis some praise in Peers to write at all.   720
Yet, did or Taste or Reason sway the times,
Ah! who would take their titles with their rhymes?
ROSCOMMON! SHEFFIELD! with your spirits fled,
No future laurels deck a noble head;
No Muse will cheer, with renovating smile,
The paralytic puling of CARLISLE.
The puny schoolboy and his early lay
Men pardon, if his follies pass away;

But who forgives the Senior's ceaseless verse,
Whose hairs grow hoary as his rhymes grow worse?   730
What heterogeneous honours deck the Peer!
Lord, rhymester, petit-maître, pamphleteer!
So dull in youth, so drivelling in his age,
His scenes alone had damned our sinking stage;
But Managers for once cried, "Hold, enough!"
Nor drugged their audience with the tragic stuff.
Yet at their judgment let his Lordship laugh,
And case his volumes in congenial calf;
Yes! doff that covering, where Morocco shines,
And hang a calf-skin on those recreant lines.   740

With you, ye Druids! rich in native lead,
Who daily scribble for your daily bread:
With you I war not: GIFFORD's heavy hand
Has crushed, without remorse, your numerous band.
On "All the Talents" vent your venal spleen;
Want is your plea, let Pity be your screen.
Let Monodies on Fox regale your crew,
And Melville's Mantle prove a Blanket too!
One common Lethe waits each hapless Bard,
And, peace be with you! 'tis your best reward.   750
Such damning fame as Dunciads only give
Could bid your lines beyond a morning live;
But now at once your fleeting labours close,
With names of greater note in blest repose.
Far be't from me unkindly to upbraid
The lovely ROSA's prose in masquerade,
Whose strains, the faithful echoes of her mind,
Leave wondering comprehension far behind.
Though Crusca's bards no more our journals fill,
Some stragglers skirmish round the columns still;   760
Last of the howling host which once was Bell's,
MATILDA snivels yet, and HAFIZ yells;
And MERRY's metaphors appear anew,
Chained to the signature of O. P. Q.

When some brisk youth, the tenant of a stall,
Employs a pen less pointed than his awl,
Leaves his snug shop, forsakes his store of shoes,
St Crispin quits, and cobbles for the Muse,
Heavens! how the vulgar stare! how crowds applaud!

How ladies read, and Literati laud!   770
If, 'chance, some wicked wag should pass his jest,
'Tis sheer ill-nature—don't the world know best?
Genius must guide when wits admire the rhyme,
And CAPEL LOFFT declares 'tis quite sublime.
Hear, then, ye happy sons of needless trade!
Swains! quit the plough, resign the useless spade!
Lo! BURNS and BLOOMFIELD, nay, a greater far,
GIFFORD was born beneath an adverse star,
Forsook the labours of a servile state,
Stemmed the rude storm, and triumphed over Fate: 780
Then why no more? if Phœbus smiled on you,
BLOOMFIELD! why not on brother Nathan too?
Him too the Mania, not the Muse, has seized;
Not inspiration, but a mind diseased:
And now no Boor can seek his last abode,
No common be inclosed without an ode.
Oh! since increased refinement deigns to smile
On Britain's sons, and bless our genial Isle,
Let Poesy go forth, pervade the whole,
Alike the rustic, and mechanic soul!   790
Ye tuneful cobblers! still your notes prolong,
Compose at once a slipper and a song;
So shall the fair your handywork peruse,
Your sonnets sure shall please—perhaps your shoes.
May Moorland weavers boast Pindaric skill,
And tailors' lays be longer than their bill!
While punctual beaux reward the grateful notes,
And pay for poems—when they pay for coats.

To the famed throng now paid the tribute due,
Neglected Genius! let me turn to you.   800
Come forth, oh CAMPBELL! give thy talents scope;
Who dares aspire if thou must cease to hope?
And thou, melodious ROGERS! rise at last,
Recall the pleasing memory of the past;
Arise! let blest remembrance still inspire,
And strike to wonted tones thy hallowed lyre;
Restore Apollo to his vacant throne,
Assert thy country's honour and thine own.
What! must deserted Poesy still weep
Where her last hopes with pious COWPER sleep?   810
Unless, perchance, from his cold bier she turns,

To deck the turf that wraps her minstrel, BURNS!
No! though Contempt hath marked the spurious brood,
The race who rhyme from folly, or for food,
Yet still some genuine sons 'tis hers to boast,
Who, least affecting, still affect the most:
Feel as they write, and write but as they feel—
Bear witness GIFFORD, SOTHEBY, MACNEIL.

"Why slumbers GIFFORD?" once was asked in vain;
Why slumbers GIFFORD? let us ask again.   820
Are there no follies for his pen to purge?
Are there no fools whose backs demand the scourge?
Are there no sins for Satire's Bard to greet?
Stalks not gigantic Vice in every street?
Shall Peers or Princes tread Pollution's path,
And 'scape alike the Law's, and Muse's wrath,
Nor blaze with guilty glare through future time,
Eternal beacons of consummate crime?
Arouse thee, GIFFORD! be thy promise claimed,
Make bad men better, or at least ashamed.   830

Unhappy WHITE! while life was in its spring,
And thy young Muse just waved her joyous wing,
The Spoiler swept that soaring Lyre away,
Which else had sounded an immortal lay.
Oh! what a noble heart was here undone,
When Science' self destroyed her favourite son!
Yes, she too much indulged thy fond pursuit,
She showed the seeds, but Death has reaped the fruit.
'Twas thine own Genius gave the final blow,
And helped to plant the wound that laid thee low: 840
So the struck Eagle, stretched upon the plain,
No more through rolling clouds to soar again,
Viewed his own feather on the fatal dart,
And winged the shaft that quivered in his heart;
Keen were his pangs, but keener far to feel
He nursed the pinion which impelled the steel;
While the same plumage that had warmed his nest
Drank the last life-drop of his bleeding breast.

There be who say, in these enlightened days,
That splendid lies are all the poet's praise;   850
That strained Invention, ever on the wing,

Alone impels the modern Bard to sing:
'Tis true, that all who rhyme—nay, all who write,
Shrink from that fatal word to Genius—Trite;
Yet Truth sometimes will lend her noblest fires,
And decorate the verse herself inspires:
This fact in Virtue's name let CRABBE attest:
Though Nature's sternest Painter, yet the best.

And here let SHEE and Genius find a place,
Whose pen and pencil yield an equal grace;   860
To guide whose hand the sister Arts combine,
And trace the Poet's or the Painter's line;
Whose magic touch can bid the canvas glow,
Or pour the easy rhyme's harmonious flow;
While honours, doubly merited, attend
The Poet's rival, but the Painter's friend.

Blest is the man who dares approach the bower
Where dwelt the Muses at their natal hour;
Whose steps have pressed, whose eye has marked afar,
The clime that nursed the sons of song and war,   870
The scenes which Glory still must hover o'er,
Her place of birth, her own Achaian shore.
But doubly blest is he whose heart expands
With hallowed feelings for those classic lands;
Who rends the veil of ages long gone by,
And views their remnants with a poet's eye!
WRIGHT! 'twas thy happy lot at once to view
Those shores of glory, and to sing them too;
And, sure, no common Muse inspired thy pen
To hail the land of Gods and Godlike men.   880

And you, associate Bards! who snatched to light
Those gems too long withheld from modern sight;
Whose mingling taste combined to cull the wreath
While Attic flowers Aonian odours breathe,
And all their renovated fragrance flung,
To grace the beauties of your native tongue;
Now let those minds, that nobly could transfuse
The glorious Spirit of the Grecian Muse,
Though soft the echo, scorn a borrowed tone:
Resign Achaia's lyre, and strike your own.   890

Let these, or such as these, with just applause,
Restore the Muse's violated laws;
But not in flimsy DARWIN'S pompous chime,
That mighty master of unmeaning rhyme,
Whose gilded cymbals, more adorned than clear,
The eye delighted, but fatigued the ear,
In show the simple lyre could once surpass,
But now, worn down, appear in native brass;
While all his train of hovering sylphs around
Evaporate his similes and sound: 900
Him let them shun, with him let tinsel die:
False glare attracts, but more offends the eye.

Yet let them not to vulgar WORDSWORTH stoop,
The meanest object of the lowly group,
Whose verse, of all but childish prattle void,
Seems blessed harmony to LAMB and LLOYD:
Let them—but hold, my Muse, nor dare to teach
A strain far, far beyond thy humble reach:
The native genius with their being given
Will point the path, and peal their notes to heaven.   910

And thou, too, SCOTT! resign to minstrels rude
The wilder Slogan of a Border feud:
Let others spin their meagre lines for hire;
Enough for Genius, if itself inspire!
Let SOUTHEY sing, altho' his teeming muse,
Prolific every spring, be too profuse;
Let simple WORDSWORTH chime his childish verse,
And brother COLERIDGE lull the babe at nurse;
Let Spectre-mongering LEWIS aim, at most,
To rouse the Galleries, or to raise a ghost;   920
Let MOORE still sigh; let STRANGFORD steal from MOORE,
And swear that CAMOËNS sang such notes of yore;
Let HAYLEY hobble on, MONTGOMERY rave,
And godly GRAHAME chant a stupid stave;
Let sonneteering BOWLES his strains refine,
And whine and whimper to the fourteenth line;
Let STOTT, CARLISLE, MATILDA, and the rest
Of Grub Street, and of Grosvenor Place the best,
Scrawl on, till Death release us from the strain,
Or Common Sense assert her rights again;   930

But Thou, with powers that mock the aid of praise,
Should'st leave to humbler Bards ignoble lays:
Thy country's voice, the voice of all the Nine,
Demand a hallowed harp—that harp is thine.
Say! will not Caledonia's annals yield
The glorious record of some nobler field,
Than the vile foray of a plundering clan,
Whose proudest deeds disgrace the name of man?
Or Marmion's acts of darkness, fitter food
For SHERWOOD's outlaw tales of ROBIN HOOD?   940
Scotland! still proudly claim thy native Bard,
And be thy praise his first, his best reward!
Yet not with thee alone his name should live,
But own the vast renown a world can give;
Be known, perchance, when Albion is no more,
And tell the tale of what she was before;
To future times her faded fame recall,
And save her glory, though his country fall.

Yet what avails the sanguine Poet's hope,
To conquer ages, and with time to cope?   950
New eras spread their wings, new nations rise,
And other Victors fill th' applauding skies;
A few brief generations fleet along,
Whose sons forget the Poet and his song:
E'en now, what once-loved Minstrels scarce may claim
The transient mention of a dubious name!
When Fame's loud trump hath blown its noblest blast,
Though long the sound, the echo sleeps at last;
And Glory, like the Phœnix midst her fires,
Exhales her odours, blazes, and expires.   960

Shall hoary Granta call her sable sons,
Expert in science, more expert at puns?
Shall these approach the Muse? ah, no! she flies,
Even from the tempting ore of Seaton's prize;
Though Printers condescend the press to soil
With rhyme by HOARE, and epic blank by HOYLE:—
Not him whose page, if still upheld by whist,
Requires no sacred theme to bid us list.
Ye! who in Granta's honours would surpass,
Must mount her Pegasus, a full-grown ass;   970

A foal well worthy of her ancient Dam,
Whose Helicon is duller than her Cam.

There CLARKE, still striving piteously "to please,"
Forgetting doggerel leads not to degrees,
A would-be Satirist, a hired Buffoon,
A monthly scribbler of some low lampoon,
Condemned to drudge, the meanest of the mean,
And furbish falsehoods for a magazine,
Devotes to scandal his congenial mind;
Himself a living libel on mankind.   980

Oh! dark asylum of a Vandal race!
At once the boast of learning, and disgrace!
So lost to Phœbus, that nor HODGSON's verse
Can make thee better, nor poor HEWSON's worse.
But where fair Isis rolls her purer wave,
The partial Muse delighted loves to lave;
On her green banks a greener wreath she wove,
To crown the Bards that haunt her classic grove;
Where RICHARDS wakes a genuine poet's fires,
And modern Britons glory in their Sires.   990

For me, who, thus unasked, have dared to tell
My country, what her sons should know too well,
Zeal for her honour bade me here engage
The host of idiots that infest her age;
No just applause her honoured name shall lose,
As first in freedom, dearest to the Muse.
Oh! would thy bards but emulate thy fame,
And rise more worthy, Albion, of thy name!
What Athens was in science, Rome in power,
What Tyre appeared in her meridian hour,   1000
'Tis thine at once, fair Albion! to have been—
Earth's chief Dictatress, Ocean's lovely Queen:
But Rome decayed, and Athens strewed the plain,
And Tyre's proud piers lie shattered in the main;
Like these, thy strength may sink in ruin hurled,
And Britain fall, the bulwark of the world.
But let me cease, and dread Cassandra's fate,
With warning ever scoffed at, till too late;
To themes less lofty still my lay confine,
And urge thy Bards to gain a name like thine.   1010

Then, hapless Britain! be thy rulers blest,
The Senate's oracles, the people's jest!
Still hear thy motley orators dispense
The flowers of rhetoric, though not of sense,
While CANNING's colleagues hate him for his wit,
And old dame PORTLAND fills the place of PITT.

Yet once again, adieu! ere this the sail
That wafts me hence is shivering in the gale;
And Afric's coast and Calpe's adverse height,
And Stamboul's minarets must greet my sight: 1020
Thence shall I stray through Beauty's native clime,
Where Kaff is clad in rocks, and crowned with snows sublime.
But should I back return, no tempting press
Shall drag my journal from the desk's recess;
Let coxcombs, printing as they come from far,
Snatch his own wreath of Ridicule from Carr;
Let ABERDEEN and ELGIN still pursue
The shade of fame through regions of Virtù;
Waste useless thousands on their Phidian freaks,
Misshapen monuments and maimed antiques;   1030
And make their grand saloons a general mart
For all the mutilated blocks of art:
Of Dardan tours let Dilettanti tell,
I leave topography to rapid GELL;
And, quite content, no more shall interpose
To stun the public ear—at least with Prose.

Thus far I've held my undisturbed career,
Prepared for rancour, steeled 'gainst selfish fear;
This thing of rhyme I ne'er disdained to own—
Though not obtrusive, yet not quite unknown: 1040
My voice was heard again, though not so loud,
My page, though nameless, never disavowed;
And now at once I tear the veil away:—
Cheer on the pack! the Quarry stands at bay,
Unscared by all the din of MELBOURNE house,
By LAMB's resentment, or by HOLLAND's spouse,
By JEFFREY's harmless pistol, HALLAM's rage,
Edina's brawny sons and brimstone page.
Our men in buckram shall have blows enough,
And feel they too are "penetrable stuff":   1050

And though I hope not hence unscathed to go,
Who conquers me shall find a stubborn foe.
The time hath been, when no harsh sound would fall
From lips that now may seem imbued with gall;
Nor fools nor follies tempt me to despise
The meanest thing that crawled beneath my eyes:
But now, so callous grown, so changed since youth,
I've learned to think, and sternly speak the truth;
Learned to deride the critic's starch decree,
And break him on the wheel he meant for me;   1060
To spurn the rod a scribbler bids me kiss,
Nor care if courts and crowds applaud or hiss:
Nay more, though all my rival rhymesters frown,
I too can hunt a Poetaster down;
And, armed in proof, the gauntlet cast at once
To Scotch marauder, and to Southern dunce.
Thus much I've dared; if my incondite lay
Hath wronged these righteous times, let others say:
This, let the world, which knows not how to spare,
Yet rarely blames unjustly, now declare.   1070

POSTCRIPT TO THE SECOND EDITION

I HAVE been informed, since the present edition went to the
press, that my trusty and well-beloved cousins, the Edinburgh
Reviewers, are preparing a most vehement critique on my poor,
gentle, *unresisting* Muse, whom they have already so be-deviled
with their ungodly ribaldry;

> "Tantæne animis cœlestibus Iræ!"

I suppose I must say of JEFFREY as Sir ANDREW AGUECHEEK saith,
"an I had known he was so cunning of fence, I had seen him
damned ere I had fought him." What a pity it is that I shall be
beyond the Bosphorus before the next number has passed the
Tweed! But I yet hope to light my pipe with it in Persia.

My Northern friends have accused me, with justice, of personality towards their great literary Anthropophagus, JEFFREY; but
what else was to be done with him and his dirty pack, who feed

by "lying and slandering," and slake their thirst by "evil speaking"? I have adduced facts already well known, and of JEFFREY's mind I have stated my free opinion, nor has he thence sustained any injury:—what scavenger was ever soiled by being pelted with mud? It may be said that I quit England because I have censured there "persons of honour and wit about town"; but I am coming back again, and their vengeance will keep hot till my return. Those who know me can testify that my motives for leaving England are very different from fears, literary or personal: those who do not, may one day be convinced. Since the publication of this thing, my name has not been concealed; I have been mostly in London, ready to answer for my transgressions, and in daily expectation of sundry cartels; but, alas! "the age of chivalry is over," or, in the vulgar tongue, there is no spirit now-a-days.

There is a youth ycleped Hewson Clarke (subaudi *esquire*), a sizer of Emmanuel College, and, I believe, a denizen of Berwick-upon-Tweed, whom I have introduced in these pages to much better company than he has been accustomed to meet; he is, notwithstanding, a very sad dog, and for no reason that I can discover, except a personal quarrel with a bear, kept by me at Cambridge to sit for a fellowship, and whom the jealousy of his Trinity contemporaries prevented from success, has been abusing me, and, what is worse, the defenceless innocent above mentioned, in the *Satirist* for one year and some months. I am utterly unconscious of having given him any provocation; indeed, I am guiltless of having heard his name, till coupled with the *Satirist*. He has therefore no reason to complain, and I dare say that, like Sir Fretful Plagiary, he is rather *pleased* than otherwise. I have now mentioned all who have done me the honour to notice me and mine, that is, my bear and my book, except the editor of the *Satirist,* who, it seems, is a gentleman—God wot! I wish he could impart a little of his gentility to his subordinate scribblers. I hear that Mr. JERNINGHAM is about to take up the cudgels for his Mæcenas, Lord Carlisle. I hope not: he was one of the few, who, in the very short intercourse I had with him, treated me with kindness when a boy; and whatever he may say or do, "pour on, I will endure." I have nothing further to add, save a general note of thanksgiving to readers, purchasers, and publishers, and in the words of *Scott,* I wish

"To all and each a fair good night,
And rosy dreams and slumbers light."

THE CURSE OF MINERVA

——"Pallas te hoc vulnere, Pallas
Immolat, et pœnam scelerato ex sanguine sumit."
—*Æneid*, lib. xii. ll. 948, 949.

ATHENS: CAPUCHIN CONVENT,
March 17, 1811.

SLOW sinks, more lovely ere his race be run,
Along Morea's hills the setting Sun;
Not, as in northern climes, obscurely bright,
But one unclouded blaze of living light;
O'er the hushed deep the yellow beam he throws,
Gilds the green wave that trembles as it glows;
On old Ægina's rock and Hydra's isle
The God of gladness sheds his parting smile;
O'er his own regions lingering loves to shine,
Though there his altars are no more divine.   10
Descending fast, the mountain-shadows kiss
Thy glorious Gulf, unconquered Salamis!
Their azure arches through the long expanse,
More deeply purpled, meet his mellowing glance,
And tenderest tints, along their summits driven,
Mark his gay course, and own the hues of Heaven;
Till, darkly shaded from the land and deep,
Behind his Delphian rock he sinks to sleep.

On such an eve his palest beam he cast
When, Athens! here thy Wisest looked his last.   20
How watched thy better sons his farewell ray,
That closed their murdered Sage's latest day!
Not yet—not yet—Sol pauses on the hill,
The precious hour of parting lingers still;
But sad his light to agonizing eyes,
And dark the mountain's once delightful dyes;
Gloom o'er the lovely land he seemed to pour,
The land where Phœbus never frowned before;
But ere he sunk below Cithæron's head,
The cup of Woe was quaffed—the Spirit fled;   30

The soul of Him that scorned to fear or fly,
Who lived and died as none can live or die.

But lo! from high Hymettus to the plain
The Queen of Night asserts her silent reign;
No murky vapour, herald of the storm,
Hides her fair face, or girds her glowing form;
With cornice glimmering as the moonbeams play,
There the white column greets her grateful ray,
And bright around, with quivering beams beset,
Her emblem sparkles o'er the Minaret: 40
The groves of olive scattered dark and wide,
Where meek Cephisus sheds his scanty tide,
The cypress saddening by the sacred mosque,
The gleaming turret of the gay kiosk,
And sad and sombre 'mid the holy calm,
Near Theseus' fane, yon solitary palm;
All, tinged with varied hues, arrest the eye;
And dull were his that passed them heedless by.

Again the Ægean, heard no more afar,
Lulls his chafed breast from elemental war: 5C
Again his waves in milder tints unfold
Their long expanse of sapphire and of gold,
Mixed with the shades of many a distant isle
That frown, where gentler Ocean deigns to smile.

As thus, within the walls of Pallas' fane,
I marked the beauties of the land and main,
Alone, and friendless, on the magic shore,
Whose arts and arms but live in poets' lore;
Oft as the matchless dome I turned to scan,
Sacred to Gods, but not secure from Man,   60
The Past returned, the Present seemed to cease,
And Glory knew no clime beyond her Greece!

Hour rolled along, and Dian's orb on high
Had gained the centre of her softest sky;
And yet unwearied still my footsteps trod
O'er the vain shrine of many a vanished God:
But chiefly, Pallas! thine, when Hecate's glare
Checked by thy columns, fell more sadly fair
O'er the chill marble, where the startling tread

Thrills the lone heart like echoes from the dead.   70
Long had I mused, and treasured every trace
The wreck of Greece recorded of her race,
When, lo! a giant-form before me strode,
And Pallas hailed me in her own Abode!

Yes, 'twas Minerva's self; but, ah! how changed,
Since o'er the Dardan field in arms she ranged!
Not such as erst, by her divine command,
Her form appeared from Phidias' plastic hand:
Gone were the terrors of her awful brow,
Her idle Ægis bore no Gorgon now;   80
Her helm was dinted, and the broken lance
Seemed weak and shaftless e'en to mortal glance;
The Olive Branch, which still she deigned to clasp,
Shrunk from her touch, and withered in her grasp;
And, ah! though still the brightest of the sky,
Celestial tears bedimmed her large blue eye;
Round the rent casque her owlet circled slow,
And mourned his mistress with a shriek of woe!

"Mortal!"—'twas thus she spake—"that blush of shame
Proclaims thee Briton, once a noble name;   90
First of the mighty, foremost of the free,
New honoured *less* by all, and *least* by me:
Chief of thy foes shall Pallas still be found.
Seek'st thou the cause of loathing?—look around.
Lo! here, despite of war and wasting fire,
I saw successive Tyrannies expire;
'Scaped from the ravage of the Turk and Goth,
Thy country sends a spoiler worse than both.
Survey this vacant, violated fane;
Recount the relics torn that yet remain: 100
These Cecrops placed, *this* Pericles adorned,
That Adrian reared when drooping Science mourned.
What more I owe let Gratitude attest—
Know, Alaric and Elgin did the rest.
That all may learn from whence the plunderer came,
The insulted wall sustains his hated name:
For Elgin's fame thus grateful Pallas pleads,
Below, his name—above, behold his deeds!
Be ever hailed with equal honour here
The Gothic monarch and the Pictish peer: 110

Arms gave the first his right, the last had none,
But basely stole what less barbarians won.
So when the Lion quits his fell repast,
Next prowls the Wolf, the filthy Jackal last:
Flesh, limbs, and blood the former make their own,
The last poor brute securely gnaws the bone.
Yet still the Gods are just, and crimes are crossed:
See here what Elgin won, and what he lost!
Another name with *his* pollutes my shrine:
Behold where Dian's beams disdain to shine!   120
Some retribution still might Pallas claim,
When Venus half avenged Minerva's shame."

She ceased awhile, and thus I dared reply,
To soothe the vengeance kindling in her eye:
"Daughter of Jove! in Britain's injured name,
A true-born Briton may the deed disclaim.
Frown not on England; England owns him not;
Athena, no! thy plunderer was a Scot.
Ask'st thou the difference? From fair Phyle's towers
Survey Bœotia;—Caledonia's ours.   130
And, well I know, within that bastard land
Hath Wisdom's goddess never held command;
A barren soil, where Nature's germs, confined
To stern sterility, can stint the mind;
Whose thistle well betrays the niggard earth,
Emblem of all to whom the Land gives birth;
Each genial influence nurtured to resist;
A land of meanness, sophistry, and mist.
Each breeze from foggy mount and marshy plain
Dilutes with drivel every drizzly brain,   140
Till, burst at length, each wat'ry head o'erflows,
Foul as their soil, and frigid as their snows:
Then thousand schemes of petulance and pride
Despatch her scheming children far and wide;
Some East, some West, some—everywhere but North!
In quest of lawless gain, they issue forth.
And thus—accurséd be the day and year!—
She sent a Pict to play the felon here.
Yet Caledonia claims some native worth,
As dull Bœotia gave a Pindar birth;   150
So may her few, the lettered and the brave,
Bound to no clime and victors of the grave.

Shake off the sordid dust of such a land,
And shine like children of a happier strand;
As once, of yore, in some obnoxious place,
Ten names (if found) had saved a wretched race."

"Mortal!" the blue-eyed maid resumed, "once more
Bear back my mandate to thy native shore.
Though fallen, alas! this vengeance yet is mine,
To turn my counsels far from lands like thine.   160
Hear then in silence Pallas' stern behest;
Hear and believe, for Time will tell the rest.

"First on the head of him who did this deed
My curse shall light,—on him and all his seed:
Without one spark of intellectual fire,
Be all the sons as senseless as the sire;
It one with wit the parent brood disgrace,
Believe him bastard of a brighter race:
Still with his hireling artists let him prate,
And Folly's praise repay for Wisdom's hate;   170
Long of their Patron's gusto let them tell,
Whose noblest, *native* gusto is—to sell:
To sell, and make—may Shame record the day!—
The State—receiver of his pilfered prey.
Meantime, the flattering, feeble dotard, West,
Europe's worst dauber, and poor Britain's best,
With palsied hand shall turn each model o'er,
And own himself an infant of fourscore.
Be all the Bruisers culled from all St Giles',
That Art and Nature may compare their styles;   180
While brawny brutes in stupid wonder stare,
And marvel at his Lordship's 'stone shop' there.
Round the thronged gate shall sauntering coxcombs creep
To lounge and lucubrate, to prate and peep;
While many a languid maid, with longing sigh,
On giant statues casts the curious eye;
The room with transient glance appears to skim,
Yet marks the mighty back and length of limb;
Mourns o'er the difference of *now* and *then;*
Exclaims, 'These Greeks indeed were proper men!'   190
Draws slight comparisons of *these* with *those,*
And envies Laïs all her Attic beaux.
When shall a modern maid have swains like these?

Alas! Sir Harry is no Hercules!
And last of all, amidst the gaping crew,
Some calm spectator, as he takes his view,
In silent indignation mixed with grief,
Admires the plunder, but abhors the thief.
Oh, loathed in life, nor pardoned in the dust,
May Hate pursue his sacrilegious lust!   200
Linked with the fool that fired the Ephesian dome,
Shall vengeance follow far beyond the tomb,
And Eratostratus and Elgin shine
In many a branding page and burning line;
Alike reserved for aye to stand accursed,
Perchance the second blacker than the first.

"So let him stand, through ages yet unborn,
Fixed statue on the pedestal of Scorn;
Though not for him alone revenge shall wait,
But fits thy country for her coming fate: 210
Hers were the deeds that taught her lawless son
To do what oft Britannia's self had done.
Look to the Baltic—blazing from afar,
Your old ally yet mourns perfidious war.
Not to such deeds did Pallas lend her aid,
Or break the compact which herself had made;
Far from such counsels, from the faithless field
She fled—but left behind her Gorgon shield,
A fatal gift that turned your friends to stone,
And left lost Albion hated and alone.   220

"Look to the East, where Ganges' swarthy race
Shall shake your tyrant empire to its base;
Lo! there Rebellion rears her ghastly head,
And glares the Nemesis of native dead;
Till Indus rolls a deep purpureal flood,
And claims his long arrear of northern blood.
So may ye perish!—Pallas, when she gave
Your free-born rights, forbade ye to enslave.

"Look on your Spain!—she clasps the hand she hates,
But boldly clasps, and thrusts you from her gates.   230
Bear witness, bright Barossa! thou canst tell
Whose were the sons that bravely fought and fell.

But Lusitania, kind and dear ally,
Can spare a few to fight, and sometimes fly.
Oh glorious field! by Famine fiercely won,
The Gaul retires for once, and all is done!
But when did Pallas teach, that one retreat
Retrieved three long Olympiads of defeat?

"Look last at home—ye love not to look there
On the grim smile of comfortless despair: 240
Your city saddens: loud though Revel howls,
Here Famine faints, and yonder Rapine prowls.
See all alike of more or less bereft;
No misers tremble when there's nothing left.
'Blest paper credit'—who shall dare to sing?
It clogs like lead Corruption's weary wing.
Yet Pallas plucked each Premier by the ear,
Who Gods and men alike disdained to hear;
But one, repentant o'er a bankrupt state,
On Pallas calls,—but calls, alas! too late: 250
Then raves for**; to that Mentor bends,
Though he and Pallas never yet were friends.
Him Senates hear, whom never yet they heard,
Contemptuous once, and now no less absurd.
So, once of yore, each reasonable frog,
Swore faith and fealty to his sovereign 'log.'
Thus hailed your rulers their patrician clod,
As Egypt chose an onion for a God.

"Now fare ye well! enjoy your little hour;
Go, grasp the shadow of your vanished power;   260
Gloss o'er the failure of each fondest scheme;
Your strength a name, your bloated wealth a dream.
Gone is that Gold, the marvel of mankind,
And Pirates barter all that's left behind.
No more the hirelings, purchased near and far,
Crowd to the ranks of mercenary war.
The idle merchant on the useless quay
Droops o'er the bales no bark may bear away;
Or, back returning, sees rejected stores
Rot piecemeal on his own encumbered shores: 270
The starved mechanic breaks his rusting loom,
And desperate mans him 'gainst the coming doom.

Then in the Senates of your sinking state
Show me the man whose counsels may have weight.
Vain is each voice where tones could once command;
E'en factions cease to charm a factious land:
Yet jarring sects convulse a sister Isle,
And light with maddening hands the mutual pile.

 " 'Tis done, 'tis past—since Pallas warns in vain;
The Furies seize her abdicated reign: 280
Wide o'er the realm they wave their kindling brands,
And wring her vitals with their fiery hands.
But one convulsive struggle still remains,
And Gaul shall weep ere Albion wear her chains,
The bannered pomp of war, the glittering files,
O'er whose gay trappings stern Bellona smiles;
The brazen trump, the spirit-stirring drum,
That bid the foe defiance ere they come;
The hero bounding at his country's call,
The glorious death that consecrates his fall,   290
Swell the young heart with visionary charms,
And bid it antedate the joys of arms.
But know, a lesson you may yet be taught,
With death alone are laurels cheaply bought;
Not in the conflict Havoc seeks delight,
His day of mercy is the day of fight.
But when the field is fought, the battle won,
Though drenched with gore, his woes are but begun:
His deeper deeds as yet ye know by name;
The slaughtered peasant and the ravished dame,   300
The rifled mansion and the foe-reaped field,
Ill suit with souls at home, untaught to yield.
Say with what eye along the distant down
Would flying burghers mark the blazing town?
How view the column of ascending flames
Shake his red shadow o'er the startled Thames?
Nay, frown not, Albion! for the torch was thine
That lit such pyres from Tagus to the Rhine:
Now should they burst on thy devoted coast,
Go, ask thy bosom who deserves them most?   310
The law of Heaven and Earth is life for life,
And she who raised, in vain regrets, the strife."

           [*First publ., 1815.*]

THE WALTZ:

AN APOSTROPHIC HYMN

BY HORACE HORNEM, ESQ.

"Qualis in Eurotæ ripis, aut per juga Cynthi,
Exercet DIANA choros."
—VIRGIL. *Æneid.* i. 498, 499.

"Such on Eurotas' banks, or Cynthus' height,
Diana seems: and so she charms the sight,
When in the dance the graceful goddess leads
The quire of nymphs, and overtops their heads."
—DRYDEN's *Virgil.*

TO THE PUBLISHER

SIR,—I am a country Gentleman of a midland county. I might have been a Parliament-man for a certain borough; having had the offer of as many votes as General T. at the general election in 1812. But I was all for domestic happiness; as, fifteen years ago, on a visit to London, I married a middle-aged Maid of Honour. We lived happily at Hornem Hall till last Season, when my wife and I were invited by the Countess of Waltzaway (a distant relation of my Spouse) to pass the winter in town. Thinking no harm, and our Girls being come to a marriageable (or, as they call it, *marketable*) age, and having besides a Chancery suit inveterately entailed upon the family estate, we came up in our old chariot,—of which, by the bye, my wife grew so ashamed in less than a week, that I was obliged to buy a second-hand barouche, of which I might mount the box, Mrs. H. says, if I could drive, but never see the inside—that place being reserved for the Honourable Augustus Tiptoe, her partner-general and Opera-knight. Hearing great praises of Mrs. H.'s dancing (she was famous for birthnight minuets in the latter end of the last century), I unbooted, and went to a ball at the Countess's, expecting to see a country dance, or, at most, Cotillons, reels, and all the old paces to the newest tunes. But, judge of my surprise, on arriving, to see poor dear Mrs. Hornem with her arms half round the loins of a huge hussar-looking gentleman I never set eyes on before; and his, to say truth, rather more than half round her waist, turning round, and round, to a d——d see-saw up-and-down sort of tune, that reminded me of the "Black Joke," only more "*affettuoso*," till it made me quite giddy with wondering they were not so. By and by they stopped a bit, and I thought they would sit or fall down:—but no; with Mrs. H.'s hand on his shoulder, "*Quam familiariter*" (as Terence said, when I was at school,) they walked about a minute, and then at it again, like two cock-chafers spitted on the same bodkin. I asked what all this meant, when, with a loud laugh, a child no older than our Wilhelmina (a name I never heard but in the *Vicar of Wakefield*, though her mother would call her after the Princes of Swappenbach,) said, "L—d! Mr. Hornem, can't you see they're valtzing?" or waltzing (I forget which); and then up she got, and her mother and sister, and away they went, and round-abouted it till supper-time. Now that I know what it is, I like it of all things, and so does Mrs. H. (though I have broken my shins, and four times overturned Mrs. Hornem's maid, in practising the preliminary steps in a morning). Indeed, so much do I like it, that having a turn for rhyme, tastily displayed in some election ballads, and songs in honour of all the victories (but till lately I have had little practice in that way,) I sat down, and with the aid of William Fitzgerald, Esq., and a few hints from Dr. Busby, (whose recitations I attend, and am monstrous fond of Master Busby's manner of delivering his father's late successful "Drury Lane Address,") I composed the following hymn, wherewithal to make my sentiments known to the Public; whom, nevertheless, I heartily despise, as well as the critics. I am, Sir, yours, etc., etc.

HORACE HORNEM.

MUSE of the many-twinkling feet! whose charms
Are now extended up from legs to arms;
Terpsichore!—too long misdeemed a maid—
Reproachful term—bestowed but to upbraid—
Henceforth in all the bronze of brightness shine,
The least a Vestal of the Virgin Nine.
Far be from thee and thine the name of Prude:
Mocked yet triumphant; sneered at, unsubdued;
Thy legs must move to conquer as they fly,
If but thy coats are reasonably high!   10
Thy breast—if bare enough—requires no shield;
Dance forth—*sans armour* thou shalt take the field
And own—impregnable to *most* assaults,
Thy not too lawfully begotten "Waltz."

Hail, nimble Nymph! to whom the young hussar,
The whiskered votary of Waltz and War,
His night devotes, despite of spur and boots;
A sight unmatched since Orpheus and his brutes:
Hail, spirit-stirring Waltz!—beneath whose banners
A modern hero fought for modish manners;   20
On Hounslow's heath to rival Wellesley's fame,
Cocked, fired, and missed his man—but gained his aim;
Hail, moving Muse! to whom the fair one's breast
Gives all it can, and bids us take the rest.
Oh! for the flow of Busby, or of Fitz,
The latter's loyalty, the former's wits,
To "energise the object I pursue,"
And give both Belial and his Dance their due!

Imperial Waltz! imported from the Rhine
(Famed for the growth of pedigrees and wine),   30
Long be thine import from all duty free,
And Hock itself be less esteemed than thee;
In some few qualities alike—for Hock
Improves our cellar—*thou* our living stock.
The head to Hock belongs—thy subtler art
Intoxicates alone the heedless heart:
Through the full veins thy gentler poison swims,
And wakes to Wantonness the willing limbs.

Oh, Germany! how much to thee we owe,
As heaven-born Pitt can testify below,   40
Ere cursed Confederation made thee France's,
And only left us thy d—d debts and dances!
Of subsidies and Hanover bereft,
We bless thee still—for George the Third is left!
Of kings the best—and last, not least in worth,
For graciously begetting George—the Fourth.
To Germany, and Highnesses serene,
Who owe us millions—don't we owe the Queen?
To Germany, what owe we not besides?
So oft bestowing Brunswickers and brides;   50
Who paid for vulgar, with her royal blood,
Drawn from the stem of each Teutonic stud:
Who sent us—so be pardoned all her faults—
A dozen dukes, some kings, a Queen—and Waltz.

But peace to her—her Emperor and Diet,
Though now transferred to Buonapartè's "fiat"!
Back to my theme—O muse of Motion! say,
How first to Albion found thy Waltz her way?

Borne on the breath of Hyperborean gales,
From Hamburg's port (while Hamburg yet had *mails*),   60
Ere yet unlucky Fame—compelled to creep
To snowy Gottenburg—was chilled to sleep;
Or, starting from her slumbers, deigned arise,
Heligoland! to stock thy mart with lies;
While unburnt Moscow yet had news to send,
Nor owed her fiery Exit to a friend,
She came—Waltz came—and with her certain sets
Of true despatches, and as true Gazettes;
Then flamed of Austerlitz the blest despatch,
Which *Moniteur* nor *Morning Post* can match;   70
And—almost crushed beneath the glorious news—
Ten plays, and forty tales of Kotzebue's;
One envoy's letters, six composers' airs,
And loads from Frankfort and from Leipsic fairs;
Meiners' four volumes upon Womankind,
Like Lapland witches to ensure a wind;
Brunck's heaviest tome for ballast, and, to back it,
Of Heynè, such as should not sink the packet.

Fraught with this cargo—and her fairest freight,
Delightful Waltz, on üptoe for a Mate,   80
The welcome vessel reached the genial strand,
And round her flocked the daughters of the land.
Not decent David, when, before the ark,
His grand *Pas-seul* excited some remark;
Not love-lorn Quixote, when his Sancho thought
The knight's *Fandango* friskier than it ought;
Not soft Herodias, when, with winning tread,
Her nimble feet danced off another's head;
Not Cleopatra on her Galley's Deck,
Displayed so much of *leg* or more of *neck*,   90
Than Thou, ambrosial Waltz, when first the Moon
Beheld thee twirling to a Saxon tune!

To You, ye husbands of ten years! whose brows
Ache with the annual tributes of a spouse;

To you of nine years less, who only bear
The budding sprouts of those that you *shall* wear,
With added ornaments around them rolled
Of native brass, or law-awarded gold;
To You, ye Matrons, ever on the watch
To mar a son's, or make a daughter's match;   100
To You, ye children of—whom chance accords—
Always the Ladies, and *sometimes* their Lords;
To You, ye single gentlemen, who seek
Torments for life, or pleasures for a week;
As Love or Hymen your endeavours guide,
To gain your own, or snatch another's bride;—
To one and all the lovely Stranger came,
And every ball-room echoes with her name.

   Endearing Waltz!—to thy more melting tune
Bow Irish Jig, and ancient Rigadoon.   115
Scotch reels, avaunt! and Country-dance forego
Your future claims to each fantastic toe!
Waltz—Waltz alone—both legs and arms demands,
Liberal of feet, and lavish of her hands;
Hands which may freely range in public sight
Where ne'er before—but—pray "put out the light":
Methinks the glare of yonder chandelier
Shines much too far—or I am much too near;
And true, though strange—Waltz whispers this remark,
"My slippery steps are safest in the dark!"   120
But here the Muse with due decorum halts,
And lends her longest petticoat to "Waltz."

   Observant Travellers of every time!
Ye Quartos published upon every clime!
O say, shall dull *Romaika's* heavy round,
Fandango's wriggle, or *Bolero's* bound;
Can Egypt's *Almas*—tantalising group—
Columbia's caperers to the warlike Whoop—
Can aught, from cold Kamschatka to Cape Horn,
With Waltz compare, or after Waltz be born?   130
Ah, no! from Morier's pages down to Galt's,
Each tourist pens a paragraph for "Waltz."

   Shades of those Belles whose reign began of yore,
With George the Third's—and ended long before!—

Though in your daughters' daughters yet you thrive,
Burst from your lead, and be yourselves alive!
Back to the Ball-room speed your spectred host,
Fool's Paradise is dull to that you lost.
No treacherous powder bids Conjecture quake:
No stiff-starched stays make meddling fingers ache;   140
Transferred to those ambiguous things that ape
Goats in their visage, women in their shape;)
No damsel faints when rather closely pressed,
But more caressing seems when most caressed;
Superfluous Hartshorn, and reviving Salts,
Both banished by the sovereign cordial "Waltz."

Seductive Waltz!—though on thy native shore
Even Werter's self proclaimed thee half a whore;
Werter—to decent vice though much inclined,
Yet warm, not wanton; dazzled, but not blind—   150
Though gentle Genlis, in her strife with Staël,
Would even proscribe thee from a Paris ball;
The fashion hails, from Countesses to Queens—
And maids and valets waltz behind the scenes;
Wide and more wide thy witching circle spreads,
And turns—if nothing else—at least our *heads;*
With thee even clumsy cits attempt to bounce,
And cockneys practise what they can't pronounce.
Gods! how the glorious theme my strain exalts,
And Rhyme finds partner Rhyme in praise of "Waltz"!   160

Blest was the time Waltz chose for her *debut!*
The Court, the Regent, like herself were new;
New face for friends, for foes some new rewards;
New ornaments for black—and royal Guards;
New laws to hang the rogues that roared for bread;
New coins (most new) to follow those that fled;
New victories—nor can we prize them less,
Though Jenky wonders at his own success;
New wars, because the old succeed so well,
That most survivors envy those who fell;   170
New mistresses—no, old—and yet 'tis true,
Though they be *old,* the *thing* is something new;
Each new, quite new—(except some ancient tricks),
New white-sticks—gold-sticks—broom-sticks—*all new sticks!*
With vests or ribands—decked alike in hue,

New troopers strut, new turncoats blush in blue:
So saith the Muse: my ——, what say you?
Such was the time when Waltz might best maintain
Her new preferments in this novel reign:
Such was the time, nor ever yet was such;   186
Hoops are *no more*, and petticoats *not much;*
Morals and Minuets, Virtue and her stays,
And tell-tale powder—all have had their days.
The Ball begins—the honours of the house
First duly done by daughter or by spouse,
Some Potentate—or royal or serene—
With Kent's gay grace, or sapient Gloster's mien,
Leads forth the ready dame, whose rising flush
Mignt once have been mistaken for a blush.
From where the garb just leaves the bosom free,   196
That spot where hearts were once supposed to be;
Round all the confines of the yielded waist,
The strangest hand may wander undisplaced:
The lady's in return may grasp as much
As princely paunches offer to her touch.
Pleased round the chalky floor how well they trip,
One hand reposing on the royal hip!
The other to the shoulder no less royal
Ascending with affection truly loyal!
Thus front to front the partners move or stand,   206
The foot may rest, but none withdraw the hand;
And all in turn may follow in their rank,
The Earl of—Asterisk—and Lady—Blank;
Sir—Such-a-one—with those of Fashion's host,
For whose blest surnames—vide "Morning Post":
(Or for that impartial print too late,
Search Doctors' Commons six months from my date)--
Thus all and each, in movement swift or slow,
The genial contact gently undergo;
Till some might marvel, with the modest Turk,   216
If "nothing follows all this palming work"?
True, honest Mirza!—you may trust my rhyme--
Something does follow at a fitter time;
The breast thus publicly resigned to man,
In private may resist him—if it can.

   O ye who loved our Grandmothers of yore,
Fitzpatrick, Sheridan, and many more!

And thou, my Prince! whose sovereign taste and will
It is to love the lovely beldames still!
Thou Ghost of Queensberry! whose judging Sprite   220
Satan may spare to peep a single night,
Pronounce—if ever in your days of bliss
Asmodeus struck so bright a stroke as this;
To teach the young ideas how to rise,
Flush in the check, and languish in the eyes;
Rush to the heart, and lighten through the frame,
With half-told wish, and ill-dissembled flame,
For prurient Nature still will storm the breast—
Who, tempted thus, can answer for the rest?

But ye—who never felt a single thought   230
For what our Morals are to be, or ought;
Who wisely wish the charms you view to reap,
Say—would you make those beauties quite so cheap?
Hot from the hands promiscuously applied,
Round the slight waist, or down the glowing side,
Where were the rapture then to clasp the form
From this lewd grasp and lawless contact warm?
At once Love's most endearing thought resign,
To press the hand so pressed by none but thine;
To gaze upon that eye which never met   240
Another's ardent look without regret;
Approach the lip which all, without restraint,
Come near enough—if not to touch—to taint;
If such thou lovest—love her then no more,
Or give—like her—caresses to a score;
Her Mind with these is gone, and with it go
The little left behind it to bestow.

Voluptuous Waltz! and dare I thus blaspheme?
Thy bard forgot thy praises were his theme.
Terpsichore forgive!—at every Ball   250
My wife *now* waltzes—and my daughters *shall;*
My son—(or stop—'tis needless to inquire—
These little accidents should ne'er transpire;
Some ages hence our genealogic tree
Will wear as green a bough for him as me)—
Waltzing shall rear, to make our name amends,
Grandsons for me—in heirs to all his friends.
[*First publ., Feb. 18, 1813.*]

THE VISION OF JUDGMENT

BY QUEVEDO REDIVIVUS

SUGGESTED BY THE COMPOSITION SO ENTITLED BY THE AUTHOR OF "WAT TYLER"

"A Daniel come to judgment! yea, a Daniel!
I thank thee, Jew, for teaching me that word."

PREFACE

IT HATH been wisely said, that "One fool makes many;" and it hath been poetically observed—

"[That] fools rush in where angels fear to tread."
—POPE'S *Essay on Criticism.*

If Mr. Southey had not rushed in where he had no business, and where he never was before, and never will be again, the following poem would not have been written. It is not impossible that it may be as good as his own, seeing that it cannot, by any species of stupidity, natural or acquired, be *worse*. The gross flattery, the dull impudence, the renegado intolerance, and impious cant, of the poem by the author of "Wat Tyler," are something so stupendous as to form the sublime of himself— containing the quintessence of his own attributes.

So much for his poem—a word on his preface. In this preface it has pleased the magnanimous Laureate to draw the picture of a supposed "Satanic School," the which he doth recommend to the notice of the legislature; thereby adding to his other laurels the ambition of those of an informer. If there exists any, where, except in his imagination, such a School, is he not suffi, ciently armed against it by his own intense vanity? The truth is that there are certain writers whom Mr. S. imagines, like Scrub, to have "talked of *him;* for they laughed consumedly."

I think I know enough of most of the writers to whom he is supposed to allude, to assert, that they, in their individual capacities, have done more good, in the charities of life, to their fellow, creatures, in any one year, than Mr. Southey has done harm to himself by his absurdities in his whole life; and this is saying a great deal. But I have a few questions to ask.

1stly, Is Mr. Southey the author of *Wat Tyler?*

2ndly, Was he not refused a remedy at law by the highest judge of his beloved England, because it was a blasphemous and seditious publication?

3rdly, Was he not entitled by William Smith, in full parliament, "a rancorous renegado?"

4thly, Is he not poet laureate, with his own lines on Martin the regicide staring him in the face?

And, 5thly, Putting the four preceding items together, with what conscience dare *he* call the attention of the laws to the publications of others, be they what they may?

I say nothing of the cowardice of such a proceeding; its meanness speaks for itself; but I wish to touch upon the *motive*, which is neither more nor less than that Mr. S. has been laughed at a little in some recent publications, as he was of yore in the *Anti-jacobin*, by his present patrons. Hence all this "skimble scamble stuff" about "Satanic," and so forth. However, it is worthy of him—"*qualis ab incepto.*"

If there is anything obnoxious to the political opinions of a portion of the public in the following poem, they may thank Mr. Southey. He might have written hexameters, as he has written everything else, for aught that the writer cared—had they been upon another subject. But to attempt to canonise a monarch, who, whatever were his household virtues, was neither a successful nor a patriot king,—inasmuch as several years of his reign passed in war with America and Ireland, to say nothing of the aggression upon France—like all other exaggeration, necessarily begets opposition. In whatever manner he may be spoken of in this new *Vision*, his *public* career will not be more favourably transmitted by history. Of his private virtues (although a little expensive to the nation) there can be no doubt.

With regard to the supernatural personages treated of, I can only say that I know as much about them and (as an honest man) have a better right to talk of them than Robert Southey. I have also treated them more tolerantly. The way in which that poor insane creature, the Laureate deals about his judgments in the next world, is like his own judgment in this. If it was not completely ludicrous, it would be something worse. I don't think that there is much more to say at present.

QUEVEDO REDIVIVUS.

P.S.—It is possible that some readers may object, in these objectionable times, to the freedom with which saints, angels, and spiritual persons discourse in this *Vision*. But, for precedents upon such points, I must refer him to Fielding's *Journey from this World to the next,* and to the Visions of myself, the said Quevedo, in Spanish or translated. The reader is also requested to observe, that no doctrinal tenets are insisted upon or discussed; that the person of the Deity is carefully withheld from sight, which is more than can be said for the Laureate, who hath thought proper to make him talk, not "like a school-divine," but like the unscholarlike Mr. Southey. The whole action passes on the outside of heaven; and Chaucer's *Wife of Bath,* Pulci's *Morgante Maggiore,* Swift's *Tale of a Tub,* and the other works above referred to, are cases in point of the freedom with which saints, etc., may be permitted to converse in works not intended to be serious.

Q. R.

❋ * ❋ Mr. Southey being, as he says, a good Christian and vindictive, threatens, I understand, a reply to this our answer. It is to be hoped that his visionary faculties will in the meantime have acquired a little more judgment, properly so called: otherwise he will get himself into new dilemmas. These apostate jacobins furnish rich rejoinders. Let him take a specimen. Mr. Southey laudeth grievously "one Mr. Landor," who cultivates much private renown in the shape of Latin verses; and not long ago, the poet laureate dedicated to him, it appeareth, one of his fugitive lyrics, upon the strength of a poem called *"Gebir."* Who could suppose, that in this same Gebir the aforesaid Savage Landor (for such is his grim cognomen) putteth into the infernal regions no less a person than the hero of his friend Mr. Southey's heaven, —yea, even George the Third! See also how personal Savage becometh, when he hath a mind. The following is his portrait of our late gracious sovereign:—

(Prince Gebir having descended into the infernal regions, the shades of his royal ancestors are, at his request, called up to his view; and he exclaims to his ghostly guide)—

"'Aroar, what wretch that nearest us? what wretch
Is that with eyebrows white and slanting brow?
Listen! him yonder who, bound down supine,

Shrinks yelling from that sword there, engine-hung;
He too amongst my ancestors! I hate
The despot, but the dastard I despise.
Was he our countryman?'

       'Alas, O king!
Iberia bore him, but the breed accurst
Inclement winds blew blighting from north-east.'
'He was a warrior then, nor feared the gods?'
'Gebir, he feared the Demons, not the gods,
Though them indeed his daily face adored;
And was no warrior, yet the thousand lives
Squandered, as stones to exercise a sling,
And the tame cruelty and cold caprice—
 Oh madness of mankind! addressed, adored!'"
    Gebir [*Works, etc.*, 1876, vii. 17].

I omit noticing some edifying Ithyphallics of Savagius, wishing to keep the proper veil over them, if his grave but somewhat indiscreet worshipper will suffer it; but certainly these teachers of "great moral lessons" are apt to be found in strange company.

I

SAINT PETER sat by the celestial gate:
 His keys were rusty, and the lock was dull.
So little trouble had been given of late;
 Not that the place by any means was full,
But since the Gallic era "eighty-eight"
 The Devils had ta'en a longer, stronger pull,
And "a pull altogether," as they say
At sea—which drew most souls another way.

II

The Angels all were singing out of tune,
 And hoarse with having little else to do,
Excepting to wind up the sun and moon,
 Or curb a runaway young star or two,
Or wild colt of a comet, which too soon
 Broke out of bounds o'er the ethereal blue,
Splitting some planet with its playful tail,
As boats are sometimes by a wanton whale.

III

The Guardian Seraphs had retired on high,
　　Finding their charges past all care below;
Terrestrial business filled nought in the sky
　　Save the Recording Angel's black bureau;
Who found, indeed, the facts to multiply
　　With such rapidity of vice and woe,
That he had stripped off both his wings in quills,
And yet was in arrear of human ills.

IV

His business so augmented of late years,
　　That he was forced, against his will, no doubt,
(Just like those cherubs, earthly ministers,)
　　For some resource to turn himself about,
And claim the help of his celestial peers,
　　To aid him ere he should be quite worn out
By the increased demand for his remarks:
Six Angels and twelve Saints were named his clerks.

V

This was a handsome board—at least for Heaven;
　　And yet they had even then enough to do,
So many Conquerors' cars were daily driven,
　　So many kingdoms fitted up anew;
Each day, too, slew its thousands six or seven,
　　Till at the crowning carnage, Waterloo,
They threw their pens down in divine disgust—
The page was so besmeared with blood and dust.

VI

This by the way; 'tis not mine to record
　　What Angels shrink from: even the very Devil
On this occasion his own work abhorred,
　　So surfeited with the infernal revel:
Though he himself had sharpened every sword,
　　It almost quenched his innate thirst of evil.

(Here Satan's sole good work deserves insertion—
'Tis, that he has both Generals in reversion.)

VII

Let's skip a few short years of hollow peace,
  Which peopled earth no better, Hell as wont,
And Heaven none—they form the tyrant's lease,
  With nothing but new names subscribed upon 't;
'Twill one day finish: meantime they increase,
  "With seven heads and ten horns," and all in front,
Like Saint John's foretold beast; but ours are born
Less formidable in the head than horn.

VIII

In the first year of Freedom's second dawn
  Died George the Third; although no tyrant, one
Who shielded tyrants, till each sense withdrawn
  Left him nor mental nor external sun:
A better farmer ne'er brushed dew from lawn,
  A worse king never left a realm undone!
He died—but left his subjects still behind,
One half as mad—and t'other no less blind.

IX

He died! his death made no great stir on earth:
  His burial made some pomp; there was profusion
Of velvet—gilding—brass—and no great dearth
  Of aught but tears—save those shed by collusion:
For these things may be bought at their true worth;
  Of elegy there was the due infusion—
Bought also; and the torches, cloaks and banners,
Heralds, and relics of old Gothic manners,

X

Formed a sepulchral melodrame. Of all
  The fools who flocked to swell or see the show,
Who cared about the corpse? The funeral
  Made the attraction, and the black the woe.
There throbbed not there a thought which pierced the pall,

And when the gorgeous coffin was laid low.
It seemed the mockery of hell to fold
The rottenness of eighty years in gold.

XI

So mix his body with the dust! It might
   Return to what it *must* far sooner, were
The natural compound left alone to fight
   Its way back into earth, and fire, and air;
But the unnatural balsams merely blight
   What Nature made him at his birth, as bare
As the mere million's base unmummied clay—
Yet all his spices but prolong decay.

XII

He's dead—and upper earth with him has done,
   He's buried; save the undertaker's bill,
Or lapidary scrawl, the world is gone
   For him, unless he left a German will:
But where's the proctor who will ask his son?
   In whom his qualities are reigning still,
Except that household virtue, most uncommon,
Of constancy to a bad, ugly woman.

XIII

"God save the king!" It is a large economy
   In God to save the like; but if he will
Be saving, all the better; for not one am I
   Of those who think damnation better still:
I hardly know too if not quite alone am I
   In this small hope of bettering future ill
By circumscribing, with some slight restriction,
The eternity of Hell's hot jurisdiction.

XIV

I know this is unpopular; I know
   'Tis blasphemous; I know one may be damned
For hoping no one else may e'er be so;
   I know my catechism; I know we're crammed

With the best doctrines till we quite o'erflow;
  I know that all save England's Church have shammed,
And that the other twice two hundred churches
And synagogues have made a *damned* bad purchase.

XV

God help us all! God help me too! I am,
  God knows, as helpless as the Devil can wish,
And not a whit more difficult to damn,
  Than is to bring to land a late-hooked fish,
Or to the butcher to purvey the lamb;
  Not that I'm fit for such a noble dish,
As one day will be that immortal fry
Of almost every body born to die.

XVI

Saint Peter sat by the celestial gate,
  And nodded o'er his keys: when, lo! there came
A wondrous noise he had not heard of late—
  A rushing sound of wind, and stream, and flame;
In short, a roar of things extremely great,
  Which would have made aught save a Saint exclaim,
But he, with first a start and then a wink,
Said, "There's another star gone out, I think!"

XVII

But ere he could return to his repose,
  A Cherub flapped his right wing o'er his eyes—
At which Saint Peter yawned, and rubbed his nose:
  "Saint porter," said the angel, "prithee rise!"
Waving a goodly wing, which glowed, as glows
  An earthly peacock's tail, with heavenly dyes:
To which the saint replied, "Well, what's the matter?
Is Lucifer come back with all this clatter?"

XVIII

"No," quoth the Cherub: "George the Third is dead."
  "And who *is* George the Third?" replied the apostle:
"*What George? What Third?*" "The King of England," said

The angel. "Well! he won't find kings to jostle
Him on his way; but does he wear his head?
    Because the last we saw here had a tustle,
And ne'er would have got into Heaven's good graces,
Had he not flung his head in all our faces.

XIX

"He was—if I remember—King of France;
    That head of his, which could not keep a crown
On earth, yet ventured in my face to advance
    A claim to those of martyrs—like my own:
If I had had my sword, as I had once
    When I cut ears off, I had cut him down;
But having but my *keys*, and not my brand,
I only knocked his head from out his hand.

XX

"And then he set up such a headless howl,
    That all the Saints came out and took him in;
And there he sits by Saint Paul, cheek by jowl;
    That fellow Paul—the parvenù! The skin
Of Saint Bartholomew, which makes his cowl
    In heaven, and upon earth redeemed his sin,
So as to make a martyr, never sped
Better than did this weak and wooden head.

XXI

"But had it come up here upon its shoulders,
    There would have been a different tale to tell:
The fellow-feeling in the Saint's beholders
    Seems to have acted on them like a spell;
And so this very foolish head Heaven solders
    Back on its trunk: it may be very well,
And seems the custom here to overthrow
Whatever has been wisely done below."

XXII

The Angel answered, "Peter! do not pout:
    The King who comes has head and all entire,

And never knew much what it was about—
He did as doth the puppet—by its wire,
And will be judged like all the rest, no doubt:
    My business and your own is not to inquire
Into such matters, but to mind our cue—
Which is to act as we are bid to do."

XXIII

While thus they spake, the angelic caravan,
    Arriving like a rush of mighty wind,
Cleaving the fields of space, as doth the swan
    Some silver stream (say Ganges, Nile, or Inde,
Or Thames, or Tweed), and midst them an old man
    With an old soul, and both extremely blind,
Halted before the gate, and, in his shroud,
Seated their fellow-traveller on a cloud.

XXIV

But bringing up the rear of this bright host
    A Spirit of a different aspect waved
His wings, like thunder-clouds above some coast
    Whose barren beach with frequent wrecks is paved;
His brow was like the deep when tempest-tossed;
    Fierce and unfathomable thoughts engraved
Eternal wrath on his immortal face,
And *where* he gazed a gloom pervaded space.

XXV

As he drew near, he gazed upon the gate
    Ne'er to be entered more by him or Sin,
With such a glance of supernatural hate,
    As made Saint Peter wish himself within;
He pottered with his keys at a great rate,
    And sweated through his Apostolic skin:
Of course his perspiration was but ichor,
Or some such other spiritual liquor.

XXVI

The very Cherubs huddled all together,
　Like birds when soars the falcon; and they felt
A tingling to the tip of every feather,
　And formed a circle like Orion's belt
Around their poor old charge; who scarce knew whither
　His guards had led him, though they gently dealt
With Royal Manes (for by many stories,
And true, we learn the Angels all are Tories).

XXVII

As things were in this posture, the gate flew
　Asunder, and the flashing of its hinges
Flung over space an universal hue
　Of many-coloured flame, until its tinges
Reached even our speck of earth, and made a new
　Aurora borealis spread its fringes
O'er the North Pole; the same seen, when ice-bound,
By Captain Parry's crew, in "Melville's Sound."

XXVIII

And from the gate thrown open issued beaming
　A beautiful and mighty Thing of Light,
Radiant with glory, like a banner streaming
　Victorious from some world-o'erthrowing fight:
My poor comparisons must needs be teeming
　With earthly likenesses, for here the night
Of clay obscures our best conceptions, saving
Johanna Southcote, or Bob Southey raving.

XXIX

'Twas the Archangel Michael: all men know
　The make of Angels and Archangels, since
There's scarce a scribbler has not one to show,
　From the fiends' leader to the Angels' Prince.
There also are some altar-pieces, though
　I really can't say that they much evince

One's inner notions of immortal spirits;
But let the connoisseurs explain *their* merits.

XXX

Michael flew forth in glory and in good;
   A goodly work of him from whom all Glory
And Good arise; the portal past—he stood;
   Before him the young Cherubs and Saints hoary—
(I say *young*, begging to be understood
   By looks, not years; and should be very sorry
To state, they were not older than St. Peter,
But merely that they seemed a little sweeter).

XXXI

The Cherubs and the Saints bowed down before
   That arch-angelic Hierarch, the first
Of Essences angelical who wore
   The aspect of a god; but this ne'er nursed
Pride in his heavenly bosom, in whose core
   No thought, save for his Maker's service, durst
Intrude—however glorified and high,
He knew him but the Viceroy of the sky.

XXXII

He and the sombre, silent Spirit met—
   They knew each other both for good and ill;
Such was their power, that neither could forget
   His former friend and future foe; but still
There was a high, immortal, proud regret
   In either's eye, as if 'twere less their will
Than destiny to make the eternal years
Their date of war, and their "Champ Clos" the spheres.

XXXIII

But here they were in neutral space: we know
   From Job, that Satan hath the power to pay
A heavenly visit thrice a-year or so;
   And that the "Sons of God," like those of clay,
Must keep him company; and we might show

From the same book, in how polite a way
The dialogue is held between the Powers
Of Good and Evil—but 'twould take up hours.

XXXIV

And this is not a theologic tract,
    To prove with Hebrew and with Arabic,
If Job be allegory or a fact,
    But a true narrative; and thus I pick
From out the whole but such and such an act
    As sets aside the slightest thought of trick.
'Tis every tittle true, beyond suspicion,
And accurate as any other vision.

XXXV

The spirits were in neutral space, before
    The gate of Heaven; like eastern thresholds is
The place where Death's grand cause is argued o'er
    And souls despatched to that world or to this;
And therefore Michael and the other wore
    A civil aspect: though they did not kiss,
Yet still between his Darkness and his Brightness
There passed a mutual glance of great politeness.

XXXVI

The Archangel bowed, not like a modern beau,
    But with a graceful oriental bend,
Pressing one radiant arm just where below
    The heart in good men is supposed to tend;
He turned as to an equal, not too low,
    But kindly; Satan met his ancient friend
With more hauteur, as might an old Castilian
Poor Noble meet a mushroom rich civilian.

XXXVII

He merely bent his diabolic brow
    An instant; and then raising it, he stood
In act to assert his right or wrong, and show
    Cause why King George by no means could or should

Make out a case to be exempt from woe
    Eternal, more than other kings, endued
With better sense and hearts, whom History mentions,
Who long have "paved Hell with their good intentions."

XXXVIII

Michael began: "What wouldst thou with this man,
    Now dead, and brought before the Lord? What ill
Hath he wrought since his mortal race began,
    That thou canst claim him? Speak! and do thy will,
If it be just: if in this earthly span
    He hath been greatly failing to fulfil
His duties as a king and mortal, say,
And he is thine; if not—let him have way."

XXXIX

"Michael!" replied the Prince of Air, "even here
    Before the gate of Him thou servest, must
I claim my subject: and will make appear
    That as he was my worshipper in dust,
So shall he be in spirit, although dear
    To thee and thine, because nor wine nor lust
Were of his weaknesses; yet on the throne
He reigned o'er millions to serve me alone.

XL

"Look to *our* earth, or rather *mine*; it was,
    Once, more thy master's: but I triumph not
In this poor planet's conquest; nor, alas!
    Need he thou servest envy me my lot:
With all the myriads of bright worlds which pass
    In worship round him, he may have forgot
Yon weak creation of such paltry things:
I think few worth damnation save their kings,

XLI

"And these but as a kind of quit-rent, to
    Assert my right as Lord: and even had
I such an inclination, 'twere (as you

Well know) superfluous: they are grown so bad,
That Hell has nothing better left to do
    Than leave them to themselves: so much more mad
And evil by their own internal curse,
Heaven cannot make them better, nor I worse.

XLII

"Look to the earth, I said, and say again:
    When this old, blind, mad, helpless, weak, poor worm
Began in youth's first bloom and flush to reign,
    The world and he both wore a different form,
And much of earth and all the watery plain
    Of Ocean called him king: through many a storm
His isles had floated on the abyss of Time;
For the rough virtues chose them for their clime.

XLIII

"He came to his sceptre young; he leaves it old:
    Look to the state in which he found his realm,
And left it; and his annals too behold,
    How to a minion first he gave the helm;
How grew upon his heart a thirst for gold,
    The beggar's vice, which can but overwhelm
The meanest hearts; and for the rest, but glance
Thine eye along America and France.

XLIV

" 'Tis true, he was a tool from first to last
    (I have the workmen safe); but as a tool
So let him be consumed. From out the past
    Of ages, since mankind have known the rule
Of monarchs—from the bloody rolls amassed
    Of Sin and Slaughter—from the Cæsars' school,
Take the worst pupil; and produce a reign
More drenched with gore, more cumbered with the slain.

XLV

"He ever warred with freedom and the free:
    Nations as men, home subjects, foreign foes,

So that they uttered the word 'Liberty!'
    Found George the Third their first opponent. Whose
History was ever stained as his will be
    With national and individual woes?
I grant his household abstinence; I grant
His neutral virtues, which most monarchs want;

XLVI

"I know he was a constant consort; own
    He was a decent sire, and middling lord.
All this is much, and most upon a throne;
    As temperance, if at Apicius' board,
Is more than at an anchorite's supper shown.
    I grant him all the kindest can accord;
And this was well for him, but not for those
Millions who found him what Oppression chose.

XLVII

"The New World shook him off; the Old yet groans
    Beneath what he and his prepared, if not
Completed: he leaves heirs on many thrones
    To all his vices, without what begot
Compassion for him—his tame virtues; drones
    Who sleep, or despots who have now forgot
A lesson which shall be retaught them, wake
Upon the thrones of earth; but let them quake!

XLVIII

"Five millions of the primitive, who hold
    The faith which makes ye great on earth, implored
A *part* of that vast *all* they held of old,—
    Freedom to worship—not alone your Lord,
Michael, but you, and you, Saint Peter! Cold
    Must be your souls, if you have not abhorred
The foe to Catholic participation
In all the license of a Christian nation.

XLIX

"True! he allowed them to pray God; but as
  A consequence of prayer, refused the law
Which would have placed them upon the same base
  With those who did not hold the Saints in awe."
But here Saint Peter started from his place
  And cried, "You may the prisoner withdraw:
Ere Heaven shall ope her portals to this Guelph,
While I am guard, may I be damned myself!

L

'Sooner will I with Cerberus exchange
  My office (and *his* is no sinecure)
Than see this royal Bedlam-bigot range
  The azure fields of Heaven, of that be sure!"
"Saint!" replied Satan, "you do well to avenge
  The wrongs he made your satellites endure;
And if to this exchange you should be given,
I'll try to coax *our* Cerberus up to Heaven!"

LI

Here Michael interposed: "Good Saint! and Devil!
  Pray, not so fast; you both outrun discretion.
Saint Peter! you were wont to be more civil:
  Satan! excuse this warmth of his expression,
And condescension to the vulgar's level:
  Even Saints sometimes forget themselves in session.
Have you got more to say?"—"No."—"If you please,
I'll trouble you to call your witnesses."

LII

Then Satan turned and waved his swarthy hand,
  Which stirred with its electric qualities
Clouds farther off than we can understand,
  Although we find him sometimes in our skies;
Infernal thunder shook both sea and land
  In all the planets—and Hell's batteries

Let off the artillery, which Milton mentions
As one of Satan's most sublime inventions.

LIII

This was a signal unto such damned souls
    As have the privilege of their damnation
Extended far beyond the mere controls
    Of worlds past, present, or to come; no station
Is theirs particularly in the rolls
    Of Hell assigned; but where their inclination
Or business carries them in search of game,
They may range freely—being damned the same.

LIV

They are proud of this—as very well they may,
    It being a sort of knighthood, or gilt key
Stuck in their loins; or like to an "entré"
    Up the back stairs, or such free-masonry.
I borrow my comparisons from clay,
    Being clay myself. Let not those spirits be
Offended with such base low likenesses;
We know their posts are nobler far than these.

LV

When the great signal ran from Heaven to Hell—
    About ten million times the distance reckoned
From our sun to its earth, as we can tell
    How much time it takes up, even to a second,
For every ray that travels to dispel
    The fogs of London, through which, dimly beaconed,
The weathercocks are gilt some thrice a year,
If that the *summer* is not too severe:

LVI

I say that I can tell—'twas half a minute;
    I know the solar beams take up more time
Ere, packed up for their journey, they begin it;
    But then their Telegraph is less sublime,
And if they ran a race, they would not win it

'Gainst Satan's couriers bound for their own clime
The sun takes up some years for every ray
To reach its goal—the Devil not half a day.

LVII

Upon the verge of space, about the size
   Of half-a-crown, a little speck appeared
(I've seen a something like it in the skies
   In the Ægean, ere a squall); it neared,
And, growing bigger, took another guise;
   Like an aërial ship it tacked, and steered,
Or *was* steered (I am doubtful of the grammar
Of the last phrase, which makes the stanza stammer;

LVIII

But take your choice): and then it grew a cloud;
   And so it was—a cloud of witnesses.
But such a cloud! No land ere saw a crowd
   Of locusts numerous as the heavens saw these;
They shadowed with their myriads Space; their loud
   And varied cries were like those of wild geese,
(If nations may be likened to a goose),
And realised the phrase of "Hell broke loose."

LIX

Here crashed a sturdy oath of stout John Bull,
   Who damned away his eyes as heretofore:
There Paddy brogued "By Jasus!"—"What's your wull?"
   The temperate Scot exclaimed: the French ghost swore
In certain terms I shan't translate in full,
   As the first coachman will; and 'midst the war,
The voice of Jonathan was heard to express,
"*Our* President is going to war, I guess."

LX

Besides there were the Spaniard, Dutch, and Dane;
   In short, an universal shoal of shades
From Otaheite's isle to Salisbury Plain,
   Of all climes and professions, years and trades,

Ready to swear against the good king's reign,
   Bitter as clubs in cards are against spades:
All summoned by this grand "subpœna," to
Try if kings mayn't be damned like me or you.

LXI

When Michael saw this host, he first grew pale,
   As Angels can; next, like Italian twilight,
He turned all colours—as a peacock's tail,
   Or sunset streaming through a Gothic skylight
In some old abbey, or a trout not stale,
   Or distant lightning on the horizon *by* night,
Or a fresh rainbow, or a grand review
Of thirty regiments in red, green, and blue.

LXII

Then he addressed himself to Satan: "Why—
   My good old friend, for such I deem you, thougl
Our different parties make us fight so shy,
   I ne'er mistake you for a *personal* foe;
Our difference is *political*, and I
   Trust that, whatever may occur below,
You know my great respect for you: and this
Makes me regret whate'er you do amiss—

LXIII

"Why, my dear Lucifer, would you abuse
   My call for witnesses? I did not mean
That you should half of Earth and Hell produce;
   'Tis even superfluous, since two honest, clean,
True testimonies are enough: we lose
   Our Time, nay, our Eternity, between
The accusation and defence: if we
Hear both, 'twill stretch our immortality."

LXIV

Satan replied, "To me the matter is
   Indifferent, in a personal point of view:
I can have fifty better souls than this

With far less trouble than we have gone through
Already; and I merely argued his
  Late Majesty of Britain's case with you
Upon a point of form: you may dispose
Of him; I've kings enough below, God knows!"

LXV

Thus spoke the Demon (late called "multi-faced"
  By multo-scribbling Southey). "Then we'll call
One or two persons of the myriads placed
  Around our congress, and dispense with all
The rest," quoth Michael: "Who may be so graced
  As to speak first? there's choice enough—who shall
It be?" Then Satan answered, "There are many;
But you may choose Jack Wilkes as well as any."

LXVI

A merry, cock-eyed, curious-looking Sprite
  Upon the instant started from the throng,
Dressed in a fashion now forgotten quite;
  For all the fashions of the flesh stick long
By people in the next world; where unite
  All the costumes since Adam's, right or wrong,
From Eve's fig-leaf down to the petticoat,
Almost as scanty, of days less remote.

LXVII

The Spirit looked around upon the crowds
  Assembled, and exclaimed, "My friends of all
The spheres, we shall catch cold amongst these clouds;
  So let's to business: why this general call?
If those are freeholders I see in shrouds,
  And 'tis for an election that they bawl,
Behold a candidate with unturned coat!
Saint Peter, may I count upon your vote?"

LXVIII

"Sir," replied Michael, "you mistake; these things
  Are of a former life, and what we do

Above is more august; to judge of kings
  Is the tribunal met: so now you know."
"Then I presume those gentlemen with wings"
  Said Wilkes, "are Cherubs; and that soul below
Looks much like George the Third, but to my mind
A good deal older—bless me! is he blind?"

LXIX

"He is what you behold him, and his doom
  Depends upon his deeds," the Angel said;
"If you have aught to arraign in him, the tomb
  Gives licence to the humblest beggar's head
To lift itself against the loftiest."—"Some,"
  Said Wilkes, "don't wait to see them laid in lead,
For such a liberty—and I, for one,
Have told them what I thought beneath the sun."

LXX

"*Above* the sun repeat, then, what thou hast
  To urge against him," said the Archangel. "Why,"
Replied the Spirit, "since old scores are past,
  Must I turn evidence? In faith, not I.
Besides, I beat him hollow at the last,
  With all his Lords and Commons: in the sky
I don't like ripping up old stories, since
His conduct was but natural in a prince.

LXXI

'Foolish, no doubt, and wicked, to oppress
  A poor unlucky devil without a shilling;
But then I blame the man himself much less
  Than Bute and Grafton, and shall be unwilling
To see him punished here for their excess,
  Since they were both damned long ago, and still in
Their place below: for me, I have forgiven,
And vote his *habeas corpus* into Heaven."

LXXII

"Wilkes," said the Devil, "I understand all this;
    You turned to half a courtier ere you died,
And seem to think it would not be amiss
    To grow a whole one on the other side
Of Charon's ferry; you forget that *his*
    Reign is concluded; whatsoe'er betide,
He won't be sovereign more: you've lost your labour,
For at the best he will but be your neighbour.

LXXIII

"However, I knew what to think of it,
    When I beheld you in your jesting way,
Flitting and whispering round about the spit
    Where Belial, upon duty for the day,
With Fox's lard was basting William Pitt,
    His pupil; I knew what to think, I say:
That fellow even in Hell breeds farther ills;
I'll have him *gagged*—'twas one of his own Bills.

LXXIV

"Call Junius!" From the crowd a shadow stalked,
    And at the name there was a general squeeze,
So that the very ghosts no longer walked
    In comfort, at their own aërial ease,
But were all rammed, and jammed (but to be balked,
    As we shall see), and jostled hands and knees,
Like wind compressed and pent within a bladder,
Or like a human colic, which is sadder.

LXXV

The shadow came—a tall, thin, grey-haired figure,
    That looked as it had been a shade on earth;
Quick in its motions, with an air of vigour,
    But nought to mark its breeding or its birth;
Now it waxed little, then again grew bigger,
    With now an air of gloom, or savage mirth;

But as you gazed upon its features, they
Changed every instant—to *what,* none could say.

LXXVI

The more intently the ghosts gazed, the less
  Could they distinguish whose the features were;
The Devil himself seemed puzzled even to guess;
  They varied like a dream—now here, now there;
And several people swore from out the press,
  They knew him perfectly; and one could swear
He was his father; upon which another
Was sure he was his mother's cousin's brother:

LXXVII

Another, that he was a duke, or knight,
  An orator, a lawyer, or a priest,
A nabob, a man-midwife; but the wight
  Mysterious changed his countenance at least
As oft as they their minds: though in full sight
  He stood, the puzzle only was increased;
The man was a phantasmagoria in
Himself—he was so volatile and thin.

LXXIII

The moment that you had pronounced him *one,*
  Presto! his face changed, and he was another;
And when that change was hardly well put on,
  It varied, till I don't think his own mother
(If that he had a mother) would her son
  Have known, he shifted so from one to t'other;
Till guessing from a pleasure grew a task,
At this epistolary "Iron Mask."

LXXIX

For sometimes he like Cerberus would seem—
  "Three gentlemen at once" (as sagely says
Good Mrs. Malaprop); then you might deem
  That he was not even *one;* now many rays
Were flashing round him; and now a thick steam

Hid him from sight—like fogs on London days:
Now Burke, now Tooke, he grew to people's fancies,
And certes often like Sir Philip Francis.

LXXX

I've an hypothesis—'tis quite my own;
    I never let it out till now, for fear
Of doing people harm about the throne,
    And injuring some minister or peer,
On whom the stigma might perhaps be blown;
    It is—my gentle public, lend thine ear!
'Tis, that what Junius we are wont to call,
Was *really—truly*—nobody at all.

LXXXI

I don't see wherefore letters should not be
    Written without hands, since we daily view
Them written without heads; and books, we see,
    Are filled as well without the latter too:
And really till we fix on somebody
    For certain sure to claim them as his due,
Their author, like the Niger's mouth, will bother
The world to say if *there* be mouth or author.

LXXXII

"And who and what art thou?" the Archangel said.
    "For *that* you may consult my title-page,"
Replied this mighty shadow of a shade:
    "If I have kept my secret half an age,
I scarce shall tell it now."—"Canst thou upbraid,"
    Continued Michael, "George Rex, or allege
Aught further?" Junius answered, "You had better
First ask him for *his* answer to my letter:

LXXXIII

"My charges upon record will outlast
    The brass of both his epitaph and tomb."
"Repent'st thou not," said Michael, "of some past
    Exaggeration? something which may doom

Thyself if false, as him if true? Thou wast
  Too bitter—is it not so?—in thy gloom
Of passion?"—"Passion!" cried the phantom dim,
"I loved my country, and I hated him.

LXXXIV

"What I have written, I have written: let
  The rest be on his head or mine!" So spoke
Old *"Nominis Umbra"*; and while speaking yet,
  Away he melted in celestial smoke.
Then Satan said to Michael, "Don't forget
  To call George Washington, and John Horne Tooke,
And Franklin;"—but at this time there was heard
A cry for room, though not a phantom stirred.

LXXXV

At length with jostling, elbowing, and the aid
  Of Cherubim appointed to that post,
The devil Asmodeus to the circle made
  His way, and looked as if his journey cost
Some trouble. When his burden down he laid,
  "What's this?" cried Michael; "why, 'tis not a ghost?"
"I know it," quoth the Incubus; "but he
Shall be one, if you leave the affair to me.

LXXXVI

"Confound the renegado! I have sprained
  My left wing, he's so heavy; one would think
Some of his works about his neck were chained.
  But to the point; while hovering o'er the brink
Of Skiddaw (where as usual it still rained),
  I saw a taper, far below me, wink,
And stooping, caught this fellow at a libel—
No less on History—than the Holy Bible.

LXXXVII

"The former is the Devil's scripture, and
  The latter yours, good Michael: so the affair
Belongs to all of us, you understand.

I snatched him up just as you see him there,
And brought him off for sentence out of hand:
I've scarcely been ten minutes in the air—
At least a quarter it can hardly be:
I dare say that his wife is still at tea."

LXXXVIII

Here Satan said, "I know this man of old,
And have expected him for some time here;
A sillier fellow you will scarce behold,
Or more conceited in his petty sphere:
But surely it was not worth while to fold
Such trash below your wing, Asmodeus dear:
We had the poor wretch safe (without being bored
With carriage) coming of his own accord.

LXXXIX

"But since he's here, let's see what he has done."
"Done!" cried Asmodeus, "he anticipates
The very business you are now upon,
And scribbles as if head clerk to the Fates.
Who knows to what his ribaldry may run,
When such an ass as this, like Balaam's, prates?"
"Let's hear," quoth Michael, "what he has to say:
You know we're bound to that in every way."

XC

Now the Bard, glad to get an audience, which
By no means often was his case below,
Began to cough, and hawk, and hem, and pitch
His voice into that awful note of woe
To all unhappy hearers within reach
Of poets when the tide of rhyme's in flow;
But stuck fast with his first hexameter,
Not one of all whose gouty feet would stir.

XCI

But ere the spavined dactyls could be spurred
Into recitative, in great dismay

Both Cherubim and Seraphim were heard
　　To murmur loudly through their long array;
And Michael rose ere he could get a word
　　Of all his foundered verses under way,
And cried, "For God's sake stop, my friend! 'twere best—
'Non Di, non homines'—you know the rest."

XCII

A general bustle spread throughout the throng,
　　Which seemed to hold all verse in detestation;
The Angels had of course enough of song
　　When upon service; and the generation
Of ghosts had heard too much in life, not long
　　Before, to profit by a new occasion:
The Monarch, mute till then, exclaimed, "What! what!
Pye come again? No more—no more of that!"

XCIII

The tumult grew; an universal cough
　　Convulsed the skies, as during a debate,
When Castlereagh has been up long enough
　　(Before he was first minister of state,
I mean—the slaves hear now); some cried "Off, off!"
　　As at a farce; till, grown quite desperate.
The Bard Saint Peter prayed to interpose
(Himself an author) only for his prose.

XCIV

The varlet was not an ill-favoured knave;
　　A good deal like a vulture in the face,
With a hook nose and a hawk's eye, which gave
　　A smart and sharper-looking sort of grace
To his whole aspect, which, though rather grave,
　　Was by no means so ugly as his case;
But that, indeed, was hopeless as can be,
Quite a poetic felony "de se."

XCV

Then Michael blew his trump, and stilled the noise
  With one still greater, as is yet the mode
On earth besides; except some grumbling voice,
  Which now and then will make a slight inroad
Upon decorous silence, few will twice
  Lift up their lungs when fairly overcrowed
And now the Bard could plead his own bad cause,
With all the attitudes of self-applause.

XCVI

He said—(I only give the heads)—he said,
  He meant no harm in scribbling; 'twas his way
Upon all topics; 'twas, besides, his bread,
  Of which he buttered both sides; 'twould delay
Too long the assembly (he was pleased to dread),
  And take up rather more time than a day,
To name his works—he would but cite a few—
"Wat Tyler"—"Rhymes on Blenheim"—"Waterloo."

XCVII

He had written praises of a Regicide;
  He had written praises of all kings whatever;
He had written for republics far and wide,
  And then against them bitterer than ever;
For pantisocracy he once had cried
  Aloud, a scheme less moral than 'twas clever;
Then grew a hearty anti-jacobin—
Had turned his coat—and would have turned his skin.

XCVIII

He had sung against all battles, and again
  In their high praise and glory; he had called
Reviewing "the ungentle craft," and then
  Became as base a critic as e'er crawled—
Fed, paid, and pampered by the very men
  By whom his muse and morals had been mauled:

He had written much blank verse, and blanker prose,
And more of both than any body knows.

XCIX

He had written Wesley's life:—here turning round
   To Satan, "Sir, I'm ready to write yours,
In two octavo volumes, nicely bound,
   With notes and preface, all that most allures
The pious purchaser; and there's no ground
   For fear, for I can choose my own reviewers:
So let me have the proper documents,
That I may add you to my other saints."

C

Satan bowed, and was silent. "Well, if you,
   With amiable modesty, decline
My offer, what says Michael? There are few
   Whose memoirs could be rendered more divine.
Mine is a pen of all work; not so new
   As it was once, but I would make you shine
Like your own trumpet. By the way, my own
Has more of brass in it, and is as well blown.

CI

"But talking about trumpets, here's my 'Vision'!
   Now you shall judge, all people—yes—you shall
Judge with my judgment! and by my decision
   Be guided who shall enter heaven or fall.
I settle all these things by intuition,
   Times present, past, to come—Heaven—Hell—and all,
Like King Alfonso. When I thus see double,
I save the Deity some worlds of trouble."

CII

He ceased, and drew forth an MS.; and no
   Persuasion on the part of Devils, Saints,
Or Angels, now could stop the torrent; so
   He read the first three lines of the contents;
But at the fourth, the whole spiritual show

Had vanished, with variety of scents,
Ambrosial and sulphureous, as they sprang,
Like lightning, off from his "melodious twang."

CIII

Those grand heroics acted as a spell;
    The Angels stopped their ears and plied their pinions;
The Devils ran howling, deafened, down to Hell;
    The ghosts fled, gibbering, for their own dominions—
(For 'tis not yet decided where they dwell,
    And I leave every man to his opinions);
Michael took refuge in his trump—but, lo!
His teeth were set on edge, he could not blow!

CIV

Saint Peter, who has hitherto been known
    For an impetuous saint, upraised his keys,
And at the fifth line knocked the poet down;
    Who fell like Phaeton, but more at ease,
Into his lake, for there he did not drown;
    A different web being by the Destinies
Woven for the Laureate's final wreath, whene'er
Reform shall happen either here or there.

CV

He first sank to the bottom—like his works,
    But soon rose to the surface—like himself;
For all corrupted things are buoyed like corks,
    By their own rottenness, light as an elf,
Or wisp that flits o'er a morass: he lurks,
    It may be, still, like dull books on a shelf,
In his own den, to scrawl some "Life" or "Vision,"
As Welborn says—"the Devil turned precisian."

CVI

As for the rest, to come to the conclusion
    Of this true dream, the telescope is gone
Which kept my optics free from all delusion,
    And showed me what I in my turn have shown;

All I saw farther, in the last confusion,
  Was, that King George slipped into Heaven for one;
And when the tumult dwindled to a calm,
I left him practising the hundredth psalm.

R[avenn]a, October 4, 1821.
[*First publ., Oct. 22, 1822.*]

TALES

THE GIAOUR

A FRAGMENT OF A TURKISH TALE

[This, the first of Byron's Oriental Tales, had some factual basis, as Byron took care to hint. He said that while at Athens he had rescued a girl, who, according to Turkish custom, as a punishment for infidelity, had been sewed in a sack and was going to be cast in the sea.]

> "One fatal remembrance—one sorrow that throws
> Its bleak shade alike o'er our joys and our woes—
> To which Life nothing darker nor brighter can bring,
> For which joy hath no balm—and affliction no sting."
> —MOORE.

TO

SAMUEL ROGERS, Esq.

AS A SLIGHT BUT MOST SINCERE TOKEN
OF ADMIRATION OF HIS GENIUS,
RESPECT FOR HIS CHARACTER,
AND GRATITUDE FOR HIS FRIENDSHIP,

THIS PRODUCTION IS INSCRIBED

BY HIS OBLIGED

AND AFFECTIONATE SERVANT,

BYRON.

LONDON, May, 1813.

ADVERTISEMENT

THE tale which these disjointed fragments present is founded upon circumstances now less common in the East than formerly;

439

either because the ladies are more circumspect than in the
"olden time," or because the Christians have better fortune, or
less enterprise. The story, when entire, contained the adventures
of a female slave, who was thrown, in the Mussulman manner,
into the sea for infidelity, and avenged by a young Venetian, her
lover, at the time the Seven Islands were possessed by the Republic of Venice, and soon after the Arnauts were beaten back
from the Morea, which they had ravaged for some time subsequent to the Russian invasion. The desertion of the Mainotes, on
being refused the plunder of Misitra, led to the abandonment of
that enterprise, and to the desolation of the Morea, during which
the cruelty exercised on all sides was unparalleled even in the
annals of the faithful.

THE GIAOUR

No BREATH of air to break the wave
That rolls below the Athenian's grave,
That tomb which, gleaming o'er the cliff,
First greets the homeward-veering skiff
High o'er the land he saved in vain:
When shall such Hero live again?

    .   .   .   .   o

Fair clime! where every season smiles
Benignant o'er those blessèd isles,
Which, seen from far Colonna's height,
Make glad the heart that hails the sight,   10
And lend to loneliness delight.
There mildly dimpling, Ocean's cheek
Reflects the tints of many a peak
Caught by the laughing tides that lave
These Edens of the Eastern wave:
And if at times a transient breeze
Break the blue crystal of the seas,
Or sweep one blossom from the trees,
How welcome is each gentle air
That wakes and wafts the odours there!   20
For there the Rose, o'er crag or vale,
Sultana of the Nightingale,
   The maid for whom his melody,
   His thousand songs are heard on high,

Blooms blushing to her lover's tale:
His queen, the garden queen, his Rose,
Unbent by winds, unchilled by snows,
Far from the winters of the west,
By every breeze and season blest,
Returns the sweets by Nature given   30
In softest incense back to Heaven;
And grateful yields that smiling sky
Her fairest hue and fragrant sigh.
And many a summer flower is there,
And many a shade that Love might share,
And many a grotto, meant for rest,
That holds the pirate for a guest;
Whose bark in sheltering cove below
Lurks for the passing peaceful prow,
Till the gay mariner's guitar   40
Is heard, and seen the Evening Star;
'Then stealing with the muffled oar,
Far shaded by the rocky shore,
Rush the night-prowlers on the prey,
And turn to groans his roundelay.
Strange—that where Nature loved to trace,
As if for Gods, a dwelling place,
And every charm and grace hath mixed
Within the Paradise she fixed,
There man, enamoured of distress,   50
Should mar it into wilderness,
And trample, brute-like, o'er each flower
That tasks not one laborious hour;
Nor claims the culture of his hand
To bloom along the fairy land,
But springs as to preclude his care,
And sweetly woos him—but to spare!
Strange—that where all is Peace beside,
There Passion riots in her pride,
And Lust and Rapine wildly reign   60
To darken o'er the fair domain.
It is as though the Fiends prevailed
Against the Seraphs they assailed,
And, fixed on heavenly thrones, should dwell
The freed inheritors of Hell;
So soft the scene, so formed for joy,
So curst the tyrants that destroy!

He who hath bent him o'er the dead
Ere the first day of Death is fled,
The first dark day of Nothingness,   **70**
The last of Danger and Distress,
(Before Decay's effacing fingers
Have swept the lines where Beauty lingers,)
And marked the mild angelic air,
The rapture of Repose that's there,
The fixed yet tender traits that streak
The languor of the placid cheek,
And—but for that sad shrouded eye,
    That fires not, wins not, weeps not, now,
    And but for that chill, changeless brow,   **80**
Where cold Obstruction's apathy
Appals the gazing mourner's heart,
As if to him it could impart
The doom he dreads, yet dwells upon;
Yes, but for these and these alone,
Some moments, aye, one treacherous hour,
He still might doubt the Tyrant's power;
So fair, so calm, so softly sealed,
The first, last look by Death revealed!
Such is the aspect of this shore;   **90**
'Tis Greece, but living Greece no more!
So coldly sweet, so deadly fair,
We start, for Soul is wanting there.
Hers is the loveliness in death,
That parts not quite with parting breath,
But beauty with that fearful bloom,
That hue which haunts it to the tomb,
Expression's last receding ray,
A gilded Halo hovering round decay,
The farewell beam of Feeling past away!   **100**
Spark of that flame, perchance of heavenly birth,
Which gleams, but warms no more its cherished earth!

    Clime of the unforgotten brave!
    Whose land from plain to mountain-cave
    Was Freedom's home or Glory's grave!
    Shrine of the mighty! can it be,
    That this is all remains of thee?
    Approach, thou craven crouching slave:
        Say, is not this Thermopylæ?

These waters blue that round you lave,— 110
  Oh servile offspring of the free—
Pronounce, what sea, what shore is this?
The gulf, the rock of Salamis!
These scenes, their story not unknown,
Arise, and make again your own;
Snatch from the ashes of your Sires
The embers of their former fires;
And he who in the strife expires
Will add to theirs a name of fear
That Tyranny shall quake to hear, 120
And leave his sons a hope, a fame,
They too will rather die than shame:
For Freedom's battle once begun,
Bequeathed by bleeding Sire to Son,
Though baffled oft is ever won.
Bear witness, Greece, thy living page!
Attest it many a deathless age!
While kings, in dusty darkness hid,
Have left a nameless pyramid,
Thy Heroes, though the general doom 130
Hath swept the column from their tomb,
A mightier monument command,
The mountains of their native land!
There points thy Muse to stranger's eye
The graves of those that cannot die!
'Twere long to tell, and sad to trace,
Each step from Splendour to Disgrace;
Enough—no foreign foe could quell
Thy soul, till from itself it fell;
Yet—Self-abasement paved the way 140
To villain-bonds and despot sway.

What can he tell who treads thy shore?
  No legend of thine olden time,
No theme on which the Muse might soar
High as thine own in days of yore,
  When man was worthy of thy clime.
The hearts within thy valleys bred,
The fiery souls that might have led
  Thy sons to deeds sublime,
Now crawl from cradle to the Grave, 150
Slaves—nay, the bondsmen of a Slave,

And callous, save to crime;
Stained with each evil that pollutes
Mankind, where least above the brutes;
Without even savage virtue blest,
Without one free or valiant breast,
Still to the neighbouring ports they waft
Proverbial wiles, and ancient craft;
In this the subtle Greek is found,
For this, and this alone, renowned,   160
In vain might Liberty invoke
The spirit to its bondage broke,
Or raise the neck that courts the yoke:
No more her sorrows I bewail,
Yet this will be a mournful tale,
And they who listen may believe,
Who heard it first had cause to grieve.

     .   .   .   .   .

Far, dark, along the blue sea glancing,
The shadows of the rocks advancing
Start on the Fisher's eye like boat   170
Of island-pirate or Mainote;
And fearful for his light caïque,
He shuns the near but doubtful creek:
Though worn and weary with his toil,
And cumbered with his scaly spoil,
Slowly, yet strongly, plies the oar,
Till Port Leone's safer shore
Receives him by the lovely light
That best becomes an Eastern night.

     .   .   .   .   .

Who thundering comes on blackest steed,   180
With slackened bit and hoof of speed?
Beneath the clattering iron's sound
The caverned Echoes wake around
In lash for lash, and bound for bound;
The foam that streaks the courser's side
Seems gathered from the Ocean-tide:
Though weary waves are sunk to rest,
There's none within his rider's breast;
And though to-morrow's tempest lower,

'Tis calmer than thy heart, young Giaour! 190
I know thee not, I loathe thy race,
But in thy lineaments I trace
What Time shall strengthen, not efface:
Though young and pale, that sallow front
Is scathed by fiery Passion's brunt;
Though bent on earth thine evil eye,
As meteor-like thou glidest by,
Right well I view and deem thee one
Whom Othman's sons should slay or shun.

On—on he hastened, and he drew 200
My gaze of wonder as he flew:
Though like a Demon of the night
He passed, and vanished from my sight,
His aspect and his air impressed
A troubled memory on my breast,
And long upon my startled ear
Rung his dark courser's hoofs of fear.
He spurs his steed; he nears the steep,
That, jutting, shadows o'er the deep;
He winds around; he hurries by; 210
The rock relieves him from mine eye;
For, well I ween, unwelcome he
Whose glance is fixed on those that flee;
And not a star but shines too bright
On him who takes such timeless flight.
He wound along; but ere he passed
One glance he snatched, as if his last,
A moment checked his wheeling steed,
A moment breathed him from his speed,
A moment on his stirrup stood— 220
Why looks he o'er the olive wood?
The Crescent glimmers on the hill,
The Mosque's high lamps are quivering still:
Though too remote for sound to wake
In echoes of the far tophaike,
The flashes of each joyous peal
Are seen to prove the Moslem's zeal.
To-night, set Rhamazani's sun;
To-night, the Bairam feast's begun;
To-night—but who and what art thou 230

Of foreign garb and fearful brow?
And what are these to thine or thee,
That thou shouldst either pause or flee?

He stood—some dread was on his face,
Soon Hatred settled in its place:
It rose not with the reddening flush
Of transient Anger's hasty blush,
But pale as marble o'er the tomb,
Whose ghastly whiteness aids its gloom.
His brow was bent, his eye was glazed;   240
He raised his arm, and fiercely raised,
And sternly shook his hand on high,
As doubting to return or fly;
Impatient of his flight delayed,
Here loud his raven charger neighed—
Down glanced that hand, and grasped his blade;
That sound had burst his waking dream,
As Slumber starts at owlet's scream.
The spur hath lanced his courser's sides;
Away—away—for life he rides: 250
Swift as the hurled on high jerreed
Springs to the touch his startled steed;
The rock is doubled, and the shore
Shakes with the clattering tramp no more;
The crag is won, no more is seen
His Christian crest and haughty mien.
'Twas but an instant he restrained
That fiery barb so sternly reined;
'Twas but a moment that he stood,
Then sped as if by Death pursued;   260
But in that instant o'er his soul
Winters of Memory seemed to roll,
And gather in that drop of time
A life of pain, an age of crime.
O'er him who loves, or hates, or fears,
Such moment pours the grief of years:
What felt *he* then, at once opprest
By all that most distracts the breast?
That pause, which pondered o'er his fate,
Oh, who its dreary length shall date!   270
Though in Time's record nearly nought,
It was Eternity to Thought!

For infinite as boundless space
The thought that Conscience must embrace,
Which in itself can comprehend
Woe without name, or hope, or end.

The hour is past, the Giaour is gone;
And did he fly or fall alone?
Woe to that hour he came or went!
The curse for Hassan's sin was sent 280
To turn a palace to a tomb;
He came, he went, like the Simoom,
That harbinger of Fate and gloom,
Beneath whose widely-wasting breath
The very cypress droops to death—
Dark tree, still sad when others' grief is fled,
The only constant mourner o'er the dead!

The steed is vanished from the stall;
No serf is seen in Hassan's hall;
The lonely Spider's thin gray pall 290
Waves slowly widening o'er the wall;
The Bat builds in his Haram bower,
And in the fortress of his power
The owl usurps the beacon-tower;
The wild-dog howls o'er the fountain's brim,
With baffled thirst, and famine, grim;
For the stream had shrunk from its marble bed,
Where the weeds and the desolate dust are spread.
'Twas sweet of yore to see it play
And chase the sultriness of day, 300
As springing high the silver dew
In whirls fantastically flew,
And flung luxurious coolness round
The air, and verdure o'er the ground.
'Twas sweet, when cloudless stars were bright,
To view the wave of watery light,
And hear its melody by night.
And oft had Hassan's Childhood played
Around the verge of that cascade;
And oft upon his mother's breast 310
That sound had harmonized his rest;
And oft had Hassan's Youth along
Its bank been soothed by Beauty's song;

And softer seemed each melting tone
Of Music mingled with its own.
But ne'er shall Hassan's Age repose
Along the brink at Twilight's close:
The stream that filled that font is fled—
The blood that warmed his heart is shed!
And here no more shall human voice   320
Be heard to rage, regret, rejoice.
The last sad note that swelled the gale
Was woman's wildest funeral wail:
That quenched in silence, all is still,
But the lattice that flaps when the wind is shrill:
Though raves the gust, and floods the rain,
No hand shall close its clasp again.
On desert sands 'twere joy to scan
The rudest steps of fellow man,
So here the very voice of Grief   330
Might wake an Echo like relief—
At least 'twould say, "All are not gone;
There lingers Life, though but in one"—
For many a gilded chamber's there,
Which Solitude might well forbear,
Within that dome as yet Decay
Hath slowly worked her cankering way—
But gloom is gathered o'er the gate,
Nor there the Fakir's self will wait;
Nor there will wandering Dervise stay,   340
For Bounty cheers not his delay;
Nor there will weary stranger halt
To bless the sacred "bread and salt."
Alike must Wealth and Poverty
Pass heedless and unheeded by
For Courtesy and Pity died
With Hassan on the mountain side.
His roof, that refuge unto men,
Is Desolation's hungry den.
The guest flies the hall, and the vassal from labour,   350
Since his turban was cleft by the infidel's sabre!

.   .   .   .   .

I hear the sound of coming feet,
But not a voice mine ear to greet;
More near—each turban I can scan,

And silver-sheathèd ataghan;
The foremost of the band is seen
An Emir by his garb of green:
"Ho! who art thou?"—"This low salam
Replies of Moslem faith I am.
The burthen ye so gently bear, 360
Seems one that claims your utmost care,
And, doubtless, holds some precious freight—
My humble bark would gladly wait."

"Thou speakest sooth: thy skiff unmoor,
And waft us from the silent shore;
Nay, leave the sail still furled, and ply
The nearest oar that's scattered by,
And midway to those rocks where sleep
The channelled waters dark and deep.
Rest from your task—so—bravely done, 370
Our course has been right swiftly run;
Yet 'tis the longest voyage, I trow,
That one of—   .   .   .

.   .   .   .   .   .

Sullen it plunged, and slowly sank,
The calm wave rippled to the bank;
I watched it as it sank, methought
Some motion from the current caught
Bestirred it more,—'twas but the beam
That checkered o'er the living stream:
I gazed, till vanishing from view, 380
Like lessening pebble it withdrew;
Still less and less, a speck of white
That gemmed the tide, then mocked the sight;
And all its hidden secrets sleep,
Known but to Genii of the deep,
Which, trembling in their coral caves,
They dare not whisper to the waves.

.   .   .   .   .   .

As rising on its purple wing
The insect queen of Eastern spring,
O'er emerald meadows of Kashmeer 890
Invites the young pursuer near,
And leads him on from flower to flower

A weary chase and wasted hour,
Then leaves him, as it soars on high,
With panting heart and tearful eye:
So Beauty lures the full-grown child,
With hue as bright, and wing as wild:
A chase of idle hopes and fears,
Begun in folly, closed in tears.
If won, to equal ills betrayed,   **400**
Woe waits the insect and the maid;
A life of pain, the loss of peace,
From infant's play, and man's caprice:
The lovely toy so fiercely sought
Hath lost its charm by being caught,
For every touch that wooed its stay
Hath brushed its brightest hues away,
Till charm, and hue, and beauty gone,
'Tis left to fly or fall alone.
With wounded wing, or bleeding breast,   **410**
Ah! where shall either victim rest?
Can this with faded pinion soar
From rose to tulip as before?
Or Beauty, blighted in an hour,
Find joy within her broken bower?
No: gayer insects fluttering by
Ne'er droop the wing o'er those that die.
And lovelier things have mercy shown
To every failing but their own,
And every woe a tear can claim   **420**
Except an erring Sister's shame.

.   .   .   .   .   .

The Mind, that broods o'er guilty woes,
  Is like the Scorpion girt by fire;
In circle narrowing as it glows,
The flame around their captive close,
Till inly searched by thousand throes,
  And maddening in her ire,
One sad and sole relief she knows—
The sting she nourished for her foes,
Whose venom never yet was vain,   **430**
Gives but one pang, and cures all pain,
And darts into her desperate brain:
So do the dark in soul expire,

Or live like Scorpion girt by fire;
So writhes the mind Remorse hath riven,
Unfit for earth, undoomed for heaven,
Darkness above, despair beneath,
Around it flame, within it death!

Black Hassan from the Haram flies,   440
Nor bends on woman's form his eyes;
The unwonted chase each hour employs,
Yet shares he not the hunter's joys.
Not thus was Hassan wont to fly
When Leila dwelt in his Serai.
Doth Leila there no longer dwell?
That tale can only Hassan tell:
Strange rumours in our city say
Upon that eve she fled away
When Rhamazan's last sun was set   450
And flashing from each Minaret
Millions of lamps proclaimed the feast
Of Bairam through the boundless East.
'Twas then she went as to the bath,
Which Hassan vainly searched in wrath;
For she was flown her master's rage
In likeness of a Georgian page,
And far beyond the Moslem's power
Had wronged him with the faithless Giaour.
Somewhat of this had Hassan deemed;
But still so fond, so fair she seemed,   460
Too well he trusted to the slave
Whose treachery deserved a grave:
And on that eve had gone to Mosque,
And thence to feast in his Kiosk.
Such is the tale his Nubians tell,
Who did not watch their charge too well;
But others say, that on that night,
By pale Phingari's trembling light,
The Giaour upon his jet-black steed
Was seen, but seen alone to speed   470
With bloody spur along the shore,
Nor maid nor page behind him bore.

Her eye's dark charm 'twere vain to tell,
But gaze on that of the Gazelle,
It will assist thy fancy well;
As large, as languishingly dark,
But Soul beamed forth in every spark
That darted from beneath the lid,
Bright as the jewel of Giamschid.
Yea, *Soul,* and should our prophet say   480
That form was nought but breathing clay,
By Alla! I would answer nay;
Though on Al-Sirat's arch I stood,
Which totters o'er the fiery flood,
With Paradise within my view,
And all his Houris beckoning through.
Oh! who young Leila's glance could read
And keep that portion of his creed
Which saith that woman is but dust,
A soulless toy for tyrant's lust?   490
On her might Muftis gaze, and own
That through her eye the Immortal shone;
On her fair cheek's unfading hue
The young pomegranate's blossoms strew
Their bloom in blushes ever new;
Her hair in hyacinthine flow,
When left to roll its folds below,
As midst her handmaids in the hall
She stood superior to them all,
Hath swept the marble where her feet   500
Gleamed whiter than the mountain sleet
Ere from the cloud that gave it birth
It fell, and caught one stain of earth.
The cygnet nobly walks the water;
So moved on earth Circassia's daughter,
The loveliest bird of Franguestan!
As rears her crest the ruffled Swan,
    And spurns the wave with wings of pride,
When pass the steps of stranger man
    Along the banks that bound her tide;   510
Thus rose fair Leila's whiter neck:—
Thus armed with beauty would she check
Intrusion's glance, till Folly's gaze
Shrunk from the charms it meant to praise.
Thus high and graceful was her gait;

Her heart as tender to her mate;
Her mate—stern Hassan, who was he?
Alas! that name was not for thee!

.   .   .   .   .   .

Stern Hassan hath a journey ta'en
With twenty vassals in his train,   520
Each armed, as best becomes a man,
With arquebuss and ataghan;
The chief before, as decked for war,
Bears in his belt the scimitar
Stained with the best of Arnaut blood,
When in the pass the rebels stood,
And few returned to tell the tale
Of what befell in Parne's vale.
The pistols which his girdle bore
Were those that once a Pasha wore,   530
Which still, though gemmed and bossed with gold,
Even robbers tremble to behold.
'Tis said he goes to woo a bride
More true than her who left his side;
The faithless slave that broke her bower,
And—worse than faithless—for a Giaour!

.   .   .   .   .   .

The Sun's last rays are on the hill,
And sparkle in the fountain rill,
Whose welcome waters, cool and clear,
Draw blessings from the mountaineer: 540
Here may the loitering merchant Greek
Find that repose 'twere vain to seek
In cities lodged too near his lord,
And trembling for his secret hoard—
Here may he rest where none can see,
In crowds a slave, in deserts free;
And with forbidden wine may stain
The bowl a Moslem must not drain.

.   .   .   .   .   .

The foremost Tartar's in the gap,
Conspicuous by his yellow cap;   550
The rest in lengthening line the while

Wind slowly through the long defile:
Above, the mountain rears a peak,
Where vultures whet the thirsty beak,
And theirs may be a feast to-night,
Shall tempt them down ere morrow's light;
Beneath, a river's wintry stream
Has shrunk before the summer beam,
And left a channel bleak and bare,
Save shrubs that spring to perish there: 560
Each side the midway path there lay
Small broken crags of granite gray,
By time, or mountain lightning, riven
From summits clad in mists of heaven;
For where is he that hath beheld
The peak of Liakura unveiled?

　　　.　　.　　.　　.　　.　　.

They reach the grove of pine at last;
"Bismillah! now the peril's past;
For yonder view the opening plain,
And there we'll prick our steeds amain:"   570
The Chiaus spake, and as he said,
A bullet whistled o'er his head;
The foremost Tartar bites the ground!
　Scarce had they time to check the rein,
Swift from their steeds the riders bound;
　But three shall never mount again:
Unseen the foes that gave the wound,
　The dying ask revenge in vain.
With steel unsheathed, and carbine bent,
Some o'er their courser's harness leant,   580
　Half sheltered by the steed;
Some fly beneath the nearest rock,
And there await the coming shock,
　Nor tamely stand to bleed
Beneath the shaft of foes unseen,
Who dare not quit their craggy screen.
Stern Hassan only from his horse
Disdains to light, and keeps his course,
Till fiery flashes in the van
Proclaim too sure the robber-clan   590
Have well secured the only way
Could now avail the promised prey;

Then curled his very beard with ire,
  And glared his eye with fiercer fire;
"Though far and near the bullets hiss,
I've scaped a bloodier hour than this."
And now the foe their covert quit,
And call his vassals to submit;
But Hassan's frown and furious word
 Are dreaded more than hostile sword,   600
Nor of his little band a man
Resigned carbine or ataghan,
Nor raised the craven cry, Amaun!
In fuller sight, more near and near,
The lately ambushed foes appear,
And, issuing from the grove, advance
Some who on battle-charger prance.
Who leads them on with foreign brand
Far flashing in his red right hand?
" 'Tis he! 'tis he! I know him now;   610
I know him by his pallid brow;
I know him by the evil eye
That aids his envious treachery;
I know him by his jet-black barb;
Though now arrayed in Arnaut garb,
Apostate from his own vile faith,
It shall not save him from the death:
'Tis he! well met in any hour,
Lost Leila's love—acccurséd Giaour!"

As rolls the river into Ocean,   620
In sable torrent wildly streaming;
  As the sea-tide's opposing motion,
In azure column proudly gleaming,
Beats back the current many a rood,
In curling foam and mingling flood,
While eddying whirl, and breaking wave,
Roused by the blast of winter, rave;
Through sparkling spray, in thundering clash,
The lightnings of the waters flash
In awful whiteness o'er the shore,   630
That shines and shakes beneath the roar;
Thus—as the stream and Ocean greet,
With waves that madden as they meet—
Thus join the bands, whom mutual wrong,

And fate, and fury, drive along.
The bickering sabres' shivering jar;
  And pealing wide or ringing near
  Its echoes on the throbbing ear,
The deathshot hissing from afar;
The shock, the shout, the groan of war,   **640**
  Reverberate along that vale,
  More suited to the shepherd's tale:
Though few the numbers—theirs the strife,
That neither spares nor speaks for life!
Ah! fondly youthful hearts can press,
To seize and share the dear caress;
But Love itself could never pant
For all that Beauty sighs to grant
With half the fervour Hate bestows
Upon the last embrace of foes,   **650**
When grappling in the fight they fold
Those arms that ne'er shall lose their hold:
Friends meet to part; Love laughs at faith;
True foes, once met, are joined till death!

  .   .   .

  With sabre shivered to the hilt,
Yet dripping with the blood he spilt;
Yet strained within the severed hand
Which quivers round that faithless brand;
His turban far behind him rolled,
And cleft in twain its firmest fold: **660**
His flowing robe by falchion torn,
And crimson as those clouds of morn
That, streaked with dusky red, portend
The day shall have a stormy end;
A stain on every bush that bore
A fragment of his palampore;
His breast with wounds unnumbered riven,
His back to earth, his face to Heaven,
Fall'n Hassan lies—his unclosed eye
Yet lowering on his enemy,   **670**
As if the hour that sealed his fate
Surviving left his quenchless hate;
And o'er him bends that foe with brow
As dark as his that bled below.

  .   .   .

"Yes, Leila sleeps beneath the wave,
But his shall be a redder grave;
Her spirit pointed well the steel
Which taught that felon heart to feel.
He called the Prophet, but his power
Was vain against the vengeful Giaour: 680
He called on Alla—but the word
Arose unheeded or unheard.
Thou Paynim fool! could Leila's prayer
Be passed, and thine accorded there?
I watched my time, I leagued with these,
The traitor in his turn to seize;
My wrath is wreaked, the deed is done,
And now I go,—but go alone."

.   .   .   .   .   ‹
.   .   .   .   .   •

The browsing camels' bells are tinkling:
His mother looked from her lattice high—   690
  She saw the dews of eve besprinkling
The pasture green beneath her eye,
  She saw the planets faintly twinkling:
" 'Tis twilight—sure his train is nigh."
She could not rest in the garden-bower,
But gazed through the grate of his steepest tower.
"Why comes he not? his steeds are fleet,
Nor shrink they from the summer heat;
Why sends not the Bridegroom his promised gift?
Is his heart more cold, or his barb less swift?   700
Oh, false reproach! yon Tartar now
Has gained our nearest mountain's brow,
And warily the steep descends,
And now within the valley bends;
And he bears the gift at his saddle bow—
How could I deem his courser slow?
Right well my largess shall repay
His welcome speed, and weary way."

  The Tartar lighted at the gate,
But scarce upheld his fainting weight!   710
His swarthy visage spake distress,
But this might be from weariness;

His garb with sanguine spots was dyed,
But these might be from his courser's side;
He drew the token from his vest—
Angel of Death! 'Tis Hassan's cloven crest!
His calpac rent—his caftan red—
"Lady, a fearful bride thy Son hath wed:
Me, not from mercy, did they spare,
But this empurpled pledge to bear.   720
Peace to the brave! whose blood is spilt:
Woe to the Giaour! for his the guilt."

.   .   .   .   .   *

A Turban carved in coarsest stone,
A Pillar with rank weeds o'ergrown,
Whereon can now be scarcely read
The Koran verse that mourns the dead,
Point out the spot where Hassan fell
A victim in that lonely dell.
There sleeps as true as Osmanlie
As e'er at Mecca bent the knee;   730
As ever scorned forbidden wine,
Or prayed with face towards the shrine,
In orisons resumed anew
At solemn sound of "Alla Hu!"
Yet died he by a stranger's hand,
And stranger in his native land;
Yet died he as in arms he stood,
And unavenged, at least in blood.
But him the maids of Paradise
   Impatient to their halls invite,   740
And the dark heaven of Houris' eyes
   On him shall glance for ever bright;
They come—their kerchiefs green they wave,
And welcome with a kiss the brave!
Who falls in battle 'gainst a Giaour
Is worthiest an immortal bower.

.   .   .   .   .   *

But thou, false Infidel! shall writhe
Beneath avenging Monkir's scythe;
And from its torments 'scape alone
To wander round lost Eblis' throne;   750
And fire unquenched, unquenchable,

Around, within, thy heart shall dwell;
Nor ear can hear nor tongue can tell
The tortures of that inward hell!
But first, on earth as Vampire sent,
Thy corse shall from its tomb be rent:
Then ghastly haunt thy native place,
And suck the blood of all thy race;
There from thy daughter, sister, wife,
At midnight drain the stream of life;   760
Yet loathe the banquet which perforce
Must feed thy livid living corse:
Thy victims ere they yet expire
Shall know the demon for their sire,
As cursing thee, thou cursing them,
Thy flowers are withered on the stem.
But one that for thy crime must fall,
The youngest, most beloved of all,
Shall bless thee with a *father's* name—
That word shall wrap thy heart in flame!   770
Yet must thou end thy task, and mark
Her cheek's last tinge, her eye's last spark,
And the last glassy glance must view
Which freezes o'er its lifeless blue;
Then with unhallowed hand shalt tear
The tresses of her yellow hair,
Of which in life a lock when shorn
Affection's fondest pledge was worn,
But now is borne away by thee,
Memorial of thine agony!   780
Wet with thine own best blood shall drip
Thy gnashing tooth and haggard lip;
Then stalking to thy sullen grave,
Go—and with Gouls and Afrits rave;
Till these in horror shrink away
From Sceptre more accursed than they!

.   .   .   .   .   .

"How name ye yon lone Caloyer?
   His features I have scanned before
In mine own land: 'tis many a year,
   Since, dashing by the lonely shore,   790
I saw him urge as fleet a steed
As ever served a horseman's need.

But once I saw that face, yet then
It was so marked with inward pain,
I could not pass it by again;
It breathes the same dark spirit now,
As death were stamped upon his brow.

" 'Tis twice three years at summer tide
    Since first among our freres he came;
And here it soothes him to abide   800
    For some dark deed he will not name.
But never at our Vesper prayer,
Nor e'er before Confession chair
Kneels he, nor recks he when arise
Incense or anthem to the skies,
But broods within his cell alone,
His faith and race alike unknown.
The sea from Paynim land he crost,
And here ascended from the coast;
Yet seems he not of Othman race,   810
But only Christian in his face:
I'd judge him some stray renegade,
Repentant of the change he made,
Save that he shuns our holy shrine,
Nor tastes the sacred bread and wine.
Great largess to these walls he brought,
And thus our Abbot's favour bought;
But were I Prior, not a day
Should brook such stranger's further stay,
Or pent within our penance cell   820
Should doom him there for aye to dwell.
Much in his visions mutters he
Of maiden whelmed beneath the sea;
Of sabres clashing, foemen flying,
Wrongs avenged, and Moslem dying.
On cliff he hath been known to stand
And rave as to some bloody hand
Fresh severed from its parent limb,
Invisible to all but him,
Which beckons onward to his grave,   830
And lures to leap into the wave."

Dark and unearthly is the scowl
That glares beneath his dusky cowl:
The flash of that dilating eye
Reveals too much of times gone by;
Though varying, indistinct its hue,
Oft will his glance the gazer rue,
For in it lurks that nameless spell,
Which speaks, itself unspeakable,
A spirit yet unquelled and high,   840
That claims and keeps ascendancy;
And like the bird whose pinions quake,
But cannot fly the gazing snake,
Will others quail beneath his look,
Nor 'scape the glance they scarce can brook:
From him the half-affrighted Friar
When met alone would fain retire,
As if that eye and bitter smile
Transferred to others fear and guile:
Not oft to smile descendeth he,   850
And when he doth 'tis sad to see
That he but mocks at Misery.
How that pale lip will curl and quiver!
Then fix once more as if for ever;
As if his sorrow or disdain
Forbade him e'er to smile again.
Well were it so—such ghastly mirth
From joyaunce ne'er derived its birth.
But sadder still it were to trace
What once were feelings in that face: 860
Time hath not yet the features fixed,
But brighter traits with evil mixed;
And there are hues not always faded,
Which speak a mind not all degraded
Even by the crimes through which it waded·
The common crowd but see the gloom
Of wayward deeds, and fitting doom;
The close observer can espy
A noble soul, and lineage high:
Alas! though both bestowed in vain,   870
Which Grief could change, and Guilt could stain,
It was no vulgar tenement
To which such lofty gifts were lent,
Ana still with little less than dread

On such the sight is riveted.
The roofless cot, decayed and rent,
　Will scarce delay the passer-by;
The tower by war or tempest bent,
While yet may frown one battlement,
　Demands and daunts the stranger's eye;　　880
Each ivied arch, and pillar lone,
Pleads haughtily for glories gone!

"His floating robe around him folding,
　Slow sweeps he through the columned aisle;
With dread beheld, with gloom beholding
　The rites that sanctify the pile.
But when the anthem shakes the choir,
And kneel the monks, his steps retire;
By yonder lone and wavering torch
His aspect glares within the porch;　　890
There will he pause till all is done—
And hear the prayer, but utter none.
See—by the half-illumined wall
His hood fly back, his dark hair fall,
That pale brow wildly wreathing round,
As if the Gorgon there had bound
The sablest of the serpent-braid
That o'er her fearful forehead strayed:
For he declines the convent oath,
And leaves those locks unhallowed growth,　　900
But wears our garb in all beside;
And, not from piety but pride,
Gives wealth to walls that never heard
Of his one holy vow nor word.
Lo!—mark ye, as the harmony
Peals louder praises to the sky,
That livid cheek, that stony air
Of mixed defiance and despair!
Saint Francis, keep him from the shrine!
Else may we dread the wrath divine　　910
Made manifest by awful sign.
If ever evil angel bore
The form of mortal, such he wore:
By all my hope of sins forgiven,
Such looks are not of earth nor heaven!"

To Love the softest hearts are prone,
But such can ne'er be all his own;
Too timid in his woes to share,
Too meek to meet, or brave despair;
And sterner hearts alone may feel   920
The wound that Time can never heal.
The rugged metal of the mine
Must burn before its surface shine,
But plunged within the furnace-flame,
It bends and melts—though still the same;
Then tempered to thy want, or will,
'Twill serve thee to defend or kill—
A breast-plate for thine hour of need,
Or blade to bid thy foeman bleed;
But if a dagger's form it bear,   930
Let those who shape its edge, beware!
Thus Passion's fire, and Woman's art,
Can turn and tame the sterner heart;
From these its form and tone are ta'en,
And what they make it, must remain,
But break—before it bend again.

    .   .   .   .   .   .

If solitude succeed to grief,
Release from pain is slight relief;
The vacant bosom's wilderness
Might thank the pang that made it less.   940
We loathe what none are left to share:
Even bliss—'twere woe alone to bear;
The heart once left thus desolate
Must fly at last for ease—to hate.
It is as if the dead could feel
The icy worm around them steal,
And shudder, as the reptiles creep
To revel o'er their rotting sleep,
Without the power to scare away
The cold consumers of their clay!   950
It is as if the desert bird,
    Whose beak unlocks her bosom's stream
    To still her famished nestlings' scream,
Nor mourns a life to them transferred,

Should rend her rash devoted breast,
And find them flown her empty nest.
The keenest pangs the wretched find
   Are rapture to the dreary void—
The leafless desert of the mind,
   The waste of feelings unemployed.   960
Who would be doomed to gaze upon
A sky without a cloud or sun?
Less hideous far the tempest's roar,
Than ne'er to brave the billows more—
Thrown, when the war of winds is o'er,
A lonely wreck on Fortune's shore,
'Mid sullen calm, and silent bay,
Unseen to drop by dull decay;—
Better to sink beneath the shock
Than moulder piecemeal on the rock!   970

‘   .   .   .   .   ʿ

"Father! thy days have passed in peace,
   'Mid counted beads, and countless prayer,
To bid the sins of others cease,
   Thyself without a crime or care,
   Save transient ills that all must bear,
Has been thy lot from youth to age;
And thou wilt bless thee from the rage
Of passions fierce and uncontrolled,
Such as thy penitents unfold,
Whose secret sins and sorrows rest   980
Within thy pure and pitying breast.
My days, though few, have passed below
In much of Joy, but more of Woe;
Yet still in hours of love or strife,
I've 'scaped the weariness of Life:
Now leagued with friends, now girt by foes,
I loathed the languor of repose.
Now, nothing left to love or hate,
No more with hope or pride elate,
I'd rather be the thing that crawls   990
Most noxious o'er a dungeon's walls,
Than pass my dull, unvarying days,
Condemned to meditate and gaze.
Yet, lurks a wish within my breast
For rest—but not to feel 'tis rest.

Soon shall my Fate that wish fulfil;
   And I shall sleep without the dream
Of what I was, and would be still,
   Dark as to thee my deeds may seem:
My memory now is but the tomb   1000
Of joys long dead; my hope, their doom:
Though better to have died with those
Than bear a life of lingering woes.
My spirit shrunk not to sustain
The searching throes of ceaseless pain;
Nor sought the self-accorded grave
Of ancient fool and modern knave:
Yet death I have not feared to meet;
And in the field it had been sweet,
Had Danger wooed me on to move   1010
The slave of Glory, not of Love.
I've braved it—not for Honour's boast;
I smile at laurels won or lost;
To such let others carve their way,
For high renown, or hireling pay:
But place again before my eyes
Aught that I deem a worthy prize—
The maid I love, the man I hate—
And I will hunt the steps of fate,
To save or slay, as these require,   1020
Through rending steel, and rolling fire:
Nor needst thou doubt this speech from one
Who would but do—what he *hath* done.
Death is but what the haughty brave,
The weak must bear, the wretch must crave;
Then let life go to Him who gave:
I have not quailed to Danger's brow
When high and happy—need I *now?*

     .   .   .   .   .   .

"I loved her, Friar! nay, adored—
   But these are words that all can use—   1030
I proved it more in deed than word;
There's blood upon that dinted sword,
   A stain its steel can never lose:
'Twas shed for her, who died for me.
   It warmed the heart of one abhorred:
Nay, start not—no—nor bend thy knee.

Nor midst my sin such act record;
Thou wilt absolve me from the deed,
For he was hostile to thy creed!
The very name of Nazarene   1040
Was wormwood to his Paynim spleen.
Ungrateful fool! since but for brands
Well wielded in some hardy hands,
And wounds by Galileans given—
The surest pass to Turkish heaven—
For him his Houris still might wait
Impatient at the Prophet's gate.
I loved her—Love will find its way
Through paths where wolves would fear to prey;
And if it dares enough, 'twere hard   1050
If Passion met not some reward—
No matter how, or where or why,
I did not vainly seek, nor sigh:
Yet sometimes, with remorse, in vain
I wish she had not loved again.
She died—I dare not tell thee how;
But look—'tis written on my brow!
There read of Cain the curse and crime,
In characters unworn by Time:
Still, ere thou dost condemn me, pause;   1060
Not mine the act, though I the cause.
Yet did he but what I had done
Had she been false to more than one.
Faithless to him—he gave the blow;
But true to me—I laid him low:
Howe'er deserved her doom might be
Her treachery was truth to me;
To me she gave her heart, that all
Which Tyranny can ne'er enthrall;
And I, alas! too late to save!   1070
Yet all I then could give, I gave—
'Twas some relief—our foe a grave.
His death sits lightly; but her fate
Has made me—what thou well mayst hate.
    His doom was sealed—he knew it well,
Warned by the voice of stern Taheer,
Deep in whose darkly boding ear
The deathshot pealed of murder near,
    As filed the troop to where they fell!

He died too in the battle broil,   1086
A time that heeds nor pain nor toil:
One cry to Mahomet for aid,
One prayer to Alla all he made.
He knew and crossed me in the fray—
I gazed upon him where he lay,
And watched his spirit ebb away:
Though pierced like pard by hunter's steel,
He felt not half that now I feel.
I searched, but vainly searched, to find
The workings of a wounded mind;   1090
Each feature of that sullen corse
Betrayed his rage, but no remorse.
Oh, what had Vengeance given to trace
Despair upon his dying face!—
The late repentance of that hour
When Penitence hath lost her power
To tear one terror from the grave,
And will not soothe, and cannot save.

     .   .   .   .   .   .

"The cold in clime are cold in blood,
   Their love can scarce deserve the name;   1100
But mine was like the lava flood
   That boils in Ætna's breast of flame.
I cannot prate in puling strain
Of Ladye-love, and Beauty's chain:
If changing cheek, and scorching vein,
Lips taught to writhe, but not complain,
If bursting heart, and maddening brain,
And daring deed, and vengeful steel,
And all that I have felt and feel,
Betoken love—that love was mine,   1110
And shown by many a bitter sign.
'Tis true, I could not whine nor sigh,
I knew but to obtain or die.
I die—but first I have possessed,
And come what may, I *have been* blessed.
Shall I the doom I sought upbraid?
No—reft of all, yet undismayed
But for the thought of Leila slain,
Give me the pleasure with the pain,
So would I live and love again.   1120

I grieve, but not, my holy Guide!
For him who dies, but her who died:
She sleeps beneath the wandering wave—
Ah! had she but an earthly grave,
This breaking heart and throbbing head
Should seek and share her narrow bed.
She was a form of Life and Light,
That, seen, became a part of sight;
And rose, where'er I turned mine eye,
The Morning-star of Memory!   1130

"Yes, Love indeed is light from Heaven;
    A spark of that immortal fire
With angels shared, by Alla given,
    To lift from earth our low desire.
Devotion wafts the mind above,
But Heaven itself descends in Love—
A feeling from the Godhead caught,
To wean from self each sordid thought;
A ray of Him who formed the whole—
A Glory circling round the soul!   1140
I grant *my* love imperfect, all
That mortals by the name miscall:
Then deem it evil, what thou wilt—
But say, oh say, *hers* was not Guilt!
She was my Life's unerring Light:
That quenched—what beam shall break my night?
Oh! would it shone to lead me still,
Although to death or deadliest ill!
Why marvel ye, if they who lose
    This present joy, this future hope,   1150
    No more with sorrow meekly cope;
In phrensy then their fate accuse;
In madness do those fearful deeds
    That seem to add but Guilt to Woe?
Alas! the breast that inly bleeds
    Hath nought to dread from outward blow:
Who falls from all he knows of bliss,
Cares little into what abyss.
Fierce as the gloomy vulture's now
    To thee, old man, my deeds appear: 1160
I read abhorrence on thy brow,

And this too was I born to bear!
'Tis true, that, like that bird of prey,
With havock have I marked my way:
But this was taught me by the dove,
To die—and know no second love.
This lesson yet hath man to learn,
Taught by the thing he dares to spurn:
The bird that sings within the brake,
The swan that swims upon the lake,   1170
One mate, and one alone, will take.
And let the fool still prone to range,
And sneer on all who cannot change,
Partake his jest with boasting boys;
I envy not his varied joys,
But deem such feeble, heartless man,
Less than yon solitary swan,—
Far, far beneath the shallow maid
He left believing and betrayed.
Such shame at least was never mine—   1180
Leila! each thought was only thine!
My good, my guilt, my weal, my woe,
My hope on high—my all below.
Earth holds no other like to thee,
Or, if it doth, in vain for me:
For worlds I dare not view the dame
Resembling thee, yet not the same.
The very crimes that mar my youth,
This bed of death—attest my truth!
'Tis all too late—thou wert, thou art   1190
The cherished madness of my heart!

"And she was lost—and yet I breathed,
   But not the breath of human life:
A serpent round my heart was wreathed,
   And stung my every thought to strife.
Alike all time—abhorred all place—
Shuddering I shrank from Nature's face,
Where every hue that charmed before
The blackness of my bosom wore.
The rest thou dost already know,   1200
And all my sins, and half my woe.
But talk no more of penitence;

Thou seest I soon shall part from hence;
And if thy holy tale were true,
The deed that's done canst *thou* undo?
Think me not thankless—but this grief
Looks not to priesthood for relief.
My soul's estate in secret guess:
But wouldst thou pity more, say less.
When thou canst bid my Leila live, 1210
Then will I sue thee to forgive;
Then plead my cause in that high place
Where purchased masses proffer grace.
Go, when the hunter's hand hath wrung
From forest-cave her shrieking young,
And calm the lonely lioness:
But soothe not—mock not *my* distress!

"In earlier days, and calmer hours,
 When heart with heart delights to blend,
Where bloom my native valley's bowers, 1220
 I had—Ah! have I now—a friend!
To him this pledge I charge thee send,
 Memorial of a youthful vow;
I would remind him of my end:
 Though souls absorbed like mine allow
Brief thought to distant Friendship's claim,
Yet dear to him my blighted name.
'Tis strange—he prophesied my doom,
 And I have smiled—I then could smile—
When Prudence would his voice assume, 1230
 And warn—I recked not what—the while:
But now Remembrance whispers o'er
Those accents scarcely marked before.
Say—that his bodings came to pass,
 And he will start to hear their truth,
 And wish his words had not been sooth:
Tell him—unheeding as I was,
 Through many a busy bitter scene
 Of all our golden youth had been,
In pain, my faltering tongue had tried 1240
To bless his memory—ere I died;
But Heaven in wrath would turn away,
If Guilt should for the guiltless pray.

I do not ask him not to blame,
Too gentle he to wound my name;
And what have I to do with Fame?
I do not ask him not to mourn,
Such cold request might sound like scorn;
And what than Friendship's manly tear
May better grace a brother's bier? 1255
But bear this ring, his own of old,
And tell him—what thou dost behold!
The withered frame, the ruined mind,
The wrack by passion left behind,
A shrivelled scroll, a scattered leaf,
Seared by the autumn blast of Grief!

. . . . .

"Tell me no more of Fancy's gleam,
No, Father, no, 'twas not a dream;
Alas! the dreamer first must sleep,—
I only watched, and wished to weep; 1260
But could not, for my burning brow
Throbbed to the very brain as now:
I wished but for a single tear,
As something welcome, new, and dear:
I wished it then, I wish it still;
Despair is stronger than my will.
Waste not thine orison—despair
Is mightier than thy pious prayer:
I would not, if I might, be blest;
I want no Paradise, but rest. 1270
'Twas then—I tell thee—Father! then
I saw her; yes, she lived again,
And shining in her white symar,
As through yon pale gray cloud the star
Which now I gaze on, as on her,
Who looked and looks far lovelier;
Dimly I view its trembling spark;
To-morrow's night shall be more dark;
And I, before its rays appear,
That lifeless thing the living fear. 1280
I wander—Father! for my soul
Is fleeting towards the final goal.
I saw her—Friar! and I rose

Forgetful of our former woes;
And rushing from my couch, I dart,
And clasp her to my desperate heart;
I clasp—what is it that I clasp?
No breathing form within my grasp,
No heart that beats reply to mine—
Yet, Leila! yet the form is thine!　　　　　　　1290
And art thou, dearest, changed so much
As meet my eye, yet mock my touch?
Ah! were thy beauties e'er so cold,
I care not—so my arms enfold
The all they ever wished to hold.
Alas! around a shadow prest
They shrink upon my lonely breast;
Yet still 'tis there! In silence stands,
And beckons with beseeching hands!
With braided hair, and bright-black eye—　　　1300
I knew 'twas false—she could not die!
But *he* is dead! within the dell
I saw him buried where he fell;
He comes not—for he cannot break
From earth;—why then art *thou* awake?
They told me wild waves rolled above
The face I view—the form I love;
They told me—'twas a hideous tale!—
I'd tell it, but my tongue would fail:
If true, and from thine ocean-cave　　　　　　1310
Thou com'st to claim a calmer grave,
Oh! pass thy dewy fingers o'er
This brow that then will burn no more;
Or place them on my hopeless heart:
But, Shape or Shade! whate'er thou art,
In mercy ne'er again depart!
Or farther with thee bear my soul
Than winds can waft or waters roll!

.　　　　.　　　　.　　　　.　　　　.　　　　.

"Such is my name, and such my tale.
　　Confessor! to thy secret ear　　　　　　　1320
I breathe the sorrows I bewail,
　　And thank thee for the generous tear
This glazing eye could never shed.
Then lay me with the humblest dead,

And, save the cross above my head,
Be neither name nor emblem spread,
By prying stranger to be read,
Or stay the passing pilgrim's tread."
He passed—nor of his name and race
He left a token or a trace,   1330
Save what the Father must not say
Who shrived him on his dying day:
This broken tale was all we knew
Of her he loved, or him he slew.

[*First publ., Dec. 27, 1813.*]

THE BRIDE OF ABYDOS

A Turkish Tale

[This poem, whose narrative is better handled than that of the
snakelike *Giaour*, was written, so Byron boasted, in four nights.
It sold 6,000 copies in a month.]

"Had we never loved sae kindly,
Had we never loved sae blindly,
Never met—or never parted,
We had ne'er been broken-hearted."

—BURNS

TO
THE RIGHT HONOURABLE

LORD HOLLAND,

THIS TALE
IS INSCRIBED, WITH
EVERY SENTIMENT OF REGARD
AND RESPECT,
BY HIS GRATEFULLY OBLIGED
AND SINCERE FRIEND,

BYRON

CANTO THE FIRST

I

KNOW ye the land where the cypress and myrtle
  Are emblems of deeds that are done in their clime?
Where the rage of the vulture, the love of the turtle,
  Now melt into sorrow, now madden to crime?
Know ye the land of the cedar and vine,
Where the flowers ever blossom, the beams ever shine;
Where the light wings of Zephyr, oppressed with perfume,
Wax faint o'er the gardens of Gúl in her bloom;
Where the citron and olive are fairest of fruit,
And the voice of the nightingale never is mute;   10
Where the tints of the earth, and the hues of the sky,
In colour though varied, in beauty may vie,
And the purple of Ocean is deepest in dye;
Where the virgins are soft as the roses they twine,
And all, save the spirit of man, is divine—
'Tis the clime of the East—'tis the land of the Sun—
Can he smile on such deeds as his children have done?
Oh! wild as the accents of lovers' farewell
Are the hearts which they bear, and the tales which they tell.

II

  Begirt with many a gallant slave,   20
  Apparelled as becomes the brave,
  Awaiting each his Lord's behest
  To guide his steps, or guard his rest,
  Old Giaffir sate in his Divan:
    Deep thought was in his agéd eye;
  And though the face of Mussulman
    Not oft betrays to standers by
  The mind within, well skilled to hide
  All but unconquerable pride,
  His pensive cheek and pondering brow   30
  Did more than he was wont avow.

III

'Let the chamber be cleared."—The train disappeared—
  "Now call me the chief of the Haram guard"—
With Giaffir is none but his only son,
    And the Nubian awaiting the sire's award.
    "Haroun—when all the crowd that wait
    Are passed beyond the outer gate,
    (Woe to the head whose eye beheld
    My child Zuleika's face unveiled!)
Hence, lead my daughter from her tower—   40
Her fate is fixed this very hour;
Yet not to her repeat my thought—
By me alone be duty taught!"

"Pacha! to hear is to obey."—
No more must slave to despot say—
Then to the tower had ta'en his way:
But here young Selim silence brake,
    First lowly rendering reverence meet;
And downcast looked, and gently spake,
    Still standing at the Pacha's feet: 50
For son of Moslem must expire,
Ere dare to sit before his sire!
"Father! for fear that thou shouldst chide
My sister, or her sable guide—
Know—for the fault, if fault there be,
Was mine—then fall thy frowns on me!
So lovelily the morning shone,
    That—let the old and weary sleep—
I could not; and to view alone
    The fairest scenes of land and deep,   60
With none to listen and reply
To thoughts with which my heart beat high
Were irksome—for whate'er my mood,
In sooth I love not solitude;
I on Zuleika's slumber broke,
    And, as thou knowest that for me
    Soon turns the Haram's grating key,
Before the guardian slaves awoke
We to the cypress groves had flown,
And made earth, main, and heaven our own!   70

There lingered we, beguiled too long
With Mejnoun's tale, or Sadi's song;
Till I, who heard the deep tambour
Beat thy Divan's approaching hour,
To thee, and to my duty true,
Warned by the sound, to greet thee flew:
But there Zuleika wanders yet—
Nay, Father, rage not—nor forget
That none can pierce that secret bower
But those who watch the women's tower."   80

IV

"Son of a slave"—the Pacha said—
"From unbelieving mother bred,
Vain were a father's hope to see
Aught that beseems a man in thee.
Thou, when thine arm should bend the bow,
    And hurl the dart, and curb the steed,
    Thou, Greek in soul if not in creed,
Must pore where babbling waters flow,
And watch unfolding roses blow.
Would that yon Orb, whose matin glow   90
Thy listless eyes so much admire,
Would lend thee something of his fire!
Thou, who would'st see this battlement
by Christian cannon piecemeal rent;
Nay, tamely view old Stambol's wall
Before the dogs of Moscow fall,
Nor strike one stroke for life and death
Against the curs of Nazareth!
Go—let thy less than woman's hand
Assume the distaff—not the brand.   100
But, Haroun!—to my daughter speed:
And hark—of thine own head take heed—
If thus Zuleika oft takes wing—
Thou see'st yon bow—it hath a string!"

V

No sound from Selim's lip was heard,
    At least that met old Giaffir's ear,
But every frown and every word

Pierced keener than a Christian's sword.
  "Son of a slave!—reproached with fear!
Those gibes had cost another dear.   110
Son of a slave! and *who* my Sire?"
  Thus held his thoughts their dark career;
And glances ev'n of more than ire
  Flash forth, then faintly disappear.
Old Giaffir gazed upon his son
  And started; for within his eye
He read how much his wrath had done;
He saw rebellion there begun:
  "Come hither, boy—what, no reply?
I mark thee—and I know thee too;   120
But there be deeds thou dar'st not do:
But if thy beard had manlier length,
And if thy hand had skill and strength,
I'd joy to see thee break a lance,
Albeit against my own perchance."
As sneeringly these accents fell,
On Selim's eye he fiercely gazed:
  That eye returned him glance for glance,
And proudly to his Sire's was raised,
  Till Giaffir's quailed and shrunk askance—   130
And why—he felt, but durst not tell.
"Much I misdoubt this wayward boy
Will one day work me more annoy:
I never loved him from his birth,
And—but his arm is little worth,
And scarcely in the chase could cope
With timid fawn or antelope,
Far less would venture into strife
Where man contends for fame and life—
I would not trust that look or tone: 140
No—nor the blood so near my own.
That blood—he hath not heard—no more—
I'll watch him closer than before.
He is an Arab to my sight,
Or Christian crouching in the fight—
But hark! I hear Zuleika's voice;
  Like Houris' hymn it meets mine ear:
She is the offspring of my choice;
  Oh! more than ev'n her mother dear,
With all to hope, and nought to fear—   150

My Peri! ever welcome here!
Sweet as the desert fountain's wave
To lips just cooled in time to save—
    Such to my longing sight art thou;
Nor can they waft to Mecca's shrine
More thanks for life, than I for thine,
    Who blest thy birth and bless thee now."

VI

Fair, as the first that fell of womankind,
    When on that dread yet lovely serpent smiling,
Whose Image then was stamped upon her mind—   160
    But once beguiled—and ever more beguiling;
Dazzling, as that, oh! too transcendent vision
    To Sorrow's phantom-peopled slumber given,
When heart meets heart again in dreams Elysian,
    And paints the lost on Earth revived in Heaven;
Soft, as the memory of buried love—
Pure, as the prayer which Childhood wafts above,
Was she—the daughter of that rude old Chief,
Who met the maid with tears—but not of grief.

Who hath not proved how feebly words essay   170
To fix one spark of Beauty's heavenly ray?
Who doth not feel, until his failing sight
Faints into dimness with its own delight,
His changing cheek, his sinking heart confess
The might—the majesty of Loveliness?
Such was Zuleika—such around her shone
The nameless charms unmarked by her alone—
The light of Love, the purity of Grace,
The mind, the Music breathing from her face,
The heart whose softness harmonized the whole,   180
And oh! that eye was in itself a Soul!

Her graceful arms in meekness bending
    Across her gently-budding breast;
At one kind word those arms extending
    To clasp the neck of him who blest
    His child caressing and carest,
Zuleika came—and Giaffir felt
His purpose half within him melt:

Not that against her fancied weal
His heart though stern could ever feel; 190
Affection chained her to that heart;
Ambition tore the links apart.

VII

"Zuleika! child of Gentleness!
How dear this very day must tell,
When I forget my own distress,
In losing what I love so well,
To bid thee with another dwell:
Another! and a braver man
Was never seen in battle's van.
We Moslem reck not much of blood: 200
But yet the line of Carasman
Unchanged, unchangeable hath stood
First of the bold Timariot bands
That won and well can keep their lands.
Enough that he who comes to woo
Is kinsman of the Bey Oglou:
His years need scarce a thought employ;
I would not have thee wed a boy.
And thou shalt have a noble dower;
And his and my united power 210
Will laugh to scorn the death-firman,
Which others tremble but to scan,
And teach the messenger what fate
The bearer of such boon may wait.
And now thou know'st thy father's will—
All that thy sex hath need to know:
'Twas mine to teach obedience still—
The way to love, thy Lord may show.'

VIII

In silence bowed the virgin's head;
And if her eye was filled with tears 220
That stifled feeling dare not shed,
And changed her cheek from pale to red,
And red to pale, as through her ears
Those wingéd words like arrows sped,
What could such be but maiden fears?

So bright the tear in Beauty's eye,
Love half regrets to kiss it dry;
So sweet the blush of Bashfulness,
Even Pity scarce can wish it less!

Whate'er it was the sire forgot;   230
Or if remembered, marked it not;
Thrice clapped his hands, and called his steed,
    Resigned his gem-adorned chibouque,
And mounting featly for the mead,
    With Maugrabee and Mamaluke,
    His way amid his Delis took,
To witness many an active deed
With sabre keen, or blunt jerreed.
The Kislar only and his Moors
Watch well the Haram's massy doors.   240

IX

His head was leant upon his hand,
    His eye looked o'er the dark blue water
That swiftly glides and gently swells
Between the winding Dardanelles;
But yet he saw nor sea nor strand,
Nor even his Pacha's turbaned band
    Mix in the game of mimic slaughter,
Careering cleave the folded felt
With sabre stroke right sharply dealt;
Nor marked the javelin-darting crowd,   250
Nor heard their Ollahs wild and loud—
    He thought but of old Giaffir's daughter!

X

No word from Selim's bosom broke;
One sigh Zuleika's thought bespoke:
Still gazed he through the lattice grate,
Pale, mute, and mournfully sedate.
To him Zuleika's eye was turned,
But little from his aspect learned:
Equal her grief, yet not the same;
Her heart confessed a gentler flame: 260
But yet that heart, alarmed or weak,

She knew not why, forbade to speak.
Yet speak she must—but when essay?
"How strange he thus should turn away!
Not thus we e'er before have met;
Not thus shall be our parting yet."
Thrice paced she slowly through the room,
    And watched his eye—it still was fixed:
    She snatched the urn wherein was mixed
The Persian Atar-gul's perfume,   270
And sprinkled all its odours o'er
The pictured roof and marble floor:
The drops, that through his glittering vest
The playful girl's appeal addressed,
Unheeded o'er his bosom flew,
As if that breast were marble too.
"What, sullen yet? it must not be—
Oh! gentle Selim, this from thee!"
She saw in curious order set
    The fairest flowers of Eastern land—   280
"He loved them once; may touch them yet,
    If offered by Zuleika's hand."
The childish thought was hardly breathed
Before the rose was plucked and wreathed;
The next fond moment saw her seat
Her fairy form at Selim's feet:
"This rose to calm my brother's cares
A message from the Bulbul bears;
It says to-night he will prolong
For Selim's ear his sweetest song;   290
And though his note is somewhat sad,
He'll try for once a strain more glad,
With some faint hope his altered lay
May sing these gloomy thoughts away.

XI

"What! not receive my foolish flower?
    Nay then I am indeed unblest:
On me can thus thy forehead lower?
    And know'st thou not who loves thee best?
Oh, Selim dear! oh, more than dearest!
Say, is it me thou hat'st or fearest?   300
Come, lay thy head upon my breast,

And I will kiss thee into rest,
Since words of mine, and songs must fail,
Ev'n from my fabled nightingale.
I knew our sire at times was stern,
But this from thee had yet to learn:
Too well I know he loves thee not;
But is Zuleika's love forgot?
Ah! deem I right? the Pacha's plan—
This kinsman Bey of Carasman   310
Perhaps may prove some foe of thine.
If so, I swear by Mecca's shrine,—
If shrines that ne'er approach allow
To woman's step admit her vow,—
Without thy free consent—command—
The Sultan should not have my hand!
Think'st thou that I could bear to part
With thee, and learn to halve my heart?
Ah! were I severed from thy side,
Where were thy friend—and who my guide?   326
Years have not seen, Time shall not see,
The hour that tears my soul from thee:
Even Azrael, from his deadly quiver
    When flies that shaft, and fly it must,
That parts all else, shall doom for ever
    Our hearts to undivided dust!"

XII

He lived—he breathed—he moved—he felt;
He raised the maid from where she knelt;
His trance was gone, his keen eye shone
With thoughts that long in darkness dwelt;   330
With thoughts that burn—in rays that melt.
As the stream late concealed
    By the fringe of its willows,
When it rushes revealed
    In the light of its billows;
As the bolt bursts on high
    From the black cloud that bound it,
Flashed the soul of that eye
    Through the long lashes round it.
A war-horse at the trumpet's sound,   340

A lion roused by heedless hound,
A tyrant waked to sudden strife
By graze of ill-directed knife,
Starts not to more convulsive life
Than he, who heard that vow, displayed,
And all, before repressed, betrayed:
"Now thou art mine, for ever mine,
With life to keep, and scarce with life resign;
Now thou art mine, that sacred oath,
Though sworn by one, hath bound us both.   350
Yes, fondly, wisely hast thou done;
That vow hath saved more heads than one:
But blench not thou—thy simplest tress
Claims more from me than tenderness;
I would not wrong the slenderest hair
That clusters round thy forehead fair,
For all the treasures buried far
Within the caves of Istakar.
This morning clouds upon me lowered,
Reproaches on my head were showered,   360
And Giaffir almost called me coward!
Now I have motive to be brave;
The son of his neglected slave,
Nay, start not, 'twas the term he gave,
May show, though little apt to vaunt,
A heart his words not deeds can daunt.
His son, indeed!—yet, thanks to thee,
Perchance I am, at least shall be;
But let our plighted secret vow
Be only known to us as now.   370
I know the wretch who dares demand
From Giaffir thy reluctant hand;
More ill-got wealth, a meaner soul
Holds not a Musselim's control;
Was he not bred in Egripo?
A viler race let Israel show!
But let that pass—to none be told
Our oath; the rest shall time unfold.
To me and mine leave Osman Bey!
I've partisans for Peril's day: 380
Think not I am what I appear;
I've arms—and friends—and vengeance near."

XIII

"Think not thou art what thou appearest!
  My Selim, thou art sadly changed:
This morn I saw thee gentle—dearest—
  But now thou'rt from thyself estranged.
My love thou surely knew'st before,
It ne'er was less—nor can be more.
To see thee—hear thee—near thee stay—
  And hate the night—I know not why,   390
Save that we meet not but by day;
  With thee to live, with thee to die,
  I dare not to my hope deny:
Thy cheek—thine eyes—thy lips to kiss—
Like this—and this—no more than this;
For, Allah! sure thy lips are flame:
  What fever in thy veins is flushing?
My own have nearly caught the same,
  At least I feel my cheek, too, blushing.
To soothe thy sickness, watch thy health,   400
Partake, but never waste thy wealth,
Or stand with smiles unmurmuring by,
And lighten half thy poverty;
Do all but close thy dying eye,
For that I could not live to try;
To these alone my thoughts aspire:
More can I do? or thou require?
But, Selim, thou must answer why
We need so much of mystery?
The cause I cannot dream nor tell,   410
But be it, since thou say'st 'tis well;
Yet what thou mean'st by 'arms' and 'friends,'
Beyond my weaker sense extends.
I meant that Giaffir should have heard
  The very vow I plighted thee;
His wrath would not revoke my word:
  But surely he would leave me free.
  Can this fond wish seem strange in me,
To be what I have ever been?
What other hath Zuleika seen   420
From simple childhood's earliest hour?
  What other can she seek to see

Than thee, companion of her bower,
   The partner of her infancy?
These cherished thoughts with life begun,
   Say, why must I no more avow?
What change is wrought to make me shun
The truth—my pride, and thine till now?
To meet the gaze of stranger's eyes
Our law—our creed—our God denies;   430
Nor shall one wandering thought of mine
At such, our Prophet's will, repine:
No! happier made by that decree,
He left me all in leaving thee.
Deep were my anguish, thus compelled
To wed with one I ne'er beheld:
This wherefore should I not reveal?
Why wilt thou urge me to conceal?
I know the Pacha's haughty mood
To thee hath never boded good;   444
And he so often storms at nought,
Allah! forbid that e'er he ought!
And why I know not, but within
My heart concealment weighs like sin.
If then such secrecy be crime,
   And such it feels while lurking here;
Oh, Selim! tell me yet in time,
   Nor leave me thus to thoughts of fear.
Ah! yonder see the Tchocadar,
My father leaves the mimic war;   450
I tremble now to meet his eye—
Say, Selim, canst thou tell me why?"

XIV

"Zuleika—to thy tower's retreat
Betake thee—Giaffir I can greet:
And now with him I fain must prate
Of firmans, imposts, levies, state.
There's fearful news from Danube's banks,
Our Vizier nobly thins his ranks,
For which the Giaour may give him thanks!
Our Sultan hath a shorter way   460
Such costly triumph to repay.
But, mark me, when the twilight drum

Hath warned the troops to food and sleep,
Unto thy cell will Selim come;
   Then softly from the Haram creep
   Where we may wander by the deep:
   Our garden battlements are steep;
Nor these will rash intruder climb
To list our words, or stint our time;
And if he doth, I want not steel   **470**
Which some have felt, and more may feel.
Then shalt thou learn of Selim more
Than thou hast heard or thought before:
Trust me Zuleika—fear not me!
Thou know'st I hold a Haram key."

"Fear thee, my Selim! ne'er till now
Did words like this——"
                 "Delay not thou;
I keep the key—and Haroun's guard
Have *some,* and hope of *more* reward.
To-night, Zuleika, thou shalt hear   **480**
My tale, my purpose, and my fear:
I am not, Jove! what I appear."

CANTO THE SECOND

I

The winds are high on Helle's wave,
  As on that night of stormy water
When Love, who sent, forgot to save
The young—the beautiful—the brave—
  The lonely hope of Sestos' daughter.
Oh! when alone along the sky
Her turret-torch was blazing high,
Though rising gale, and breaking foam,   **490**
And shrieking sea-birds warned him home;
And clouds aloft and tides below,
With signs and sounds, forbade to go,
He could not see, he would not hear,
Or sound or sign foreboding fear;
His eye but saw that light of Love,

The only star it hailed above;
His ear but rang with Hero's song,
"Ye waves, divide not lovers long!"—
That tale is old, but Love anew 500
May nerve young hearts to prove as true.

II

The winds are high and Helle's tide
  Rolls darkly heaving to the main;
And Night's descending shadows hide
  That field with blood bedewed in vain,
The desert of old Priam's pride;
  The tombs, sole relics of his reign,
All—save immortal dreams that could beguile
The blind old man of Scio's rocky isle!

III

Oh! yet—for there my steps have been; 510
  These feet have pressed the sacred shore,
These limbs that buoyant wave hath borne—
Minstrel! with thee to muse, to mourn,
  To trace again those fields of yore,
Believing every hillock green
  Contains no fabled hero's ashes,
And that around the undoubted scene
  Thine own "broad Hellespont" still dashes,
Be long my lot! and cold were he
Who there could gaze denying thee! 520

IV

The Night hath closed on Helle's stream,
  Nor yet hath risen on Ida's hill
That Moon, which shone on his high theme:
No warrior chides her peaceful beam,
  But conscious shepherds bless it still.
Their flocks are grazing on the Mound
  Of him who felt the Dardan's arrow:
That mighty heap of gathered ground
Which Ammon's son ran proudly round,

By nations raised, by monarchs crowned,   530
  Is now a lone and nameless barrow!
  Within—thy dwelling-place how narrow!
Without—can only strangers breathe
The name of him that *was* beneath:
Dust long outlasts the storied stone;
But Thou—thy very dust is gone!

v

Late, late to-night will Dian cheer
The swain, and chase the boatman's fear;
Till then—no beacon on the cliff
May shape the course of struggling skiff;   540
The scattered lights that skirt the bay,
All, one by one, have died away;
The only lamp of this lone hour
Is glimmering in Zuleika's tower.
Yes! there is light in that lone chamber,
  And o'er her silken ottoman
Are thrown the fragrant beads of amber,
  O'er which her fairy fingers ran;
Near these, with emerald rays beset,
(How could she thus that gem forget?)   550
Her mother's sainted amulet,
Whereon engraved the Koorsee text,
Could smooth this life, and win the next;
And by her Comboloio lies
A Koran of illumined dyes;
And many a bright emblazoned rhyme
By Persian scribes redeemed from Time;
And o'er those scrolls, not oft so mute,
Reclines her now neglected lute;
And round her lamp of fretted gold   560
Bloom flowers in urns of China's mould;
The richest work of Iran's loom,
And Sheeraz' tribute of perfume;
All that can eye or sense delight
  Are gathered in that gorgeous room:
  But yet it hath an air of gloom.
She, of this Peri cell the sprite,
What doth she hence, and on so rude a night?

VI

Wrapt in the darkest sable vest,
   Which none save noblest Moslem wear,   575
To guard from winds of Heaven the breast
   As Heaven itself to Selim dear,
With cautious steps the thicket threading,
   And starting oft, as through the glade
   The gust its hollow moanings made,
Till, on the smoother pathway treading,
More free her timid bosom beat,
   The maid pursued her silent guide;
And though her terror urged retreat,
   How could she quit her Selim's side?   580
   How teach her tender lips to chide?

VII

They reached at length a grotto, hewn
   By nature, but enlarged by art,
Where oft her lute she wont to tune,
   And oft her Koran conned apart;
And oft in youthful reverie
She dreamed what Paradise might be:
Where Woman's parted soul shall go
Her Prophet had disdained to show;
But Selim's mansion was secure,   590
Nor deemed she, could he long endure
His bower in other worlds of bliss
Without *her*, most beloved in this!
Oh! who so dear with him could dwell?
What Houri soothe him half so well?

VIII

Since last she visited the spot
Some change seemed wrought within the grot:
It might be only that the night
Disguised things seen by better light: 600
That brazen lamp but dimly threw
A ray of no celestial hue;
But in a nook within the cell

Her eye on stranger objects fell.
There arms were piled, not such as wield
The turbaned Delis in the field;
But brands of foreign blade and hilt,
And one was red—perchance with guilt!
Ah! how without can blood be spilt?
A cup too on the board was set
That did not seem to hold sherbet.   610
What may this mean? she turned to see
Her Selim—"Oh! can this be he?"

                    IX

His robe of pride was thrown aside,
   His brow no high-crowned turban bore,
But in its stead a shawl of red,
   Wreathed lightly round, his temples wore:
That dagger, on whose hilt the gem
Were worthy of a diadem,
No longer glittered at his waist,
Where pistols unadorned were braced;   620
And from his belt a sabre swung,
And from his shoulder loosely hung
The cloak of white, the thin capote
That decks the wandering Candiote;
Beneath—his golden plated vest
Clung like a cuirass to his breast;
The greaves below his knee that wound
With silvery scales were sheathed and bound.
But were it not that high command
Spake in his eye, and tone, and hand,   630
All that a careless eye could see
In him was some young Galiongée.

                    X

"I said I was not what I seemed;
   And now thou see'st my words were true:
I have a tale thou hast not dreamed,
   If sooth—its truth must others rue.
My story now 'twere vain to hide,
I must not see thee Osman's bride:
But had not thine own lips declared

How much of that young heart I shared,   640
I could not, must not, yet have shown
The darker secret of my own.
In this I speak not now of love;
That—let Time—Truth—and Peril prove:
But first—Oh! never wed another—·
Zuleika! I am not thy brother!"

XI

"Oh! not my brother!—yet unsay—
  God! am I left alone on earth
To mourn—I dare not curse—the day
  That saw my solitary birth?   650
Oh! thou wilt love me now no more!
  My sinking heart foreboded ill:
But know *me* all I was before,
  Thy sister—friend—Zuleika still.
Thou led'st me here perchance to kill;
  If thou hast cause for vengeance, see!
My breast is offered—take thy fill!
  Far better with the dead to be
  Than live thus nothing now to thee:
Perhaps far worse, for now I know   660
Why Giaffir always seemed thy foe;
And I, alas! am Giaffir's child,
For whom thou wert contemned, reviled.
If not thy sister—would'st thou save
My life—Oh! bid me be thy slave!"

XII

"My slave, Zuleika!—nay, I'm thine:
  But, gentle love, this transport calm,
Thy lot shall yet be linked with mine;
I swear it by our Prophet's shrine,
  And be that thought thy sorrow's balm.   670
So may the Koran verse displayed
Upon its steel direct my blade,
In danger's hour to guard us both,
As I preserve that awful oath!
The name in which thy heart hath prided
  Must change; but, my Zuleika, know,

That tie is widened, not divided,
  Although thy Sire's my deadliest foe.
My father was to Giaffir all
  That Selim late was deemed to thee;   680
That brother wrought a brother's fall,
  But spared, at least, my infancy!
And lulled me with a vain deceit
That yet a like return may meet.
He reared me, not with tender help,
  But like the nephew of a Cain;
He watched me like a lion's whelp,
  That gnaws and yet may break his chain.
  My father's blood in every vein
Is boiling! but for thy dear sake   690
No present vengeance will I take;
  Though here I must no more remain.
But first, beloved Zuleika! hear
How Giaffir wrought this deed of fear.

                    XIII

'How first their strife to rancour grew,
  If Love or Envy made them foes,
It matters little if I knew;
In fiery spirits, slights, though few
  And thoughtless, will disturb repose.
In war Abdallah's arm was strong,   700
Remembered yet in Bosniac song,
And Paswan's rebel hordes attest
How little love they bore such guest:
His death is all I need relate,
The stern effect of Giaffir's hate;
And how my birth disclosed to me,
Whate'er beside it makes, hath made me free.

                    XIV

"When Paswan, after years of strife,
At last for power, but first for life,
In Widdin's walls too proudly sate,   710
Our Pachas rallied round the state;
Not last nor least in high command,

Each brother led a separate band;
They gave their Horse-tails to the wind,
  And mustering in Sophia's plain
Their tents were pitched, their post assigned;
  To one, alas! assigned in vain!
What need of words? the deadly bowl,
  By Giaffir's order drugged and given,
With venom subtle as his soul,   **720**
  Dismissed Abdallah's hence to Heaven.
Reclined and feverish in the bath,
  He, when the hunter's sport was up,
But little deemed a brother's wrath
  To quench his thirst had such a cup:
The bowl a bribed attendant bore;
He drank one draught, nor needed more!
If thou my tale, Zuleika, doubt,
Call Haroun—he can tell it out.

             XV

"The deed once done, and Paswan's feud   **730**
In part suppressed, though ne'er subdued,
  Abdallah's Pachalick was gained:—
Thou know'st not what in our Divan
Can wealth procure for worse than man—
  Abdallah's honours were obtained
By him a brother's murder stained;
'Tis true, the purchase nearly drained
His ill-got treasure, soon replaced.
Would'st question whence? Survey the waste,
And ask the squalid peasant how   **740**
His gains repay his broiling brow!—
Why me the stern Usurper spared,
Why thus with me his palace shared,
I know not. Shame—regret—remorse—
And little fear from infant's force;
Besides, adoption as a son
By him whom Heaven accorded none,
Or some unknown cabal, caprice,
Preserved me thus;—but not in peace;
He cannot curb his haughty mood,   **750**
Nor I forgive a father's blood.

XVI

"Within thy Father's house are foes;
  Not all who break his bread are true:
To these should I my birth disclose,
  His days—his very hours were few:
They only want a heart to lead,
A hand to point them to the deed.
But Haroun only knows, or knew
This tale, whose close is almost nigh:
He in Abdallah's palace grew,   760
  And held that post in his Serai
  Which holds he here—he saw him die;
But what could single slavery do?
Avenge his lord? alas! too late;
Or save his son from such a fate?
He chose the last, and when elate
  With foes subdued, or friends betrayed,
Proud Giaffir in high triumph sate,
He led me helpless to his gate,
  And not in vain, it seems, essayed   770
  To save the life for which he prayed.
The knowledge of my birth secured
  From all and each, but most from me—
Thus Giaffir's safety was ensured.
  Removed he too from Roumelie
To this our Asiatic side,
Far from our seats by Danube's tide,
  With none but Haroun, who retains
Such knowledge—and that Nubian feels
  A Tyrant's secrets are but chains,   780
From which the captive gladly steals,
And this and more to me reveals:
Such still to guilt just Allah sends—
Slaves, tools, accomplices—no friends!

XVII

"All this, Zuleika, harshly sounds;
  But harsher still my tale must be:
Howe'er my tongue thy softness wounds,
  Yet I must prove all truth to thee.

I saw thee start this garb to see,
Yet it is one I oft have worn, 790
 And long must wear: this Galiongée,
To whom thy plighted vow is sworn,
 Is leader of those pirate hordes,
 Whose laws and lives are on their swords;
To hear whose desolating tale
Would make thy waning cheek more pale:
Those arms thou see'st my band have brought,
The hands that wield are not remote;
This cup too for the rugged knaves
 Is filled—once quaffed, they ne'er repine: 800
Our Prophet might forgive the slaves;
 They're only infidels in wine.

XVIII

"What could I be? Proscribed at home,
And taunted to a wish to roam;
And listless left—for Giaffir's fear
Denied the courser and the spear—
Though oft—Oh, Mahomet! how oft!—
In full Divan the despot scoffed,
As if *my* weak unwilling hand
Refused the bridle or the brand: 810
He ever went to war alone,
And pent me here untried—unknown;
To Haroun's care with women left,
By hope unblest, of fame bereft,
While thou—whose softness long endeared,
Though it unmanned me, still had cheered—
To Brusa's walls for safety sent,
Awaited'st there the field's event.
Haroun, who saw my spirit pining
 Beneath inaction's sluggish yoke, 820
His captive, though with dread resigning,
 My thraldom for a season broke,
On promise to return before
The day when Giaffir's charge was o'er.
'Tis vain—my tongue can not impart
My almost drunkenness of heart,
When first this liberated eye
Surveyed Earth—Ocean—Sun—and Sky—

As if my Spirit pierced them through,
And all their inmost wonders knew!   830
One word alone can paint to thee
That more than feeling—I was Free!
E'er for thy presence ceased to pine;
The World—nay, Heaven itself was mine!

XIX

"The shallop of a trusty Moor
Conveyed me from this idle shore;
I longed to see the isles that gem
Old Ocean's purple diadem:
I sought by turns, and saw them all;
    But when and where I joined the crew,   840
With whom I'm pledged to rise or fall,
    When all that we design to do
Is done, 'twill then be time more meet
To tell thee, when the tale's complete.

XX

" 'Tis true, they are a lawless brood,
But rough in form, nor mild in mood;
And every creed, and every race,
With them hath found—may find a place:
But open speech, and ready hand,
Obedience to their Chief's command;   850
A soul for every enterprise,
That never sees with Terror's eyes;
Friendship for each, and faith to all,
And vengeance vowed for those who fall,
Have made them fitting instruments
For more than e'en my own intents.
And some—and I have studied all
    Distinguished from the vulgar rank—
But chiefly to my council call
    The wisdom of the cautious Frank:—   860
And some to higher thoughts aspire;
    The last of Lambro's patriots there
    Anticipated freedom share;
And oft around the cavern fire

On visionary schemes debate,
To snatch the Rayahs from their fate.
So let them ease their hearts with prate
Of equal rights, which man ne'er knew;
I have a love for freedom too.
Aye! let me like the ocean-Patriarch roam,   870
Or only know on land the Tartar's home!
My tent on shore, my galley on the sea,
Are more than cities and Serais to me:
Borne by my steed, or wafted by my sail,
Across the desert, or before the gale,
Bound where thou wilt, my barb! or glide, my prow!
But be the Star that guides the wanderer, Thou!
Thou, my Zuleika, share and bless my bark;
The Dove of peace and promise to mine ark!
Or, since that hope denied in worlds of strife,   880
Be thou the rainbow to the storms of life!
The evening beam that smiles the clouds away,
And tints to-morrow with prophetic ray!
Blest—as the Muezzin's strain from Mecca's wall
To pilgrims pure and prostrate at his call;
Soft—as the melody of youthful days,
That steals the trembling tear of speechless praise;
Dear—as his native song to Exile's ears,
Shall sound each tone thy long-loved voice endears.
For thee in those bright isles is built a bower   890
Blooming as Aden in its earliest hour.
A thousand swords, with Selim's heart and hand,
Wait—wave—defend—destroy—at thy command!
Girt by my band, Zuleika at my side,
The spoil of nations shall bedeck my bride.
The Haram's languid years of listless ease
Are well resigned for cares—for joys like these:
Not blind to Fate, I see, where'er I rove,
Unnumbered perils,—but one only love!
Yet well my toils shall that fond breast repay,   900
Though Fortune frown, or falser friends betray.
How dear the dream in darkest hours of ill,
Should all be changed, to find thee faithful still!
Be but thy soul, like Selim's, firmly shown;
To thee be Selim's tender as thine own;
To soothe each sorrow, share in each delight,
Blend every thought, do all—but disunite!

Once free, 'tis mine our horde again to guide;
Friends to each other, foes to aught beside:
Yet there we follow but the bent assigned   911
By fatal Nature to man's warring kind:
Mark! where his carnage and his conquests cease!
He makes a solitude, and calls it—peace!
I, like the rest, must use my skill or strength,
But ask no land beyond my sabre's length:
Power sways but by division—her resource
The blest alternative of fraud or force!
Ours be the last; in time Deceit may come
When cities cage us in a social home:
There ev'n thy soul might err—how oft the heart   920
Corruption shakes which Peril could not part!
And Woman, more than Man, when Death or Woe,
Or even Disgrace, would lay her lover low,
Sunk in the lap of Luxury will shame—
Away suspicion!—*not* Zuleika's name!
But life is hazard at the best; and here
No more remains to win, and much to fear:
Yes, fear!—the doubt, the dread of losing thee,
By Osman's power, and Giaffir's stern decree.
That dread shall vanish with the favouring gale,   930
Which Love to-night hath promised to my sail:
No danger daunts the pair his smile hath blest—
Their steps still roving, but their hearts at rest.
With thee all toils are sweet, each clime hath charms;
Earth—sea alike—our world within our arms!
Aye—let the loud winds whistle o'er the deck,
So that those arms cling closer round my neck:
The deepest murmur of this lip shall be,
No sigh for safety, but a prayer for thee!
The war of elements no fears impart   940
To Love, whose deadliest bane is human Art.
There lie the only rocks our course can check;
Here moments menace—*there* are years of wreck!
But hence ye thoughts that rise in Horror's shape!
This hour bestows, or ever bars escape.
Few words remain of mine my tale to close;
Of thine but *one* to waft us from our foes;
Yea—foes—to me will Giaffir's hate decline?
And is not Osman, who would part us, thine?

XXI

"His head and faith from doubt and death   950
  Returned in time my guard to save;
  Few heard, none told, that o'er the wave
From isle to isle I roved the while:
And since, though parted from my band
Too seldom now I leave the land,
No deed they've done, nor deed shall do,
Ere I have heard and doomed it too:
I form the plan—decree the spoil—
'Tis fit I oftener share the toil.
But now too long I've held thine ear;   960
Time presses—floats my bark—and here
We leave behind but hate and fear.
To-morrow Osman with his train
Arrives—to-night must break thy chain:
And would'st thou save that haughty Bey,—
  Perchance *his* life who gave thee thine,—
With me this hour away—away!
  But yet, though thou art plighted mine,
Would'st thou recall thy willing vow,
Appalled by truths imparted now,   970
Here rest I—not to see thee wed:
But be that peril on *my* head!"

XXII

Zuleika, mute and motionless,
Stood like that Statue of Distress,
When, her last hope for ever gone,
The Mother hardened into stone;
All in the maid that eye could see
Was but a younger Niobé.
But ere her lip, or even her eye,
Essayed to speak, or look reply,   980
Beneath the garden's wicket porch
Far flashed on high a blazing torch!
Another—and another—and another—
"Oh! fly—no more—yet now my more than brother!"
Far, wide, through every thicket spread,

The fearful lights are gleaming red,
Nor these alone—for each right hand
Is ready with a sheathless brand.
They part—pursue—return, and wheel
With searching flambeau, shining steel;　　990
And last of all, his sabre waving,
Stern Giaffir in his fury raving:
And now almost they touch the cave—
Oh! must that grot be Selim's grave?

XXIII

Dauntless he stood—" 'Tis come—soon past—
One kiss, Zuleika—'tis my last:
　But yet my band not far from shore
May hear this signal, see the flash;
Yet now too few—the attempt were rash:
　No matter—yet one effort more."　　1000
Forth to the cavern mouth he stept;
　His pistol's echo rang on high,
Zuleika started not, nor wept,
　Despair benumbed her breast and eye!—
"They hear me not, or if they ply
Their oars, 'tis but to see me die;
That sound hath drawn my foes more nigh.
Then forth my father's scimitar,
Thou ne'er hast seen less equal war!
Farewell, Zuleika!—Sweet! retire:　　1010
　Yet stay within—here linger safe,
　At thee his rage will only chafe.
Stir not—lest even to thee perchance
Some erring blade or ball should glance.
Fear'st thou for him?—may I expire
If in this strife I seek thy sire!
No—though by him that poison poured;
No—though again he call me coward!
But tamely shall I meet their steel?
No—as each crest save _his_ may feel!"　　1020

XXIV

One bound he made, and gained the sand:
　Already at his feet had sunk

The foremost of the prying band,
  A gasping head, a quivering trunk:
Another falls—but round him close
A swarming circle of his foes;
From right to left his path he cleft,
  And almost met the meeting wave:
His boat appears—not five oars' length—
His comrades strain with desperate strength—   1030
  Oh! are they yet in time to save?
His feet the foremost breakers lave;
His band are plunging in the bay,
Their sabres glitter through the spray;
Wet—wild—unwearied to the strand
They struggle—now they touch the land!
They come—'tis but to add to slaughter—
His heart's best blood is on the water.

XXV

Escaped from shot, unharmed by steel,
Or scarcely grazed its force to feei,   1040
Had Selim won, betrayed, beset,
To where the strand and billows met;
There as his last step left the land,
And the last death-blow dealt his hand—
Ah! wherefore did he turn to look
  For her his eye but sought in vain?
That pause, that fatal gaze he took,
  Hath doomed his death, or fixed his chain.
Sad proof, in peril and in pain,
How late will Lover's hope remain!   1050
His back was to the dashing spray;
Behind, but close, his comrades lay,
When, at the instant, hissed the ball—
"So may the foes of Giaffir fall!"
Whose voice is heard? whose carbine rang?
Whose bullet through the night-air sang,
Too nearly, deadly aimed to err?
'Tis thine—Abdallah's Murderer!
The father slowly rued thy hate,
The son hath found a quicker fate: 1060
Fast from his breast the blood is bubbling,
The whiteness of the sea-foam troubling—

If aught his lips essayed to groan,
The rushing billows choked the tone!

XXVI

Morn slowly rolls the clouds away;
    Few trophies of the fight are there:
The shouts that shook the midnight-bay
Are silent; but some signs of fray
    That strand of strife may bear,
And fragments of each shivered brand;   1070
Steps stamped; and dashed into the sand
The print of many a struggling hand
    May there be marked; nor far remote
    A broken torch, an oarless boat;
And tangled on the weeds that heap
The beach where shelving to the deep
    There lies a white capote!
'Tis rent in twain—one dark-red stain
The wave yet ripples o'er in vain:
    But where is he who wore?   1080
Ye! who would o'er his relics weep,
Go, seek them where the surges sweep
Their burthen round Sigæum's steep
    And cast on Lemnos' shore:
The sea-birds shriek above the prey,
O'er which their hungry beaks delay,
As shaken on his restless pillow,
His head heaves with the heaving billow;
That hand, whose motion is not life,
Yet feebly seems to menace strife,   1090
Flung by the tossing tide on high,
    Then levelled with the wave—
What recks it, though that corse shall lie
    Within a living grave?
The bird that tears that prostrate form
Hath only robbed the meaner worm;
The only heart, the only eye
Had bled or wept to see him die,
Had seen those scattered limbs composed,
    And mourned above his turban-stone,   1100
That heart hath burst—that eye was closed—
    Yea—closed before his own!

XXVII

By Helle's stream there is a voice of wail!
And Woman's eye is wet—Man's cheek is pale:
Zuleika! last of Giaffir's race,
   Thy destined lord is come too late:
He sees not—ne'er shall see thy face!
      Can he not hear
The loud Wul-wulleh warn his distant ear?
   Thy handmaids weeping at the gate,   1110
   The Koran-chanters of the Hymn of Fate.
   The silent slaves with folded arms that wait,
Sighs in the hall, and shrieks upon the gale,
      Tell him thy tale!
Thou didst not view thy Selim fall!
   That fearful moment when he left the cave
      Thy heart grew chill:
   He was thy hope—thy joy—thy love—thine all,
   And that last thought on him thou could'st not save
      Sufficed to kill;   1120
Burst forth in one wild cry—and all was still.
   Peace to thy broken heart—and virgin grave!
Ah! happy! but of life to lose the worst!
That grief—though deep—though fatal—was thy first!
Thrice happy! ne'er to feel nor fear the force
Of absence—shame—pride—hate—revenge—remorse!
And, oh! that pang where more than Madness lies,
The Worm that will not sleep—and never dies!
Thought of the gloomy day and ghastly night,
That dreads the darkness, and yet loathes the light,   1130
That winds around, and tears the quivering heart!
Ah! wherefore not consume it—and depart!
Woe to thee, rash and unrelenting Chief!
   Vainly thou heap'st the dust upon thy head,
   Vainly the sackcloth o'er thy limbs dost spread:
   By that same hand Abdallah—Selim bled.
Now let it tear thy beard in idle grief:
Thy pride of heart, thy bride for Osman's bed,
She, whom thy Sultan had but seen to wed,
      Thy Daughter's dead!   1140
   Hope of thine age, thy twilight's lonely beam,
   The Star hath set that shone on Helle's stream

What quenched its ray?—the blood that thou hast shed!
Hark! to the hurried question of Despair:
"Where is my child?"—an Echo answers—
   "Where?"

XXVIII

Within the place of thousand tombs
  That shine beneath, while dark above
The sad but living cypress glooms
  And withers not, though branch and leaf
Are stamped with an eternal grief,   1150
  Like early unrequited Love,
One spot exists, which ever blooms,
  Ev'n in that deadly grove—
A single rose is shedding there
Its lonely lustre, meek and pale:
It looks as planted by Despair—
  So white—so faint—the slightest gale
Might whirl the leaves on high;
  And yet, though storms and blight assail,
And hands more rude than wintry sky   1160
  May wring it from the stem—in vain—
  To-morrow sees it bloom again!
The stalk some Spirit gently rears,
And waters with celestial tears;
  For well may maids of Helle deem
That this can be no earthly flower,
Which mocks the tempest's withering hour,
And buds unsheltered by a bower;
Nor droops, though Spring refuse her shower,
  Nor woos the Summer beam: 1170
To it the livelong night there sings
  A Bird unseen—but not remote:
Invisible his airy wings,
But soft as harp that Houri strings
  His long entrancing note!
It were the Bulbul; but his throat,
  Though mournful, pours not such a strain:
For they who listen cannot leave
The spot, but linger there and grieve,
  As if they loved in vain!   1180
And yet so sweet the tears they shed,
'Tis sorrow so unmixed with dread.

They scarce can bear the morn to break
  That melancholy spell,
And longer yet would weep and wake,
  He sings so wild and well!
But when the day-blush bursts from high
Expires that magic melody.
And some have been who could believe,
(So fondly youthful dreams deceive,   1190
  Yet harsh be they that blame,)
That note so piercing and profound
Will shape and syllable its sound
  Into Zuleika's name.
'Tis from her cypress summit heard,
That melts in air the liquid word:
'Tis from her lowly virgin earth
That white rose takes its tender birth.
There late was laid a marble stone;
Eve saw it placed—the Morrow gone!   1200
It was no mortal arm that bore
That deep fixed pillar to the shore;
For there, as Helle's legends tell,
Next morn 'twas found where Selim fell;
Lashed by the tumbling tide, whose wave
Denied his bones a holier grave:
And there by night, reclined, 'tis said,
Is seen a ghastly turbaned head:
  And hence extended by the billow,
  'Tis named the "Pirate-phantom's pillow!"   1210
  Where first it lay that mourning flower
  Hath flourished; flourisheth this hour,
Alone and dewy—coldly pure and pale;
As weeping Beauty's cheek at Sorrow's tale!

          [First publ., Nov. 29, 1813.]

THE CORSAIR

A TALE

[With this poem Byron reached an unprecedented height of popularity, for John Murray, the publisher, wrote that 10,000 copies had been sold on the first day of publication.]

——"I suoi pensieri in lui dormir non ponno."
—TASSO, *Gerusalemme Liberata*, Canto X.
[stanza lxxviii. line 8].

TO THOMAS MOORE, ESQ.

MY DEAR MOORE,

      I DEDICATE to you the last production with which I shall trespass on public patience, and your indulgence, for some years; and I own that I feel anxious to avail myself of this latest and only opportunity of adorning my pages with a name, consecrated by unshaken public principle, and the most undoubted and various talents. While Ireland ranks you among the firmest of her patriots; while you stand alone the first of her bards in her estimation, and Britain repeats and ratifies the decree, permit one, whose only regret, since our first acquaintance, has been the years he had lost before it commenced, to add the humble but sincere suffrage of friendship, to the voice of more than one nation. It will at least prove to you, that I have neither forgotten the gratification derived from your society, nor abandoned the prospect of its renewal, whenever your leisure or inclination allows you to atone to your friends for too long an absence. It is said among those friends, I trust truly, that you are engaged in the composition of a poem whose scene will be laid in the East; none can do those scenes so much justice. The wrongs of your own country, the magnificent and fiery spirit of her sons, the beauty and feeling of her daughters, may there be found; and Collins, when he denominated his Oriental his Irish Eclogues, was not aware how true, at least, was a part of his parallel. Your imagination will create a warmer sun, and less clouded sky; but wildness, tenderness, and originality, are part of your national claim of oriental descent, to which you have already thus far proved your title more clearly than the most zealous of your country's antiquarians.

May I add a few words on a subject on which all men are supposed to be fluent, and none agreeable?—Self. I have written much, and published more than enough to demand a longer silence than I now meditate: but, for some years to come, it is my intention to tempt no further the award of "Gods, men, nor columns." In the present composition I have attempted not the most difficult, but, perhaps, the best adapted measure to our language, the good old and now neglected heroic couplet. The stanza of Spenser is perhaps too slow and dignified for narrative; though, I confess, it is the measure most after my own heart; Scott alone, of the present generation, has hitherto completely triumphed over the fatal facility of the octosyllabic verse; and this is not the least victory of his fertile and mighty genius: in blank verse, Milton, Thomson, and our dramatists, are the beacons that shine along the deep, but warn us from the rough and barren rock on which they are kindled. The heroic couplet is not the most popular measure certainly; but as I did not deviate into the other from a wish to flatter what is called public opinion, I shall quit it without further apology, and take my chance once more with that versification, in which I have hitherto published nothing but compositions whose former circulation is part of my present, and will be of my future regret.

With regard to my story, and stories in general, I should have been glad to have rendered my personages more perfect and amiable, if possible, inasmuch as I have been sometimes criticised, and considered no less responsible for their deeds and qualities than if all had been personal. Be it so—if I have deviated into the gloomy vanity of "drawing from self," the pictures are probably like, since they are unfavourable: and if not, those who know me are undeceived, and those who do not, I have little interest in undeceiving. I have no particular desire that any but my acquaintance should think the author better than the beings of his imagining; but I cannot help a little surprise, and perhaps amusement, at some odd critical exceptions in the present instance, when I see several bards (far more deserving, I allow) in very reputable plight, and quite exempted from all participation in the faults of those heroes, who, nevertheless, might be found with little more morality than *The Giaour*, and perhaps—but no—I must admit Childe Harold to be a very repulsive personage; and as to his identity, those who like it must give him whatever "alias" they please.

If, however, it were worth while to remove the impression, it might be of some service to me, that the man who is alike the delight of his readers and his friends, the poet of all circles, and the idol of his own, permits me here and elsewhere to subscribe myself,

Most truly,
And affectionately,
His obedient servant,
BYRON.
January 2, 1814.

CANTO THE FIRST

"—— nessun maggior dolore,
Che ricordarsi del tempo felice
Nella miseria,——"
—DANTE, *Inferno*, v. 121.

I

"O'ER the glad waters of the dark blue sea,
Our thoughts as boundless, and our souls as free,
Far as the breeze can bear, the billows foam,
Survey our empire, and behold our home!
These are our realms, no limits to their sway—
Our flag the sceptre all who meet obey.
Ours the wild life in tumult still to range
From toil to rest, and joy in every change.
Oh, who can tell? not thou, luxurious slave!
Whose soul would sicken o'er the heaving wave;   1r
Not thou, vain lord of Wantonness and Ease!
Whom Slumber soothes not—Pleasure cannot please—
Oh, who can tell, save he whose heart hath tried,
And danced in triumph o'er the waters wide,
The exulting sense—the pulse's maddening play,
That thrills the wanderer of that trackless way?
That for itself can woo the approaching fight,
And turn what some deem danger to delight;
That seeks what cravens shun with more than zeal,
And where the feebler faint can only feel—   20
Feel—to the rising bosom's inmost core,
Its hope awaken and its spirit soar?
No dread of Death—if with us die our foes—

Save that it seems even duller than repose;
Come when it will—we snatch the life of Life—
When lost—what recks it—by disease or strife?
Let him who crawls, enamoured of decay,
Cling to his couch, and sicken years away;
Heave his thick breath, and shake his palsied head;
Ours the fresh turf, and not the feverish bed,—   30
While gasp by gasp he falters forth his soul,
Ours with one pang—one bound—escapes control.
His corse may boast its urn and narrow cave,
And they who loathed his life may gild his grave:
Ours are the tears, though few, sincerely shed,
When Ocean shrouds and sepulchres our dead.
For us, even banquets fond regret supply
In the red cup that crowns our memory;
And the brief epitaph in Danger's day,
When those who win at length divide the prey,   40
And cry, Remembrance saddening o'er each brow,
How had the brave who fell exulted *now!*"

II

Such were the notes that from the Pirate's isle
Around the kindling watch-fire rang the while:
Such were the sounds that thrilled the rocks along,
And unto ears as rugged seemed a song!
In scattered groups upon the golden sand,
They game—carouse—converse—or whet the brand;
Select the arms—to each his blade assign,
And, careless, eye the blood that dims its shine;   50
Repair the boat, replace the helm or oar,
While others straggling muse along the shore;
For the wild bird the busy springes set,
Or spread beneath the sun the dripping net:
Gaze where some distant sail a speck supplies,
With all the thirsting eye of Enterprise;
Tell o'er the tales of many a night of toil,
And marvel where they next shall seize a spoil:
No matter where—their Chief's allotment this;
Theirs to believe no prey nor plan amiss.   60
But who that CHIEF? his name on every shore
Is famed and feared—they ask and know no more.
With these he mingles not but to command;

Few are his words, but keen his eye and hand.
Ne'er seasons he with mirth their jovial mess,
But they forgive his silence for success.
Ne'er for his lip the purpling cup they fill,
That goblet passes him untasted still—
And for his fare—the rudest of his crew
Would that, in turn, have passed untasted too;   70
Earth's coarsest bread, the garden's homeliest roots,
And scarce the summer luxury of fruits,
His short repast in humbleness supply
With all a hermit's board would scarce deny.
But while he shuns the grosser joys of sense,
His mind seems nourished by that abstinence.
"Steer to that shore!" they sail. "Do this!"—'tis done:—
"Now form and follow me!"—the spoil is won.
Thus prompt his accents and his actions still,
And all obey and few inquire his will;   80
To such, brief answer and contemptuous eye
Convey reproof, nor further deign reply.

III

"A sail!—a sail!"—a promised prize to Hope!
Her nation—flag—how speaks the telescope?
No prize, alas! but yet a welcome sail:
The blood-red signal glitters in the gale.
Yes—she is ours—a home-returning bark—
Blow fair, thou breeze!—she anchors ere the dark.
Already doubled is the cape—our bay
Receives that prow which proudly spurns the spray.   90
How gloriously her gallant course she goes!
Her white wings flying—never from her foes—
She walks the waters like a thing of Life,
And seems to dare the elements to strife.
Who would not brave the battle-fire, the wreck,
To move the monarch of her peopled deck!

IV

Hoarse o'er her side the rustling cable rings:
The sails are furled, and anchoring round she swings;
And gathering loiterers on the land discern

Her boat descending from the latticed stern.   100
'Tis manned—the oars keep concert to the strand,
Till grates her keel upon the shallow sand.
Hail to the welcome shout!—the friendly speech!
When hand grasps hand uniting on the beach;
The smile, the question, and the quick reply,
And the Heart's promise of festivity!

V

The tidings spread, and gathering grows the crowd:
The hum of voices, and the laughter loud,
And Woman's gentler, anxious tone is heard—
Friends'—husbands'—lovers' names in each dear word: 110
"Oh! are they safe? we ask not of success—
But shall we see them? will their accents bless?
From where the battle roars, the billows chafe,
They doubtless boldly did—but who are safe?
Here let them haste to gladden and surprise,
And kiss the doubt from these delighted eyes!"

VI

"Where is our Chief? for him we bear report—
And doubt that joy—which hails our coming—short;
Yet thus sincere—'tis cheering, though so brief;
But, Juan! instant guide us to our Chief: 120
Our greeting paid, we'll feast on our return,
And all shall hear what each may wish to learn."
Ascending slowly by the rock-hewn way,
To where his watch-tower beetles o'er the bay,
By bushy brake, the wild flowers blossoming,
And freshness breathing from each silver spring,
Whose scattered streams from granite basins burst,
Leap into life, and sparkling woo your thirst;
From crag to cliff they mount—Near yonder cave,
What lonely straggler looks along the wave?   130
In pensive posture leaning on the brand,
Not oft a resting-staff to that red hand?
" 'Tis he—'tis Conrad—here—as wont—alone;
On—Juan! on—and make our purpose known.
The bark he views—and tell him we would greet

His ear with tidings he must quickly meet:
We dare not yet approach—thou know'st his mood,
When strange or uninvited steps intrude."

VII

Him Juan sought, and told of their intent;—
He spake not, but a sign expressed assent: 140
These Juan calls—they come—to their salute
He bends him slightly, but his lips are mute.
"These letters, Chief, are from the Greek—the spy,
Who still proclaims our spoil or peril nigh:
Whate'er his tidings, we can well report,
Much that"—"Peace, peace!"—he cuts their prating short.
Wondering they turn abashed, while, each to each,
Conjecture whispers in his muttering speech:
They watch his glance with many a stealing look,
To gather how that eye the tidings took;   150
But, this as if he guessed, with head aside,
Perchance from some emotion, doubt, or pride,
He read the scroll—"My tablets, Juan, hark—
Where is Gonsalvo?"
                        "In the anchored bark."
"There let him stay—to him this order bear—
Back to your duty—for my course prepare:
Myself this enterprise to-night will share."
"To-night, Lord Conrad?"
                                "Aye! at set of sun:
The breeze will freshen when the day is done.
My corslet—cloak—one hour and we are gone.   160
Sling on thy bugle—see that free from rust
My carbine-lock springs worthy of my trust;
Be the edge sharpened of my boarding-brand,
And give its guard more room to fit my hand.
This let the Armourer with speed dispose;
Last time, it more fatigued my arm than foes;
Mark that the signal-gun be duly fired,
To tell us when the hour of stay's expired."

VIII

They make obeisance, and retire in haste,
Too soon to seek again the watery waste: 170

Yet they repine not—so that Conrad guides;
And who dare question aught that he decides?
That man of loneliness and mystery,
Scarce seen to smile, and seldom heard to sigh;
Whose name appals the fiercest of his crew,
And tints each swarthy cheek with sallower hue;
Still sways their souls with that commanding art
That dazzles, leads, yet chills the vulgar heart.
What is that spell, that thus his lawless train
Confess and envy—yet oppose in vain!   180
What should it be, that thus their faith can bind?
The power of Thought—the magic of the Mind!
Linked with success, assumed and kept with skill,
That moulds another's weakness to its will;
Wields with their hands, but, still to these unknown,
Makes even their mightiest deeds appear his own.
Such hath it been—shall be—beneath the Sun
The many still must labour for the one!
'Tis Nature's doom—but let the wretch who toils,
Accuse not—hate not—*him* who wears the spoils.   190
Oh! if he knew the weight of splendid chains,
How light the balance of his humbler pains!

IX

Unlike the heroes of each ancient race,
Demons in act, but Gods at least in face,
In Conrad's form seems little to admire,
Though his dark eyebrow shades a glance of fire:
Robust but not Herculean—to the sight
No giant frame sets forth his common height;
Yet, in the whole, who paused to look again,
Saw more than marks the crowd of vulgar men;   20
They gaze and marvel how—and still confess
That thus it is, but why they cannot guess.
Sun-burnt his cheek, his forehead high and pale
The sable curls in wild profusion veil;
And oft, perforce, his rising lip reveals
The haughtier thought it curbs, but scarce conceals.
Though smooth his voice, and calm his general mien,
Still seems there something he would not have seen:
His features' deepening lines and varying hue

At times attracted, yet perplexed the view,   210
As if within that murkiness of mind
Worked feelings fearful, and yet undefined;
Such might it be—that none could truly tell—
Too close inquiry his stern glance would quell.
There breathe but few whose aspect might defy
The full encounter of his searching eye;
He had the skill, when Cunning's gaze would seek
To probe his heart and watch his changing cheek,
At once the observer's purpose to espy,
And on himself roll back his scrutiny,   220
Lest he to Conrad rather should betray
Some secret thought, than drag that Chief's to-day.
There was a laughing Devil in his sneer,
That raised emotions both of rage and fear;
And where his frown of hatred darkly fell,
Hope withering fled—and Mercy sighed farewell!

X

Slight are the outward signs of evil thought,
Within—within—'twas there the spirit wrought!
Love shows all changes—Hate, Ambition, Guile,
Betray no further than the bitter smile;   230
The lip's least curl, the lightest paleness thrown
Along the governed aspect, speak alone
Of deeper passions; and to judge their mien,
He, who would see, must be himself unseen.
Then—with the hurried tread, the upward eye,
The clenchéd hand, the pause of agony,
That listens, starting, lest the step too near
Approach intrusive on that mood of fear:
Then—with each feature working from the heart,
With feelings, loosed to strengthen—not depart: 240
That rise—convulse—contend—that freeze or glow,
Flush in the cheek, or damp upon the brow;
Then—Stranger! if thou canst, and tremblest not,
Behold his soul—the rest that soothes his lot!
Mark how that lone and blighted bosom sears
The scathing thought of execrated years!
Behold—but who hath seen, or e'er shall see,
Man as himself—the secret spirit free?

XI

Yet was not Conrad thus by Nature sent
To lead the guilty—Guilt's worst instrument—   250
His soul was changed, before his deeds had driven
Him forth to war with Man and forfeit Heaven.
Warped by the world in Disappointment's school,
In words too wise—in conduct *there* a fool;
Too firm to yield, and far too proud to stoop,
Doomed by his very virtues for a dupe,
He cursed those virtues as the cause of ill,
And not the traitors who betrayed him still;
Nor deemed that gifts bestowed on better men
Had left him joy, and means to give again.   260
Feared—shunned—belied—ere Youth had lost her force,
He hated Man too much to feel remorse,
And thought the voice of Wrath a sacred call,
To pay the injuries of some on all.
He knew himself a villain—but he deemed
The rest no better than the thing he seemed;
And scorned the best as hypocrites who hid
Those deeds the bolder spirit plainly did.
He knew himself detested, but he knew
The hearts that loathed him, crouched and dreaded too.   270
Lone, wild, and strange, he stood alike exempt
From all affection and from all contempt:
His name could sadden, and his acts surprise;
But they that feared him dared not to despise:
Man spurns the worm, but pauses ere he wake
The slumbering venom of the folded snake:
The first may turn, but not avenge the blow;
The last expires, but leaves no living foe;
Fast to the doomed offender's form it clings,
And he may crush—not conquer—still it stings!   280

XII

None are all evil—quickening round his heart,
One softer feeling would not yet depart:
Oft could he sneer at others as beguiled
By passions worthy of a fool or child;

Yet 'gainst that passion vainly still he strove,
And even in him it asks the name of Love!
Yes, it was love—unchangeable—unchanged,
Felt but for one from whom he never ranged;
Though fairest captives daily met his eye,
He shunned, nor sought, but coldly passed them by;   **290**
Though many a beauty drooped in prisoned bower,
None ever soothed his most unguarded hour.
Yes—it was Love—if thoughts of tenderness,
Tried in temptation, strengthened by distress,
Unmoved by absence, firm in every clime,
And yet—Oh more than all!—untired by Time;
Which nor defeated hope, nor baffled wile,
Could render sullen were She near to smile,
Nor rage could fire, nor sickness fret to vent
On her one murmur of his discontent;   **300**
Which still would meet with joy, with calmness part,
Less that his look of grief should reach her heart;
Which nought removed, nor menaced to remove—
If there be Love in mortals—this was Love!
He was a villain—aye, reproaches shower
On him—but not the Passion, nor its power,
Which only proved—all other virtues gone—
Not Guilt itself could quench this loveliest one!

XIII

He paused a moment—till his hastening men
Passed the first winding downward to the glen.   **310**
"Strange tidings!—many a peril have I passed,
Nor know I why this next appears the last!
Yet so my heart forebodes, but must not fear,
Nor shall my followers find me falter here.
'Tis rash to meet—but surer death to wait,
Till, here, they hunt us to undoubted fate;
And, if my plan but hold, and Fortune smile,
We'll furnish mourners for our funeral pile.
Aye, let them slumber—peaceful be their dreams!
More ne'er awoke them with such brilliant beams   **320**
As kindle high to-night (but blow, thou breeze!)
To warm these slow avengers of the seas.

Now to Medora—Oh! my sinking heart,
Long may her own be lighter than thou art!
Yet was I brave—mean boast where all are brave!
Ev'n insects sting for aught they seek to save—
This common courage which with brutes we share,
That owes its deadliest efforts to Despair,
Small merit claims—but 'twas my nobler hope
To teach my few with numbers still to cope; 330
Long have I led them—not to vainly bleed:
No medium now—we perish or succeed!
So let it be—it irks not me to die;
But thus to urge them whence they cannot fly.
My lot hath long had little of my care,
But chafes my pride thus baffled in the snare:
Is this my skill? my craft? to set at last
Hope, Power, and Life upon a single cast?
Oh, Fate!—accuse thy folly—not thy fate;
She may redeem thee still—nor yet too late." 340

XIV

Thus with himself communion held he, till
He reached the summit of his tower-crowned hill:
There at the portal paused—for wild and soft
He heard those accents never heard too oft!
Through the high lattice far yet sweet they rung,
And these the notes his Bird of Beauty sung:

1

"Deep in my soul that tender secret dwells,
    Lonely and lost to light for evermore,
Save when to thine my heart responsive swells,
    Then trembles into silence as before. 350

2

"There, in its centre, a sepulchral lamp
    Burns the slow flame, eternal—but unseen;
Which not the darkness of Despair can damp,
    Though vain its ray as it had never been.

3

"Remember me—Oh! pass not thou my grave
　　Without one thought whose relics there recline:
The only pang my bosom dare not brave
　　Must be to find forgetfulness in thine.

4

"My fondest—faintest—latest accents hear—
　　Grief for the dead not Virtue can reprove;　　　　360
Then give me all I ever asked—a tear,
　　The first—last—sole reward of so much love!"

He passed the portal, crossed the corridor,
And reached the chamber as the strain gave o'er:
"My own Medora! sure thy song is sad—"

"In Conrad's absence would'st thou have it glad
Without thine ear to listen to my lay,
Still must my song my thoughts, my soul betray:
Still must each accent to my bosom suit,
My heart unhushed—although my lips were mute!　　370
Oh! many a night on this lone couch reclined,
My dreaming fear with storms hath winged the wind,
And deemed the breath that faintly fanned thy sail
The murmuring prelude of the ruder gale;
Though soft—it seemed the low prophetic dirge,
That mourned thee floating on the savage surge:
Still would I rise to rouse the beacon fire,
Lest spies less true should let the blaze expire;
And many a restless hour outwatched each star,
And morning came—and still thou wert afar.　　　380
Oh! how the chill blast on my bosom blew,
And day broke dreary on my troubled view,
And still I gazed and gazed—and not a prow
Was granted to my tears—my truth—my vow!
At length—'twas noon—I hailed and blest the mast
That met my sight—it neared—Alas! it passed!
Another came—Oh God! 'twas thine at last!
Would that those days were over; wilt thou ne'er,

My Conrad! learn the joys of peace to share?
Sure thou hast more than wealth, and many a home   390
As bright as this invites us not to roam:
Thou know'st it is not peril that I fear,
I only tremble when thou are not here;
Then not for mine, but that far dearer life,
Which flies from love and languishes for strife—
How strange that heart, to me so tender still,
Should war with Nature and its better will!"

"Yea, strange indeed—that heart hath long been changed;
Worm-like 'twas trampled—adder-like avenged—
Without one hope on earth beyond thy love,   400
And scarce a glimpse of mercy from above.
Yet the same feeling which thou dost condemn,
My very love to thee is hate to them,
So closely mingling here, that disentwined,
I cease to love thee when I love Mankind:
Yet dread not this—the proof of all the past
Assures the future that my love will last;
But—Oh, Medora! nerve thy gentler heart;
This hour again—but not for long—we part."

"This hour we part!—my heart foreboded this: 410
Thus ever fade my fairy dreams of bliss.
This hour—it cannot be—this hour away!
Yon bark hath hardly anchored in the bay:
Her consort still is absent, and her crew
Have need of rest before they toil anew;
My love! thou mock'st my weakness; and wouldst steel
My breast before the time when it must feel;
But trifle now no more with my distress,
Such mirth hath less of play than bitterness.
Be silent, Conrad!—dearest! come and share   420
The feast these hands delighted to prepare;
Light toil! to cull and dress thy frugal fare!
See, I have plucked the fruit that promised best,
And where not sure, perplexed, but pleased, I guessed
At such as seemed the fairest; thrice the hill
My steps have wound to try the coolest rill;
Yes! thy Sherbet to-night will sweetly flow,
See how it sparkles in its vase of snow!
The grape's gay juice thy bosom never cheers;

Thou more than Moslem when the cup appears: 430
Think not I mean to chide—for I rejoice
What others deem a penance is thy choice.
But come, the board is spread; our silver lamp
Is trimmed, and heeds not the Sirocco's damp:
Then shall my handmaids while the time along,
And join with me the dance, or wake the song;
Or my guitar, which still thou lov'st to hear,
Shall soothe or lull—or, should it vex thine ear,
We'll turn the tale, by Ariosto told,
Of fair Olympia loved and left of old.   440
Why, thou wert worse than he who broke his vow
To that lost damsel, should thou leave me *now*—
Or even that traitor chief—I've seen thee smile,
When the clear sky showed Ariadne's Isle,
Which I have pointed from these cliffs the while:
And thus half sportive—half in fear—I said,
Lest Time should raise that doubt to more than dread,
Thus Conrad, too, will quit me for the main:
And he deceived me—for—he came again!"

"Again, again—and oft again—my Love!   450
If there be life below, and hope above,
He will return—but, now, the moments bring
The time of parting with redoubled wing:
The why, the where—what boots it now to tell?
Since all must end in that wild word—Farewell!
Yet would I fain—did time allow—disclose—
Fear not—these are no formidable foes!
And here shall watch a more than wonted guard,
For sudden siege and long defence prepared:
Nor be thou lonely, though thy Lord's away,   460
Our matrons and thy handmaids with thee stay;
And this thy comfort—that, when next we meet,
Security shall make repose more sweet.
List!—'tis the bugle!"—Juan shrilly blew—
"One kiss—one more—another—Oh! Adieu!"
She rose—she sprung—she clung to his embrace,
Till his heart heaved beneath her hidden face:
He dared not raise to his that deep-blue eye,
Which downcast drooped in tearless agony.
Her long fair hair lay floating o'er his arms,   470
In all the wildness of dishevelled charms;

Scarce beat that bosom where his image dwelt
So full—*that* feeling seemed almost unfelt!
Hark—peals the thunder of the signal-gun!
It told 'twas sunset, and he cursed that sun.
Again—again—that form he madly pressed,
Which mutely clasped, imploringly caressed!
And tottering to the couch his bride he bore,
One moment gazed—as if to gaze no more;
Felt that for him Earth held but her alone,   480
Kissed her cold forehead—turned—is Conrad gone?

XV

"And is he gone?"—on sudden solitude
How oft that fearful question will intrude!
" 'Twas but an instant passed, and here he stood!
And now"—without the portal's porch she rushed,
And then at length her tears in freedom gushed;
Big, bright, and fast, unknown to her they fell;
But still her lips refused to send—"Farewell!"
For in that word—that fatal word—howe'er
We promise—hope—believe—there breathes Despair.   49r
O'er every feature of that still, pale face,
Had Sorrow fixed what Time can ne'er erase:
The tender blue of that large loving eye
Grew frozen with its gaze on vacancy,
Till—Oh, how far!—it caught a glimpse of him,
And then it flowed, and phrensied seemed to swim
Through those long, dark, and glistening lashes dewed
With drops of sadness oft to be renewed.
"He's gone!"—against her heart that hand is driven,
Convulsed and quick—then gently raised to Heaven: 500
She looked and saw the heaving of the main;
The white sail set—she dared not look again;
But turned with sickening soul within the gate—
"It is no dream—and I am desolate!"

XVI

From crag to crag descending, swiftly sped
Stern Conrad down, nor once he turned his head;
But shrunk whene'er the windings of his way
Forced on his eye what he would not survey,

His lone, but lovely dwelling on the steep,
That hailed him first when homeward from the deep:　510
And she—the dim and melancholy Star,
Whose ray of Beauty reached him from afar,
On her he must not gaze, he must not think—
There he might rest—but on Destruction's brink:
Yet once almost he stopped and nearly gave
His fate to chance, his projects to the wave:
But no—it must not be—a worthy chief
May melt, but not betray to Woman's grief.
He sees his bark, he notes how fair the wind,
And sternly gathers all his might of mind:　520
Again he hurries on—and as he hears
The clang of tumult vibrate on his ears,
The busy sounds, the bustle of the shore,
The shout, the signal, and the dashing oar;
As marks his eye the seaboy on the mast,
The anchors rise, the sails unfurling fast,
The waving kerchiefs of the crowd that urge
That mute Adieu to those who stem the surge;
And more than all, his blood-red flag aloft,
He marvelled how his heart could seem so soft.　530
Fire in his glance, and wildness in his breast,
He feels of all his former self possest;
He bounds—he flies—until his footsteps reach
The verge where ends the cliff, begins the beach,
There checks his speed; but pauses less to breathe
The breezy freshness of the deep beneath,
Than there his wonted statelier step renew;
Nor rush, disturbed by haste, to vulgar view:
For well had Conrad learned to curb the crowd,
By arts that veil, and oft preserve the proud;　540
His was the lofty port, the distant mien,
That seems to shun the sight—and awes if seen:
The solemn aspect, and the high-born eye,
That checks low mirth, but lacks not courtesy;
All these he wielded to command assent:
But where he wished to win, so well unbent,
That Kindness cancelled fear in those who heard,
And others' gifts showed mean beside his word.
When echoed to the heart as from his own
His deep yet tender melody of tone:　550
But such was foreign to his wonted mood.

He cared not what he softened, but subdued;
The evil passions of his youth had made
Him value less who loved—than what obeyed.

XVII

Around him mustering ranged his ready guard:
Before him Juan stands—"Are all prepared?"
"They are—nay more—embarked: the latest boat
Waits but my Chief——"
       "My sword, and my capote!"
Soon firmly girded on, and lightly slung,
His belt and cloak were o'er his shoulders flung: 560
"Call Pedro here!" He comes—and Conrad bends,
With all the courtesy he deigned his friends;
"Receive these tablets, and peruse with care,
Words of high trust and truth are graven there;
Double the guard, and when Anselmo's bark
Arrives, let him alike these orders mark:
In three days (serve the breeze) the sun shall shine
On our return—till then all peace be thine!"
This said, his brother Pirate's hand he wrung,
Then to his boat with haughty gesture sprung. 570
Flashed the dipt oars, and sparkling with the stroke,
Around the waves' phosphoric brightness broke;
They gain the vessel—on the deck he stands,—
Shrieks the shrill whistle, ply the busy hands—
He marks how well the ship her helm obeys,
How gallant all her crew, and deigns to praise.
His eyes of pride to young Gonsalvo turn—
Why doth he start, and inly seem to mourn?
Alas! those eyes beheld his rocky tower,
And live a moment o'er the parting hour; 580
She—his Medora—did she mark the prow?
Ah! never loved he half so much as now!
But much must yet be done ere dawn of day—
Again he mans himself and turns away;
Down to the cabin with Gonsalvo bends,
And there unfolds his plan—his means, and ends;
Before them burns the lamp, and spreads the chart,
And all that speaks and aids the naval art;
They to the midnight watch protract debate;
To anxious eyes what hour is ever late? 590

Meantime, the steady breeze serenely blew,
And fast and falcon-like the vessel flew;
Passed the high headlands of each clustering isle,
To gain their port—long—long ere morning smile:
And soon the night-glass through the narrow bay
Discovers where the Pacha's galleys lay.
Count they each sail, and mark how there supine
The lights in vain o'er heedless Moslem shine.
Secure, unnoted, Conrad's prow passed by,
And anchored where his ambush meant to lie;   600
Screened from espial by the jutting cape,
That rears on high its rude fantastic shape.
Then rose his band to duty—not from sleep—
Equipped for deeds alike on land or deep;
While leaned their Leader o'er the fretting flood,
And calmly talked—and yet he talked of blood!

CANTO THE SECOND

"Conosceste i dubbiosi desiri?"
—DANTE, *Inferno*, v. 120.

I

IN CORON's bay floats many a galley light,
Through Coron's lattices the lamps are bright,
For Seyd, the Pacha, makes a feast to-night:
A feast for promised triumph yet to come,   610
When he shall drag the fettered Rovers home;
This hath he sworn by Allah and his sword,
And faithful to his firman and his word,
His summoned prows collect along the coast,
And great the gathering crews, and loud the boast;
Already shared the captives and the prize,
Though far the distant foe they thus despise;
'Tis but to sail—no doubt to-morrow's Sun
Will see the Pirates bound—their haven won!
Meantime the watch may slumber, if they will,   620
Nor only wake to war, but dreaming kill.
Though all, who can, disperse on shore and seek
To flesh their glowing valour on the Greek;
How well such deed becomes the turbaned brave—

To bare the sabre's edge before a slave!
Infest his dwelling—but forbear to slay,
Their arms are strong, yet merciful to-day,
And do not deign to smite because they may!
Unless some gay caprice suggests the blow,
To keep in practice for the coming foe. 630
Revel and rout the evening hours beguile,
And they who wish to wear a head must smile;
For Moslem mouths produce their choicest cheer,
And hoard their curses, till the coast is clear.

II

High in his hall reclines the turbaned Seyd;
Around—the bearded chiefs he came to lead.
Removed the banquet, and the last pilaff—
Forbidden draughts, 'tis said, he dared to quaff,
Though to the rest the sober berry's juice
The slaves bear round for rigid Moslems' use; 640
The long chibouque's dissolving cloud supply,
While dance the Almas to wild minstrelsy.
The rising morn will view the chiefs embark;
But waves are somewhat treacherous in the dark:
And revellers may more securely sleep
On silken couch than o'er the rugged deep:
Feast there who can—nor combat till they must,
And less to conquest than to Korans trust;
And yet the numbers crowded in his host
Might warrant more than even the Pacha's boast. 651

III

With cautious reverence from the outer gate
Slow stalks the slave, whose office there to wait,
Bows his bent head—his hand salutes the floor,
Ere yet his tongue the trusted tidings bore:
"A captive Dervise, from the Pirate's nest
Escaped, is here—himself would tell the rest."
He took the sign from Seyd's assenting eye,
And led the holy man in silence nigh.
His arms were folded on his dark-green vest,
His step was feeble, and his look deprest; 660
Yet worn he seemed of hardship more than years,

And pale his cheek with penance, not from fears.
Vowed to his God—his sable locks he wore,
And these his lofty cap rose proudly o'er:
Around his form his loose long robe was thrown,
And wrapt a breast bestowed on heaven alone;
Submissive, yet with self-possession manned,
He calmly met the curious eyes that scanned,
And question of his coming fain would seek,
Before the Pacha's will allowed to speak.   670

IV

"Whence com'st thou, Dervise?"
                              "From the Outlaw's den
A fugitive—"
              "Thy capture where and when?"
"From Scalanova's port to Scio's isle,
The Saick was bound; but Allah did not smile
Upon our course—the Moslem merchant's gains
The Rovers won; our limbs have worn their chains.
I had no death to fear, nor wealth to boast,
Beyond the wandering freedom which I lost;
At length a fisher's humble boat by night
Afforded hope, and offered chance of flight;   680
I seized the hour, and find my safety here—
With thee—most mighty Pacha! who can fear?"

"How speed the outlaws? stand they well prepared,
Their plundered wealth, and robber's rock, to guard?
Dream they of this our preparation, doomed
To view with fire their scorpion nest consumed?"
"Pacha! the fettered captive's mourning eye,
That weeps for flight, but ill can play the spy;
I only heard the reckless waters roar,
Those waves that would not bear me from the shore;   690
I only marked the glorious Sun and sky,
Too bright—too blue—for my captivity;
And felt that all which Freedom's bosom cheers
Must break my chain before it dried my tears.
This mayst thou judge, at least, from my escape,
They little deem of aught in Peril's shape;
Else vainly had I prayed or sought the chance
That leads me here—if eyed with vigilance:

The careless guard that did not see me fly,
May watch as idly when thy power is nigh. 700
Pacha! my limbs are faint—and nature craves
Food for my hunger, rest from tossing waves:
Permit my absence—peace be with thee! Peace
With all around!—now grant repose—release."

"Stay, Dervise! I have more to question—stay,
I do command thee—sit—dost hear?—obey!
More I must ask, and food the slaves shall bring;
Thou shalt not pine where all are banqueting:
The supper done—prepare thee to reply,
Clearly and full—I love not mystery." 710
'Twere vain to guess what shook the pious man,
Who looked not lovingly on that Divan;
Nor showed high relish for the banquet prest,
And less respect for every fellow guest.
'Twas but a moment's peevish hectic passed
Along his cheek, and tranquillised as fast:
He sate down in silence, and his look
Resumed the calmness which before forsook:
The feast was ushered in—but sumptuous fare
He shunned as if some poison mingled there. 720
For one so long condemned to toil and fast,
Methinks he strangely spares the rich repast.
"What ails thee, Dervise? eat—dost thou suppose
This feast a Christian's? or my friends thy foes?
Why dost thou shun the salt? that sacred pledge,
Which, once partaken, blunts the sabre's edge,
Makes even contending tribes in peace unite,
And hated hosts seem brethren to the sight!"

"Salt seasons dainties—and my food is still
The humblest root, my drink the simplest rill; 730
And my stern vow and Order's laws oppose
To break or mingle bread with friends or foes;
It may seem strange—if there be aught to dread,
That peril rests upon my single head;
But for thy sway—nay more—thy Sultan's throne,
I taste nor bread nor banquet—save alone;
Infringed our Order's rule, the Prophet's rage
To Mecca's dome might bar my pilgrimage."

"Well—as thou wilt—ascetic as thou art—
One question answer; then in peace depart.   740
How many?—Ha! it cannot sure be day?
What Star—what Sun is bursting on the bay?
It shines a lake of fire!—away—away!
Ho! treachery! my guards! my scimitar!
The galleys feed the flames—and I afar!
Accurséd Dervise!—these thy tidings—thou
Some villain spy—seize—cleave him—slay him now!"

Up rose the Dervise with that burst of light,
Nor less his change of form appalled the sight:
Up rose that Dervise—not in saintly garb,   750
But like a warrior bounding on his barb,
Dashed his high cap, and tore his robe away—
Shone his mailed breast, and flashed his sabre's ray!
His close but glittering casque, and sable plume,
More glittering eye, and black brow's sabler gloom,
Glared on the Moslems' eyes some Afrit Sprite,
Whose demon death-blow left no hope for fight.
The wild confusion, and the swarthy glow
Of flames on high, and torches from below;
The shriek of terror, and the mingling yell—   760
For swords began to clash, and shouts to swell—
Flung o'er that spot of earth the air of Hell!
Distracted, to and fro, the flying slaves
Behold but bloody shore and fiery waves;
Nought heeded they the Pacha's angry cry,
They seize that Dervise!—seize on Zatanai!
He saw their terror—checked the first despair
That urged him but to stand and perish there,
Since far too early and too well obeyed,
The flame was kindled ere the signal made;   770
He saw their terror—from his baldric drew
His bugle—brief the blast—but shrilly blew;
'Tis answered—"Well ye speed, my gallant crew!
Why did I doubt their quickness of career?
And deem design had left me single here?"
Sweeps his long arm—that sabre's whirling sway
Sheds fast atonement for its first delay;
Completes his fury, what their fear begun,
And makes the many basely quail to one.

The cloven turbans o'er the chamber spread,   780
And scarce an arm dare rise to guard its head:
Even Seyd, convulsed, o'erwhelmed, with rage, surprise,
Retreats before him, though he still defies.
No craven he—and yet he dreads the blow,
So much Confusion magnifies his foe!
His blazing galleys still distract his sight,
He tore his beard, and foaming fled the fight;
For now the pirates passed the Haram gate,
And burst within—and it were death to wait;
Where wild Amazement shrieking—kneeling—throws   79ʋ
The sword aside—in vain—the blood o'erflows!
The Corsairs pouring, haste to where within
Invited Conrad's bugle, and the din
Of groaning victims, and wild cries for life,
Proclaimed how well he did the work of strife.
They shout to find him grim and lonely there,
A glutted tiger mangling in his lair!
But short their greeting, shorter his reply—
" 'Tis well—but Seyd escapes—and he must die—
Much hath been done—but more remains to do—   800
Their galleys blaze—why not their city too?"

                              V

Quick at the word they seized him each a torch,
And fire the dome from minaret to porch.
A stern delight was fixed in Conrad's eye,
But sudden sunk—for on his ear the cry
Of women struck, and like a deadly knell
Knocked at that heart unmoved by Battle's yell.
"Oh! burst the Haram—wrong not on your lives
One female form—remember—*we* have wives.
On them such outrage Vengeance will repay;   810
Man is our foe, and such 'tis ours to slay:
But still we spared—must spare the weaker prey.
Oh! I forgot—but Heaven will not forgive
If at my word the helpless cease to live;
Follow who will—I go—we yet have time
Our souls to lighten of at least a crime."
He climbs the crackling stair—he bursts the door,
Nor feels his feet glow scorching with the floor;

His breath choked gasping with the volumed smoke,
But still from room to room his way he broke.   820
They search—they find—they save: with lusty arms
Each bears a prize of unregarded charms;
Calm their loud fears, sustain their sinking frames
With all the care defenceless Beauty claims:
So well could Conrad tame their fiercest mood,
And check the very hands with gore imbrued.
But who is she? whom Conrad's arms convey,
From reeking pile and combat's wreck, away—
Who but the love of him he dooms to bleed?
The Haram queen—but still the slave of Seyd!   830

VI

Brief time had Conrad now to greet Gulnare,
Few words to reassure the trembling Fair;
For in that pause Compassion snatched from War,
The foe before retiring, fast and far,
With wonder saw their footsteps unpursued,
First slowlier fled—then rallied—then withstood.
This Seyd perceives, then first perceives how few,
Compared with his, the Corsair's roving crew,
And blushes o'er his error, as he eyes
The ruin wrought by Panic and Surprise.   840
Alla il Alla! Vengeance swells the cry—
Shame mounts to rage that must atone or die!
And flame for flame and blood for blood must tell,
The tide of triumph ebbs that flowed too well—
When Wrath returns to renovated strife,
And those who fought for conquest strike for life.
Conrad beheld the danger—he beheld
His followers faint by freshening foes repelled:
"One effort—one—to break the circling host!"
They form—unite—charge—waver—all is lost!   850
Within a narrower ring compressed, beset,
Hopeless, not heartless, strive and struggle yet—
Ah! now they fight in firmest file no more,
Hemmed in—cut off—cleft down and trampled o'er;
But each strikes singly—silently—and home,
And sinks outwearied rather than o'ercome—
His last faint quittance rendering with his breath,
Till the blade glimmers in the grasp of Death!

VII

But first, ere came the rallying host to blows,
And rank to rank, and hand to hand oppose,   860
Gulnare and all her Haram handmaids freed,
Safe in the dome of one who held their creed,
By Conrad's mandate safely were bestowed,
And dried those tears for life and fame that flowed:
And when that dark-eyed lady, young Gulnare,
Recalled those thoughts late wandering in despair,
Much did she marvel o'er the courtesy
That smoothed his accents, softened in his eye—
'Twas strange—*that* robber thus with gore bedewed,
Seemed gentler then than Seyd in fondest mood.   870
The Pacha wooed as if he deemed the slave
Must seem delighted with the heart he gave;
The Corsair vowed protection, soothed affright,
As if his homage were a Woman's right.
"The wish is wrong—nay, worse for female—vain:
Yet much I long to view that Chief again;
If but to thank for, what my fear forgot,
The life—my loving Lord remembered not!"

VIII

And him she saw, where thickest carnage spread,
But gathered breathing from the happier dead;   880
Far from his band, and battling with a host
That deem right dearly won the field he lost,
Felled—bleeding—baffled of the death he sought,
And snatched to expiate all the ills he wrought;
Preserved to linger and to live in vain,
While Vengeance pondered o'er new plans of pain,
And stanched the blood she saves to shed again—
But drop by drop, for Seyd's unglutted eye
Would doom him ever dying—ne'er to die!
Can this be he? triumphant late she saw,   890
When his red hand's wild gesture waved a law!
'Tis he indeed—disarmed but undeprest,
His sole regret the life he still possest;

His wounds too slight, though taken with that will,
Which would have kissed the hand that then could kill.
Oh were there none, of all the many given,
To send his soul—he scarcely asked to Heaven?
Must he alone of all retain his breath,
Who more than all had striven and struck for death?
He deeply felt—what mortal hearts must feel,   900
When thus reversed on faithless Fortune's wheel,
For crimes committed, and the victor's threat
Of lingering tortures to repay the debt—
He deeply, darkly felt; but evil Pride
That led to perpetrate—now serves to hide.
Still in his stern and self-collected mien
A conqueror's more than captive's air is seen,
Though faint with wasting toil and stiffening wound,
But few that saw—so calmly gazed around:
Though the far shouting of the distant crowd,   910
Their tremors o'er, rose insolently loud,
The better warriors who beheld him near,
Insulted not the foe who taught them fear;
And the grim guards that to his durance led,
In silence eyed him with a secret dread.

IX

The Leech was sent—but not in mercy—there,
To note how much the life yet left could bear;
He found enough to load with heaviest chain,
And promise feeling for the wrench of Pain;
To-morrow—yea—to-morrow's evening Sun   920
Will, sinking, see Impalement's pangs begun,
And rising with the wonted blush of morn
Behold how well or ill those pangs are borne.
Of torments this the longest and the worst,
Which adds all other agony to thirst,
That day by day Death still forbears to slake,
While famished vultures flit around the stake.
"Oh! water—water!"—smiling Hate denies
The victim's prayer, for if he drinks he dies.
This was his doom;—the Leech, the guard, were gone,   930
And left proud Conrad fettered and alone.

X

'Twere vain to paint to what his feelings grew—
It even were doubtful if their victim knew.
There is a war, a chaos of the mind,
When all its elements convulsed—combined—
Lie dark and jarring with perturbéd force,
And gnashing with impenitent Remorse—
That juggling fiend, who never spake before,
But cries "I warned thee!" when the deed is o'er.
Vain voice! the spirit burning but unbent,   **940**
May writhe—rebel—the weak alone repent!
Even in that lonely hour when most it feels,
And, to itself, all—all that self reveals,—
No single passion, and no ruling thought
That leaves the rest, as once, unseen, unsought,
But the wild prospect when the Soul reviews,
All rushing through their thousand avenues—
Ambition's dreams expiring, Love's regret,
Endangered Glory, Life itself beset;
The joy untasted, the contempt or hate   **950**
'Gainst those who fain would triumph in our fate;
The hopeless past, the hasting future driven
Too quickly on to guess if Hell or Heaven;
Deeds—thoughts—and words, perhaps remembered not
So keenly till that hour, but ne'er forgot;
Things light or lovely in their acted time,
But now to stern Reflection each a crime:
The withering sense of Evil unrevealed,
Not cankering less because the more concealed—
All, in a word, from which all eyes must start—   **960**
That opening sepulchre, the naked heart
Bares with its buried woes—till Pride awake,
To snatch the mirror from the soul, and break.
Aye, Pride can veil, and Courage brave it all—
All—all—before—beyond—the deadliest fall.
Each hath some fear, and he who least betrays,
The only hypocrite deserving praise:
Not the loud recreant wretch who boasts and flies,—
But he who looks on Death—and silent dies:
So, steeled by pondering o'er his far career,   **970**
He half-way meets Him should he menace near!

XI

In the high chamber of his highest tower
Sate Conrad, fettered in the Pacha's power.
His palace perished in the flame—this fort
Contained at once his captive and his court.
Not much could Conrad of his sentence blame,
His foe, if vanquished, had but shared the same:—
Alone he sate—in solitude had scanned
His guilty bosom, but that breast he manned:
One thought alone he could not—dared not meet—   980
"Oh, how these tidings will Medora greet?"
Then—only then—his clanking hands he raised,
And strained with rage the chain on which he gazed:
But soon he found, or feigned, or dreamed relief,
And smiled in self-derision of his grief,
"And now come Torture when it will, or may—
More need of rest to nerve me for the day!"
This said, with languor to his mat he crept,
And, whatso'er his visions, quickly slept.

'Twas hardly midnight when that fray begun,   990
For Conrad's plans matured, at once were done,
And Havoc loathes so much the waste of time,
She scarce had left an uncommitted crime.
One hour beheld him since the tide he stemmed—
Disguised—discovered—conquering—ta'en—condemned—
A Chief on land—an outlaw on the deep—
Destroying—saving—prisoned—and asleep!

XII

He slept in calmest seeming, for his breath
Was hushed so deep—Ah! happy if in death!
He slept—Who o'er his placid slumber bends?   1000
His foes are gone—and here he hath no friends;
Is it some Seraph sent to grant him grace?
No, 'tis an earthly form with heavenly face!
Its white arm raised a lamp—yet gently hid,
Lest the ray flash abruptly on the lid
Of that closed eye, which opens but to pain,
And once unclosed—but once may close again.

That form, with eye so dark, and cheek so fair,
And auburn waves of gemmed and braided hair;
With shape of fairy lightness—naked foot, 1010
That shines like snow, and falls on earth as mute—
Through guards and dunnest night how came it there?
Ah! rather ask what will not Woman dare?
Whom Youth and Pity lead like thee, Gulnare!
She could not sleep—and while the Pacha's rest
In muttering dreams yet saw his pirate-guest,
She left his side—his signet-ring she bore,
Which oft in sport adorned her hand before—
And with it, scarcely questioned, won her way
Through drowsy guards that must that sign obey. 1020
Worn out with toil, and tired with changing blows,
Their eyes had envied Conrad his repose;
And chill and nodding at the turret door,
They stretch their listless limbs, and watch no more;
Just raised their heads to hail the signet-ring,
Nor ask or what or who the sign may bring.

XIII

She gazed in wonder, "Can he calmly sleep,
While other eyes his fall or ravage weep?
And mine in restlessness are wandering here—
What sudden spell hath made this man so dear? 1030
True—'tis to him my life, and more, I owe,
And me and mine he spared from worse than woe:
'Tis late to think—but soft—his slumber breaks—
How heavily he sighs!—he starts—awakes!"
He raised his head, and dazzled with the light,
His eye seemed dubious if it saw aright:
He moved his hand—the grating of his chain
Too harshly told him that he lived again.
"What is that form? if not a shape of air,
Methinks, my jailor's face shows wondrous fair!" 1040
"Pirate! thou know'st me not, but I am one,
Grateful for deeds thou hast too rarely done;
Look on me—and remember her, thy hand
Snatched from the flames, and thy more fearful band.
I come through darkness—and I scarce know why—
Yet not to hurt—I would not see thee die."

"If so, kind lady! thine the only eye
That would not here in that gay hope delight:
Theirs is the chance—and let them use their right.
But still I thank their courtesy or thine,   1050
That would confess me at so fair a shrine!"
Strange though it seem—yet with extremest grief
Is linked a mirth—it doth not bring relief—
That playfulness of Sorrow ne'er beguiles,
And smiles in bitterness—but still it smiles;
And sometimes with the wisest and the best,
Till even the scaffold echoes with their jest!
Yet not the joy to which it seems akin—
It may deceive all hearts, save that within.
Whate'er it was that flashed on Conrad, now   1060
A laughing wildness half unbent his brow:
And these his accents had a sound of mirth,
As if the last he could enjoy on earth;
Yet 'gainst his nature—for through that short life,
Few thoughts had he to spare from gloom and strife.

                                    XIV

"Corsair! thy doom is named—but I have power
To soothe the Pacha in his weaker hour.
Thee would I spare—nay more—would save thee now,
But this—Time—Hope—nor even thy strength allow;
But all I can,—I will—at least delay   1070
The sentence that remits thee scarce a day.
More now were ruin—even thyself were loth
The vain attempt should bring but doom to both."

"Yes!—loth indeed:—my soul is nerved to all,
Or fall'n too low to fear a further fall:
Tempt not thyself with peril—me with hope
Of flight from foes with whom I could not cope:
Unfit to vanquish—shall I meanly fly,
The one of all my band that would not die?
Yet there is one—to whom my Memory clings,   1080
Till to these eyes her own wild softness springs.
My sole resources in the path I trod
Were these—my bark—my sword—my love—my God!
The last I left in youth!—He leaves me now—
And Man but works his will to lay me low.

I have no thought to mock his throne with prayer
Wrung from the coward crouching of Despair;
It is enough—I breathe—and I can bear.
My sword is shaken from the worthless hand
That might have better kept so true a brand;   1090
My bark is sunk or captive—but my Love—
For her in sooth my voice would mount above:
Oh! she is all that still to earth can bind—
And this will break a heart so more than kind,
And blight a form—till thine appeared, Gulnare!
Mine eye ne'er asked if others were as fair."
"Thou lov'st another then?—but what to me
Is this?—'tis nothing—nothing e'er can be:
But yet—thou lov'st—and—-Oh! I envy those
Whose hearts on hearts as faithful can repose,   1100
Who never feel the void—the wandering thought
That sighs o'er visions—such as mine hath wrought.'

"Lady—methought thy love was his, for whom
This arm redeemed thee from a fiery tomb."

"My love stern Seyd's! Oh—No—No—not my love—
Yet much this heart, that strives no more, once strove
To meet his passion—but it would not be.
I felt—I feel—Love dwells with—with the free.
I am a slave, a favoured slave at best,
To share his splendour, and seem very blest!   1110
Oft must my soul the question undergo,
Of—'Dost thou love?' and burn to answer, 'No!'
Oh! hard it is that fondness to sustain,
And struggle not to feel averse in vain;
But harder still the heart's recoil to bear,
And hide from one—perhaps another there.
He takes the hand I give not—nor withhold—
Its pulse nor checked—nor quickened—calmly cold:
And when resigned, it drops a lifeless weight
From one I never loved enough to hate.   1120
No warmth these lips return by his imprest,
And chilled Remembrance shudders o'er the rest.
Yes—had I ever proved that Passion's zeal,
The change to hatred were at least—to feel:
But still—he goes unmourned—returns unsought—·
And oft when present—absent from my thought.

Or when Reflection comes—and come it must—
I fear that henceforth 'twill but bring disgust;
I am his slave—but, in despite of pride,
'Twere worse than bondage to become his bride. 1130
Oh! that this dotage of his breast would cease!
Or seek another and give mine release,
But yesterday—I could have said, to peace!
Yes, if unwonted fondness now I feign,
Remember—Captive! 'tis to break thy chain;
Repay the life that to thy hand I owe;
To give thee back to all endeared below,
Who share such love as I can never know.
Farewell—Morn breaks—and I must now away.
Twill cost me dear—but dread no death to-day!" 1146

XV

She pressed his fettered fingers to her heart,
And bowed her head, and turned her to depart,
And noiseless as a lovely dream is gone.
And was she here? and is he now alone?
What gem hath dropped and sparkles o'er his chain?
The tear most sacred, shed for others' pain,
That starts at once—bright—pure—from Pity's mine,
Already polished by the hand divine!
Oh! too convincing—dangerously dear—
In Woman's eye the unanswerable tear! 1150
That weapon of her weakness she can wield,
To save, subdue—at once her spear and shield:
Avoid it—Virtue ebbs and Wisdom errs,
Too fondly gazing on that grief of hers!
What lost a world, and bade a hero fly?
The timid tear in Cleopatra's eye.
Yet be the soft Triumvir's fault forgiven;
By this—how many lose not earth—but Heaven!
Consign their souls to Man's eternal foe,
And seal their own to spare some Wanton's woe! 1160

XVI

'Tis Morn—and o'er his altered features play
The beams—without the Hope of yesterday.
What shall he be ere night? perchance a thing

O'er which the raven flaps her funeral wing,
By his closed eye unheeded and unfelt,
While sets that Sun, and dews of Evening melt,
Chill, wet, and misty round each stiffened limb,
Refreshing earth—reviving all but him!

CANTO THE THIRD

"—come vedi, ancor non m'abbandona."
—DANTE, *Inferno*, v. 105.

I

SLOW sinks, more lovely ere his race be run,
Along Morea's hills the setting Sun;   1170
Not, as in Northern climes, obscurely bright,
But one unclouded blaze of living light!
O'er the hushed deep the yellow beam he throws,
Gilds the green wave, that trembles as it glows.
On old Ægina's rock, and Idra's isle,
The God of gladness sheds his parting smile;
O'er his own regions lingering, loves to shine,
Though there his altars are no more divine.
Descending fast the mountain shadows kiss
Thy glorious gulf, unconquered Salamis!   1180
Their azure arches through the long expanse
More deeply purpled meet his mellowing glance,
And tenderest tints, along their summits driven,
Mark his gay course, and own the hues of Heaven:
Till, darkly shaded from the land and deep,
Behind his Delphian cliff he sinks to sleep.

On such an eve, his palest beam he cast,
When—Athens! here thy Wisest looked his last.
How watched thy better sons his farewell ray,
That closed their murdered Sage's latest day!   1190
Not yet—not yet—Sol pauses on the hill—
The precious hour of parting lingers still;
But sad his light to agonizing eyes,
And dark the mountain's once delightful dyes:
Gloom o'er the lovely land he seemed to pour,
The land, where Phœbus never frowned before:

But ere he sunk below Cithæron's head,
The cup of woe was quaffed—the Spirit fled;
The Soul of him who scorned to fear or fly—
Who lived and died, as none can live or die!   1200

But lo! from high Hymettus to the plain,
The Queen of night asserts her silent reign:
No murky vapour, herald of the storm,
Hides her fair face, nor girds her glowing form;
With cornice glimmering as the moon-beams play,
There the white column greets her grateful ray,
And bright around with quivering beams beset,
Her emblem sparkles o'er the Minaret:
The groves of olive scattered dark and wide
Where meek Cephisus pours his scanty tide;   1210
The cypress saddening by the sacred Mosque,
The gleaming turret of the gay Kiosk;
And, dun and sombre 'mid the holy calm,
Near Theseus' fane yon solitary palm,
All tinged with varied hues arrest the eye—
And dull were his that passed them heedless by.

Again the Ægean, heard no more afar,
Lulls his chafed breast from elemental war;
Again his waves in milder tints unfold
Their long array of sapphire and of gold,   1220
Mixed with the shades of many a distant isle,
That frown—where gentler Ocean seems to smile.

II

Not now my theme—why turn my thoughts to thee?
Oh! who can look along thy native sea,
Nor dwell upon thy name, whate'er the tale,
So much its magic must o'er all prevail?
Who that beheld that Sun upon thee set,
Fair Athens! could thine evening face forget?
Not he—whose heart nor time nor distance frees,
Spell-bound within the clustering Cyclades!   1230
Nor seems this homage foreign to its strain,
His Corsair's isle was once thine own domain—
Would that with freedom it were thine again!

IU

The Sun hath sunk--and, darker than the night,
Sinks with its beam upon the beacon height
Medora's heart—the third day's come and gone—
With it he comes not—sends not—faithless one!
The wind was fair though light! and storms were none.
Last eve Anselmo's bark returned, and yet
His only tidings that they had not met!   1240
Though wild, as now, far different were the tale
Had Conrad waited for that single sail.
The night-breeze freshens—she that day had passed
In watching all that Hope proclaimed a mast;
Sadly she sate on high—Impatience bore
At last her footsteps to the midnight shore,
And there she wandered, heedless of the spray
That dashed her garments oft, and warned away:
She saw not, felt not this—nor dared depart,
Nor deemed it cold—her chill was at her heart;   1250
Till grew such certainty from that suspense—
His very Sight had shocked from life or sense!

It came at last—a sad and shattered boat,
Whose inmates first beheld whom first they sought;
Some bleeding—all most wretched—these the few—
Scarce knew they how escaped—*this* all they knew.
In silence, darkling, each appeared to wait
His fellow's mournful guess at Conrad's fate:
Something they would have said; but seemed to fear
To trust their accents to Medora's ear.   1260
She saw at once, yet sunk not—trembled not—
Beneath that grief, that loneliness of lot;
Within that meek fair form were feelings high,
That deemed not, till they found, their energy.
While yet was Hope they softened, fluttered, wept—
All lost—that Softness died not—but it slept;
And o'er its slumber rose that Strength which said,
"With nothing left to love, there's nought to dread."
'Tis more than Nature's—like the burning might
Delirium gathers from the fever's height.   1270

"Silent you stand—nor would I hear you tell
What—speak not—breathe not—for I know it well—
Yet would I ask—almost my lip denies
The—quick your answer—tell me where he lies."

"Lady! we know not—scarce with life we fled;
But here is one denies that he is dead:
He saw him bound; and bleeding—but alive."

She heard no further—'twas in vain to strive—
So throbbed each vein—each thought—till then withstood;
Her own dark soul these words at once subdued: 1280
She totters—falls—and senseless had the wave
Perchance but snatched her from another grave;
But that with hands though rude, yet weeping eyes,
They yield such aid as Pity's haste supplies:
Dash o'er her deathlike cheek the ocean dew,
Raise, fan, sustain—till life returns anew;
Awake her handmaids, with the matrons leave
That fainting form o'er which they gaze and grieve;
Then seek Anselmo's cavern, to report
The tale too tedious—when the triumph short.   1290

IV

In that wild council words waxed warm and strange,
With thoughts of ransom, rescue, and revenge;
All, save repose or flight: still lingering there
Breathed Conrad's spirit, and forbade despair;
What'er his fate—the breasts he formed and led
Will save him living, or appease him dead.
Woe to his foes! there yet survive a few,
Whose deeds are daring, as their hearts are true.

V

Within the Haram's secret chamber sate
Stern Seyd, still pondering o'er his Captive's fate;   1300
His thoughts on love and hate alternate dwell,
Now with Gulnare, and now in Conrad's cell;
Here at his feet the lovely slave reclined
Surveys his brow—would soothe his gloom of mind;
While many an anxious glance her large dark eye

Sends in its idle search for sympathy,
His only bends in seeming o'er his beads,
But inly views his victim as he bleeds.
"Pacha! the day is thine; and on thy crest
Sits Triumph—Conrad taken—fall'n the rest!   1310
His doom is fixed—he dies; and well his fate
Was earned—yet much too worthless for thy hate:
Methinks, a short release, for ransom told
With all his treasure, not unwisely sold;
Report speaks largely of his pirate-hoard—
Would that of this my Pacha were the lord!
While baffled, weakened by this fatal fray—
Watched—followed—he were then an easier prey;
But once cut off—the remnant of his band
Embark their wealth, and seek a safer strand."   1320

"Gulnare!—if for each drop of blood a gem
Were offered rich as Stamboul's diadem;
If for each hair of his a massy mine
Of virgin ore should supplicating shine;
If all our Arab tales divulge or dream
Of wealth were here—that gold should not redeem!
It had not now redeemed a single hour,
But that I know him fettered, in my power;
And, thirsting for revenge, I ponder still
On pangs that longest rack—and latest kill."   1330

"Nay, Seyd! I seek not to restrain thy rage.
Too justly moved for Mercy to assuage;
My thoughts were only to secure for thee
His riches—thus released, he were not free:
Disabled—shorn of half his might and band,
His capture could but wait thy first command."

"His capture *could!*—and shall I then resign
One day to him—the wretch already mine?
Release my foe!—at whose remonstrance?—thine!
Fair suitor!—to thy virtuous gratitude,   1340
That thus repays this Giaour's relenting mood,
Which thee and thine alone of all could spare—
No doubt, regardless—if the prize were fair—
My thanks and praise alike are due—now hear!
I have a counsel for thy gentler ear:

I do mistrust thee, Woman! and each word
Of thine stamps truth on all Suspicion heard.
Borne in his arms through fire from yon Serai—
Say, wert thou lingering there with him to fly?
Thou need'st not answer—thy confession speaks,   1350
Already reddening on thy guilty cheeks:
Then—Lovely Dame—bethink thee! and beware:
'Tis not *his* life alone may claim such care!
Another word and—nay—I need no more.
Accurséd was the moment when he bore
Thee from the flames, which better far—but no—
I then had mourned thee with a lover's woe—
Now 'tis thy lord that warns—deceitful thing!
Know'st thou that I can clip thy wanton wing?
In words alone I am not wont to chafe: 1360
Look to thyself—nor deem thy falsehood safe!"

He rose—and slowly, sternly thence withdrew,
Rage in his eye, and threats in his adieu:
Ah! little recked that Chief of womanhood—
Which frowns ne'er quelled, nor menaces subdued;
And little deemed he what thy heart, Gulnare!
When soft could feel—and when incensed could dare!
His doubts appeared to wrong—nor yet she knew
How deep the root from whence Compassion grew—
She was a slave—from such may captives claim   1370
A fellow-feeling, differing but in name;
Still half unconscious—heedless of his wrath,
Again she ventured on the dangerous path,
Again his rage repelled—until arose
That strife of thought, the source of Woman's woes!

VI

Meanwhile—long—anxious—weary—still the same
Rolled day and night: his soul could Terror tame—
This fearful interval of doubt and dread,
When every hour might doom him worse than dead;
When every step that echoed by the gate,   1380
Might entering lead where axe and stake await;
When every voice that grated on his ear
Might be the last that he could ever hear;
Could Terror tame—that Spirit stern and high

Had proved unwilling as unfit to die;
'Twas worn—perhaps decayed—yet silent bore
That conflict, deadlier far than all before:
The heat of fight, the hurry of the gale,
Leave scarce one thought inert enough to quail:
But bound and fixed in fettered solitude,   1390
To pine, the prey of every changing mood;
To gaze on thine own heart—and meditate
Irrevocable faults, and coming fate—
Too late the last to shun—the first to mend—
To count the hours that struggle to thine end,
With not a friend to animate, and tell
To other ears that Death became thee well;
Around thee foes to forge the ready lie,
And blot Life's latest scene with calumny;
Before thee tortures, which the Soul can dare,   1400
Yet doubts how well the shrinking flesh may bear
But deeply feels a single cry would shame—
To Valour's praise thy last and dearest claim;
The life thou leav'st below, denied above
By kind monopolists of heavenly love,
And—more than doubtful Paradise—thy Heaven
Of earthly hope, thy loved one from thee riven!
Such were the thoughts that outlaw must sustain,
And govern pangs surpassing mortal pain:
And those sustained he—boots it well or ill?   1410
Since not to sink beneath, is something still!

VII

The first day passed—he saw not her—Gulnare—
The second, third—and still she came not there:
But what her words avouched, her charms had done,
Or else he had not seen another Sun.
The fourth day rolled along, and with the night
Came storm and darkness in their mingling might.
Oh! how he listened to the rushing deep,
That ne'er till now so broke upon his sleep;
And his wild Spirit wilder wishes sent,   1420
Roused by the roar of his own element!
Oft had he ridden on that wingéd wave,
And loved its roughness for the speed it gave;
And now its dashing echoed on his ear,

A long known voice—alas! too vainly near!
Loud sung the wind above; and, doubly loud,
Shook o'er his turret cell the thunder-cloud;
And flashed the lightning by the latticed bar,
To him more genial than the Midnight Star:
Close to the glimmering grate he dragged his chain,   1430
And hoped *that* peril might not prove in vain.
He raised his iron hand to Heaven, and prayed
One pitying flash to mar the form it made:
His steel and impious prayer attract alike—
The storm rolled onward, and disdained to strike;
Its peal waxed fainter—ceased—he felt alone,
As if some faithless friend had spurned his groan!

VIII

The midnight passed—and to the massy door
A light step came—it paused—it moved once more;
Slow turns the grating bolt and sullen key: 1440
'Tis as his heart foreboded—that fair She!
Whate'er her sins, to him a Guardian Saint,
And beauteous still as hermit's hope can paint;
Yet changed since last within that cell she came,
More pale her cheek, more tremulous her frame:
On him she cast her dark and hurried eye,
Which spoke before her accents—"Thou must die!
Yes, thou must die—there is but one resource,
The last—the worst—if torture were not worse."

'Lady! I look to none; my lips proclaim   1450
What last proclaimed they—Conrad still the same:
Why should'st thou seek an outlaw's life to spare,
And change the sentence I deserve to bear?
Well have I earned—nor here alone—the meed
Of Seyd's revenge, by many a lawless deed."

"Why should I seek? because—Oh! didst thou not
Redeem my life from worse than Slavery's lot?
Why should I seek?—hath Misery made thee blind
To the fond workings of a woman's mind?
And must I say?—albeit my heart rebel   1460
With all that Woman feels, but should not tell—
Because—despite thy crimes—that heart is moved:

It feared thee—thanked thee—pitied—maddened—loved.
Reply not, tell not now thy tale again,
Thou lov'st another—and I love in vain:
Though fond as mine her bosom, form more fair,
I rush through peril which she would not dare.
If that thy heart to hers were truly dear,
Were I thine own—thou wert not lonely here:
An outlaw's spouse—and leave her Lord to roam! 1470
What hath such gentle dame to do with home?
But speak not now—o'er thine and o'er my head
Hangs the keen sabre by a single thread;
If thou hast courage still, and would'st be free,
Receive this poniard—rise and follow me!"

"Aye—in my chains! my steps will gently tread,
With these adornments, o'er such slumbering head!
Thou hast forgot—is this a garb for flight?
Or is that instrument more fit for fight?"

"Misdoubting Corsair! I have gained the guard, 1480
Ripe for revolt, and greedy for reward.
A single word of mine removes that chain:
Without some aid how here could I remain?
Well, since we met, hath sped my busy time,
If in aught evil, for thy sake the crime:
The crime—'tis none to punish those of Seyd.
That hated tyrant, Conrad—he must bleed!
I see thee shudder, but my soul is changed—
Wronged—spurned—reviled—and it shall be avenged—
Accused of what till now my heart disdained— 1490
Too faithful, though to bitter bondage chained.
Yes, smile!—but he had little cause to sneer,
I was not treacherous then—nor thou too dear:
But he has said it—and the jealous well,—
Those tyrants—teasing—tempting to rebel,—
Deserve the fate their fretting lips foretell.
I never loved—he bought me—somewhat high—
Since with me came a heart he could not buy.
I was a slave unmurmuring; he hath said,
But for his rescue I with thee had fled. 1500
'Twas false thou know'st—but let such Augurs rue,
Their words are omens Insult renders true.
Nor was thy respite granted to my prayer;

This fleeting grace was only to prepare
New torments for thy life—and my despair.
Mine, too, he threatens; but his dotage still
Would fain reserve me for his lordly will:
When wearier of these fleeting charms and me,
There yawns the sack—and yonder rolls the sea!
What, am I then a toy for dotard's play,   1510
To wear but till the gilding frets away?
I saw thee—loved thee—owe thee all—would save,
If but to show how grateful is a slave.
But had he not thus menaced fame and life,—
And well he keeps his oaths pronounced in strife—
I still had saved thee—but the Pacha spared.
Now I am all thine own—for all prepared:
Thou lov'st me not—nor know'st—or but the worst.
Alas! *this* love—*that* hatred—are the first—
Oh! could'st thou prove my truth, thou would'st not start, 1520
Nor fear the fire that lights an Eastern heart;
'Tis now the beacon of thy safety—now
It points within the port a Mainote prow:
But in one chamber, where our path must lead,
There sleeps—he must not wake—the oppressor Seyd!"

"Gulnare—Gulnare—I never felt till now
My abject fortune, withered fame so low:
Seyd is mine enemy; had swept my band
From earth with ruthless but with open hand,
And therefore came I, in my bark of war,   1530
To smite the smiter with the scimitar;
Such is my weapon—not the secret knife;
Who spares a Woman's seeks not Slumber's life.
Thine saved I gladly, Lady—not for this;
Let me not deem that mercy shown amiss.
Now fare thee well—more peace be with thy breast!
Night wears apace, my last of earthly rest!"

"Rest! rest! by sunrise must thy sinews shake,
And thy limbs writhe around the ready stake,—
I heard the order—saw—I will not see—   1540
If thou wilt perish, I will fall with thee.
My life—my love—my hatred—all below
Are on this cast—Corsair! 'tis but a blow!

Without it flight were idle—how evade
His sure pursuit?—my wrongs too unrepaid,
My youth disgraced—the long, long wasted years,
One blow shall cancel with our future fears;
But since the dagger suits thee less than brand,
I'll try the firmness of a female hand.
The guards are gained—one moment all were o'er—   1550
Corsair! we meet in safety or no more;
If errs my feeble hand, the morning cloud
Will hover o'er thy scaffold, and my shroud."

IX

She turned, and vanished ere he could reply,
But his glance followed far with eager eye;
And gathering, as he could, the links that bound
His form, to curl their length, and curb their sound,
Since bar and bolt no more his steps preclude,
He, fast as fettered limbs allow, pursued.
'Twas dark and winding, and he knew not where   1560
That passage led; nor lamp nor guard was there:
He sees a dusky glimmering—shall he seek
Or shun that ray so indistinct and weak?
Chance guides his steps—a freshness seems to bear
Full on his brow, as if from morning air;
He reached an open gallery—on his eye
Gleamed the last star of night, the clearing sky:
Yet scarcely heeded these—another light
From a lone chamber struck upon his sight.
Towards it he moved; a scarcely closing door   1570
Revealed the ray within, but nothing more.
With hasty step a figure outward passed,
Then paused, and turned—and paused—'tis She at last!
No poniard in that hand, nor sign of ill—
"Thanks to that softening heart—she could not kill!"
Again he looked, the wildness of her eye
Starts from the day, abrupt and fearfully.
She stopped—threw back her dark far-floating hair,
That nearly veiled her face and bosom fair,
As if she late had bent her leaning head   1580
Above some object of her doubt or dread.
They meet—upon her brow—unknown—forgot—

Her hurrying hand had left—'twas but a spot—
Its hue was all he saw, and scarce withstood—
Oh! slight but certain pledge of crime—'tis Blood!

X

He had seen battle—he had brooded lone
O'er promised pangs to sentenced Guilt foreshown;
He had been tempted—chastened—and the chain
Yet on his arms might ever there remain:
But ne'er from strife—captivity—remorse—   1590
From all his feelings in their inmost force—
So thrilled, so shuddered every creeping vein,
As now they froze before that purple stain.
That spot of blood, that light but guilty streak,
Had banished all the beauty from her cheek!
Blood he had viewed—could view unmoved—but then
It flowed in combat, or was shed by men!

XI

" 'Tis done—he nearly waked—but it is done.
Corsair! he perished—thou art dearly won.
All words would now be vain—away—away!   1600
Our bark is tossing—'tis already day.
The few gained over, now are wholly mine,
And these thy yet surviving band shall join:
Anon my voice shall vindicate my hand,
When once our sail forsakes this hated strand."

XII

She clapped her hands, and through the gallery pour,
Equipped for flight, her vassals—Greek and Moor;
Silent but quick they stoop, his chains unbind;
Once more his limbs are free as mountain wind!
But on his heavy heart such sadness sate,   1610
As if they there transferred that iron weight.
No words are uttered—at her sign, a door
Reveals the secret passage to the shore;
The city lies behind—they speed, they reach
The glad waves dancing on the yellow beach;
And Conrad following, at her beck, obeyed,

Nor cared he now if rescued or betrayed;
Resistance were as useless as if Seyd
Yet lived to view the doom his ire decreed.

XIII

Embarked—the sail unfurled—the light breeze blew—   1620
How much had Conrad's memory to review!
Sunk he in contemplation, till the Cape,
Where last he anchored, reared its giant shape.
Ah!—since that fatal night, though brief the time,
Had swept an age of terror, grief, and crime.
As its far shadow frowned above the mast,
He veiled his face, and sorrowed as he passed;
He thought of all—Gonsalvo and his band,
His fleeting triumph and his failing hand;
He thought on her afar, his lonely bride: 1630
He turned and saw—Gulnare, the Homicide!

XIV

She watched his features till she could not bear
Their freezing aspect and averted air;
And that strange fierceness foreign to her eye
Fell quenched in tears, too late to shed or dry.
She knelt beside him and his hand she pressed,
"Thou may'st forgive though Allah's self detest;
But for that deed of darkness what wert thou?
Reproach me—but not yet—Oh! spare me *now!*
I am not what I seem—this fearful night   1640
My brain bewildered—do not madden quite!
If I had never loved—though less my guilt—
Thou hadst not lived to—hate me—if thou wilt."

XV

She wrongs his thoughts—they more himself upbraid
Than her—though undesigned—the wretch he made;
But speechless all, deep, dark, and unexprest,
They bleed within that silent cell—his breast.
Still onward, fair the breeze, nor rough the surge,
The blue waves sport around the stern they urge;
Far on the Horizon's verge appears a speck,   1650

A spot—a mast—a sail—an arméd deck!
Their little bark her men of watch descry,
And ampler canvass woos the wind from high;
She bears her down majestically near,
Speed on her prow, and terror in her tier;
A flash is seen—the ball beyond her bow
Booms harmless, hissing to the deep below.
Up rose keen Conrad from his silent trance,
A long, long absent gladness in his glance;
" 'Tis mine—my blood-red flag again—again—   1660
I am not all deserted on the main!"
They own the signal, answer to the hail,
Hoist out the boat at once, and slacken sail.
" 'Tis Conrad! Conrad!" shouting from the deck,
Command nor Duty could their transport check!
With light alacrity and gaze of Pride,
They view him mount once more his vessel's side;
A smile relaxing in each rugged face,
Their arms can scarce forbear a rough embrace.
He, half forgetting danger and defeat,   1670
Returns their greeting as a Chief may greet,
Wrings with a cordial grasp Anselmo's hand,
And feels he yet can conquer and command!

XVI

These greetings o'er, the feelings that o'erflow,
Yet grieve to win him back without a blow;
They sailed prepared for vengeance—had they known
A woman's hand secured that deed her own,
She were their Queen—less scrupulous are they
Than haughty Conrad how they win their way.
With many an asking smile, and wondering stare,   1680
They whisper round, and gaze upon Gulnare;
And her, at once above—beneath her sex,
Whom blood appalled not, their regards perplex.
To Conrad turns her faint imploring eye,
She drops her veil, and stands in silence by;
Her arms are meekly folded on that breast,
Which—Conrad safe—to Fate resigned the rest.
Though worse than frenzy could that bosom fill,
Extreme in love or hate, in good or ill,
The worst of crimes had left her Woman still!   1690

XVII

This Conrad marked, and felt—ah! could he less?—
Hate of that deed—but grief for her distress;
What she has done no tears can wash away,
And Heaven must punish on its angry day:
But—it was done: he knew, whate'er her guilt,
For him that poniard smote, that blood was spilt;
And he was free!—and she for him had given
Her all on earth, and more than all in heaven!
And now he turned him to that dark-eyed slave
Whose brow was bowed beneath the glance he gave,   1700
Who now seemed changed and humbled, faint and meek,
But varying oft the colour of her cheek
To deeper shades of paleness—all its red
That fearful spot which stained it from the dead!
He took that hand—it trembled—now too late—
So soft in love—so wildly nerved in hate;
He clasped that hand—it trembled—and his own
Had lost its firmness, and his voice its tone.
"Gulnare!"—but she replied not—"dear Gulnare!"
She raised her eye—her only answer there—   1710
At once she sought and sunk in his embrace:
If he had driven her from that resting-place,
His had been more or less than mortal heart,
But—good or ill—it bade her not depart.
Perchance, but for the bodings of his breast,
His latest virtue then had joined the rest.
Yet even Medora might forgive the kiss
That asked from form so fair no more than this,
The first, the last that Frailty stole from Faith—
To lips where Love had lavished all his breath,   1720
To lips—whose broken sighs such fragrance fling,
As he had fanned them freshly with his wing!

XVIII

They gain by twilight's hour their lonely isle.
To them the very rocks appear to smile;
The haven hums with many a cheering sound,
The beacons blaze their wonted stations round,
The boats are darting o'er the curly bay,

And sportive Dolphins bend them through the spray;
Even the hoarse sea-bird's shrill, discordant shriek,
Greets like the welcome of his tuneless beak!   1730
Beneath each lamp that through its lattice gleams,
Their fancy paints the friends that trim the beams.
Oh! what can sanctify the joys of home,
Like Hope's gay glance from Ocean's troubled foam?

XIX

The lights are high on beacon and from bower,
And 'midst them Conrad seeks Medora's tower:
He looks in vain—'tis strange—and all remark,
Amid so many, hers alone is dark.
'Tis strange—of yore its welcome never failed,
Nor now, perchance, extinguished—only veiled.   1740
With the first boat descends he for the shore,
And looks impatient on the lingering oar.
Oh! for a wing beyond the falcon's flight,
To bear him like an arrow to that height!
With the first pause the resting rowers gave,
He waits not—looks not—leaps into the wave,
Strives through the surge, bestrides the beach, and high
Ascends the path familiar to his eye.

He reached his turret door—he paused—no sound
Broke from within; and all was night around.   1750
He knocked, and loudly—footstep nor reply
Announced that any heard or deemed him nigh;
He knocked, but faintly—for his trembling hand
Refused to aid his heavy heart's demand.
The portal opens—'tis a well-known face—
But not the form he panted to embrace.
Its lips are silent—twice his own essayed,
And failed to frame the question they delayed;
He snatched the lamp—its light will answer all—
It quits his grasp, expiring in the fall.   176.
He would not wait for that reviving ray—
As soon could he have lingered there for day;
But, glimmering through the dusky corridor,
Another chequers o'er the shadowed floor;
His steps the chamber gain—his eyes behold
All that his heart believed not—yet foretold!

XX

He turned not—spoke not—sunk not—fixed his look,
And set the anxious frame that lately shook:
He gazed—how long we gaze despite of pain,
And know, but dare not own, we gaze in vain!   1770
In life itself she was so still and fair,
That Death with gentler aspect withered there;
And the cold flowers her colder hand contained,
In that last grasp as tenderly were strained
As if she scarcely felt, but feigned a sleep—
And made it almost mockery yet to weep:
The long dark lashes fringed her lids of snow,
And veiled—Thought shrinks from all that lurked below—
Oh! o'er the eye Death most exerts his might,
And hurls the Spirit from her throne of light;   1780
Sinks those blue orbs in that long last eclipse,
But spares, as yet, the charm around her lips—
Yet, yet they seem as they forebore to smile,
And wished repose,—but only for a while;
But the white shroud, and each extended tress,
Long, fair—but spread in utter lifelessness,
Which, late the sport of every summer wind,
Escaped the baffled wreath that strove to bind;
These—and the pale pure cheek, became the bier—
But She is nothing—wherefore is he here?   1790

XXI

He asked no question—all were answered now
By the first glance on that still, marble brow.
It was enough—she died—what recked it how?
The love of youth, the hope of better years,
The source of softest wishes, tenderest fears,
The only living thing he could not hate,
Was reft at once—and he deserved his fate,
But did not feel it less;—the Good explore,
For peace, those realms where Guilt can never soar:
The proud, the wayward—who have fixed below   1800
Their joy, and find this earth enough for woe,
Lose in that one their all—perchance a mite—
But who in patience parts with all delight?

Full many a stoic eye and aspect stern
Mask hearts where Grief hath little left to learn;
And many a withering thought lies hid, not lost,
In smiles that least befit who wear them most.

XXII

By those, that deepest feel, is ill exprest
The indistinctness of the suffering breast;
Where thousand thoughts begin to end in one,　　1810
Which seeks from all the refuge found in none;
No words suffice the secret soul to show,
For Truth denies all eloquence to Woe.
On Conrad's stricken soul Exhaustion prest,
And Stupor almost lulled it into rest;
So feeble now—his mother's softness crept
To those wild eyes, which like an infant's wept:
It was the very weakness of his brain,
Which thus confessed without relieving pain.
None saw his trickling tears—perchance, if seen,　　1820
That useless flood of grief had never been:
Nor long they flowed—he dried them to depart,
In helpless—hopeless—brokenness of heart:
The Sun goes forth, but Conrad's day is dim:
And the night cometh—ne'er to pass from him.
There is no darkness like the cloud of mind,
On Grief's vain eye—the blindest of the blind!
Which may not—dare not see—but turns aside
To blackest shade—nor will endure a guide!

XXIII

His heart was formed for softness—warped to wrong,　　1830
Betrayed too early, and beguiled too long;
Each feeling pure—as falls the dropping dew
Within the grot—like that had hardened too;
Less clear, perchance, its earthly trials passed
But sunk, and chilled, and petrified at last.
Yet tempests wear, and lightning cleaves the rock;
If such his heart, so shattered it the shock.
There grew one flower beneath its rugged brow,
Though dark the shade—it sheltered—saved till now.

The thunder came—that bolt hath blasted both,   1840
The Granite's firmness, and the Lily's growth:
The gentle plant hath left no leaf to tell
Its tale, but shrunk and withered where it fell;
And of its cold protector, blacken round
But shivered fragments on the barren ground.

XXIV

'Tis morn—to venture on his lonely hour
Few dare; though now Anselmo sought his tower.
He was not there, nor seen along the shore;
Ere night, alarmed, their isle is traversed o'er:
Another morn—another bids them seek,   1850
And shout his name till Echo waxeth weak;
Mount—grotto—cavern—valley searched in vain,
They find on shore a sea-boat's broken chain:
Their hope revives—they follow o'er the main.
'Tis idle all—moons roll on moons away,
And Conrad comes not, came not since that day:
Nor trace nor tidings of his doom declare
Where lives his grief, or perished his despair!
Long mourned his band whom none could mourn beside;
And fair the monument they gave his Bride: 1860
For him they raise not the recording stone—
His death yet dubious, deeds too widely known;
He left a Corsair's name to other times,
Linked with one virtue, and a thousand crimes.
                    [First publ., Feb. 1, 1814.]

THE PRISONER OF CHILLON

[The poem was written in the summer of 1816, after Byron
and Shelley had made a trip by boat to the head of Lake Geneva
and had visited the Chateau of Chillon. Though Byron's account
is based on a story of François Bonivard which he picked up on
the spot and which is inaccurate both as to historical events and
characters, it has not failed to be one of the most gripping of his
poetic tales, for which reason probably it is the most widely
known. Bonivard was once incarcerated in the dungeon of Chillon for four years (1532–1536) for his political activities against

Duke Charles III of Savoy, but so far as is known no brothers died with him. He was not chained but walked about so much that he wore a path in the rock.]

SONNET ON CHILLON

ETERNAL Spirit of the chainless Mind!
   Brightest in dungeons, Liberty! thou art:
   For there thy habitation is the heart—
The heart which love of thee alone can bind;
And when thy sons to fetters are consigned—
   To fetters, and the damp vault's dayless gloom,
   Their country conquers with their martyrdom,
And Freedom's fame finds wings on every wind.
Chillon! thy prison is a holy place,
   And thy sad floor an altar—for 'twas trod,
Until his very steps have left a trace
   Worn, as if thy cold pavement were a sod,
By Bonnivard!—May none those marks efface!
   For they appeal from tyranny to God.

ADVERTISEMENT

WHEN this poem was composed, I was not sufficiently aware of the history of Bonnivard, or I should have endeavoured to dignify the subject by an attempt to celebrate his courage and his virtues. With some account of his life I have been furnished, by the kindness of a citizen of that republic, which is still proud of the memory of a man worthy of the best age of ancient freedom:—

"François de Bonnivard, fils de Louis de Bonnivard, originaire de Seyssel et Seigneur de Lunes, naquit en 1496. Il fit ses études à Turin: en 1510 Jean Aimé de Bonnivard, son oncle, lui résigna le Prieuré de St. Victor, qui aboutissoit aux murs de Genève, et qui formait un bénéfice considérable. . . .

"Ce grand homme—(Bonnivard mérite ce titre par la force de son âme, la droiture de son cœur, la noblesse de ses intentions, la sagesse de ses conseils, le courage de ses démarches, l'étendue de ses connaissances, et la vivacité de son esprit),—ce grand homme, qui excitera l'admiration de tous ceux qu'une vertu héroïque peut encore émouvoir, inspirera encore la plus vive reconnaissance dans les cœurs des Génevois qui aiment Genève. Bonnivard en fut toujours un des plus fermes appuis: pour assurer la liberté de notre République, il ne craignit pas de perdre souvent la sienne; il oublia son repos; il méprisa ses richesses; il ne négligea rien pour affermir le bonheur d'une patrie qu'il honora de son choix: dès ce moment il la chérit comme le plus zélé de ses citoyens; il la servit avec l'intrépidité d'un héros, et il écrivit son Histoire avec la naïveté d'un philosophe et la chaleur d'un patriote.

"Il dit dans le commencement de son Histoire de Genève, que, *dès qu'il eut commencé de lire l'histoire des nations, il se sentit entraîné par son goût pour les Républiques, dont il épousa toujours les intérêts:* c'est ce goût pour la liberté qui lui fit sans doute adopter Genève pour sa patrie. . . .

"Bonnivard, encore jeune, s'annonça hautement comme le défenseur de Genève contre le Duc de Savoye et l'Evêque. . . .

"En 1519, Bonnivard devient le martyr de sa patrie: Le Duc de Savoye étant entré dans Genève avec cinq cents hommes, Bonnivard craint le ressentiment du Duc; il voulut se retirer à Fribourg pour en éviter les suites; mais il fut trahi par deux hommes qui l'accompagnaient, et conduit par ordre du Prince à Grolée, où il resta prisonnier pendant deux ans. Bonnivard était malheureux dans ses voyages: comme ses malheurs n'avaient point ralenti son zèle pour Genève, il était toujours un ennemi redoutable pour ceux qui la menaçaient, et par conséquent il devait être exposé à leurs coups. Il fut rencontré en 1530 sur le Jura par des voleurs, qui le dépouillèrent, et qui le mirent encore entre les mains du Duc de Savoye: ce Prince le fit enfermer dans le Château de Chillon, où il resta sans être interrogé jusques en 1536; il fut alors delivré par les Bernois, qui s'emparèrent du Pays-de-Vaud.

"Bonnivard, en sortant de sa captivité, eut le plaisir de trouver Genève libre et réformée: la République s'empressa de lui témoigner sa reconnaissance, et de le dédommager des maux qu'il avoit soufferts; elle le reçut Bourgeois de la ville au mois de Juin, 1536; elle lui donna la maison habitée autrefois par le Vicaire-Général, et elle lui assigna une pension de deux cents écus d'or tant qu'il séjournerait à Genève. Il fut admis dans le Conseil des Deux-Cent en 1537.

"Bonnivard n'a pas fini d'être utile: après avoir travaillé à rendre Genève libre, il réussit à la rendre tolérante. Bonnivard engagea le Conseil à accorder [aux ecclésiastiques et aux paysans] un tems

suffisant pour examiner les propositions qu'on leur faisait; il réussit
par sa douceur: on prêche toujours le Christianisme avec succès
quand on le prêche avec charité. . . .

"Bonnivard fut savant: ses manuscrits, qui sont dans la bibliothèque publique, prouvent qu'il avait bien lu les auteurs clas-
siques Latins, et qu'il avait approfondi la théologie et l'histoire.
Ce grand homme aimait les sciences, et il croyait qu'elles pou-
vaient faire la gloire de Genève; aussi il ne négligea rien pour les
fixer dans cette ville naissante; en 1551 il donna sa bibliothèque
au public; elle fut le commencement de notre bibliothèque publique; et ces livres sont en partie les rares et belles éditions du
quinzième siècle qu'on voit dans notre collection. Enfin, pendant
la même année, ce bon patriote institua la République son
héritière, à condition qu'elle employerait ses biens à entretenir
le collège dont on projettait la fondation.

"Il paraît que Bonnivard mourut en 1570; mais on ne peut
l'assurer, parce qu'il y a une lacune dans le Nécrologe depuis
le mois de Juillet, 1570, jusques en 1571."—[*Histoire Littéraire
de Geneve,* par Jean Sénebier (1741–1809), 1786, i. 131–137.]

I

My hair is grey, but not with years,
    Nor grew it white
    In a single night,
As men's have grown from sudden fears:
My limbs are bowed, though not with toil,
    But rusted with a vile repose,
For they have been a dungeon's spoil,
    And mine has been the fate of those
To whom the goodly earth and air
Are banned, and barred—forbidden fare;   10
But this was for my father's faith
I suffered chains and courted death;
That father perished at the stake
For tenets he would not forsake;
And for the same his lineal race
In darkness found a dwelling place;
We were seven—who now are one,
    Six in youth, and one in age,
Finished as they had begun,
    Proud of Persecution's rage;   20
One in fire, and two in field,

Their belief with blood have sealed,
Dying as their father died,
For the God their foes denied;—
Three were in a dungeon cast,
Of whom this wreck is left the last.

II

There are seven pillars of Gothic mould,
In Chillon's dungeons deep and old,
There are seven columns, massy and grey,
Dim with a dull imprisoned ray,   30
A sunbeam which hath lost its way,
And through the crevice and the cleft
Of the thick wall is fallen and left;
Creeping o'er the floor so damp,
Like a marsh's meteor lamp:
And in each pillar there is a ring,
    And in each ring there is a chain;
That iron is a cankering thing,
    For in these limbs its teeth remain,
With marks that will not wear away,   40
Till I have done with this new day,
Which now is painful to these eyes,
Which have not seen the sun so rise
For years—I cannot count them o'er,
I lost their long and heavy score
When my last brother dropped and died,
And I lay living by his side.

III

They chained us each to a column stone,
And we were three—yet, each alone;
We could not move a single pace,   5C
We could not see each other's face,
But with that pale and livid light
That made us strangers in our sight:
And thus together—yet apart,
Fettered in hand, but joined in heart,
'Twas still some solace in the dearth
Of the pure elements of earth,
To hearken to each other's speech,

And each turn comforter to each
With some new hope, or legend old,   60
Or song heroically bold;
But even these at length grew cold.
Our voices took a dreary tone,
An echo of the dungeon stone,
  A grating sound, not full and free,
  As they of yore were wont to be:
  It might be fancy—but to me
They never sounded like our own.

IV

I was the eldest of the three,
  And to uphold and cheer the rest   70
  I ought to do—and did my best—
And each did well in his degree.
  The youngest, whom my father loved,
Because our mother's brow was given
To him, with eyes as blue as heaven—
  For him my soul was sorely moved:
And truly might it be distressed
To see such bird in such a nest;
For he was beautiful as day—
  (When day was beautiful to me   80
  As to young eagles, being free)—
  A polar day, which will not see
A sunset till its summer's gone,
  Its sleepless summer of long light,
The snow-clad offspring of the sun:
  And thus he was as pure and bright,
And in his natural spirit gay,
With tears for naught but others' ills,
And then they flowed like mountain rills,
Unless he could assuage the woe   90
Which he abhorred to view below.

V

The other was as pure of mind,
But formed to combat with his kind;
Strong in his frame, and of a mood
Which 'gainst the world in war had stood.

And perished in the foremost rank
   With joy:—but not in chains to pine:
His spirit withered with their clank,
   I saw it silently decline—
   And so perchance in sooth did mine: 100
But yet I forced it on to cheer
Those relics of a home so dear.
He was a hunter of the hills,
   Had followed there the deer and wolf
   To him this dungeon was a gulf,
And fettered feet the worse of ills.

VI

   Lake Leman lies by Chillon's walls:
A thousand feet in depth below
Its massy waters meet and flow;
Thus much the fathom-line was sent   110
From Chillon's snow-white battlement,
   Which round about the wave inthralls:
A double dungeon wall and wave
Have made—and like a living grave.
Below the surface of the lake
The dark vault lies wherein we lay:
We heard it ripple night and day;
   Sounding o'er our heads it knocked;
And I have felt the winter's spray
Wash through the bars when winds were high   120
And wanton in the happy sky;
   And then the very rock hath rocked,
   And I have felt it shake, unshocked,
Because I could have smiled to see
The death that would have set me free.

VII

I said my nearer brother pined,
I said his mighty heart declined,
He loathed and put away his food;
It was not that 'twas coarse and rude,
For we were used to hunter's fare,   130
And for the like had little care:
The milk drawn from the mountain goat

Was changed for water from the moat,
Our bread was such as captives' tears
Have moistened many a thousand years,
Since man first pent his fellow men
Like brutes within an iron den;
But what were these to us or him?
These wasted not his heart or limb;
My brother's soul was of that mould   140
Which in a palace had grown cold,
Had his free breathing been denied
The range of the steep mountain's side;
But why delay the truth?—he died.
I saw, and could not hold his head,
Nor reach his dying hand—nor dead,—
Though hard I strove, but strove in vain,
To rend and gnash my bonds in twain.
He died—and they unlocked his chain,
And scooped for him a shallow grave   150
Even from the cold earth of our cave.
I begged them, as a boon, to lay
His corse in dust whereon the day
Might shine—it was a foolish thought,
But then within my brain it wrought,
That even in death his freeborn breast
In such a dungeon could not rest.
I might have spared my idle prayer—
They coldly laughed—and laid him there:
The flat and turfless earth above   160
The being we so much did love;
His empty chain above it leant,
Such Murder's fitting monument!

VIII

But he, the favourite and the flower,
Most cherished since his natal hour,
His mother's image in fair face,
The infant love of all his race,
His martyred father's dearest thought,
My latest care, for whom I sought
To hoard my life, that his might be   170
Less wretched now, and one day free;
He, too, who yet had held untired

A spirit natural or inspired—
He, too, was struck, and day by day
Was withered on the stalk away.
Oh, God! it is a fearful thing
To see the human soul take wing
In any shape, in any mood:
I've seen it rushing forth in blood,
I've seen it on the breaking ocean   180
Strive with a swoln convulsive motion,
I've seen the sick and ghastly bed
Of Sin delirious with its dread:
But these were horrors—this was woe
Unmixed with such—but sure and slow:
He faded, and so calm and meek,
So softly worn, so sweetly weak,
So tearless, yet so tender—kind,
And grieved for those he left behind;
With all the while a cheek whose bloom   190
Was as a mockery of the tomb,
Whose tints as gently sunk away
As a departing rainbow's ray;
An eye of most transparent light,
That almost made the dungeon bright;
And not a word of murmur—not
A groan o'er his untimely lot,—
A little talk of better days,
A little hope my own to raise,
For I was sunk in silence—lost   200
In this last loss, of all the most;
And then the sighs he would suppress
Of fainting Nature's feebleness,
More slowly drawn, grew less and less:
I listened, but I could not hear;
I called, for I was wild with fear;
I knew 'twas hopeless, but my dread
Would not be thus admonishéd;
I called, and thought I heard a sound—
I burst my chain with one strong bound,   210
And rushed to him:—I found him not,
I only stirred in this black spot,
I only lived, I only drew
The accurséd breath of dungeon-dew;
The last, the sole, the dearest link

Between me and the eternal brink,
Which bound me to my failing race,
Was broken in this fatal place.
One on the earth, and one beneath—
My brothers—both had ceased to breathe!   225
I took that hand which lay so still,
Alas! my own was full as chill;
I had not strength to stir, or strive,
But felt that I was still alive—
A frantic feeling, when we know
That what we love shall ne'er be so.
    I know not why
    I could not die,
I had no earthly hope—but faith,
And that forbade a selfish death.   230

IX

What next befell me then and there
  I know not well—I never knew—
First came the loss of light, and air,
  And then of darkness too:
I had no thought, no feeling—none—
Among the stones I stood a stone,
And was, scarce conscious what I wist,
As shrubless crags within the mist;
For all was blank, and bleak, and grey;
It was not night—it was not day;   240
It was not even the dungeon-light,
So hateful to my heavy sight,
But vacancy absorbing space,
And fixedness—without a place;
There were no stars—no earth—no time—
No check—no change—no good—no crime—
But silence, and a stirless breath
Which neither was of life nor death;
A sea of stagnant idleness,
Blind, boundless, mute, and motionless!   250

X

A light broke in upon my brain,—
  It was the carol of a bird;

It ceased, and then it came again,
  The sweetest song ear ever heard,
And mind was thankful till my eyes
Ran over with the glad surprise,
And they that moment could not see
I was the mate of misery;
But then by dull degrees came back
My senses to their wonted track;   260
I saw the dungeon walls and floor
Close slowly round me as before,
I saw the glimmer of the sun
Creeping as it before had done,
But through the crevice where it came
That bird was perched, as fond and tame,
  And tamer than upon the tree;
A lovely bird, with azure wings,
And song that said a thousand things,
  And seemed to say them all for me!   270
I never saw its like before,
I ne'er shall see its likeness more:
It seemed like me to want a mate,
But was not half so desolate,
And it was come to love me when
None lived to love me so again,
And cheering from my dungeon's brink,
Had brought me back to feel and think.
I know not if it late were free,
  Or broke its cage to perch on mine,   280
But knowing well captivity,
  Sweet bird! I could not wish for thine!
Or if it were, in wingéd guise,
A visitant from Paradise;
For—Heaven forgive that thought! the while
Which made me both to weep and smile—
I sometimes deemed that it might be
My brother's soul come down to me;
But then at last away it flew,
And then 'twas mortal well I knew,   290
For he would never thus have flown—
And left me twice so doubly lone,—
Lone—as the corse within its shroud,
Lone—as a solitary cloud,
  A single cloud on a sunny day,

While all the rest of heaven is clear,
A frown upon the atmosphere,
That hath no business to appear
    When skies are blue, and earth is gay.

XI

A kind of change came in my fate,   300
My keepers grew compassionate;
I know not what had made them so,
They were inured to sights of woe,
But so it was:—my broken chain
With links unfastened did remain,
And it was liberty to stride
Along my cell from side to side,
And up and down, and then athwart,
And tread it over every part;
And round the pillars one by one,   310
Returning where my walk begun,
Avoiding only, as I trod,
My brothers' graves without a sod;
For if I thought with heedless tread
My step profaned their lowly bed,
My breath came gaspingly and thick,
And my crushed heart felt blind and sick.

XII

I made a footing in the wall,
    It was not therefrom to escape,
For I had buried one and all,   320
    Who loved me in a human shape;
And the whole earth would henceforth be
A wider prison unto me:
No child—no sire—no kin had I,
No partner in my misery;
I thought of this, and I was glad,
For thought of them had made me mad;
But I was curious to ascend
To my barred windows, and to bend
Once more, upon the mountains high,   330
The quiet of a loving eye.

XIII

I saw them—and they were the same,
They were not changed like me in frame;
I saw their thousand years of snow
On high—their wide long lake below,
And the blue Rhone in fullest flow;
I heard the torrents leap and gush
O'er channelled rock and broken bush;
I saw the white-walled distant town,
And whiter sails go skimming down;   340
And then there was a little isle,
Which in my very face did smile,
  The only one in view;
A small green isle, it seemed no more.
Scarce broader than my dungeon floor,
But in it there were three tall trees,
And o'er it blew the mountain breeze,
And by it there were waters flowing,
And on it there were young flowers growing,
  Of gentle breath and hue.   350
The fish swam by the castle wall,
And they seemed joyous each and all;
The eagle rode the rising blast,
Methought he never flew so fast
As then to me he seemed to fly;
And then new tears came in my eye,
And I felt troubled—and would fain
I had not left my recent chain;
And when I did descend again,
The darkness of my dim abode   360
Fell on me as a heavy load;
It was as is a new-dug grave,
Closing o'er one we sought to save,—
And yet my glance, too much opprest,
Had almost need of such a rest.

XIV

It might be months, or years, or days—
  I kept no count, I took no note—
I had no hope my eyes to raise,

And clear them of their dreary mote;
At last men came to set me free;   370
   I asked not why, and recked not where;
It was at length the same to me,
Fettered or fetterless to be,
   I learned to love despair.
And thus when they appeared at last,
And all my bonds aside were cast,
These heavy walls to me had grown
A hermitage—and all my own!
And half I felt as they were come
To tear me from a second home: 380
With spiders I had friendship made,
And watched them in their sullen trade,
Had seen the mice by moonlight play,
And why should I feel less than they?
We were all inmates of one place,
And I, the monarch of each race,
Had power to kill—yet, strange to tell!
In quiet we had learned to dwell;
My very chains and I grew friends,
So much a long communion tends   390
To make us what we are;—even I
Regained my freedom with a sigh.
               [*First publ., Dec. 5, 1816.*]

ITALIAN POEMS

BEPPO

A VENETIAN STORY

[Based on a true story then current in Venice. In a letter to John Murray, October 12, 1817, Byron says he has "written a poem (of 84 octave stanzas), humourous, in or after the excellent manner of Mr. Whistlecraft (whom I take to be Frere), on a Venetian anecdote which amused me." He himself never said more of this anecdote. Actually the story was told to Byron and his friend John Cam Hobhouse on the evening of August 29, 1817, at La Mira, on the Brenta just outside of Venice, where Marianna Segati—"pretty as an antelope," with "large black, Oriental eyes"—had established herself in Byron's house as his regular *amica*. It is perhaps ironically appropriate to the spirit of *Beppo* that it should have been told by the husband of Marianna, who, Hobhouse says, used to spend the weekends at La Mira to court another lady.

This is the anecdote as Hobhouse recorded it in his diary: ". . . dine, ride, moonlight walk with B. Zagati [*sic*] at dinner told us two singular stories . . . [the second one concerns us here] A Turk arrived at the Regina di Unghera [*sic*] inn at Venice and lodged there—he asked to speak to the mistress of the inn a buxom lady of 40 in keeping with several children and who had lost her husband many years before at sea—after some preliminaries my hostess went to the Turk who immediately shut the door and began questioning her about her family and her late husband—she told her loss—when the Turk asked if her husband had any particular mark about him she said—yes he had a scar on his shoulder—something like this said the Turk pulling down his robe—I am your husband—I have been to Turkey—I have made a large fortune and I make you three offers, either to quit your amoroso and come with me or to stay with your amoroso or to accept a pension and live alone." Hobhouse adds: The lady has not yet given an answer, but M. Zagati said—I'm sure I

would not leave my amoroso for any husband—looking at B.
This is too gross even for me."

In a little more than a month Byron had transformed this
"gross" episode which amused him into the poetic irony of
Beppo.]

Rosalind. Farewell, Monsieur Traveller; Look, you lisp, and wear
strange suits: disable all the benefits of your own country; be out of
love with your Nativity, and almost chide God for making you that
countenance you are; or I will scarce think you have swam in a
Gondola.

—*As You Like It,* act iv. sc. 1, lines 33–35.

Annotation of the Commentators.

That is, *been at Venice,* which was much visited by the young
English gentlemen of those times, and was *then* what *Paris* is *now*—
the seat of all dissoluteness.—S. A.

I

'Tis known, at least it should be, that throughout
　　All countries of the Catholic persuasion,
Some weeks before Shrove Tuesday comes about,
　　The People take their fill of recreation,
And buy repentance, ere they grow devout,
　　However high their rank, or low their station,
With fiddling, feasting, dancing, drinking, masquing,
And other things which may be had for asking.

II

The moment night with dusky mantle covers
　　The skies (and the more duskily the better),
The Time less liked by husbands than by lovers
　　Begins, and Prudery flings aside her fetter;
And Gaiety on restless tiptoe hovers,
　　Giggling with all the gallants who beset her;
And there are songs and quavers, roaring, humming,
Guitars, and every other sort of strumming.

III

And there are dresses splendid, but fantastical,
   Masks of all times and nations, Turks and Jews,
And harlequins and clowns, with feats gymnastical,
   Greeks, Romans, Yankee-doodles, and Hindoos;
All kinds of dress, except the ecclesiastical,
   All people, as their fancies hit, may choose,
But no one in these parts may quiz the Clergy,—
Therefore take heed, ye Freethinkers! I charge ye.

IV

You'd better walk about begirt with briars,
   Instead of coat and small clothes, than put on
A single stitch reflecting upon friars,
   Although you swore it only was in fun;
They'd haul you o'er the coals, and stir the fires
   Of Phlegethon with every mother's son,
Nor say one mass to cool the cauldron's bubble
That boiled your bones, unless you paid them double.

V

But saving this, you may put on whate'er
   You like by way of doublet, cape, or cloak,
Such as in Monmouth-street, or in Rag Fair,
   Would rig you out in seriousness or joke;
And even in Italy such places are,
   With prettier name in softer accents spoke,
For, bating Covent Garden, I can hit on
No place that's called "Piazza" in Great Britain.

VI

This feast is named the Carnival, which being
   Interpreted, implies "farewell to flesh"—
So called, because the name and thing agreeing,
   Through Lent they live on fish both salt and fresh
But why they usher Lent with so much glee in,
   Is more than I can tell, although I guess

'Tis as we take a glass with friends at parting,
In the Stage-Coach or Packet, just at starting.

VII

And thus they bid farewell to carnal dishes,
    And solid meats, and highly spiced ragouts,
To live for forty days on ill-dressed fishes,
    Because they have no sauces to their stews;
A thing which causes many "poohs" and "pishes,"
    And several oaths (which would not suit the Muse),
From travellers accustomed from a boy
To eat their salmon, at the least, with soy;

VIII

And therefore humbly I would recommend
    "The curious in fish-sauce," before they cross
The sea, to bid their cook, or wife, or friend,
    Walk or ride to the Strand, and buy in gross
(Or if set out beforehand, these may send
    By any means least liable to loss),
Ketchup, Soy, Chili-vinegar, and Harvey,
Or, by the Lord! a Lent will well nigh starve ye;

IX

That is to say, if your religion's Roman,
    And you at Rome would do as Romans do,
According to the proverb,—although no man,
    If foreign, is obliged to fast; and you,
If Protestant, or sickly, or a woman,
    Would rather dine in sin on a ragout—
Dine and be d—d! I don't mean to be coarse,
But that's the penalty, to say no worse.

X

Of all the places where the Carnival
    Was most facetious in the days of yore,
For dance, and song, and serenade, and ball,
    And Masque, and Mime, and Mystery, and more
Than I have time to tell now, or at all,

Venice the gem from every city bore,—
And at the moment when I fix my story,
That sea-born city was in all her glory.

XI

They've pretty faces yet, those same Venetians,
　　Black eyes, arched brows, and sweet expressions still;
Such as of old were copied from the Grecians,
　　In ancient arts by moderns mimicked ill;
And like so many Venuses of Titian's
　　(The best's at Florence—see it, if ye will,)
They look when leaning over the balcony,
Or stepped from out a picture by Giorgione,

XII

Whose tints are Truth and Beauty at their best;
　　And when you to Manfrini's palace go,
That picture (howsoever fine the rest)
　　Is loveliest to my mind of all the show;
It may perhaps be also to *your* zest,
　　And that's the cause I rhyme upon it so:
'Tis but a portrait of his Son, and Wife,
And self; but *such* a Woman! Love in Life!

XIII

Love in full and length, not love ideal,
　　No, nor ideal beauty, that fine name,
But something better still, so very real,
　　That the sweet Model must have been the same;
A thing that you would purchase, beg, or steal,
　　Wer't not impossible, besides a shame:
The face recalls some face, as 'twere with pain,
You once have seen, but ne'er will see again;

XIV

One of those forms which flit by us, when we
　　Are young, and fix our eyes on every face;
And, oh! the Loveliness at times we see
　　In momentary gliding, the soft grace,

The Youth, the Bloom, the Beauty which agree,
   In many a nameless being we retrace,
Whose course and home we knew not, nor shall know,
Like the lost Pleiad seen no more below.

XV

I said that like a picture by Giorgione
   Venetian women were, and so they *are*,
Particularly seen from a balcony,
   (For beauty's sometimes best set off afar)
And there, just like a heroine of Goldoni,
   They peep from out the blind, or o'er the bar;
And truth to say, they're mostly very pretty,
And rather like to show it, more's the pity!

XVI

For glances beget ogles, ogles sighs,
   Sighs wishes, wishes words, and words a letter,
Which flies on wings of light-heeled Mercuries,
   Who do such things because they know no better;
And then, God knows what mischief may arise,
   When Love links two young people in one fetter,
Vile assignations, and adulterous beds,
Elopements, broken vows, and hearts, and heads.

XVII

Shakespeare described the sex in Desdemona
   As very fair, but yet suspect in fame,
And to this day from Venice to Verona
   Such matters may be probably the same,
Except that since those times was never known a
   Husband whom mere suspicion could inflame
To suffocate a wife no more than twenty,
Because she had a "Cavalier Servente."

XVIII

Their jealousy (if they are ever jealous)
   Is of a fair complexion altogether,
Not like that sooty devil of Othello's

Which smothers women in a bed of feather,
But worthier of these much more jolly fellows,
    When weary of the matrimonial tether
His head for such a wife no mortal bothers,
But takes at once another, or *another's.*

XIX

Didst ever see a Gondola? For fear
    You should not, I'll describe it you exactly:
'Tis a long covered boat that's common here,
    Carved at the prow, built lightly, but compactly,
Rowed by two rowers, each called "Gondolier,"
    It glides along the water looking blackly,
Just like a coffin clapt in a canoe,
Where none can make out what you say or do.

XX

And up and down the long canals they go,
    And under the Rialto shoot along,
By night and day, all paces, swift or slow,
    And round the theatres, a sable throng,
They wait in their dusk livery of woe,—
    But not to them do woeful things belong,
For sometimes they contain a deal of fun,
Like mourning coaches when the funeral's done.

XXI

But to my story.—'Twas some years ago,
    It may be thirty, forty, more or less,
The Carnival was at its height, and so
    Were all kinds of buffoonery and dress;
A certain lady went to see the show,
    Her real name I know not, nor can guess,
And so we'll call her Laura, if you please,
Because it slips into my verse with ease.

XXII

She was not old, nor young, nor at the years
    Which certain people call a *"certain age,"*

Which yet the most uncertain age appears,
  Because I never heard, nor could engage
A person yet by prayers, or bribes, or tears,
  To name, define by speech, or write on page,
The period meant precisely by that word,—
Which surely is exceedingly absurd.

XXIII

Laura was blooming still, had made the best
  Of Time, and Time returned the compliment,
And treated her genteelly, so that, dressed,
  She looked extremely well where'er she went;
A pretty woman is a welcome guest,
  And Laura's brow a frown had rarely bent;
Indeed, she shone all smiles, and seemed to flatter
Mankind with her black eyes for looking at her.

XXIV

She was a married woman; 'tis convenient,
  Because in Christian countries 'tis a rule
To view their little slips with eyes more lenient;
  Whereas if single ladies play the fool,
(Unless within the period intervenient
  A well-timed wedding makes the scandal cool)
I don't know how they ever can get over it,
Except they manage never to discover it.

XXV

Her husband sailed upon the Adriatic,
  And made some voyages, too, in other seas,
And when he lay in Quarantine for pratique
  (A forty days' precaution 'gainst disease),
His wife would mount, at times, her highest attic,
  For thence she could discern the ship with ease:
He was a merchant trading to Aleppo,
His name Giuseppe, called more briefly, Beppo.

XXVI

He was a man as dusky as a Spaniard,
    Sunburnt with travel, yet a portly figure;
Though coloured, as it were, within a tanyard,
    He was a person both of sense and vigour—
A better seaman never yet did man yard;
    And she, although her manner showed no rigour,
Was deemed a woman of the strictest principle,
So much as to be thought almost invincible.

XXVII

But several years elapsed since they had met;
    Some people thought the ship was lost, and some
That he had somehow blundered into debt,
    And did not like the thought of steering home;
And there were several offered any bet,
    Or that he would, or that he would not come;
For most men (till by losing rendered sager)
Will back their own opinions with a wager.

XXVIII

'Tis said that their last parting was pathetic,
    As partings often are, or ought to be,
And their presentiment was quite prophetic,
    That they should never more each other see,
(A sort of morbid feeling, half poetic,
    Which I have known occur in two or three,)
When kneeling on the shore upon her sad knee
He left this Adriatic Ariadne.

XXIX

And Laura waited long, and wept a little,
    And thought of wearing weeds, as well she might;
She almost lost all appetite for victual,
    And could not sleep with ease alone at night;
She deemed the window-frames and shutters brittle
    Against a daring housebreaker or sprite,

And so she thought it prudent to connect her
With a vice-husband, *chiefly* to *protect her.*

XXX

She chose, (and what is there they will not choose,
   If only you will but oppose their choice?)
Till Beppo should return from his long cruise,
   And bid once more her faithful heart rejoice,
A man some women like, and yet abuse—
   A Coxcomb was he by the public voice;
A Count of wealth, they said, as well as quality,
And in his pleasures of great liberality.

XXXI

And then he was a Count, and then he knew
   Music, and dancing, fiddling, French and Tuscan;
The last not easy, be it known to you,
   For few Italians speak the right Etruscan.
He was a critic upon operas, too,
   And knew all niceties of sock and buskin;
And no Venetian audience could endure a
Song, scene, or air, when he cried "seccatura!"

XXXII

His "bravo" was decisive, for that sound
   Hushed "Academie" sighed in silent awe;
The fiddlers trembled as he looked around,
   For fear of some false note's detected flaw;
The "Prima Donna's" tuneful heart would bound,
   Dreading the deep damnation of his "Bah!"
Soprano, Basso, even the Contra-Alto,
Wished him five fathom under the Rialto.

XXXIII

He patronised the Improvisatori.
   Nay, could himself extemporise some stanzas,
Wrote rhymes, sang songs, could also tell a story,
   Sold pictures, and was skilful in the dance as
Italians can be, though in this their glory

Must surely yield the palm to that which France has;
In short, he was a perfect Cavaliero
And to his very valet seemed a hero.

XXXIV

Then he was faithful too, as well as amorous;
    So that no sort of female could complain,
Although they're now and then a little clamorous,
    He never put the pretty souls in pain;
His heart was one of those which most enamour us,
    Wax to receive, and marble to retain:
He was a lover of the good old school,
Who still become more constant as they cool.

XXXV

No wonder such accomplishments should turn
    A female head, however sage and steady—
With scarce a hope that Beppo could return,
    In law he was almost as good as dead, he
Nor sent, nor wrote, nor showed the least concern,
    And she had waited several years already:
And really if a man won't let us know
That he's alive, he's *dead*—or should be so.

XXXVI

Besides, within the Alps, to every woman,
    (Although, God knows, it is a grievous sin,)
'Tis, I may say, permitted to have *two* men;
    I can't tell who first brought the custom in,
But "Cavalier Serventes" are quite common
    And no one notices or cares a pin;
And we may call this (not to say the worst)
A *second* marriage which corrupts the *first*.

XXXVII

The word was formerly a "Cicisbeo,"
    But *that* is now grown vulgar and indecent;
The Spaniards call the person a *"Cortejo,"*
    For the same mode subsists in Spain, though recent;

In short it reaches from the Po to Teio,
   And may perhaps at last be o'er the sea sent
But Heaven preserve Old England from such courses!
Or what becomes of damage and divorces?

XXXVIII

However, I still think, with all due deference
   To the fair *single* part of the creation,
That married ladies should preserve the preference
   In *tête à tête* or general conversation—
And this I say without peculiar reference
   To England, France, or any other nation—
Because they know the world, and are at ease,
And being natural, naturally please.

XXXIX

'Tis true, your budding Miss is very charming,
   But shy and awkward at first coming out,
So much alarmed, that she is quite alarming,
   All Giggle, Blush—half Pertness, and half Pout;
And glancing at *Mamma*, for fear there's harm in
   What you, she, it, or they, may be about:
The Nursery still lisps out in all they utter—
Besides, they always smell of bread and butter.

XL

But "Cavalier Servente" is the phrase
   Used in politest circles to express
This supernumerary slave, who stays
   Close to the lady as a part of dress,
Her word the only law which he obeys.
   His is no sinecure, as you may guess;
Coach, servants, gondola, he goes to call,
And carries fan and tippet, gloves and shawl.

XLI

With all its sinful doings, I must say,
   That Italy's a pleasant place to me,
Who love to see the Sun shine every day,

And vines (not nailed to walls) from tree to tree
Festooned, much like the back scene of a play,
 Or melodrame, which people flock to see,
When the first act is ended by a dance
In vineyards copied from the south of France.

XLII

I like on Autumn evenings to ride out,
 Without being forced to bid my groom be sure
My cloak is round his middle strapped about,
 Because the skies are not the most secure;
I know too that, if stopped upon my route,
 Where the green alleys windingly allure,
Reeling with *grapes* red wagons choke the way,—
In England 'twould be dung, dust, or a dray.

XLIII

I also like to dine on becaficas,
 To see the Sun set, sure he'll rise to-morrow,
Not through a misty morning twinkling weak as
 A drunken man's dead eye in maudlin sorrow,
But with all Heaven t'himself; the day will break as
 Beauteous as cloudless, nor be forced to borrow
That sort of farthing candlelight which glimmers
Where reeking London's smoky cauldron simmers.

XLIV

I love the language, that soft bastard Latin,
 Which melts like kisses from a female mouth,
And sounds as if it should be writ on satin,
 With syllables which breathe of the sweet South,
And gentle liquids gliding all so pat in,
 That not a single accent seems uncouth,
Like our harsh northern whistling, grunting guttural,
Which we're obliged to hiss, and spit, and sputter all.

XLV

I like the women too (forgive my folly!),
 From the rich peasant cheek of ruddy bronze,

And large black eyes that flash on you a volley
 Of rays that say a thousand things at once,
To the high Dama's brow, more melancholy,
 But clear, and with a wild and liquid glance,
Heart on her lips, and soul within her eyes,
Soft as her clime, and sunny as her skies.

XLVI

Eve of the land which still is Paradise!
 Italian Beauty didst thou not inspire
Raphael, who died in thy embrace, and vies
 With all we know of Heaven, or can desire,
In what he hath bequeathed us?—in what guise
 Though flashing from the fervour of the Lyre,
Would *words* describe thy past and present glow,
While yet Canova can create below?

XLVII

"England! with all thy faults I love thee still,"
 I said at Calais, and have not forgot it;
I like to speak and lucubrate my fill;
 I like the government (but that is not it);
I like the freedom of the press and quill;
 I like the Habeas Corpus (when we've got it);
I like a Parliamentary debate,
Particularly when 'tis not too late;

XLVIII

I like the taxes, when they're not too many;
 I like a seacoal fire, when not too dear;
I like a beef-steak, too, as well as any;
 Have no objection to a pot of beer;
I like the weather,—when it is not rainy,
 That is, I like two months of every year.
And so God save the Regent, Church, and King!
Which means that I like all and every thing.

XLIX

Our standing army, and disbanded seamen,
  Poor's rate, Reform, my own, the nation's debt,
Our little riots, just to show we're free men,
  Our trifling bankruptcies in the Gazette,
Our cloudy climate, and our chilly women,
  All these I can forgive, and those forget,
And greatly venerate our recent glories,
And wish they were not owing to the Tories.

L

But to my tale of Laura,—for I find
  Digression is a sin, that by degrees
Becomes exceeding tedious to my mind,
  And, therefore, may the reader too displease—
The gentle reader, who may wax unkind,
  And caring little for the Author's ease,
Insist on knowing what he means—a hard
And hapless situation for a Bard.

LI

Oh! that I had the art of easy writing
  What should be easy reading! could I scale
Parnassus, where the Muses sit inditing
  Those pretty poems never known to fail,
How quickly would I print (the world delighting)
  A Grecian, Syrian, or Assyrian tale;
And sell you, mixed with western Sentimentalism,
Some samples of the *finest Orientalism*.

LII

But I am but a nameless sort of person,
  (A broken Dandy lately on my travels)
And take for rhyme, to hook my rambling verse on,
  The first that Walker's Lexicon unravels,
And when I can't find that, I put a worse on,
  Not caring as I ought for critic's cavils;

I've half a mind to tumble down to prose.
But verse is more in fashion—so here goes!

LIII

The Count and Laura made their new arrangement,
　　Which lasted, as arrangements sometimes do,
For half a dozen years without estrangement;
　　They had their little differences, too;
Those jealous whiffs, which never any change meant;
　　In such affairs there probably are few
Who have not had this pouting sort of squabble,
From sinners of high station to the rabble.

LIV

But, on the whole, they were a happy pair,
　　As happy as unlawful love could make them;
The gentleman was fond, the lady fair,
　　Their chains so slight, 'twas not worth while to break
　　　　them:
The World beheld them with indulgent air;
　　The pious only wished "the Devil take them!"
He took them not; he very often waits,
And leaves old sinners to be young ones' baits.

LV

But they were young: Oh! what without our Youth
　　Would Love be! What would Youth be without Love!
Youth lends its joy, and sweetness, vigour, truth,
　　Heart, soul, and all that seems as from above;
But, languishing with years, it grows uncouth—
　　One of few things Experience don't improve;
Which is, perhaps, the reason why old fellows
Are always so preposterously jealous.

LVI

It was the Carnival, as I have said
　　Some six and thirty stanzas back, and, so,
Laura the usual preparations made,
　　Which you do when your mind's made up to go

To-night to Mrs. Boehm's masquerade,
   Spectator, or partaker in the show;
The only difference known between the cases
Is—*here*, we have six weeks of "varnished faces."

LVII

Laura, when dressed, was (as I sang before)
   A pretty woman as was ever seen,
Fresh as the Angel o'er a new inn door,
   Or frontispiece of a new Magazine,
With all the fashions which the last month wore,
   Coloured, and silver paper leaved between
That and the title-page, for fear the Press
Should soil with parts of speech the parts of dress.

LVIII

They went to the Ridotto; 'tis a hall
   Where People dance, and sup, and dance again;
Its proper name, perhaps, were a masqued ball,
   But that's of no importance to my strain;
'Tis (on a smaller scale) like our Vauxhall,
   Excepting that it can't be spoilt by rain;
The company is "mixed" (the phrase I quote is
As much as saying, they're below your notice);

LIX

For a "mixed company" implies that, save
   Yourself and friends, and half a hundred more,
Whom you may bow to without looking grave,
   The rest are but a vulgar set, the bore
Of public places, where they basely brave
   The fashionable stare of twenty score
Of well-bred persons, called *"The World"*; but I,
Although I know them, really don't know why.

LX

This is the case in England; at least was
   During the dynasty of Dandies, now
Perchance succeeded by some other class

Of imitated Imitators:—how
Irreparably soon decline, alas!
 The Demagogues of fashion: all below
Is frail; how easily the world is lost
By Love, or War, and, now and then,—by Frost!

LXI

Crushed was Napoleon by the northern Thor,
 Who knocked his army down with icy hammer,
Stopped by the *Elements*—like a Whaler—or
 A blundering novice in his new French grammar;
Good cause had he to doubt the chance of war,
 And as for Fortune—but I dare not d—n her,
Because, were I to ponder to Infinity,
The more I should believe in her Divinity.

LXII

She rules the present, past, and all to be yet,
 She gives us luck in lotteries, love, and marriage;
I cannot say that she's done much for me yet;
 Not that I mean her bounties to disparage,
We've not yet closed accounts, and we shall see yet
 How much she'll make amends for past miscarriage;
Meantime the Goddess I'll no more importune,
Unless to thank her when she's made my fortune.

LXIII

To turn,—and to return;—the Devil take it!
 This story slips for ever through my fingers,
Because, just as the stanza likes to make it,
 It needs must be—and so it rather lingers;
This form of verse began, I can't well break it,
 But must keep time and tune like public singers;
But if I once get through my present measure,
I'll take another when I'm next at leisure.

LXIV

They went to the Ridotto ('tis a place
 To which I mean to go myself to-morrow,

Just to divert my thoughts a little space
  Because I'm rather hippish, and may borrow
Some spirits, guessing at what kind of face
  May lurk beneath each mask; and as my sorrow
Slackens its pace sometimes, I'll make, or find,
Something shall leave it half an hour behind.)

LXV

Now Laura moves along the joyous crowd,
  Smiles in her eyes, and simpers on her lips;
To some she whispers, others speaks aloud;
  To some she curtsies, and to some she dips,
Complains of warmth, and, this complaint avowed,
  Her lover brings the lemonade she sips;
She then surveys, condemns, but pities still
Her dearest friends for being dressed so ill.

LXVI

One has false curls, another too much paint,
  A third—where did she buy that frightful turban?
A fourth's so pale she fears she's going to faint,
  A fifth's look's vulgar, dowdyish, and suburban,
A sixth's white silk has got a yellow taint,
  A seventh's thin muslin surely will be her bane,
And lo! an eighth appears,—"I'll see no more!"
For fear, like Banquo's kings, they reach a score.

LXVII

Meantime, while she was thus at others gazing,
  Others were levelling their looks at her;
She heard the men's half-whispered mode of praising,
  And, till 'twas done, determined not to stir;
The women only thought it quite amazing
  That, at her time of life, so many were
Admirers still,—but "Men are so debased—
Those brazen Creatures always suit their taste."

LXVIII

For my part, now, I ne'er could understand
  Why naughty women—but I won't discuss
A thing which is a scandal to the land,
  I only don't see why it should be thus;
And if I were but in a gown and band,
  Just to entitle me to make a fuss,
I'd preach on this till Wilberforce and Romilly
Should quote in their next speeches from my homily.

LXIX

While Laura thus was seen and seeing, smiling,
  Talking, she knew not why, and cared not what,
So that her female friends, with envy broiling,
  Beheld her airs, and triumph, and all that;
And well-dressed males still kept before her filing,
  And passing bowed and mingled with her chat·
More than the rest one person seemed to stare
With pertinacity that's rather rare.

LXX

He was a Turk, the colour of mahogany;
  And Laura saw him, and at first was glad,
Because the Turks so much admire philogyny,
  Although their usage of their wives is sad;
'Tis said they use no better than a dog any
  Poor woman, whom they purchase like a pad·
They have a number, though they ne'er exhibit 'em,
Four wives by law, and concubines "ad libitum."

LXXI

They lock them up, and veil, and guard them daily,
  They scarcely can behold their male relations,
So that their moments do not pass so gaily
  As is supposed the case with northern nations;
Confinement, too, must make them look quite palely;
  And as the Turks abhor long conversations,

Their days are either passed in doing nothing,
Or bathing, nursing, making love, and clothing.

LXXII

They cannot read, and so don't lisp in criticism;
   Nor write, and so they don't affect the Muse;
Were never caught in epigram or witticism,
   Have no romances, sermons, plays, reviews,—
In Harams learning soon would make a pretty schism!
   But luckily these Beauties are no "Blues";
No bustling *Botherby* have they to show 'em
"That charming passage in the last new poem":

LXXIII

No solemn, antique gentleman of rhyme,
   Who having angled all his life for Fame,
And getting but a nibble at a time,
   Still fussily keeps fishing on, the same
Small "Triton of the minnows," the sublime
   Of Mediocrity, the furious tame,
The Echo's echo, usher of the school
Of female wits, boy bards—in short, a fool!

LXXIV

A stalking oracle of awful phrase,
   The approving *"Good!"* (by no means GOOD in law)
Humming like flies around the newest blaze,
   The bluest of bluebottles you e'er saw,
Teasing with blame, excruciating with praise,
   Gorging the little fame he gets all raw,
Translating tongues he knows not even by letter,
And sweating plays so middling, bad were better.

LXXV

One hates an author that's *all author*—fellows
   In foolscap uniforms turned up with ink,
So very anxious, clever, fine, and jealous,
   One don't know what to say to them, or think,

Unless to puff them with a pair of bellows;
 Of Coxcombry's worst coxcombs e'en the pink
Are preferable to these shreds of paper,
These unquenched snuffings of the midnight taper.

LXXVI

Of these same we see several, and of others,
 Men of the World, who know the World like Men,
Scott, Rogers, Moore, and all the better brothers,
 Who think of something else besides the pen;
But for the children of the "Mighty Mother's,"
 The would-be wits, and can't-be gentlemen,
I leave them to their daily "tea is ready,"
Smug coterie, and literary lady.

LXXVII

The poor dear Mussul*women* whom I mention
 Have none of these instructive pleasant people,
And *one* would seem to them a new invention,
 Unknown as bells within a Turkish steeple;
I think 'twould almost be worth while to pension
 (Though best-sown projects very often reap ill)
A missionary author—just to preach
Our Christian usage of the parts of speech.

LXXVIII

No Chemistry for them unfolds her gases,
 No Metaphysics are let loose in lectures,
No Circulating Library amasses
 Religious novels, moral tales, and strictures
Upon the living manners, as they pass us;
 No Exhibition glares with annual pictures;
They stare not on the stars from out their attics,
Nor deal (thank God for that!) in Mathematics.

LXXIX

Why I thank God for that is no great matter,
 I have my reasons, you no doubt suppose,
And as, perhaps, they would not highly flatter,

I'll keep them for my life (to come) in prose;
I fear I have a little turn for Satire,
  And yet methinks the older that one grows
Inclines us more to laugh than scold, though Laughter
Leaves us so doubly serious shortly after.

LXXX

Oh, Mirth and Innocence! Oh, Milk and Water!
  Ye happy mixtures of more happy days!
In these sad centuries of sin and slaughter,
  Abominable Man no more allays
His thirst with such pure beverage. No matter,
  I love you both, and both shall have my praise:
Oh, for old Saturn's reign of sugar-candy!—
Meantime I drink to your return in brandy.

LXXXI

Our Laura's Turk still kept his eyes upon her,
  Less in the Mussulman than Christian way,
Which seems to say, "Madam, I do you honour,
  And while I please to stare, you'll please to stay."
Could staring win a woman, this had won her,
  But Laura could not thus be led astray;
She had stood fire too long and well, to boggle
Even at this Stranger's most outlandish ogle.

LXXXII

The morning now was on the point of breaking,
  A turn of time at which I would advise
Ladies who have been dancing, or partaking
  In any other kind of exercise,
To make their preparation for forsaking
  The ball-room ere the Sun begins to rise,
Because when once the lamps and candles fail,
His blushes make them look a little pale.

LXXXIII

I've seen some balls and revels in my time,
  And stayed them over for some silly reason,

And then I looked (I hope it was no crime)
   To see what lady best stood out the season;
And though I've seen some thousands in their prime
   Lovely and pleasing, and who still may please on,
I never saw but one (the stars withdrawn)
Whose bloom could after dancing dare the Dawn.

LXXXIV

The name of this Aurora I'll not mention,
   Although I might, for she was nought to me
More than that patent work of God's invention,
   A charming woman, whom we like to see;
But writing names would merit reprehension,
   Yet if you like to find out this fair *She*,
At the next London or Parisian ball
You still may mark her cheek, out-blooming all.

LXXXV

Laura, who knew it would not do at all
   To meet the daylight after seven hours' sitting
Among three thousand people at a ball,
   To make her curtsey thought it right and fitting;
The Count was at her elbow with her shawl,
   And they the room were on the point of quitting,
When lo! those curséd Gondoliers had got
Just in the very place where they *should not*.

LXXXVI

In this they're like our coachmen, and the cause
   Is much the same—the crowd, and pulling, hauling,
With blasphemies enough to break their jaws,
   They make a never intermitted bawling.
At home, our Bow-street gem'men keep the laws,
   And here a sentry stands within your calling;
But for all that, there is a deal of swearing,
And nauseous words past mentioning or bearing.

LXXXVII

The Count and Laura found their boat at last,
    And homeward floated o'er the silent tide,
Discussing all the dances gone and past;
    The dancers and their dresses, too, beside;
Some little scandals eke; but all aghast
    (As to their palace-stairs the rowers glide)
Sate Laura by the side of her adorer,
When lo! the Mussulman was there before her!

LXXXVIII

"Sir," said the Count, with brow exceeding grave,
    "Your unexpected presence here will make
It necessary for myself to crave
    Its import? But perhaps 'tis a mistake;
I hope it is so; and, at once to waive
    All compliment, I hope so for *your* sake;
You understand my meaning, or you *shall*."
"Sir," (quoth the Turk) " 'tis no mistake at all:

LXXXIX

"That Lady is *my wife!*" Much wonder paints
    The lady's changing cheek, as well it might;
But where an Englishwoman sometimes faints,
    Italian females don't do so outright;
They only call a little on their Saints,
    And then come to themselves, almost, or quite;
Which saves much hartshorn, salts, and sprinkling faces,
And cutting stays, as usual in such cases.

XC

She said,—what could she say? Why, not a word;
    But the Count courteously invited in
The Stranger, much appeased by what he heard:
    "Such things, perhaps, we'd best discuss within,"
Said he; "don't let us make ourselves absurd
    In public, by a scene, nor raise a din,

For then the chief and only satisfaction
Will be much quizzing on the whole transaction."

XCI

They entered, and for Coffee called—it came,
    A beverage for Turks and Christians both,
Although the way they make it's not the same.
    Now Laura, much recovered, or less loth
To speak, cries "Beppo! what's your pagan name?
    Bless me! your beard is of amazing growth!
And how came you to keep away so long?
Are you not sensible 'twas very wrong?

XCII

"Are you *really, truly,* now a Turk?
    With any other women did you wive?
Is't true they use their fingers for a fork?
    Well, that's the prettiest Shawl—as I'm alive!
You'll give it me? They say you eat no pork.
    And how so many years did you contrive
To—Bless me! did I ever? No, I never
Saw a man grown so yellow! How's your liver?

XCIII

"Beppo! that beard of yours becomes you not;
    It shall be shaved before you're a day older:
Why do you wear it? Oh! I had forgot—
    Pray don't you think the weather here is colder?
How do I look? You shan't stir from this spot
    In that queer dress, for fear that some beholder
Should find you out, and make the story known.
How short your hair is! Lord! how grey it's grown!"

XCIV

What answer Beppo made to these demands
    Is more than I know. He was cast away
About where Troy stood once, and nothing stands;
    Became a slave of course, and for his pay
Had bread and bastinadoes, till some bands

Of pirates landing in a neighbouring bay,
He joined the rogues and prospered, and became
A renegado of indifferent fame.

XCV

But he grew rich, and with his riches grew so
    Keen the desire to see his home again,
He thought himself in duty bound to do so,
    And not be always thieving on the main;
Lonely he felt, at times, as Robin Crusoe,
    And so he hired a vessel come from Spain,
Bound for Corfu: she was a fine polacca,
Manned with twelve hands, and laden with tobacco.

XCVI

Himself, and much (heaven knows how gotten!) cash,
    He then embarked, with risk of life and limb,
And got clear off, although the attempt was rash;
    He said that *Providence* protected him—
For my part, I say nothing—lest we clash
    In our opinions:—well—the ship was trim,
Set sail, and kept her reckoning fairly on,
Except three days of calm when off Cape Bonn.

XCVII

They reached the Island, he transferred his lading,
    And self and live stock to another bottom,
And passed for a true Turkey-merchant, trading
    With goods of various names—but I've forgot 'em.
However, he got off by this evading,
    Or else the people would perhaps have shot him;
And thus at Venice landed to reclaim
His wife, religion, house, and Christian name.

XCVIII

His wife received, the Patriarch re-baptized him,
    (He made the Church a present, by the way;)
He then threw off the garments which disguised him,
    And borrowed the Count's smallclothes for a day:

His friends the more for his long absence prized him,
    Finding he'd wherewithal to make them gay,
With dinners, where he oft became the laugh of them,
For stories—but *I* don't believe the half of them.

XCIX

Whate'er his youth had suffered, his old age
    With wealth and talking made him some amends;
Though Laura sometimes put him in a rage,
    I've heard the Count and he were always friends.
My pen is at the bottom of a page,
    Which being finished, here the story ends:
'Tis to be wished it had been sooner done,
But stories somehow lengthen when begun.

                          [*First publ., Feb. 28, 1818.*]

FRANCESCA OF RIMINI

FROM THE *INFERNO* OF DANTE

CANTO THE FIFTH

'THE Land where I was born sits by the Seas
    Upon that shore to which the Po descends,
    With all his followers, in search of peace.
Love, which the gentle heart soon apprehends,
    Seized him for the fair person which was ta'en
    From me, and me even yet the mode offends.
Love, who to none beloved to love again
    Remits, seized me with wish to please, so strong,
    That, as thou see'st, yet, yet it doth remain.
Love to one death conducted us along,   10
    But Cainà waits for him our life who ended:'
    These were the accents uttered by her tongue.—
Since I first listened to these Souls offended,
    I bowed my visage, and so kept it till—
    'What think'st thou?' said the bard; when I unbended,
And recommenced: 'Alas! unto such ill
    How many sweet thoughts, what strong ecstacies,

Led these their evil fortune to fulfil!'
And then I turned unto their side my eyes,
  And said, 'Francesca, thy sad destinies   **20**
  Have made me sorrow till the tears arise.
But tell me, in the Season of sweet sighs,
  By what and how thy Love to Passion rose,
  So as his dim desires to recognize?'
Then she to me: 'The greatest of all woes
  Is to remind us of our happy days
  In misery, and that thy teacher knows.
But if to learn our Passion's first root preys
  Upon thy spirit with such Sympathy,
  I will do even as he who weeps and says.   **30**
We read one day for pastime, seated nigh,
  Of Lancilot, how Love enchained him too.
  We were alone, quite unsuspiciously.
But oft our eyes met, and our cheeks in hue
  All o'er discoloured by that reading were;
  But one point only wholly us o'erthrew;
When we read the long-sighed-for smile of her,
  To be thus kissed by such devoted lover,
  He, who from me can be divided ne'er,
Kissed my mouth, trembling in the act all over: **40**
  Accursèd was the book and he who wrote!
  That day no further leaf we did uncover.'
While thus one Spirit told us of their lot,
  The other wept, so that with Pity's thralls,
  I swooned, as if by Death I had been smote,
And fell down even as a dead body falls.

March 20, 1820.
[*First published, 1830.*]

DRAMA

MANFRED

A DRAMATIC POEM

"There are more things in heaven and earth, Horatio,
Than are dreamt of in your philosophy."

[*Hamlet,* i., 5.]

DRAMATIS PERSONÆ

MANFRED
CHAMOIS HUNTER
ABBOT OF ST. MAURICE
MANUEL
HERMAN

WITCH OF THE ALPS
ARIMANES
NEMESIS
THE DESTINIES
SPIRITS, ETC.

The Scene of the Drama is amongst the Higher Alps—partly in the Castle of Manfred, and partly in the Mountains.

ACT I

SCENE I—MANFRED *alone.—Scene, a Gothic Gallery.—Time, Midnight.*

Manfred. THE lamp must be replenished, but even then
It will not burn so long as I must watch:
My slumbers—if I slumber—are not sleep,
But a continuance of enduring thought,

Which then I can resist not: in my heart
There is a vigil, and these eyes but close
To look within; and yet I live, and bear
The aspect and the form of breathing men.
But Grief should be the Instructor of the wise;
Sorrow is Knowledge: they who know the most   10
Must mourn the deepest o'er the fatal truth—
The Tree of Knowledge is not that of Life.
Philosophy and Science, and the springs
Of Wonder, and the wisdom of the World,
I have essayed, and in my mind there is
A power to make these subject to itself—
But they avail not: I have done men good,
And I have met with good even among men—
But this availed not: I have had my foes,
And none have baffled, many fallen before me—   20
But this availed not:—Good—or evil—life—
Powers, passions—all I see in other beings,
Have been to me as rain unto the sands,
Since that all-nameless hour. I have no dread,
And feel the curse to have no natural fear,
Nor fluttering throb that beats with hopes or wishes,
Or lurking love of something on the earth.
Now to my task.—
                    Mysterious Agency!
Ye Spirits of the unbounded Universe!
Whom I have sought in darkness and in light—   30
Ye, who do compass earth about, and dwell
In subtler essence—ye, to whom the tops
Of mountains inaccessible are haunts,
And Earth's and Ocean's caves familiar things—
I call upon ye by the written charm
Which gives me power upon you—Rise! Appear!

                                        [*A pause.*

They come not yet.—Now by the voice of him
Who is the first among you—by this sign,
Which makes you tremble—by the claims of him
Who is undying,—Rise! Appear!——Appear!   40

                                        [*A pause.*

If it be so.—Spirits of Earth and Air,
Ye shall not so elude me! By a power,
Deeper than all yet urged, a tyrant-spell,

Which had its birthplace in a star condemned,
The burning wreck of a demolished world,
A wandering hell in the eternal Space;
By the strong curse which is upon my Soul,
The thought which is within me and around me,
I do compel ye to my will.—Appear!

> [*A star is seen at the darker end of the gallery;
> it is stationary; and a voice is heard singing.*

FIRST SPIRIT

Mortal! to thy bidding bowed,   **50**
From my mansion in the cloud,
Which the breath of Twilight builds,
And the Summer's sunset gilds
With the azure and vermilion,
Which is mixed for my pavilion;
Though thy quest may be forbidden,
On a star-beam I have ridden,
To thine adjuration bowed:
Mortal—be thy wish avowed!

Voice of the SECOND SPIRIT

Mont Blanc is the Monarch of mountains;   **60**
    They crowned him long ago
On a throne of rocks, in a robe of clouds,
    With a Diadem of snow.
Around his waist are forests braced,
    The Avalanche in his hand;
But ere it fall, that thundering ball
    Must pause for my command.
The Glacier's cold and restless mass
    Moves onward day by day;
But I am he who bids it pass,   **70**
    Or with its ice delay.
I am the Spirit of the place,
    Could make the mountain bow
And quiver to his caverned base—
    And what with me would'st *Thou?*

Voice of the THIRD SPIRIT

In the blue depth of the waters,
   Where the wave hath no strife,
Where the Wind is a stranger,
   And the Sea-snake hath life,
Where the Mermaid is decking   80
   Her green hair with shells,
Like the storm on the surface
   Came the sound of thy spells;
O'er my calm Hall of Coral
   The deep Echo rolled—
To the Spirit of Ocean
   Thy wishes unfold!

FOURTH SPIRIT

Where the slumbering Earthquake
   Lies pillowed on fire,
And the lakes of bitumen   90
   Rose boilingly higher;
Where the roots of the Andes
   Strike deep in the earth,
As their summits to heaven
   Shoot soaringly forth;
I have quitted my birthplace,
   Thy bidding to bide—
Thy spell hath subdued me,
   Thy will be my guide!

FIFTH SPIRIT

I am the rider of the wind,   100
   The stirrer of the storm;
The hurricane I left behind
   Is yet with lightning warm;
To speed to thee, o'er shore and sea
   I swept upon the blast:
The fleet I met sailed well—and yet
   'Twill sink ere night be past.

SIXTH SPIRIT

My dwelling is the shadow of the Night,
Why doth thy magic torture me with light?

SEVENTH SPIRIT

The Star which rules thy destiny   110
Was ruled, ere earth began, by me:
It was a World as fresh and fair
As e'er revolved round Sun in air;
Its course was free and regular,
Space bosomed not a lovelier star.
The Hour arrived—and it became
A wandering mass of shapeless flame,
A pathless Comet, and a curse,
The menace of the Universe;
Still rolling on with innate force,   120
Without a sphere, without a course,
A bright deformity on high,
The monster of the upper sky!
And Thou! beneath its influence born—
Thou worm! whom I obey and scorn—
Forced by a Power (which is not thine,
And lent thee but to make thee mine)
For this brief moment to descend,
Where these weak Spirits round thee bend
And parley with a thing like thee—   130
What would'st thou, Child of Clay! with me?

The SEVEN SPIRITS

Earth—ocean—air—night—mountains—winds—thy Star,
   Are at thy beck and bidding, Child of Clay!
Before thee at thy quest their Spirits are—
   What would'st thou with us, Son of mortals—say?
   Manfred. Forgetfulness——
   First Spirit.   Of what—of whom—and why?
   Manfred. Of that which is within me; read it there—
Ye know it—and I cannot utter it.
   Spirit. We can but give thee that which we possess:
Ask of us subjects, sovereignty, the power   140

O'er earth—the whole, or portion—or a sign
Which shall control the elements, whereof
We are the dominators,—each and all,
These shall be thine.
    Manfred.   Oblivion—self-oblivion!
Can ye not wring from out the hidden realms
Ye offer so profusely—what I ask?
    Spirit. It is not in our essence, in our skill;
But—thou may'st die.
    Manfred.   Will Death bestow it on me?
    Spirit. We are immortal, and do not forget;
We are eternal; and to us the past   150
Is, as the future, present. Art thou answered?
    Manfred. Ye mock me—but the Power which brought ye here
Hath made you mine. Slaves, scoff not at my will!
The Mind—the Spirit—the Promethean spark,
The lightning of my being, is as bright,
Pervading, and far darting as your own,
And shall not yield to yours, though cooped in clay!
Answer, or I will teach you what I am.
    Spirit. We answer—as we answered; our reply
Is even in thine own words.   160
    Manfred.   Why say ye so?
    Spirit. If, as thou say'st, thine essence be as ours,
We have replied in telling thee, the thing
Mortals call death hath nought to do with us.
    Manfred. I then have called ye from your realms in vain;
Ye cannot, or ye will not, aid me.
    Spirit.   Say—
What we possess we offer; it is thine:
Bethink ere thou dismiss us;—ask again;
Kingdom, and sway, and strength, and length of days—
    Manfred. Accursèd! what have I to do with days?
They are too long already.—Hence—begone!   170
    Spirit. Yet pause: being here, our will would do thee service;
Bethink thee, is there then no other gift
Which we can make not worthless in thine eyes?
    Manfred. No, none: yet stay—one moment, ere we part,
I would behold ye face to face. I hear
Your voices, sweet and melancholy sounds,
As Music on the waters; and I see
The steady aspect of a clear large Star—

But nothing more. Approach me as ye are,
Or one—or all—in your accustomed forms.   180
    Spirit. We have no forms, beyond the elements
Of which we are the mind and principle:
But choose a form—in that we will appear.
    Manfred. I have no choice; there is no form on earth
Hideous or beautiful to me. Let him,
Who is most powerful of ye, take such aspect
As unto him may seem most fitting—Come!
    *Seventh Spirit (appearing in the shape of a beautiful female
figure).* Behold!
    Manfred.   Oh God! if it be thus, and *thou*
Art not a madness and a mockery,
I yet might be most happy. I will clasp thee,   190
And we again will be——
                              [*The figure vanishes.*
                My heart is crushed!
                    [Manfred *falls senseless.*

(*A voice is heard in the Incantation which follows.*)

      When the Moon is on the wave,
        And the glow-worm in the grass,
      And the meteor on the grave,
        And the wisp on the morass;
      When the falling stars are shooting,
      And the answered owls are hooting,
      And the silent leaves are still
      In the shadow of the hill,
      Shall my soul be upon thine,   200
      With a power and with a sign.

      Though thy slumber may be deep,
      Yet thy Spirit shall not sleep;
      There are shades which will not vanish,
      There are thoughts thou canst not banish;
      By a Power to thee unknown,
      Thou canst never be alone;
      Thou art wrapt as with a shroud,
      Thou art gathered in a cloud;
      And for ever shalt thou dwell   210
      In the spirit of this spell.

Though thou seest me not pass by,
Thou shalt feel me with thine eye
As a thing that, though unseen,
Must be near thee, and hath been;
And when in that secret dread
Thou hast turned around thy head,
Thou shalt marvel I am not
As thy shadow on the spot,
And the power which thou dost feel   220
Shall be what thou must conceal.

And a magic voice and verse
Hath baptized thee with a curse;
And a Spirit of the air
Hath begirt thee with a snare;
In the wind there is a voice
Shall forbid thee to rejoice;
And to thee shall Night deny
All the quiet of her sky;
And the day shall have a sun,   230
Which shall make thee wish it done.

From thy false tears I did distil
An essence which hath strength to kill;
From thy own heart I then did wring
The black blood in its blackest spring;
From thy own smile I snatched the snake,
For there it coiled as in a brake;
From thy own lip I drew the charm
Which gave all these their chiefest harm;
In proving every poison known,   240
I found the strongest was thine own.

By the cold breast and serpent smile,
By thy unfathomed gulfs of guile,
By that most seeming virtuous eye,
By thy shut soul's hypocrisy;
By the perfection of thine art
Which passed for human thine own heart:
By thy delight in others' pain,
And by thy brotherhood of Cain,
I call upon thee! and compel   250
Thyself to be thy proper Hell!

And on thy head I pour the vial
Which doth devote thee to this trial;
Nor to slumber, nor to die,
Shall be in thy destiny;
Though thy death shall still seem near
To thy wish, but as a fear;
Lo! the spell now works around thee,
And the clankless chain hath bound thee;
O'er thy heart and brain together   260
Hath the word been passed—now wither!

SCENE II—*The Mountain of the Jungfrau.—Time, Morning.—*
MANFRED *alone upon the cliffs.*

Manfred. The spirits I have raised abandon me,
The spells which I have studied baffle me,
The remedy I recked of tortured me:
I lean no more on superhuman aid;
It hath no power upon the past, and for
The future, till the past be gulfed in darkness,
It is not of my search.—My Mother Earth!
And thou fresh-breaking Day, and you, ye Mountains,
Why are ye beautiful? I cannot love ye.
And thou, the bright Eye of the Universe,   10
That openest over all, and unto all
Art a delight—thou shin'st not on my heart.
And you ye crags, upon whose extreme edge
I stand, and on the torrent's brink beneath
Behold the tall pines dwindled as to shrubs
In dizziness of distance; when a leap,
A stir, a motion, even a breath, would bring
My breast upon its rocky bosom's bed
To rest for ever—wherefore do I pause?
I feel the impulse—yet I do not plunge;   20
I see the peril—yet do not recede;
And my brain reels—and yet my foot is firm:
There is a power upon me which withholds,
And makes it my fatality to live,—
If it be life to wear within myself
This barrenness of Spirit, and to be
My own Soul's sepulchre, for I have ceased
To justify my deeds unto myself—

The last infirmity of evil. Aye,
Thou winged and cloud-cleaving minister,   30
                    [*An Eagle passes.*
Whose happy flight is highest into heaven,
Well may'st thou swoop so near me—I should be
The prey, and gorge thine eaglets; thou art gone
Where the eye cannot follow thee; but thine
Yet pierces downward, onward, or above,
With a pervading vision.—Beautiful!
How beautiful is all this visible world!
How glorious in its action and itself!
But we, who name ourselves its sovereigns, we,
Half dust, half deity, alike unfit   40
To sink or soar, with our mixed essence make
A conflict of its elements, and breathe
The breath of degradation and of pride,
Contending with low wants and lofty will,
Till our Mortality predominates,
And men are—what they name not to themselves,
And trust not to each other. Hark! the note,
                    [*The Shepherd's pipe in the distance is heard.*
The natural music of the mountain reed—
For here the patriarchal days are not
A pastoral fable—pipes in the liberal air,   50
Mixed with the sweet bells of the sauntering herd;
My soul would drink those echoes. Oh, that I were
The viewless spirit of a lovely sound,
A living voice, a breathing harmony,
A bodiless enjoyment—born and dying
With the blest tone which made me!

Enter from below a CHAMOIS HUNTER

Chamois Hunter.   Even so
This way the Chamois leapt: her nimble feet
Have baffled me; my gains to-day will scarce
Repay my break-neck travail.—What is here?
Who seems not of my trade, and yet hath reached   60
A height which none even of our mountaineers,
Save our best hunters, may attain: his garb
Is goodly, his mien manly, and his air
Proud as a free-born peasant's, at this distance:—
I will approach him nearer.

Manfred (not perceiving the other). To be thus—
Grey-haired with anguish, like these blasted pines,
Wrecks of a single winter, barkless, branchless,
A blighted trunk upon a cursèd root,
Which but supplies a feeling to Decay—
And to be thus, eternally but thus,   70
Having been otherwise! Now furrowed o'er
With wrinkles, ploughed by moments, not by years
And hours, all tortured into ages—hours
Which I outlive!—Ye toppling crags of ice!
Ye Avalanches, whom a breath draws down
In mountainous o'erwhelming, come and crush me!
I hear ye momently above, beneath,
Crash with a frequent conflict; but ye pass,
And only fall on things that still would live;
On the young flourishing forest, or the hut   80
And hamlet of the harmless villager.
     Chamois Hunter. The mists begin to rise from up the valley;
I'll warn him to descend, or he may chance
To lose at once his way and life together.
     Manfred. The mists boil up around the glaciers; clouds
Rise curling fast beneath me, white and sulphury,
Like foam from the roused ocean of deep Hell,
Whose every wave breaks on a living shore,
Heaped with the damned like pebbles.—I am giddy.
     Chamois Hunter. I must approach him cautiously; if near, 90
A sudden step will startle him, and he
Seems tottering already.
     Manfred.   Mountains have fallen,
Leaving a gap in the clouds, and with the shock
Rocking their Alpine brethren; filling up
The ripe green valleys with Destruction's splinters;
Damming the rivers with a sudden dash,
Which crushed the waters into mist, and made
Their fountains find another channel—thus,
Thus, in its old age, did Mount Rosenberg—
Why stood I not beneath it?
     Chamois Hunter.   Friend! have a care,   100
Your next step may be fatal!—for the love
Of Him who made you, stand not on that brink!
     Manfred (not hearing him). Such would have been for me a
          fitting tomb;
My bones had then been quiet in their depth;

They had not then been strewn upon the rocks
For the wind's pastime—as thus—thus they shall be—
In this one plunge.—Farewell, ye opening Heavens!
Look not upon me thus reproachfully—
You were not meant for me—Earth! take these atoms!

> [*As* MANFRED *is in act to spring from the cliff,*
> *the* CHAMOIS HUNTER *seizes and retains him*
> *with a sudden grasp.*

   Chamois Hunter. Hold, madman!—though aweary of thy life,
Stain not our pure vales with thy guilty blood: 111
Away with me—I will not quit my hold.
   Manfred. I am most sick at heart—nay, grasp me not—
I am all feebleness—the mountains whirl,
Spinning around me——I grow blind——What art thou?
   Chamois Hunter. I'll answer that anon.—Away with me——
The clouds grow thicker——there—now lean on me—
Place your foot here—here, take this staff, and cling
A moment to that shrub—now give me your hand,
And hold fast my girdle—softly—well—   120
The Chalet will be gained within an hour:
Come on, we'll quickly find a surer footing,
And something like a pathway, which the torrent
Hath washed since winter.—Come, 'tis bravely done—
You should have been a hunter.—Follow me.

> [*As they descend the rocks with difficulty, the*
> *scene closes.*

ACT II

SCENE I—*A Cottage among the Bernese Alps.*—MANFRED *and*
the CHAMOIS HUNTER.

   Chamois Hunter. No—no—yet pause—thou must not yet go
    forth:
Thy mind and body are alike unfit
To trust each other, for some hours, at least;
When thou art better, I will be thy guide—
But whither?
   Manfred.   It imports not: I do know
My route full well, and need no further guidance.
   Chamois Hunter. Thy garb and gait bespeak thee of high
    lineage—

One of the many chiefs, whose castled crag
Look o'er the lower valleys—which of these
May call thee lord? I only know their portals;   **10**
My way of life leads me but rarely down
To bask by the huge hearths of those old halls,
Carousing with the vassals; but the paths,
Which step from out our mountains to their doors,
I know from childhood—which of these is thine?
   Manfred. No matter.
   Chamois Hunter.   Well, Sir, pardon me the question,
And be of better cheer. Come, taste my wine;
'Tis of an ancient vintage; many a day
'T has thawed my veins among our glaciers, now
Let it do thus for thine—Come, pledge me fairly!   **20**
   Manfred. Away, away! there's blood upon the brim!
Will it then never—never sink in the earth?
   Chamois Hunter. What dost thou mean? thy senses wander
    from thee.
   Manfred. I say 'tis blood—my blood! the pure warm stream
Which ran in the veins of my fathers, and in ours
When we were in our youth, and had one heart,
And loved each other as we should not love,
And this was shed: but still it rises up,
Colouring the clouds, that shut me out from Heaven,
Where thou art not—and I shall never be.   **30**
   Chamois Hunter. Man of strange words, and some half-
    maddening sin,
Which makes thee people vacancy, whate'er
Thy dread and sufferance be, there's comfort yet—
The aid of holy men, and heavenly patience——
   Manfred. Patience—and patience! Hence—that word was
    made
For brutes of burthen, not for birds of prey!
Preach it to mortals of a dust like thine,—
I am not of thine order.
   Chamois Hunter.   Thanks to Heaven!
I would not be of thine for the free fame
Of William Tell; but whatsoe'er thine ill,   **40**
It must be borne, and these wild starts are useless.
   Manfred. Do I not bear it?—Look on me—I live.
   Chamois Hunter. This is convulsion, and no healthful life.
   Manfred. I tell thee, man! I have lived many years,
Many long years, but they are nothing now

To those which I must number: ages—ages—
Space and eternity—and consciousness,
With the fierce thirst of death—and still unslaked!
 Chamois Hunter. Why, on thy brow the seal of middle age
Hath scarce been set; I am thine elder far.   50
 Manfred. Think'st thou existence doth depend on time?
It doth; but actions are our epochs: mine
Have made my days and nights imperishable,
Endless, and all alike, as sands on the shore,
Innumerable atoms; and one desert,
Barren and cold, on which the wild waves break,
But nothing rests, save carcasses and wrecks,
Rocks, and the salt-surf weeds of bitterness.
 Chamois Hunter. Alas! he's mad—but yet I must not leave
  him.
 Manfred. I would I were—for then the things I see   60
Would be but a distempered dream.
 Chamois Hunter.   What is it
That thou dost see, or think thou look'st upon?
 Manfred. Myself, and thee—a peasant of the Alps—
Thy humble virtues, hospitable home,
And spirit patient, pious, proud, and free;
Thy self-respect grafted on innocent thoughts;
Thy days of health, and nights of sleep: thy toils,
By danger dignified, yet guiltless; hopes
Of cheerful old age and a quiet grave,
With cross and garland over its green turf,   70
And thy grandchildren's love for epitaph!
This do I see—and then I look within—
It matters not—my Soul was scorched already!
 Chamois Hunter. And would'st thou then exchange thy lot for
  mine?
 Manfred. No, friend! I would not wrong thee, nor exchange
My lot with living being: I can bear—
However wretchedly, 'tis still to bear—
In life what others could not brook to dream,
But perish in their slumber.
 Chamois Hunter.   And with this—
This cautious feeling for another's pain,   80
Canst thou be black with evil?—say not so.
Can one of gentle thoughts have wreaked revenge
Upon his enemies?
 Manfred.   Oh! no, no, no!

My injuries came down on those who loved me—
On those whom I best loved: I never quelled
An enemy, save in my just defence—-
But my embrace was fatal.
 Chamois Hunter.   Heaven give thee rest!
And Penitence restore thee to thyself;
My prayers shall be for thee.
 Manfred.   I need them not,
But can endure thy pity. I depart—   90
'Tis time—farewell!—Here's gold, and thanks for thee—
No words—it is thy due.—Follow me not—
I know my path—the mountain peril's past:
And once again I charge thee, follow not!

             [*Exit* MANFRED.

  SCENE II—*A lower Valley in the Alps.—A Cataract.*

     Enter MANFRED.

It is not noon—the Sunbow's rays still arch
The torrent with the many hues of heaven,
And roll the sheeted silver's waving column
O'er the crag's headlong perpendicular,
And fling its line of foaming light along,
And to and fro, like the pale courser's tail,
The Giant steed, to be bestrode by Death,
As told in the Apocalypse. No eyes
But mine now drink this sight of loveliness;
I should be sole in this sweet solitude,   10
And with the Spirit of the place divide
The homage of these waters.—I will call her.

     [MANFRED *takes some of the water into the palm*
      of his hand and flings it into the air, mutter-
      ing the adjuration. After a pause, the WITCH
      OF THE ALPS *rises beneath the arch of the*
      sunbow of the torrent.

Beautiful Spirit! with thy hair of light,
And dazzling eyes of glory, in whose form
The charms of Earth's least mortal daughters grow
To an unearthly stature, in an essence
Of purer elements; while the hues of youth,—
Carnationed like a sleeping infant's cheek,
Rocked by the beating of her mother's heart,

Or the rose tints, which Summer's twilight leaves   20
Upon the lofty Glacier's virgin snow,
The blush of earth embracing with her Heaven,—
Tinge thy celestial aspect, and make tame
The beauties of the Sunbow which bends o'er thee.
Beautiful Spirit! in thy calm clear brow,
Wherein is glassed serenity of Soul,
Which of itself shows immortality,
I read that thou wilt pardon to a Son
Of Earth, whom the abstruser powers permit
At times to commune with them—if that he   30
Avail him of his spells—to call thee thus,
And gaze on thee a moment.
  Witch.   Son of Earth!
I know thee, and the Powers which give thee power!
I know thee for a man of many thoughts,
And deeds of good and ill, extreme in both,
Fatal and fated in thy sufferings.
I have expected this—what would'st thou with me?
 Manfred. To look upon thy beauty—nothing further.
The face of the earth hath maddened me, and I
Take refuge in her mysteries, and pierce   40
To the abodes of those who govern her—
But they can nothing aid me. I have sought
From them what they could not bestow, and now
I search no further.
  Witch.   What could be the quest
Which is not in the power of the most powerful,
The rulers of the invisible?
  Manfred.   A boon;—
But why should I repeat it? 'twere in vain.
 Witch. I know not that; let thy lips utter it.
  Manfred. Well, though it torture me, 'tis but the same;
My pang shall find a voice. From my youth upwards   50
My Spirit walked not with the souls of men,
Nor looked upon the earth with human eyes;
The thirst of their ambition was not mine,
The aim of their existence was not mine;
My joys—my griefs—my passions—and my powers,
Made me a stranger; though I wore the form,
I had no sympathy with breathing flesh,
Nor midst the Creatures of Clay that girded me
Was there but One who—but of her anon.

I said with men, and with the thoughts of men,   60
I held but slight communion; but instead,
My joy was in the wilderness,—to breathe
The difficult air of the iced mountain's top,
Where the birds dare not build—nor insect's wing
Flit o'er the herbless granite; or to plunge
Into the torrent, and to roll along
On the swift whirl of the new-breaking wave
Of river-stream, or ocean, in their flow.
In these my early strength exulted; or
To follow through the night the moving moon,   70
The stars and their development; or catch
The dazzling lightnings till my eyes grew dim;
Or to look, list'ning, on the scattered leaves,
While Autumn winds were at their evening song.
These were my pastimes, and to be alone;
For if the beings, of whom I was one,—
Hating to be so,—crossed me in my path,
I felt myself degraded back to them,
And all was clay again. And then I dived,
In my lone wanderings, to the caves of Death,   80
Searching its cause in its effect; and drew
From withered bones, and skulls, and heaped up dust,
Conclusions most forbidden. Then I passed
The nights of years in sciences untaught,
Save in the old-time; and with time and toil,
And terrible ordeal, and such penance
As in itself hath power upon the air,
And spirits that do compass air and earth,
Space, and the peopled Infinite, I made
Mine eyes familiar with Eternity,   90
Such as, before me, did the Magi, and
He who from out their fountain-dwellings raised
Eros and Anteros, at Gadara,
As I do thee;—and with my knowledge grew
The thirst of knowledge, and the power and joy
Of this most bright intelligence, until——
    Witch. Proceed.
    Manfred.   Oh! I but thus prolonged my words,
Boasting these idle attributes, because
As I approach the core of my heart's grief—
But—to my task. I have not named to thee   100
Father or mother, mistress, friend, or being,

With whom I wore the chain of human ties;
If I had such, they seemed not such to me—
Yet there was One——
    Witch.   Spare not thyself—proceed.
    Manfred. She was like me in lineaments—her eyes—
Her hair—her features—all, to the very tone
Even of her voice, they said were like to mine;
But softened all, and tempered into beauty:
She had the same lone thoughts and wanderings,
The quest of hidden knowledge, and a mind   110
To comprehend the Universe: nor these
Alone, but with them gentler powers than mine,
Pity, and smiles, and tears—which I had not;
And tenderness—but that I had for her;
Humility—and that I never had.
Her faults were mine—her virtues were her own—
I loved her, and destroyed her!
    Witch.   With thy hand?
    Manfred. Not with my hand, but heart, which broke her heart:
It gazed on mine, and withered. I have shed
Blood, but not hers—and yet her blood was shed;   120
I saw—and could not stanch it.
    Witch.   And for this—
A being of the race thou dost despise—
The order, which thine own would rise above,
Mingling with us and ours,—thou dost forego
The gifts of our great knowledge, and shrink'st back
To recreant mortality——Away!
    Manfred. Daughter of Air! I tell thee, since that hour—
But words are breath—look on me in my sleep,
Or watch my watchings—Come and sit by me!
My solitude is solitude no more,   130
But peopled with the Furies;—I have gnashed
My teeth in darkness till returning morn,
Then cursed myself till sunset;—I have prayed
For madness as a blessing—'tis denied me.
I have affronted Death—but in the war
Of elements the waters shrunk from me,
And fatal things passed harmless; the cold hand
Of an all-pitiless Demon held me back,
Back by a single hair, which would not break
In Fantasy, Imagination, all   140
The affluence of my soul—which one day was

A Crœsus in creation—I plunged deep,
But, like an ebbing wave, it dashed me back
Into the gulf of my unfathomed thought.
I plunged amidst Mankind—Forgetfulness
I sought in all, save where 'tis to be found—
And that I have to learn—my Sciences,
My long pursued and superhuman art,
Is mortal here: I dwell in my despair—
And live—and live for ever.
   Witch.   It may be   **150**
That I can aid thee.
   Manfred.   To do this thy power
Must wake the dead, or lay me low with them.
Do so—in any shape—in any hour—
With any torture—so it be the last.
   Witch. That is not in my province; but if thou
Wilt swear obedience to my will, and do
My bidding, it may help thee to thy wishes.
   Manfred. I will not swear—Obey! and whom? the Spirits
Whose presence I command, and be the slave
Of those who served me—Never!
   Witch.   Is this all?   **160**
Hast thou no gentler answer?—Yet bethink thee,
And pause ere thou rejectest.
   Manfred.   I have said it.
   Witch. Enough! I may retire then—say!
   Manfred.   Retire!
                     [*The* WITCH *disappears.*
   Manfred (*alone*). We are the fools of Time and Terror: Days
Steal on us, and steal from us; yet we live,
Loathing our life, and dreading still to die.
In all the days of this detested yoke—
This vital weight upon the struggling heart,
Which sinks with sorrow, or beats quick with pain,
Or joy that ends in agony or faintness—   **170**
In all the days of past and future—for
In life there is no present—we can number
How few—how less than few—wherein the soul
Forbears to pant for death, and yet draws back
As from a stream in winter, though the chill
Be but a moment's. I have one resource
Still in my science—I can call the dead,
And ask them what it is we dread to be:

The sternest answer can but be the Grave,
And that is nothing: if they answer not——   180
The buried Prophet answered to the Hag
Of Endor; and the Spartan Monarch drew
From the Byzantine maid's unsleeping spirit
An answer and his destiny—he slew
That which he loved, unknowing what he slew,
And died unpardoned—though he called in aid
The Phyxian Jove, and in Phigalia roused
The Arcadian Evocators to compel
The indignant shadow to depose her wrath,
Or fix her term of vengeance—she replied   190
In words of dubious import, but fulfilled.
If I had never lived, that which I love
Had still been living; had I never loved
That which I love would still be beautiful,
Happy and giving happiness. What is she?
What is she now?—a sufferer for my sins—
A thing I dare not think upon—or nothing.
Within few hours I shall not call in vain—
Yet in this hour I dread the thing I dare:
Until this hour I never shrunk to gaze   200
On spirit, good or evil—now I tremble,
And feel a strange cold thaw upon my heart.
But I can act even what I most abhor,
And champion human fears.—The night approaches.

                                [*Exit.*

SCENE III—*The summit of the Jungfrau Mountain.*

Enter FIRST DESTINY.

The Moon is rising broad, and round, and bright;
And here on snows, where never human foot
Of common mortal trod, we nightly tread,
And leave no traces: o'er the savage sea,
The glassy ocean of the mountain ice,
We skim its rugged breakers, which put on
The aspect of a tumbling tempest's foam
Frozen in a moment—a dead Whirlpool's image:
And this most steep fantastic pinnacle,
The fretwork of some earthquake—where the clouds   10

Pause to repose themselves in passing by—
Is sacred to our revels, or our vigils;
Here do I wait my sisters, on our way
To the Hall of Arimanes—for to-night
Is our great festival—'tis strange they come not.

A Voice without, singing.

The Captive Usurper,
    Hurled down from the throne,
Lay buried in torpor,
    Forgotten and lone;
I broke through his slumbers,   **20**
    I shivered his chain,
I leagued him with numbers—
    He's Tyrant again!
With the blood of a million he'll answer my care,
With a Nation's destruction—his flight and despair!

Second Voice, without.

The Ship sailed on, the Ship sailed fast,
But I left not a sail, and I left not a mask;
There is not a plank of the hull or the deck,
And there is not a wretch to lament o'er his wreck;
Save one, whom I held, as he swam, by the hair,   **3c**
And he was a subject well worthy my care;
A traitor on land, and a pirate at sea—
But I saved him to wreak further havoc for me!

FIRST DESTINY, *answering.*

The City lies sleeping;
    The morn, to deplore it,
May dawn on it weeping:
    Sullenly, slowly,
The black plague flew o'er it—
    Thousands lie lowly;
Tens of thousands shall perish;   **40**
    The living shall fly from
The sick they should cherish;

But nothing can vanquish
        The touch that they die from.
    Sorrow and anguish,
And evil and dread,
        Envelop a nation;
    The blest are the dead,
    Who see not the sight
        Of their own desolation;
    This work of a night—
This wreck of a realm—this deed of my doing—
For ages I've done, and shall still be renewing!

Enter the SECOND *and* THIRD DESTINIES.

The Three.

Our hands contain the hearts of men,
        Our footsteps are their graves;
    We only give to take again
        The Spirits of our slaves!
First Destiny. Welcome!—Where's Nemesis?
Second Destiny.   At some great work;
But what I know not, for my hands were full.
    Third Destiny. Behold she cometh.

Enter NEMESIS.

First Destiny.   Say, where hast thou been?   60
My Sisters and thyself are slow to-night.
    Nemesis. I was detained repairing shattered thrones—
Marrying fools, restoring dynasties—
Avenging men upon their enemies,
And making them repent their own revenge;
Goading the wise to madness; from the dull
Shaping out oracles to rule the world
Afresh—for they were waxing out of date,
And mortals dared to ponder for themselves,
To weigh kings in the balance—and to speak   70
Of Freedom, the forbidden fruit.—Away!
We have outstayed the hour—mount we our clouds!

[*Exeunt.*

Scene IV—*The Hall of Arimanes.—Arimanes on his Throne, a Globe of Fire, surrounded by the Spirits.*

Hymn of the Spirits.

Hail to our Master!—Prince of Earth and Air!
  Who walks the clouds and waters—in his hand
The sceptre of the Elements, which tear
  Themselves to chaos at his high command!
He breatheth—and a tempest shakes the sea;
  He speaketh—and the clouds reply in thunder;
He gazeth—from his glance the sunbeams flee;
  He moveth—Earthquakes rend the world asunder.
Beneath his footsteps the Volcanoes rise;
  His shadow is the Pestilence: his path   10
The comets herald through the crackling skies;
  And Planets turn to ashes at his wrath.
To him War offers daily sacrifice;
  To him Death pays his tribute; Life is his,
With all its Infinite of agonies—
  And his the Spirit of whatever is!

Enter the Destinies *and* Nemesis.

  First Destiny. Glory to Arimanes! on the earth
His power increaseth—both my sisters did
His bidding, nor did I neglect my duty!
  Second Destiny. Glory to Arimanes! we who bow   20
The necks of men, bow down before his throne!
  Third Destiny. Glory to Arimanes! we await His nod!
  Nemesis. Sovereign of Sovereigns! we are thine,
And all that liveth, more or less, is ours,
And most things wholly so; still to increase
Our power, increasing thine, demands our care,
And we are vigilant. Thy late commands
Have been fulfilled to the utmost.

Enter Manfred.

  A Spirit.   What is here?
A mortal!—Thou most rash and fatal wretch,
Bow down and worship!

 Second Spirit.   I do know the man—   30
A Magian of great power, and fearful skill!
 Third Spirit. Bow down and worship, slave!—What, know'st
  thou not
Thine and our Sovereign?—Tremble, and obey!
 All the Spirits. Prostrate thyself, and thy condemnéd clay,
Child of the Earth! or dread the worst.
 Manfred.   I know it;
And yet ye see I kneel not.
 Fourth Spirit.   'Twill be taught thee.
 Manfred. 'Tis taught already;—many a night on the earth,
On the bare ground, have I bowed down my face,
And strewed my head with ashes; I have known
The fulness of humiliation—for   40
I sunk before my vain despair, and knelt
To my own desolation.
 Fifth Spirit.   Dost thou dare
Refuse to Arimanes on his throne
What the whole earth accords, beholding not
The terror of his Glory?—Crouch! I say.
 Manfred. Bid *him* bow down to that which is above him,
The overruling Infinite—the Maker
Who made him not for worship—let him kneel,
And we will kneel together.
 The Spirits.   Crush the worm!
Tear him in pieces!—
 First Destiny. Hence! Avaunt!—he's mine.   50
Prince of the Powers invisible! This man
Is of no common order, as his port
And presence here denote: his sufferings
Have been of an immortal nature—like
Our own; his knowledge, and his powers and will,
As far as is compatible with clay,
Which clogs the ethereal essence, have been such
As clay hath seldom borne; his aspirations
Have been beyond the dwellers of the earth,
And they have only taught him what we know— 60
That knowledge is not happiness, and science
But an exchange of ignorance for that
Which is another kind of ignorance.
This is not all—the passions, attributes
Of Earth and Heaven, from which no power nor being,
Nor breath from the worm upwards is exempt,

Have pierced his heart; and in their consequence
Made him a thing—which—I who pity not,
Yet pardon those who pity. He is mine—
And thine it may be; be it so, or not—   70
No other Spirit in this region hath
A soul like his—or power upon his soul.
　　Nemesis. What doth he here then?
　　First Destiny.   Let *him* answer that.
　　Manfred. Ye know what I have known; and without powe:
I could not be amongst ye: but there are
Powers deeper still beyond—I come in quest
Of such, to answer unto what I seek.
　　Nemesis. What would'st thou?
　　Manfred.   Thou canst not reply to me.
Call up the dead—my question is for them.
　　Nemesis. Great Arimanes, doth thy will avouch   80
The wishes of this mortal?
　　Arimanes.   Yea.
　　Nemesis.   Whom wouldst thou
Uncharnel?
　　Manfred.   One without a tomb—call up
Astarte.

NEMESIS.

　　　Shadow! or Spirit!
　　　　Whatever thou art,
　　　Which still doth inherit
　　　　The whole or a part
　　　Of the form of thy birth,
　　　　Of the mould of thy clay,
　　　Which returned to the earth,   90
　　　　Re-appear to the day!
　　　Bear what thou borest,
　　　　The heart and the form,
　　　And the aspect thou worest
　　　　Redeem from the worm.
　　Appear!—Appear!—Appear!
　　Who sent thee there requires thee here!
　　　　[*The Phantom of* ASTARTE *rises and stands in
　　　　　the midst.*

　　Manfred. Can this be death? there's bloom upon her cheek;
But now I see it is no living hue,

But a strange hectic—like the unnatural red   **100**
Which Autumn plants upon the perished leaf,
It is the same! Oh, God! that I should dread
To look upon the same—Astarte!—No,
I cannot speak to her—but bid her speak—
Forgive me or condemn me.

NEMESIS.

    By the Power which hath broken
      The grave which enthralled thee,
    Speak to him who hath spoken,
      Or those who have called thee!
Manfred.   She is silent,
And in that silence I am more than answered.   **110**
   Nemesis. My power extends no further. Prince of Air!
It rests with thee alone—command her voice.
   Arimanes. Spirit—obey this sceptre!
   Nemesis.   Silent still!
She is not of our order, but belongs
To the other powers. Mortal! thy quest is vain,
And we are baffled also.
   Manfred.   Hear me, hear me—
Astarte! my belovéd! speak to me:
I have so much endured—so much endure—
Look on me! the grave hath not changed thee more
Than I am changed for Thee. Thou lovedst me   **120**
Too much, as I loved thee: we were not made
To torture thus each other—though it were
The deadliest sin to love as we have loved.
Say that thou loath'st me not—that I do bear
This punishment for both—that thou wilt be
One of the blesséd—and that I shall die;
For hitherto all hateful things conspire
To bind me in existence—in a life
Which makes me shrink from Immortality—
A future like the past. I cannot rest.   **130**
I know not what I ask, nor what I seek:
I feel but what thou art, and what I am;
And I would hear yet once before I perish
The voice which was my music—speak to me!
For I have called on thee in the still night,

Startled the slumbering birds from the hushed boughs,
And woke the mountain wolves, and made the caves
Acquainted with thy vainly echoed name,
Which answered me—many things answered me—
Spirits and men—but thou wert silent all.   140
Yet speak to me! I have outwatched the stars,
And gazed o'er heaven in vain in search of thee.
Speak to me! I have wandered o'er the earth,
And never found thy likeness—Speak to me!
Look on the fiends around—they feel for me:
I fear them not, and feel for thee alone.
Speak to me! though it be in wrath;—but say—
I reck not what—but let me hear thee once—
This once—once more!

    Phantom of Astarte. Manfred!
    Manfred.   Say on, say on—
I live but in the sound—it is thy voice!   150
    Phantom. Manfred! to-morrow ends thine earthly ills.
Farewell!
    Manfred. Yet one word more—am I forgiven?
    Phantom. Farewell!
    Manfred.   Say, shall we meet again?
    Phantom.   Farewell!
    Manfred. One word for mercy! Say thou lovest me.
    Phantom. Manfred!

                [*The Spirit of* ASTARTE *disappears.*
    Nemesis.   She's gone, and will not be recalled:
Her words will be fulfilled. Return to the earth.
    A Spirit. He is convulsed—This is to be a mortal,
And seek the things beyond mortality.
    Another Spirit. Yet, see, he mastereth himself, and makes
His torture tributary to his will.   160
Had he been one of us, he would have made
An awful Spirit.
    Nemesis.   Hast thou further question
Of our great sovereign, or his worshippers?
    Manfred. None.
    Nemesis.   Then, for a time, farewell.
    Manfred. We meet then! Where? On the earth?—
Even as thou wilt: and for the grace accorded
I now depart a debtor. Fare ye well!

                          [*Exit* MANFRED.

       (*Scene closes.*)

ACT III

Scene I—*A Hall in the Castle of Manfred.*

Manfred *and* Herman.

Manfred. What is the hour?
Herman. It wants but one till sunset,
And promises a lovely twilight.
Manfred. Say,
Are all things so disposed of in the tower
As I directed?
Herman. All, my Lord, are ready:
Here is the key and casket.
Manfred. It is well:
Thou mayst retire. [*Exit* Herman.
Manfred (alone). There is a calm upon me—
Inexplicable stillness! which till now
Did not belong to what I knew of life.
If that I did not know Philosophy
To be of all our vanities the motliest, 10
The merest word that ever fooled the ear
From out the schoolman's jargon, I should deem
The golden secret, the sought "Kalon," found,
And seated in my soul. It will not last,
But it is well to have known it, though but once:
It hath enlarged my thoughts with a new sense,
And I within my tablets would note down
That there is such a feeling. Who is there?

Re-enter Herman.

Herman. My Lord, the Abbot of St. Maurice craves
To greet your presence.

Enter the Abbot of St. Maurice.

Abbot. Peace be with Count Manfred! 20
Manfred. Thanks, holy father! welcome to these walls;
Thy presence honours them, and blesseth those
Who dwell within them.

Abbot.   Would it were so, Count!—
But I would fain confer with thee alone.
   Manfred. Herman, retire.—What would my reverend guest?
   Abbot. Thus, without prelude:—Age and zeal—my office—
And good intent must plead my privilege;
Our near, though not acquainted neighbourhood,
May also be my herald. Rumours strange,
And of unholy nature, are abroad,   30
And busy with thy name—a noble name
For centuries: may he who bears it now
Transmit it unimpaired!
   Manfred.   Proceed,—I listen.
   Abbot. 'Tis said thou holdest converse with the things
Which are forbidden to the search of man;
That with the dwellers of the dark abodes,
The many evil and unheavenly spirits
Which walk the valley of the Shade of Death,
Thou communest. I know that with mankind,
Thy fellows in creation, thou dost rarely   40
Exchange thy thoughts, and that thy solitude
Is as an Anchorite's—were it but holy.
   Manfred. And what are they who do avouch these things?
   Abbot. My pious brethren—the scared peasantry—
Even thy own vassals—who do look on thee
With most unquiet eyes. Thy life's in peril!
   Manfred. Take it.
   Abbot.   I come to save, and not destroy:
I would not pry into thy secret soul;
But if these things be sooth, there still is time
For penitence and pity: reconcile thee   50
With the true church, and through the church to Heaven.
   Manfred. I hear thee. This is my reply—whate'er
I may have been, or am, doth rest between
Heaven and myself—I shall not choose a mortal
To be my mediator—Have I sinned
Against your ordinances? prove and punish!
   Abbot. My son! I did not speak of punishment,
But penitence and pardon;—with thyself
The choice of such remains—and for the last,
Our institutions and our strong belief   60
Have given me power to smooth the path from sin
To higher hope and better thoughts; the first
I leave to Heaven,—"Vengeance is mine alone!"

So saith the Lord, and with all humbleness
His servant echoes back the awful word.
    Manfred. Old man! there is no power in holy men,
Nor charm in prayer, nor purifying form
Of penitence, nor outward look, nor fast,
Nor agony—nor, greater than all these,
The innate tortures of that deep Despair,   70
Which is Remorse without the fear of Hell,
But all in all sufficient to itself
Would make a hell of Heaven—can exorcise
From out the unbounded spirit the quick sense
Of its own sins—wrongs—sufferance—and revenge
Upon itself; there is no future pang
Can deal that justice on the self-condemned
He deals on his own soul.
    Abbot.   All this is well;
For this will pass away, and be succeeded
By an auspicious hope, which shall look up   80
With calm assurance to that blessed place,
Which all who seek may win, whatever be
Their earthly errors, so they be atoned:
And the commencement of atonement is
The sense of its necessity. Say on—
And all our church can teach thee shall be taught;
And all we can absolve thee shall be pardoned.
    Manfred. When Rome's sixth Emperor was near his last,
The victim of a self-inflicted wound,
To shun the torments of a public death   90
From senates once his slaves, a certain soldier,
With show of loyal pity, would have stanched
The gushing throat with his officious robe;
The dying Roman thrust him back, and said—
Some empire still in his expiring glance—
"It is too late—is this fidelity?"
    Abbot. And what of this?
    Manfred.   I answer with the Roman—
"It is too late!"
    Abbot.   It never can be so,
To reconcile thyself with thy own soul,
And thy own soul with Heaven. Hast thou no hope?   100
'Tis strange—even those who do despair above,
Yet shape themselves some fantasy on earth,
To which frail twig they cling, like drowning men.

Manfred. Aye—father! I have had those early visions,
And noble aspirations in my youth,
To make my own the mind of other men,
The enlightener of nations; and to rise
I knew not whither—it might be to fall;
But fall, even as the mountain-cataract,
Which having leapt from its more dazzling height,   110
Even in the foaming strength of its abyss,
(Which casts up misty columns that become
Clouds raining from the re-ascended skies,)
Lies low but mighty still.—-But this is past,
My thoughts mistook themselves.
 Abbot.   And wherefore so?
 Manfred. I could not tame my nature down; for he
Must serve who fain would sway; and soothe, and sue,
And watch all time, and pry into all place,
And be a living Lie, who would become
A mighty thing amongst the mean—and such   120
The mass are; I disdained to mingle with
A herd, though to be leader—and of wolves.
The lion is alone, and so am I.
 Abbot. And why not live and act with other men?
 Manfred. Because my nature was averse from life;
And yet not cruel; for I would not make,
But find a desolation. Like the Wind,
The red-hot breath of the most lone Simoom,
Which dwells but in the desert, and sweeps o'er
The barren sands which bear no shrubs to blast,   130
And revels o'er their wild and arid waves,
And seeketh not, so that it is not sought,
But being met is deadly,—such hath been
The course of my existence; but there came
Things in my path which are no more.
 Abbot.   Alas!
I 'gin to fear that thou art past all aid
From me and from my calling; yet so young,
I still would——
 Manfred.   Look on me! there is an order
Of mortals on the earth, who do become
Old in their youth, and die ere middle age,   140
Without the violence of warlike death;
Some perishing of pleasure—some of study—
Some worn with toil, some of mere weariness,—

Some of disease—and some insanity—
And some of withered, or of broken hearts;
For this last is a malady which slays
More than are numbered in the lists of Fate,
Taking all shapes, and bearing many names.
Look upon me! for even of all these things
Have I partaken; and of all these things   15C
One were enough; then wonder not that I
Am what I am, but that I ever was,
Or having been, that I am still on earth.
    Abbot. Yet, hear me still——
    Manfred.   Old man! I do respect
Thine order, and revere thine years; I deem
Thy purpose pious, but it is in vain:
Think me not churlish; I would spare thyself,
Far more than me, in shunning at this time
All further colloquy—and so—farewell.

                                    [*Exit* MANFRED
    Abbot. This should have been a noble creature: he   160
Hath all the energy which would have made
A goodly frame of glorious elements,
Had they been wisely mingled; as it is,
It is an awful chaos—Light and Darkness—
And mind and dust—and passions and pure thoughts
Mixed, and contending without end or order,—
All dormant or destructive. He will perish—
And yet he must not—I will try once more,
For such are worth redemption; and my duty
Is to dare all things for a righteous end.   170
I'll follow him—but cautiously, though surely.

                                    [*Exit* ABBOT

                SCENE II—*Another Chamber.*

                MANFRED *and* HERMAN.

    Herman. My lord, you bade me wait on you at sunset:
He sinks behind the mountain.
    Manfred.   Doth he so?
I will look on him.
                [MANFRED *advances to the Window of the Hall.*
                Glorious Orb! the idol
Of early nature, and the vigorous race

Of undiseased mankind, the giant sons
Of the embrace of Angels, with a sex
More beautiful than they, which did draw down
The erring Spirits who can ne'er return.—
Most glorious Orb! that wert a worship, ere 10
The mystery of thy making was revealed!
Thou earliest minister of the Almighty,
Which gladdened, on their mountain tops, the hearts
Of the Chaldean shepherds, till they poured
Themselves in orisons! Thou material God!
And representative of the Unknown—
Who chose thee for his shadow! Thou chief Star!
Centre of many stars! which mak'st our earth
Endurable, and temperest the hues
And hearts of all who walk within thy rays!
Sire of the seasons! Monarch of the climes, 20
And those who dwell in them! for near or far,
Our inborn spirits have a tint of thee
Even as our outward aspects;—thou dost rise,
And shine, and set in glory. Fare thee well!
I ne'er shall see thee more. As my first glance
Of love and wonder was for thee, then take
My latest look: thou wilt not beam on one
To whom the gifts of life and warmth have been
Of a more fatal nature. He is gone—
I follow. [*Exit* MANFRED.

SCENE III—*The Mountains—The Castle of Manfred at some
distance—A Terrace before a Tower.—Time, Twilight.*

HERMAN, MANUEL, *and other dependants of* MANFRED.

Herman. 'Tis strange enough! night after night, for years,
He hath pursued long vigils in this tower,
Without a witness. I have been within it,—
So have we all been oft-times; but from it,
Or its contents, it were impossible
To draw conclusions absolute, of aught
His studies tend to. To be sure, there is
One chamber where none enter: I would give
The fee of what I have to come these three years,
To pore upon its mysteries.
 Manuel. 'Twere dangerous; 10

Content thyself with what thou know'st already.

Herman. Ah! Manuel! thou art elderly and wise,
And couldst say much; thou hast dwelt within the castle—
How many years is't?

Manuel.   Ere Count Manfred's birth,
I served his father, whom he nought resembles.

Herman. There be more sons in like predicament!
But wherein do they differ?

Manuel.   I speak not
Of features or of form, but mind and habits;
Count Sigismund was proud, but gay and free,—
A warrior and a reveller; he dwelt not   10
With books and solitude, nor made the night
A gloomy vigil, but a festal time,
Merrier than day; he did not walk the rocks
And forests like a wolf, nor turn aside
From men and their delights.

Herman.   Beshrew the hour,
But those were jocund times! I would that such
Would visit the old walls again; they look
As if they had forgotten them.

Manuel.   These walls
Must change their chieftain first. Oh! I have seen
Some strange things in them, Herman.

Herman.   Come, be friendly;   30
Relate me some to while away our watch:
I've heard thee darkly speak of an event
Which happened hereabouts, by this same tower.

Manuel. That was a night indeed! I do remember
'Twas twilight, as it may be now, and such
Another evening:—yon red cloud, which rests
On Eigher's pinnacle, so rested then,—
So like that it might be the same; the wind
Was faint and gusty, and the mountain snows
Began to glitter with the climbing moon;   40
Count Manfred was, as now, within his tower,—
How occupied, we knew not, but with him
The sole companion of his wanderings
And watchings—her, whom of all earthly things
That lived, the only thing he seemed to love,—
As he, indeed, by blood was bound to do,
The Lady Astarte, his——

                    Hush! who comes here?

Enter the ABBOT.

Abbot. Where is your master?
Herman.   Yonder in the **tower.**
Abbot. I must speak with him.
Manuel.   'Tis impossible;
He is most private, and must not be thus   **50**
Intruded on.
   Abbot.   Upon myself I take
The forfeit of my fault, if fault there be—
But I must see him.
   Herman.   Thou hast seen him once
This eve already.
   Abbot.   Herman! I command thee,
Knock, and apprize the Count of my approach.
   Herman. We dare not.
   Abbot.   Then it seems I must be herald
Of my own purpose.
   Manuel.   Reverend father, stop—
I pray you pause.
   Abbot.   Why so?
   Manuel.   But step this way,
And I will tell you further.   [*Exeunt.*

SCENE IV—*Interior of the Tower.*

MANFRED *alone.*

The stars are forth, the moon above the tops
Of the snow-shining mountains.—Beautiful!
I linger yet with Nature, for the Night
Hath been to me a more familiar face
Than that of man; and in her starry shade
Of dim and solitary loveliness,
I learned the language of another world.
I do remember me, that in my youth,
When I was wandering,—upon such a night
I stood within the Coliseum's wall,   **10**
'Midst the chief relics of almighty Rome;
The trees which grew along the broken arches
Waved dark in the blue midnight, and the stars
Shone through the rents of ruin; from afar

The watch-dog bayed beyond the Tiber; and
More near from out the Cæsar's palace came
The owl's long cry, and, interruptedly,
Of distant sentinels the fitful song
Begun and died upon the gentle wind.
Some cypresses beyond the time-worn breach   20
Appeared to skirt the horizon, yet they stood
Within a bowshot. Where the Cæsars dwelt,
And dwell the tuneless birds of night, amidst
A grove which springs through levelled battlements,
And twines its roots with the imperial hearths,
Ivy usurps the laurel's place of growth;—
But the gladiators' bloody Circus stands,
A noble wreck in ruinous perfection,
While Cæsar's chambers, and the Augustan halls,
Grovel on earth in indistinct decay.—   30
And thou didst shine, thou rolling Moon, upon
All this, and cast a wide and tender light,
Which softened down the hoar austerity
Of rugged desolation, and filled up,
As 'twere anew, the gaps of centuries;
Leaving that beautiful which still was so,
And making that which was not—till the place
Became religion, and the heart ran o'er
With silent worship of the Great of old,—
The dead, but sceptred, Sovereigns, who still rule   40
Our spirits from their urns.
                       'Twas such a night!
'Tis strange that I recall it at this time;
But I have found our thoughts take wildest flight
Even at the moment when they should array
Themselves in pensive order.

Enter the ABBOT.

    Abbot.   My good Lord!
I crave a second grace for this approach;
But yet let not my humble zeal offend
By its abruptness—all it hath of ill
Recoils on me; its good in the effect
May light upon your head—could I say *heart*—   50
Could I touch *that,* with words or prayers, I should
Recall a noble spirit which hath wandered,

But is not yet all lost.
    Manfred.   Thou know'st me not;
My days are numbered, and my deeds recorded:
Retire, or 'twill be dangerous—Away!
    Abbot. Thou dost not mean to menace me?
    Manfred.   Not I!
I simply tell thee peril is at hand,
And would preserve thee.
    Abbot.   What dost thou mean?
    Manfred.   Look there!
What dost thou see?
    Abbot.   Nothing.
    Manfred.   Look there, I say,
And steadfastly;—now tell me what thou see'st?   61
    Abbot. That which should shake me,—but I fear it not:
I see a dusk and awful figure rise,
Like an infernal god, from out the earth;
His face wrapt in a mantle, and his form
Robed as with angry clouds: he stands between
Thyself and me—but I do fear him not.
    Manfred. Thou hast no cause—he shall not harm thee—but
His sight may shock thine old limbs into palsy.
I say to thee—Retire!
    Abbot.   And I reply—
Never—till I have battled with this fiend:—   70
What doth he here?
    Manfred.   Why—aye—what doth he here?
I did not send for him,—he is unbidden.
    Abbot. Alas! lost Mortal! what with guests like these
Hast thou to do? I tremble for thy sake:
Why doth he gaze on thee, and thou on him?
Ah! he unveils his aspect: on his brow
The thunder-scars are graven; from his eye
Glares forth the immortality of Hell—
Avaunt!—
    Manfred. Pronounce—what is thy mission?
    Spirit.   Come!
    Abbot. What art thou, unknown being? answer!—speak!   80
    Spirit. The genius of this mortal.—Come! 'tis time.
    Manfred. I am prepared for all things, but deny
The Power which summons me. Who sent thee here?
    Spirit. Thou'lt know anon—Come! come!
    Manfred.   I have commanded

Things of an essence greater far than thine,
And striven with thy masters. Get thee hence!
   Spirit. Mortal! thine hour is come—Away! I say.
   Manfred. I knew, and know my hour is come, but not
To render up my soul to such as thee:
Away! I'll die as I have lived—alone.   90
   Spirit. Then I must summon up my brethren.—Rise!
                           [*Other Spirits rise up.*
   Abbot. Avaunt! ye evil ones!—Avaunt! I say,—
Ye have no power where Piety hath power,
And I do charge ye in the name—
   Spirit.   Old man!
We know ourselves, our mission and thine order;
Waste not thy holy words on idle uses—
It were in vain: this man is forfeited.
Once more—I summon him—Away! Away!
   Manfred. I do defy ye,—though I feel my soul
Is ebbing from me, yet I do defy ye;   100
Nor will I hence, while I have earthly breath
To breathe my scorn upon ye—earthly strength
To wrestle, though with spirits; what ye take
Shall be ta'en limb by limb.
   Spirit.   Reluctant mortal!
Is this the Magian who would so pervade
The world invisible, and make himself
Almost our equal? Can it be that thou
Art thus in love with life? the very life
Which made thee wretched?
   Manfred.   Thou false fiend, thou liest!
My life is in its last hour,—*that* I know,   110
Nor would redeem a moment of that hour;
I do not combat against Death, but thee
And thy surrounding angels; my past power
Was purchased by no compact with thy crew,
But by superior science—penance, daring,
And length of watching, strength of mind, and skill
In knowledge of our Fathers—when the earth
Saw men and spirits walking side by side,
And gave ye no supremacy: I stand
Upon my strength—I do defy—deny—   124
Spurn back, and scorn ye!—
   Spirit.   But thy many crimes
Have made thee——

Manfred.   What are they to such as thee?
Must crimes be punished but by other crimes,
And greater criminals?—Back to thy hell!
Thou hast no power upon me, *that* I feel;
Thou never shalt possess me, *that* I know:
What I have done is done; I bear within
A torture which could nothing gain from thine:
The Mind which is immortal makes itself
Requital for its good or evil thoughts,—   136
Is its own origin of ill and end—
And its own place and time: its innate sense,
When stripped of this mortality, derives
No colour from the fleeting things without,
But is absorbed in sufferance or in joy,
Born from the knowledge of its own desert.
Thou didst not tempt me, and thou couldst not tempt me;
I have not been thy dupe, nor am I thy prey—
But was my own destroyer, and will be
My own hereafter.—Back, ye baffled fiends!   140
The hand of Death is on me—but not yours!
                              [*The Demons disappear.*

Abbot. Alas! how pale thou art—thy lips are white—
And thy breast heaves—and in thy gasping throat
The accents rattle: Give thy prayers to Heaven—
Pray—albeit but in thought,—but die not thus.
Manfred. 'Tis over—my dull eyes can fix thee not;
But all things swim around me, and the earth
Heaves as it were beneath me. Fare thee well—
Give me thy hand.
Abbot.   Cold—cold—even to the heart—
But yet one prayer—Alas! how fares it with thee?   150
Manfred. Old man! 'tis not so difficult to die.
                              [MANFRED *expires.*

Abbot. He's gone—his soul hath ta'en its earthless flight;
Whither? I dread to think—but he is gone.
                    [*First publ., June 16, 1817.*]

INDEX OF TITLES